THE
AIRCRAFT
CARRIER
STORY

THE
AIRCRAFT CARRIER STORY

1908–1945

GUY ROBBINS

CASSELL&CO

Cassell & Co
Wellington House, 125 Strand,
London WC2R 0BB

First published in Great Britain 2001

British Library Cataloguing-in-Publication Data
A catalogue record for this book is available from the
British Library

ISBN 0-304-35308-6

Distributed in the USA by
Sterling Publishing Co. Inc.,
387 Park Avenue South, New York, NY 10016-8810

Designed and edited by DAG Publications Ltd
Edited by Michael Boxall
Designed by David Gibbons
Typesetting and layout by Roger Chesneau

Printed in Great Britain

Contents

Abbreviations

AA	anti-aircraft		**CID**	Committee of Imperial Defence
ABE	Assessors of Bomb and Battleship Experiments		**CinC**	Commander-in-Chief
ACA	Admiral Aircraft Carriers		**CNO**	Chief of Naval Operations
ACNS	Assistant Chief of the Naval Staff		**CO**	Commanding Officer
ACTG	Advanced Carrier Training Group		**ComAirPac**	Commander Aircraft Carriers Pacific
AD	Air Department		**COWS**	Chief of the War Staff
ADAD	Assistant Director Air Department		**CS**	Cruiser Squadron
			CV	aircraft carrier (US)
AFTS	Advanced Flying Training School		**CVB**	heavy aircraft carrier (US)
			CVE	escort aircraft carrier (US)
AMC	Armed Merchant Cruiser		**DAD**	Director of the Air Department
ASAC	Assistant Superintendent of Aircraft Construction		**DAS**	Director of Air Services
BCF	Battle Cruiser Fleet		**DCNS**	Deputy Chief of the Naval Staff
BIR	Board of Invention and Research		**DLCO**	Deck Landing Control Officer
BS	Battle Squadron			
BuAer	Bureau of Aeronautics		**DNA**	Director of Naval Aviation
CAM	Catapult Aircraft Merchantman		**DNAD**	Director of Naval Air Division
CAP	Combat Air Patrol			
CAS	Chief of the Air Staff		**DNC**	Director of Naval Construction
CASU	Carrier Aircraft Service Unit			
			DNO	Director of Naval Ordnance
CFS	Central Flying School			
CIC	Combat Information Center		**DOD**	Director Operations Division

DP	Director of Plans	**RCAF**	Royal Canadian Air Force
DRC	Defence Requirements Committee	**RFC**	Royal Flying Corps
		RN	Royal Navy
EFTS	Elementary Flying Training School	**RNAS**	Royal Naval Air Service
		RNR	Royal Naval Reserve
FAA	Fleet Air Arm	**RNVR**	Royal Naval Volunteer Reserve
FAAM	Fleet Air Arm Museum		
FCS	Fighter Catapult Ship	**RNVR(A)**	Royal Naval Volunteer Reserve (Air Branch)
FDO	Fighter Direction Officer		
GFBO	Grand Fleet Battle Orders	**ROTC**	Reserve Officer Training Course
HMS	His Majesty's Ship		
ICA	Inspecting Captain of Airships	**RT**	radio telegraphy
		SAC	Superintendent of Aircraft Construction
IFF	Identification Friend or Foe		
		SFO	Senior Flying Officer
IJN	Imperial Japanese Navy	**SMS**	*Seine Majistäts Schiff* (His Majesty's Ship; German)
IJNS	Imperial Japanese Navy Ship		
		SNO	Senior Naval Officer
IWM	Imperial War Museum	**TAG**	Telegraphist Air Gunner
JCS	Joint Chiefs of Staff	**TBR**	Torpedo-Bomber-Reconnaissance
KMS	*Kriegsmarineschiff* (German Navy Ship)		
		TF	Task Force
LSO	Landing Signal Officer	**TOMCAT**	radar picket destroyer(s)
MAC	Merchant Aircraft Carrier	**TSR**	Torpedo-Spotter-Reconnaissance
MNB	Mobile Naval Base		
MONAB	Mobile Naval Air Station	**UK**	United Kingdom
NAP	Naval Aviation Pilot	**US**	United States
NAS	Naval Air Station; Naval Air Squadron	**USA**	United States of America
		USMC	United States Marine Corps
NYK	Japanese Mail Steam Company		
		USNRFC	United States Naval Reserve Flying Corps
OSK	Osaka Merchant Ship Company		
		USS	United States Ship
RAA	Rear Admiral Aircraft Carriers	**VCS**	Vulnerability of Capital Ships
RAF	Royal Air Force	**VT**	variable time (fuse)

Introduction

When the Wright brothers flew for the first time in December 1903 no one had a clear idea about the best way to take aeroplanes to sea with the fleet. Before the First World War most navies had experimented with aeroplanes but were operating seaplanes by 1914. Whether they were operated from ships and how depended on the operational requirements of each navy and the development of other types of aircraft, especially airships.

By the end of the war the Royal Navy was building carriers which could launch and recover aeroplanes and were recognisable as aircraft carriers, a term used in the Admiralty as early as 1916. However, the question of whether flush decked or island type carriers were best was unresolved. Nor had the carrier been tried in battle to attack an enemy fleet at sea or in its bases. The aircraft carrier had been developed during the First World War solely by the Royal Navy which had a considerable lead over the US and Japanese navies, both of which received British assistance.

Because of their differing strategic situations, these three navies had very contrasting approaches during the inter-war years. By 1939 the Royal Navy had been overtaken in naval aviation by the other two, mainly because it alone was handicapped by an independent air force which relegated maritime aircraft to a minor role. The question of operational capability remained open. Exercises had shown that carriers could attack fleets and shore bases, but the extent of the damage they could inflict remained debatable – as was their ability to defend themselves against land-based aircraft. Carriers continued to be largely auxiliary to battleships which remained the capital ship of the fleet.

Development by France, Germany and Italy was minimal although the former did in fact commission a carrier. Germany and Italy also started carrier construction and German representatives went to Japan to study their designs. Japan in turn pressed strongly for Germany to send air crews to Japan for training, but the Germans did not want to be drawn into such a close naval co-operation. In France, Germany and Italy unified air forces were instrumental in preventing the full development of aircraft carriers. The French carrier never fulfilled its role in the Second World War and the Italian and German carriers were never completed. Thus, while these projects are very interesting, they had little influence on the development of the carrier as the capital ship of modern navies and have been omitted for reasons of space.

The Second World War finally established the carrier as the centre of naval warfare. Large-scale air strikes against bases disabled fleets and installations and decisive naval battles took place with the opposing fleets not even in sight of each other. Above all carrier air groups proved to be a match for land-based aircraft and were able to project immense power inland. While many of these trends were pioneered by the Royal Navy, it lacked a large number of modern carriers until late in the war. There were no enemy carriers to attack in European waters and the RN had to operate in seas largely dominated by the large German and Italian land-based air forces.

Thus in the early years of the war the Fleet Air Arm largely fought a courageous, rearguard action using obsolete aircraft and carriers. In 1943 and 1944 it was largely deployed to provide support for the amphibious assaults (Madagascar, North Africa, Sicily, Salerno, Anzio and the South of France) of the Mediterranean strategy. When a carrier-based British Pacific Fleet was finally available for the Indian Ocean and Pacific it found it was only one Task Group of many in the Fast Carrier Force of a huge US Pacific Fleet and had to learn from the Americans the new techniques of a revolution in naval warfare.

The special circumstances of the Pacific theatre (huge distances, few large land masses, naval domination, Japanese inferiority, their notorious surprise attack and the loss of the American old battleships) led to the first carrier battles (with the fleets never sighting each other) in history and the development of carrier air power as the main strike force of the fleet. For the Americans necessity made the carriers their main hope and weapon in 1942, but in 1943 and 1944 their huge industrial capacity and development of carrier techniques created an undreamed of naval power able to strike and destroy Japanese forces at will.

For the Japanese the development of an élite carrier force was the foundation of their six months of victories until Midway. However, once this force was worn down the rest of the Japanese Navy was systematically destroyed by the US fast carrier fleet which was largely created in response to the Japanese example, by huge shipbuilding programmes and the freeing of the carrier admirals from the old concepts tied to the US battle force.

Thus the story of the aircraft carrier is largely that of two world wars. In the First the operational requirements of the Royal Navy were solely responsible for the development of the concept of the aircraft carrier, but the war ended before it could be proven in battle. Between the wars the British, Japanese and American navies knew they had to have carriers but mainly as an auxiliary arm to the battleships. The Pacific campaign of The Second World War was the catalyst for the development of the carrier as the capital ship of the modern navy.

1. The Royal Navy and Aircraft Carriers, 1908–1945

Although the Royal Navy had set up institutions to study and develop aviation as early as 1908, progress was somewhat unsteady because of early uncertainties about the right path to follow, the creation of the Royal Air Force in 1918, and suspicions about forming a naval air arm that would have separatist tendencies. During the Great War the technical advance of the development of the aircraft carrier did not benefit the fleet to the extent that the Admiralty had hoped and the war ended before it was able to engage the enemy with the new weapon. The realisation of its great potential was heavily dependent on the development of an independent Royal Air Force.

Early British Carrier Policy, 1908–1914

From 1903 to 1908 the Royal Navy showed interest in ship-borne man-lifting kites (for scouting, anti-mine/submarine and spotting), but little interest in kite balloons or aeroplanes. In March 1907 the Board of Admiralty rejected the Wrights' offer to sell their patents. Aeroplanes were considered too flimsy and short ranged for use at sea at that time. In 1908 successful tests with the kites at sea were abandoned in favour of airships.

The First Sea Lord, Lord Fisher and his chief technical aide, Captain R. H. Bacon DNO (Director of Naval Ordnance), were very interested in the rigid airship because of its great range and weight-carrying capacity. They also feared that Count Zeppelin, the German airship developer, would pass his expertise to the German Navy. When on 1 July 1908 Zeppelin flew his fourth rigid airship for twelve hours (240 miles) Fisher decided to forestall the Germans (as with the dreadnoughts) by developing a squadron of dirigibles and as a first step to build a prototype. Their role would be to scout the North Sea from land bases, to enable the fleet to instigate a distant blockade of German ports and force the decisive battle that Fisher hoped would eliminate the German fleet.

Lord Esher CID (Committee of Imperial Defence), appointed a Sub-Committee to co-ordinate aviation development by the Army and Navy; it approved airship development (January 1909) but left aeroplanes to private enterprise. This was mainly be-

Short aeroplane S.27 on the cruiser HMS *Hibernia*. Samson's aim was to develop aircraft that would fly-off from a platform over the fore turret of ordinary warships but land on the sea. (IWM)

cause Bacon, the naval representative, who clearly understood the possible naval uses of aircraft (air defence, scouting, spotting, anti-submarine/mine and offence), was concerned to secure funding for the rigid prototype and considered aeroplanes impractical at sea. The Army was not interested. In December 1909 Captain M. F. Sueter was appointed ICA (Inspecting Captain of Airships) to develop them.

However, while the Navy's dirigible was much delayed by design and building difficulties, the aeroplane was developing rapidly abroad. At the end of 1910 the Admiralty accepted the Royal Aero Club's offer of free pilot tuition for four naval officers. The new First Sea Lord (Sir Arthur Wilson) was not keen on airships, which he felt were susceptible to weather and difficult to navigate at sea, and refused to agree the building programme that Sueter was pressing until the prototype was successful. There were also worries that the French and Americans (Eugene Ely, a Curtiss demonstration pilot, had flown off and landed on warships in October 1910) were ahead of Great Britain in aeroplane development.

Wilson re-instituted the strategy of a close blockade of the German coast but realised that modern guns, torpedoes, submarines and mines posed a real problem to reconnaissance. He thought airships too vulnerable to coastal defences, but aeroplanes, launched from ships, ideal for reconnoitring enemy harbours. When their course ended in September 1911, the senior pilot (Lieutenant C. R. Samson) persuaded Wilson to authorise a Naval Air Station at Eastchurch and in return promised to develop the requisite techniques for flying-off from a ship.

Samson duly flew off the forecastle of the old battleship *Africa* in Sheerness harbour on 10 January 1912. His aeroplane (a Short 538) was equipped with pontoons attached to the wheels for emergency touch-down on the sea. As a result Sueter and Rear-Admiral E. C. T. Troubridge, Chief of the War Staff (COWS), suggested trials in four cruisers of the Home Fleet before issuing two machines per warship in the fleet. Further experiments involved flying-off from cruisers' decks at sea (*Hibernia*) and while under way at 10½ knots (*London*).

Unlike Ely, however, Samson never attempted to follow up these experiments by flying on to a ship despite having a technique proposed for doing so. In December 1911 Lieutenant H. A. Williamson, a submariner, forwarded a proposal to the Admiralty to convert existing warships, or even to build a new carrier, to launch and retrieve aeroplanes for fleet anti-submarine duties. This design was rejected by Samson as too complicated, but primarily because he had decided to develop seaplanes. He considered flying on to a ship too dangerous for fast machines and unnecessary for seaplanes.

Several pilots, including Cecil Grace who was to have taught Samson to fly, had been lost because of engine failure over the sea. Shorts, the main pre-war naval aircraft designer, had developed flotation bags, the forerunner of floats, for aeroplanes but these were useless in heavy seas although Lieutenant A. M. Longmore, also one of the original four pilots, like Curtiss, landed alongside a ship and took off again in harbour.

HMS *Hibernia* (1912), using a special launch platform built over the forecastle. Samson proved that aeroplanes could fly from warships at sea, 2 May 1912. (FAAM)

Samson favoured the flexibility of a sea 'aerodrome' but realised that flying from the open sea was not easy.

Sueter and other officers, after the wreck of the dirigible (September 1911), had sponsored Commander Oliver Schwann to pilot a seaplane (Avro biplane 35hp Green). They also found, despite a short hop from the water on 18 November 1911 and much experimentation with floats, that the use of seaplanes was still very problematical. Williamson had suggested using aeroplanes precisely because of the difficulties of launching seaplanes from heavy seas.

Samson's solution was to fly seaplanes from the deck and to land them beside their mother ship. Sueter and Troubridge consulted him and agreed that aeroplanes should 'start from ship, alight on water'. Samson hoped to keep the interference on the carrier to the minimum, maximise the safety and flexibility of operations, allow aircraft launches without slowing down or hoisting out, and persuade commanders that aeroplanes were reliable. However, the carrier had to turn into the wind and Samson underestimated the danger from U-boats when stopped to hoist in seaplanes. The war was far advanced before *Campania* developed hoisting in under way.

By March 1912 Shorts had developed a seaplane (S41, Admiralty No. 10) for Samson and he was the first British pilot to fly a seaplane off and on to the sea, in Portland Harbour, on 3 May. He followed this up by taking off in the open sea, having been hoisted out by *Hibernia* off Deal, on 13 May. In July Shorts devised the first folding seaplane (S63, Admiralty No. 81) which was used during the 1913 manoeuvres aboard *Hermes*.

Meanwhile Churchill had become First Lord in October 1911 and sacked Wilson in December. However, he and Battenberg (Second, later First Sea Lord) also favoured aeroplane development, halted the airship programme and disbanded the Airship Section in January. In April 1912 Churchill, in the light of successful German dirigibles, changed his mind and asked the CID to investigate the development of airships. This was finally agreed in mid 1913 despite the opposition of the Chancellor, Lloyd George, on the grounds of expense. Churchill's initial hostility to airships ensured that their development was fatally delayed, vital time was lost and never recovered for the British airship programme. British airships never challenged the Zeppelins during the First World War.

However, when Sueter was appointed Director of the Air Department (DAD) in July 1912 no one knew war was so close and his policy was to develop both aeroplanes and airships. He quickly established in August, that their roles would be command of the air, scouting, spotting, anti-submarine and offence. He also continued Samson's policy of developing seaplanes. Sueter's plan was to restart airship development, convert a ship to pioneer flying seaplanes from a deck and then design a fast fleet seaplane carrier.

Thus he gained permission to buy non-rigids for training and to build rigids for scouting. Sueter also issued a specification for a converted 10-knot carrier with a 200-

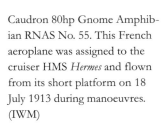

Caudron 80hp Gnome Amphibian RNAS No. 55. This French aeroplane was assigned to the cruiser HMS *Hermes* and flown from its short platform on 18 July 1913 during manoeuvres. (IWM)

foot flying-off deck and turned to a new but innovative shipbuilder, William Beardmore Ltd, to design his fleet carrier. One of their Directors, the Marquis of Graham (later Duke of Montrose), had been hand-picked by Fisher to help raise the RNVR and was already interested in aviation. It appears that in October 1912 Sueter encouraged him and his firm to submit a design for a 21-knot carrier.

Churchill authorised the conversion of a merchant ship, but sufficient funds were unavailable in the 1912/13 Estimates and the Treasury refused any extra. Sueter therefore secured permission to prepare the old cruiser *Hermes* for seaplane experiments and proposed in December, that Beardmores build a 15-knot carrier (a variant of their original design) to pioneer flying from her deck. She was to become a depot ship for destroyers once she had gained data for the fleet carrier.

The Board refused permission to build her since Churchill had ruled against any more depot ships and they required proof of the feasibility of seaplanes at sea plus further design work due to the invention by Shorts of folding seaplanes. Another factor was that the Air Department had already spent £½ million on re-starting the airship programme. The Beardmore design was therefore postponed until seaplanes were proven and funds were made available. It did, however, form the basis for later Air Department fleet carrier designs.

During the summer manoeuvres of 1913 *Hermes* proved that the latest Short folder seaplane (S63 or Admiralty No. 81) could land on and fly from the sea. This led to further carrier and torpedo aeroplanes being designed by Shorts, Sopwith and White. *Hermes* also twice launched a Caudron G.III amphibian on 28 July and 3 September from her short platform, but lacked a long deck to fly off seaplanes.

Hermes' commander (Captain G. W. Vivian) noted that extemporised carriers were of limited value (the machines needed shelter from the elements), the importance of folder seaplanes for storage, their need for strong construction to operate from the sea and the inability to guarantee taking off from the sea even in good weather. Seaworthy seaplanes were heavy and required long decks to take off. Thus the Air Department sought a carrier which could fly seaplanes from a long deck.

Another reason for providing carriers was Sueter's ambition, as a torpedo specialist, to pioneer aerial torpedoes to attack the German fleet. During a European tour in June 1912 to study airships, and while building No. 1 Rigid, he had proposed that airships carry torpedoes. With the success of *Hermes'* experiments he turned to the less vulnerable seaplane. Churchill was also very keen to develop seaplanes to attack German troop transports (there was an invasion scare in 1913) as well as their fleet. Loaded with a heavy torpedo these would require more powerful engines and to be carried close to the German ports or a fleet action.

In September 1913 Sueter and Lieutenant D. T. Hyde-Thomson, the torpedo specialist assigned to the Air Department, issued a specification for a torpedo-seaplane which they patented in March 1914. Sueter asked Sopwith to produce the seaplane and the DNO to design a lightweight 1,000lb 18-inch torpedo. In the meantime Hyde-Thomson used a Sopwith taxiplane to develop the torpedo gear at Calshot.

With the approach of war Longmore dropped a 810lb 14-inch torpedo from a 160hp Short on 28 July which was a 'stunt' since the seaplane was under-powered. The 200hp Sopwith Type C arrived in August and regularly dropped torpedoes, but proved to be too large and under-powered for carrier service.

After her trials *Hermes* was paid off into reserve in December 1913 and Churchill agreed to allocate £110,000 in that year's or the 1914/15 Estimates to convert a trials ship. Jellicoe (Second Sea Lord, assigned air development) supervised the Air Department's development of aerial requirements to enable the Third Sea Lord, Admiral A. G. H. Moore, to design a new 'aeroplane ship' for the 1915/16 programme. Churchill expected (October 1913) naval seaplanes 'from a ship at sea' to scout 'with the fleet', fight the 'enemy's aeroplanes and airships overseas' and attack the 'enemy's vulnerable points on shore'. To facilitate this he planned to buy 20 machines of two types: a fast fighter able to carry bombs to attack airships and enemy targets ashore, and a two-seater scout. In theory, the fleet was to have carrier aviation by the end of 1916.

In practice, however, money was not available in the 1913/14 Estimates and although it was available in 1914–15 it was cut to £80,000. Moreover, the fast fleet seaplane carrier was put back to the 1916/17 Estimates and would not reach the fleet until the end of 1917 at the earliest. The carrier programme was a victim of political circumstance despite the strong support of Churchill and the First (Battenberg), Second (Jellicoe) and Third (Moore) Sea Lords.

Churchill was under strong Cabinet pressure, especially from his erstwhile ally, the Chancellor of the Exchequer, to cut naval spending. Lloyd George wanted to spend the money on social reform and to encourage the Germans to end the very expensive and dangerous naval arms race. Presenting the sketch 1914/15 Estimates to the Cabinet, Churchill insisted that Great Britain should maintain her margin of dreadnought superiority over Germany (by building the *Queen Elizabeth* class, his pet project) and provoked a Cabinet crisis (December 1913–February 1914). A government crisis was averted by 'contractions, postponements and excisions' to services other than the ship-building programme.

One of these services was aviation. Since April 1912 Churchill had been fighting for funds to restart the naval airship programme. Lloyd George (who had seen Zeppelin's *LZ4* crash at Echterdingen) had postponed approval until mid 1913. The bulk of the funds were thus in the 1914/15 Estimates. For this reason, the widening capability gap being opened up by Zeppelin and Jellicoe, aviation's Supervising Sea Lord, being a keen supporter, airships got preference in the Air Department budget over the fast carrier, which was postponed. However, the rigid programme did not go unscathed since those parts that could be postponed for a year were.

Meanwhile the Air Department had to make do with the merchant ship whose conversion had been approved. They chose one on the stocks to enable the best possible conversion for aviation. She was to carry up to ten trainee pilots, bombs and torpedoes to begin training a corps of personnel qualified for the fleet. However, *Ark Royal* was not to be launched until late 1914. In July 1914 when war was imminent every effort was made to hasten her completion but she was not commissioned until 9 December. Moreover, a 10½ knot training carrier could not operate with the 20-knot fleet. She was instead sent to the Dardanelles where her lack of speed was not a handicap until the U-boats arrived.

The First World War

The Air Department's greatest success in the Great War, in terms of the whole history of naval aviation, was undoubtedly the successful solving of the problem of taking aircraft to sea with the fleet. This is now taken for granted, but the ultimate solution was by no means a foregone conclusion. In the early days the avoidance of operating aircraft from ships seemed easier and more attractive. The outbreak of war when the Air Department's plans were far from complete played a key role in the development of carriers from 1915 to 1917.

The Early War Plans, 1914–1915

In August 1914 the outbreak of hostilities precipitated a crisis in British naval aviation. In sheer numbers of aircraft the Royal Navy did not compare unfavourably with the Germans: eight airships and more than eighty land and seaplanes as opposed to one Zeppelin and nine seaplanes available for operations. The problem was the lack of aircraft with the fleet and the potential to rectify this rapidly.

All the airships were short-ranged non-rigids, bought to train crews for the projected rigids, and only suitable for anti-submarine patrols. The rigid airship programme had just been restarted and a prototype (*R9*) was building whereas the Germans had a production line developed that could quickly produce Zeppelins. With little rigid experience the British tended to overestimate German rigid airship capabilities.

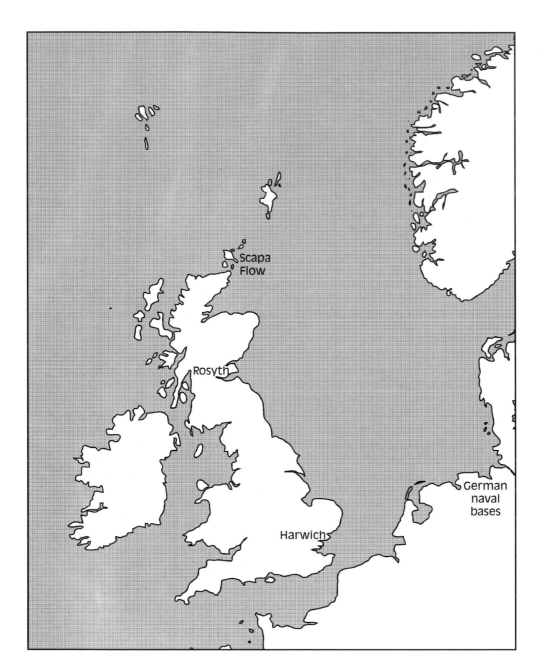

Map showing the North Sea in 1914–18.

The British preponderance in seaplanes was of little value unless they could be carried with the fleet. Moreover, *Hermes* had proven their use to be problematical unless they could be launched from decks. The development of long flying-decks, to launch seaplanes, had been seen as the next step in the development of the aircraft carrier. The Royal Navy was the only navy to have decided on this approach and had established a lead, if only in conception, in carrier aviation, but with their training carrier still converting it was unable to develop this. The war moreover worked against the early implementation of flying-off decks.

The Admiralty's air policy in August 1914 was primarily to prevent air attacks on Britain's cities, industries and naval bases which it was believed the Zeppelins would launch, so all aeroplanes and seaplanes were sent to the East Coast air stations. Throughout the war the Royal Navy had more faith in the rigid's potential than in its capabilities.

Sueter's second priority was to provide the fleet with aircraft of which it had none. The Navy could expect no rigid airships yet since the second prototype (*R9*) was still building. The few training non-rigids lacked range and all-weather capability for fleet co-operation. Seaplanes therefore had to provide the fleet's scouting and defence against the Zeppelin. Sueter's other main objective was for torpedo seaplanes to attack the German fleet and the Kiel Canal.

Carriers were not available to carry the short-ranged seaplanes. Of the carriers proposed pre-war, the training seaplane carrier *Ark Royal* had not been launched and the fast fleet seaplane carrier was not even on the drawing-board. The problem was that seaplanes heavily laden with torpedoes needed a long deck to fly off a ship (a catapult was not developed by the Royal Navy until 1916) which meant a large ship and lengthy, radical conversions.

However, most of the fast, large, mercantile ships (mainly liners) had already been allocated as Armed Merchant Cruisers to tackle commerce raiders and Churchill had ruled that the war would only last one year and all building should add to the immediate war effort especially for the next six months. Sueter therefore procured three cross-Channel ferries, *Engadine*, *Riviera* and *Empress*, of the South East and Chatham Railway, to carry torpedo-seaplanes. These were fast ships (18–21 knots) and were quickly modified at Chatham Dockyard, on the lines of *Hermes*, to carry three seaplanes each. They could also operate from the small East Coast harbours which large liners could not. Their main drawback was launching their seaplanes from the sea without a flying-off deck. It took 30 minutes to hoist out the seaplanes without damage in a seaway using derricks.

To obtain some short flying-off decks for fighter seaplanes, Sueter asked for the conversion of the *Bacchante* class cruisers on the lines of *Hermes*. As these were already assigned to patrolling, *Hermes* alone was converted but she was sunk on 31 October. This was to delay carrier development until June 1915 since only then did the Royal Navy have flying-off decks. In August 1914, with planning for a short war, Sueter was concerned merely to provide carriers immediately.

He wanted them to attack enemy ships or flagships with torpedoes, during or before a fleet action began. The carriers would be stationed astern of the fleet so as not to mask it, and would hoist out seaplanes for reconnaissance and torpedo attacks. He also planned to attack the Kiel Canal, to prevent the German fleet escaping into the Baltic, and the Zeppelin sheds while reconnoitring for the proposed torpedo raid.

The raid never took place. Sueter had to restrain the aggressive Commander C. J. L'E. Malone (his former assistant, now CO *Engadine*) and his pilots because he knew the seaplanes could not do the job. Experiments by Lieutenant R. P. Ross (Senior Pilot,

Engadine) revealed that the 160hp Type 81 Short barely lifted a 14-inch torpedo higher than 50 feet, even without a passenger, getting off the sea was very difficult and the engine unreliable. This meant even short sea flights would be very hazardous. Since a 14-inch torpedo would do little damage to a warship Sueter postponed his torpedo attack until a more powerful engine was available and in the meantime planned to reconnoitre German harbours in preparation.

Sueter's problems were exacerbated by the fact that the carriers were required for other duties. Churchill and the new COWS (Vice-Admiral F. C. D. Sturdee) had agreed on their designation as 'Torpedo Seaplane Carrying Ships'. However, Churchill thought scouting would lose the element of surprise and by October was keen to destroy the German air threat and to blockade the German fleet in its harbours or provoke it into battle. The carriers were to be instrumental in either case. They were to make bombing raids (on Zeppelin sheds and the Kiel Canal), photograph islands (Borkum or Sylt) for possible landings and, with the Grand Fleet in support, provoke a fleet action. He therefore kept all the carriers together under Admiralty control.

From October the Harwich Force (Commodore R. Y. Tyrwhitt) escorted the carriers in attempts to bomb Zeppelin sheds and reconnoitre the German coast, with the Grand Fleet under Jellicoe supporting in case German units came out to attack them. The only operations in 1914 that met with any success were the first (25 October) and the last (25 December) which launched one and seven (two S64s, three S74s and two S87s) seaplanes respectively. No Zeppelin sheds were hit, but during the latter raid other targets including ships were bombed.

The Admiralty saw great potential in the 'Christmas Raid', the first naval-air battle in history (Zeppelins and seaplanes attacked the carriers). They agreed with Malone who predicted that within six months merchant shipping in the Schillig Roads as well as naval units could well find themselves being attacked by seaplanes armed with 18- or 20-inch torpedoes or even light guns, and that naval strategy would have to change accordingly.

However, as with *Hermes* in 1913, the small *Engadine*s could not protect their seaplanes from the elements with canvas hangars, nor always launch them from the sea when required, which made Churchill impatient for better results. When Lord Fisher became First Sea Lord on 30 October 1914 the Admiralty adopted a new construction policy of completing or building warships within 1915 rather than Churchill's original six months. This allowed the conversion of ferries but not the building of a new fleet carrier.

Sueter therefore had the *Engadine*s and a larger ferry, the *Ben-my-Chree* (formerly an Isle of Man packet), permanently converted for the summer operations. *Empress* and *Ben-my-Chree* were fitted to fly-off the new Sopwith Schneider single-seat fighter seaplane, developed to attack Zeppelins. The short length of *Empress*'s platform, however, meant she was never used. In March Sueter converted a fifth seaplane carrier, *Vindex*, which was not commissioned until September.

HMS *Ben-my-Chree* (1915). One of the first 'cross-Channel' type seaplane carriers permanently converted from a ferry, she was earmarked to develop seaplane torpedo operations. (IWM)

The Air Department was also encouraged by seaplane development. Two proto-type Short S87s with Salmson engines served in the 1914 carrier operations, and during the Christmas raid the larger of the two, with 200hp engine, allowed Lt Erskine Childers to make a reconnaissance of the German harbours and proved the best rough weather seaplane. The Admiralty ordered production batches of both types, the smaller to reduce stowage space and the larger for torpedoes.

However, as expected the 200hp engine was unable to carry a torpedo and Sueter had already issued a new specification to Shorts, Sopwith and J. Samuel White for torpedo-aircraft in September 1914. Types 814, 860 and 840 had the new Sunbeam 225hp engine, but did not arrive until early 1915.

The carrier air raids were not re-started until the spring and summer of 1915 after the carriers had been modified to enable adequate stowage, and experiments in 'spot-ting' for monitor gunfire from the Belgian coast had been conducted. In May the carriers renewed the bombing of the Zeppelin sheds and photographed Borkum for Churchill's projected landing. During Operation 'TW' a Sopwith Schneider was ready on *Ben-my-Chree*'s deck to attack any Zeppelins scouting the Task Force. When one appeared, however, the machine backfired, and *Engadine*'s Schneiders could not take off from the sea fast enough, again proving the need for long decks.

In late May, after seven failed attempts, the Admiralty decided to defer operations. The seaplane carrier squadron was broken up. *Ben-my-Chree*, with *Engadine*'s key (torpedo and observer) crew, continued practice torpedo runs with the first two Type 184 seaplanes. On 21 May she sailed to assist *Ark Royal* in the Dardanelles operations, with the unofficial intention of torpedoing the German cruisers *Goeben* and *Breslau* at Constantinople. *Riviera* was assigned to spotting experiments at Sheerness. *Engadine*, *Empress* and *Vindex* were assigned to the East Coast to augment the air stations and undertake further carrier raids when ordered.

It was now clear that the Christmas seaplane raid which had so encouraged the Admiralty had only been successful because of exceptional conditions. The seaplane requirements (fine weather, smooth sea, some wind and clear skies) were also ideal for the Zeppelins which quickly found the task force, and were too demanding to allow operations to be successful regularly. As Williamson had warned in late 1911, the seaplanes could not always take off whenever they were required.

Churchill on at least two occasions (October 1914 and April 1915) suggested continuing the air raids on the German coast by changing the seaplanes into aeroplanes, the loss of their floats improving performance, and launching them from barges for instant use. Sueter, however, persuaded him that improved seaplanes could do the job. Safety was still a large factor for the pilots because engines were unreliable. The Air Department's aircraft designer, H. Booth (a theoretician), also argued that seaplanes could not be converted to aeroplanes despite conversions during the war.

The aggressive Tyrwhitt and Sueter convinced the new Board (First Lord A. J. Balfour, appointed 27 May 1915) to undertake another carrier raid. The Admiralty wished to scout the Ems for German invasion transports, and to counter Zeppelins bombing England. Sueter wanted to attack Zeppelin sheds (*LZ38* was destroyed on 7 June in her shed in Belgium by RNAS aircraft shore-based in Belgium) with the new Type 184 seaplanes. Tyrwhitt's aim was to blind the German fleet by destroying the Zeppelins which shadowed the British fleet during summer operations.

Operation 'G' (4 July) was a complete failure. Only one of five new Shorts could get off the sea and the Schneiders were unable to attack the seven Zeppelins attracted to the Harwich Force. The new Board was incensed that the seaplanes had not been tested at sea to ensure that they could take off quickly while the force was in enemy waters. Sueter was asked for an explanation by the new First Sea Lord, H. B. Jackson, and had to admit that an improved Schneider (the Sopwith Baby) was being developed. The Schneider had been developed with light floats to fly off decks, but none was available (*Ben-my-Chree* being in the Aegean).

The seaplane carriers' record was not good. In the eighteen operations attempted, only two had launched seaplanes. Of eighty-four seaplanes taken to sea, only twenty-seven were launched and only ten got off the sea. Not one Zeppelin or shed was destroyed though some reconnaissance was achieved. The Christmas Raid was an isolated success. The only other plus was the torpedoing of three Turkish merchant ships by two Short 184s of *Ben-my-Chree* flown by Flight Commander C. H. K. Edmonds and Flight Lieutenant G. B. Dacre on 12 and 17 August. However, these had a short range and low altitude when carrying a 14-inch torpedo (useless against warships) and could only do so when new. They never attacked the *Goeben*.

By contrast it seemed that the Germans had perfected Zeppelin scouting and during the summer 1915 British squadrons were constantly shadowed by airships. British admirals over-estimated their usefulness to the German war effort, but they were managing to drop bombs on the British mainland and this was not good for the Admiralty's image since it had taken over the country's aerial defence from the Army in 1914. Attempts to bomb their sheds and to entice them out to be shot down had failed. The Admiralty now abandoned carrier raids and resorted to AA guns and cruiser patrols along the coast. These too failed.

Another response was to re-start rigid airship development, in July 1915, abandoned again by Churchill the previous January to concentrate on aeroplanes and non rigids (anti-submarine duties). German rigids seemed more useful than British seaplanes. However, this second interruption to the rigid programme ensured that the British fleet would not have modern rigids until the end of the war by which time it was clear they were very vulnerable to aeroplanes.

In mid 1915 the poor carrier performance, the apparent success of the German rigids and the Board's criticism of the Air Department were disastrous for Sueter. As a result the Board appointed Rear-Admiral C. L. Vaughan Lee as Director of Air Services (DAS) to develop fleet aviation, which it felt had been neglected, and favoured airships rather than a carriers. This was just at the time when, as a result of the experience with seaplane carriers, Sueter was seeking to develop a programme of carriers of much improved design.

The Development of the Aircraft Carrier, 1915–1916

After the failure of Operation 'G', Sueter admitted that seaplanes could only take off from calm seas. When they failed to operate in conditions which did not distress picket boats it damaged the RNAS's reputation with the fleet, especially when the carriers hoisted out seaplanes in U-boat waters. Moreover, seaplanes had to fly off the deck if they were to destroy Zeppelins before they could attack or pin-point the fleet's position. He therefore reverted to his pre-war policy of flying-off all seaplanes from the deck. As existing carriers could not fly-off two-seater scouts he wanted new ones with 100ft launching decks. However, Sueter had to wait for the Grand Fleet's seaplane carrier (*Campania*) to prove that seaplanes could fly off a carrier deck (6 August).

In early August 1914 the Grand Fleet was worried by reports of enemy aircraft near its Scapa Flow base. Just before the war Churchill replaced the CinC, Grand Fleet (Callaghan) with Jellicoe (Fisher's choice) who, as a Zeppelin admirer and aviation Sea Lord, demanded aircraft for the fleet. Sueter therefore suggested providing the large, fast carrier planned for the fleet pre-war, by converting a fast liner able to operate with the fleet's modern battleships and large enough to carry eight to twelve seaplanes. Its speed at sea would make it difficult for enemy aircraft to track it.

HMS *Campania* (1915), the first Grand Fleet carrier, as fitted for two-seater seaplanes after her second refit, winter 1915/16, with long sloping deck and split forefunnel. (IWM)

A converted liner was proposed because Churchill had suspended new building and they were the fastest merchantmen of the time, but it proved difficult to find a suitable one because most were already Armed Merchant Cruisers (AMCs) and the Operations Division and COWS (Sturdee) would not release them, failing to understand the importance of speed. Finally the old *Campania* (launched 1893) was rescued from a breaker's yard, but it was 5 May 1915 before she was repaired and converted (her small holds and low decks being unsuitable for seaplane stowage) and joined the fleet under Sueter's Deputy, Captain Oliver Schwann.

In June *Campania* accompanied the fleet to sea for exercises reporting hostile vessels (Operation 'Q') during which her seaplanes were hoisted out. Schwann claimed they had proved their usefulness to the CinC before a fleet action, but identified two major problems. The seaplanes' difficulties in fixing the true position of the enemy fleet in relation to the Grand Fleet explains Jellicoe's reluctance to use seaplanes for strategic reconnaissance before the fleets were in contact. Instead they were to scout the German fleet and report its course in relation to the Grand Fleet and allow Jellicoe to deploy to cross its 'T'.

The other problem was that the seaplanes (150hp Shorts and 100hp Sopwiths) could only be launched on one day out of three. One Wight 225hp scouted over the fleet but her wireless broke down. Schwann attributed the problems to the Atlantic swell which also made hoisting in and out difficult. He suggested better seaplanes and a second carrier for when the first was hoisting out. Jellicoe asked for *Engadine* (in the Forth) but was refused.

On 13–14 July the fleet held battle exercises simulating two fleets. Again the seaplanes (including a new Short 225) failed to get off in a slight swell. Jellicoe also heard of the Sopwith Schneider's floats breaking up during Operation 'G' on 4 July. He concluded that fleet seaplanes could not take off from the sea but must fly from decks, which he and Schwann already knew from their previous jobs (Second Sea Lord preparing fleet carrier plans and ADAD supervising *Ark Royal*'s design).

In late July Jellicoe informed the Admiralty that during a fleet action seaplanes, unable to get off the sea, had to use decks. His main concern was to shoot down the Zeppelins, the German CinC's eyes. He asked for aeroplanes to fly off *Campania* and come down on the sea with flotation bags to enable the pilot to be fished out. Jellicoe wanted aeroplanes because seaplanes could not climb swiftly enough to pose a threat to the Zeppelins. The Air Department, however, still favoured seaplanes and Schwann did not want aeroplanes landing on carriers. So flying seaplanes off the deck was continued.

Schwann improved *Campania*'s seaplane holds, her derricks to lift seaplanes up to the boat deck (to spread wings and test engines) and lengthened the 120ft flying-deck by 48 feet. On 6 August Flight Lieutenant W. L. Welsh flew-off a Sopwith Schneider, with only a little fuel and a light wind in case air eddies proved dangerous. Sueter could now abandon the idea of seaplanes taking off in heavy seas. The Third Sea Lord

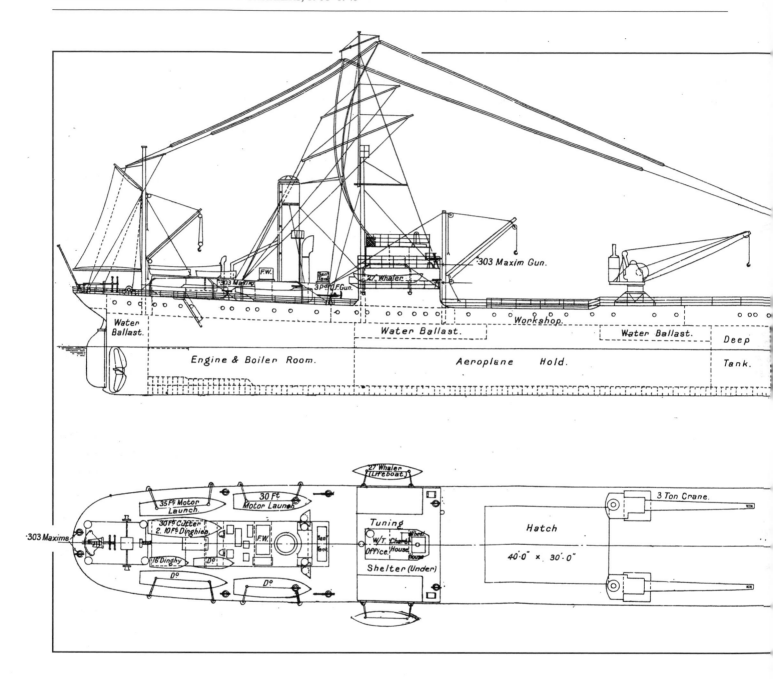

(Tudor) ordered deck launchings to fly-off all seaplanes under any sea conditions and the new First Sea Lord, Jackson, gave it high priority.

Schwann turned to flying-off two-seater seaplanes because Schneiders (weak floats, unreliable engine, no wireless or observer) and aeroplanes (shorter decks, but needed overhaul after each sea ditching or ship landing) were poor for fleet work. Two-seater seaplanes could come down on the sea but required a longer deck. He hoped high winds over the deck or acceleration by catapult would allow shorter take-offs by two-seater seaplanes. However, to fly off two-seaters *Campania* would need a 200ft deck involving extensive shipyard work.

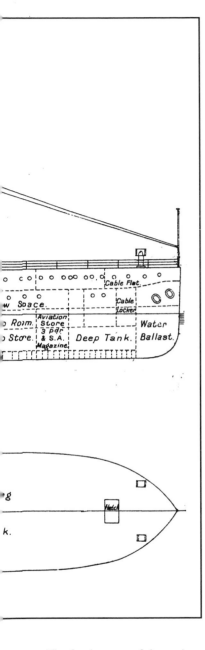

The development of the carrier (i): HMS *Ark Royal* (1915). Note the long deck to launch seaplanes and the cranes to recover them. (Royal Navy)

The fleet also needed more carriers with long decks. On 31 August, his last day as DAD, Sueter urgently proposed the building of three 28-knot seaplane carrying cruisers (100ft deck to fly-off nine seaplanes for scouting, anti-submarine and spotting duties) designed by Lieutenant Gerard Holmes RNVR, a Cunard constructor serving in *Riviera*. Sueter wanted to get the design accepted before being replaced and into the 1916 Shipbuilding Programme. In May 1915 Churchill, admitting that the Russians could not end the war quickly, again extended the Admiralty shipbuilding policy to allow new construction proposals.

When Vaughan Lee became DAS on 1 September, Tudor requested his opinion on Sueter's proposal, as the Director of Naval Construction (DNC), E. H. T. d'Eyncourt, stated that the design was over-optimistic, needed work and would take 15–18 months to build. The DAS decided to delay until he got more data on flying seaplanes off and onto ships.

Sueter had also got permission on 30 August for fighter aeroplane trials in *Vindex*, the latest 'cross-Channel' carrier conversion (authorised March 1915 and just completed with a flying-platform and hangar forward). This was a more seaworthy adaptation of *Ben-my-Chree*'s platform to fly-off seaplanes or aeroplanes against Zeppelins.

Vindex's deck was to test the principle of fast carriers providing a high wind over the deck to launch large aircraft from short decks. Her 64ft platform was designed by Holmes as a prototype of his 100ft design and he transferred to *Vindex* to determine the best flight-deck (September–November). As a result a 'Tail Directing Gear' was devised to fly the machine off safely (the torque of the engine had to be combated), deck conditions were measured for air currents and eddies, and a series of flights perfected. Two Bristol Scout fighters were stowed in the forward hangar with wings detached, and crews were trained to replace the wings and ready the aeroplanes for two flights in ten minutes. They needed a wind speed over deck of 25–30 knots to take off and for each knot the length of deck increased or decreased by six feet. A 25-knot ship needed a 30ft deck to fly-off scouts, a 20-knot 60 ft and a 15-knot 90 ft.

Similar measurements were found by *Campania*'s trials with seaplanes. After five more Schneider flights with full loads, using a widened deck and *Vindex*'s Tail Directing Gear, in November Schwann found a 200ft deck sufficient to fly-off fully loaded two-seater seaplanes, but despite Jackson's order to expedite her experiments, *Campania*'s second conversion was delayed.

In October Schwann enlisted the support of Vice-Admiral Sir George Warrender (Fleet Aviation Supervisor) and Jellicoe because he feared the Fourth Sea Lord (Lambert, transport services) wanted to return *Campania* to merchant use. Lambert was sending as many merchant auxiliaries as possible back to their trade because of the heavy losses to U-boats. The COWS (Oliver) also queried *Campania*'s alterations since she was larger than *Vindex* and the DNC's Department was overworked. Finally *Campania* was sent to Cammell Laird for her 200ft deck, but was delayed by muddle and labour shortages and her experiments did not re-start until May 1916.

Vaughan Lee also postponed consideration of Holmes' carrier design because Hugh Williamson again proposed flying on to a ship. In 1911 he transferred to the RNAS (despite a shortage of qualified submariners) and by August 1914 was overseeing *Ark Royal*'s completion. He was her Senior Pilot in the Dardanelles where her seaplanes failed to enable (by spotting) the battleship *Queen Elizabeth* to destroy the Turkish forts guarding the Dardanelles (5 March) or to discover the minefield which prevented the naval attack (18 March).

Williamson argued that the Dardanelles might have been forced if the seaplane pilots had been trained and used only for this purpose, but the fleet had no experience of seaplanes and its senior officers were not accustomed to seeking advice nor juniors to proffering it. The other problem was the poor seaplanes (Sopwiths and Wights) except Short No. 136 which could not take-off from the deck (*Ark Royal* was too slow). The aeroplanes which could, but had to ditch every time, were moved ashore instead.

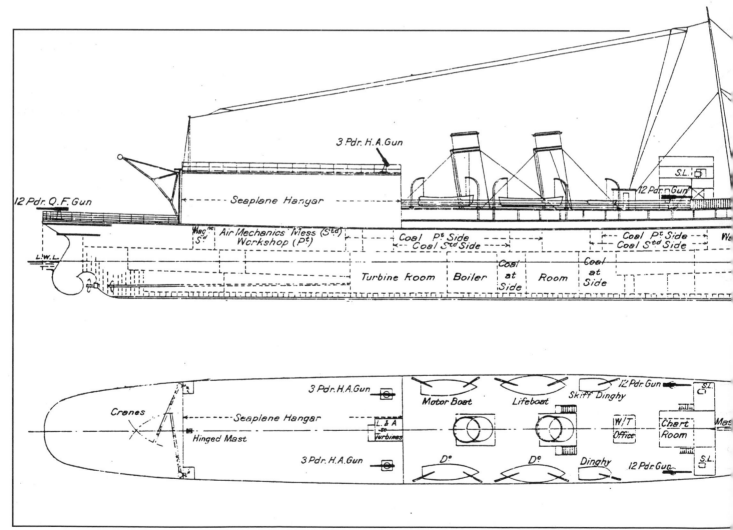

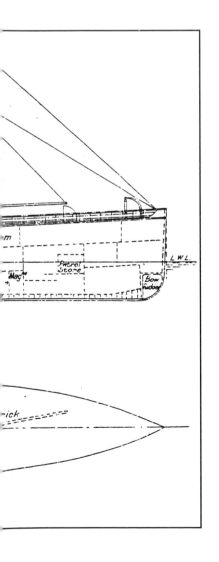

The development of the carrier (ii): HMS *Engadine* (1915), a cross-Channel ferry as refitted with a steel hangar but no flying-off deck. (Royal Navy)

On 5 March Williamson, injured in a seaplane crash, went home for treatment and was appointed to the Supply Section of the Air Department on 19 July. He tried to improve seaplane design but met resistance from Booth, the designer who told Churchill seaplanes could not be used as aeroplanes.

He therefore turned to the problems of fleet carrier aircraft when scouting and attacking Zeppelins and, as in 1911, concluded that the solution lay in superior performance of both aeroplanes and landing-on technique. His design consisted of a long deck with flying-off forward and alighting aft (aided by arrester gear) with a streamlined 'island' (for navigation, funnel and mast) on the starboard side to give a clear air flow. His explanatory model was similar to *Eagle* in the 1920s.

Williamson went to Vaughan Lee and also to the Board of Invention and Research (BIR), which Balfour set up on 5 July to organise scientific effort for the Navy and to evaluate new ideas. The senior officer on the Seaplane Sub-Committee, Squadron Commander J. W. Seddon (AD Test Pilot), was a friend who had sponsored another of his ideas, undercarriages to enable seaplanes to fly-off decks.

The Seaplane Sub-Committee was considering three proposals for launching seaplanes and preparing a 'Report . . . on the problem of Seaplanes rising from and alighting back on Ships' (18 September) for the BIR Central Committee. The Third Sea Lord had already decided on deck launching, but the Admiralty Central Committee independently decided on 23 September to ask the DNC to sketch a converted vessel ('special unit') to go with their report.

This was based on an American's (P. F. B. Biddle) proposal 'for a mother ship with a clear run fore and aft'. A direct development of existing practice, his fast, flush-decked ship, with no superstructure to create dangerous air conditions, seemed the simplest solution for launching and landing, but required 20 knots for safe alighting and 25–30 knots for employment with the battlefleet. This was close to Williamson's ideas.

The Seaplane Sub-Committee embodied Williamson's proposal into the report, but the DNC stated that Biddle's flush-decked ship was impracticable because a reliable internal combustion engine (to eliminate funnels) capable of 20 knots was not yet available. Williamson, moreover, used ship speed and arrester wires to reduce the deck length for safe landings. The BIR therefore recommended building a land deck, arrester gear, and 'island' to test the wind conditions of landing on.

Seddon also showed Williamson's model to Sueter, now Superintendent of Aircraft Construction (SAC), who recognised the originality and importance of the 'island' on the starboard side. As Williamson required advice on placing the funnels on one side of the ship, Sueter arranged for him to see Chief Constructor J. H. Narbeth (DNC's carrier designer) who saw 'no difficulty'.

The BIR performed a most valuable service in championing deck landing, to which Sueter, always ready to take advice, now committed the Air Department. At Grain it tested Williamson's arrester gear which worked well. Squadron Commander G. W.

Aldwell also tested aircraft brakes, suggested by Commander R. M. Groves (ASAC), which were adopted, together with a safety barrier of netting. Sueter hoped to test them in another 'cross-Channel' conversion (*Manxman*) but she was too small. The arrester gear feature was shelved until August 1916 when it was decided to convert a new carrier (*Argus*), with flying-on deck.

Little interest was now shown in Williamson's 'island' and the BIR's mock-up was not built. The DNC preferred two islands for navigation, accommodation, etc., and the advice of the BIR, which like Williamson appreciated the danger of superstructures causing air eddies (later proved in *Furious*), was ignored. Williamson was appointed to the Air Department's Operations Section as the DAS's Assistant and continued to recommend an 'island' carrier. The DNC later took up the idea in 1918, but made no recognition of Williamson's role. His only reward for the 'island' carrier concept was £500 from the Royal Commission on Awards to Inventors (1925).

The Air Department's policy was now to provide more fleet carriers. In January 1916 the DAS sought to convert another ferry (*Manxman*) to develop landing-on experiments at sea and then join the fleet. Sueter again (26 February) proposed to build the three carriers. A modified design allowed these, without stopping, to land aeroplanes on aft plus launch and recover large torpedo-seaplanes on a slipway aft. They were designed by Holmes (Air Department, Design Section) with help from Professor Sir John Biles, a naval architect (Glasgow University and consultant for *Dreadnought*) in January 1916.

Holmes also prepared Sueter's arguments for the renewed proposal to build three carriers, stressing that the Grand Fleet needed seaplane carriers to find and destroy Zeppelins when out of range of British shore-based machines. The aircraft had to launch from and land onto ships' decks, for reliability of launch and to avoid the danger of stopping, which existing carriers could not do.

In the meantime the DAS had also proposed (early April) converting another seagoing carrier with a flight-deck (a liner or the fleet messenger *Wahine*) or building an 'Improved cross-Channel' for the Grand Fleet. Sueter wanted to convert another eight ferries plus *Manxman*. This was a large programme for wartime, submitted in a piecemeal fashion and with the Air Department's justification poorly and diffusely presented, which was prejudicial because the Board was reluctant to add to the shipbuilding programme. When Fisher had become First Sea Lord in October 1914 he accelerated or started large numbers of submarines, destroyers and cruisers to reinforce the Grand Fleet as soon as possible, strengthened the battlecruisers and ordered monitors and landing-craft for projected assault-landings and anti-submarine escorts. With renewed unconditional U-boat warfare, merchant shipbuilding was given equal priority with warships. The shipyards also had large numbers of ships needing repair and refit, while the airship programme (rigids and their sheds, July 1915) competed for steel and workers.

Moreover, many skilled shipyard workers had enlisted in the Army or been lured away to munitions work under Lloyd George (Minister of Munitions) who had control

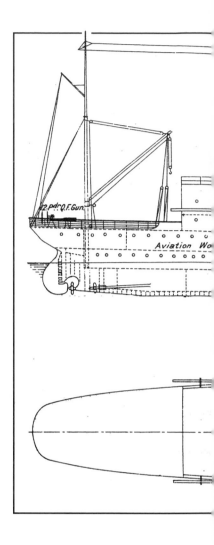

The development of the carrier (iii): HMS *Ben-my-Chree* (1915), the first ferry fitted to fly-off single-seater seaplanes and aeroplanes. (Royal Navy)

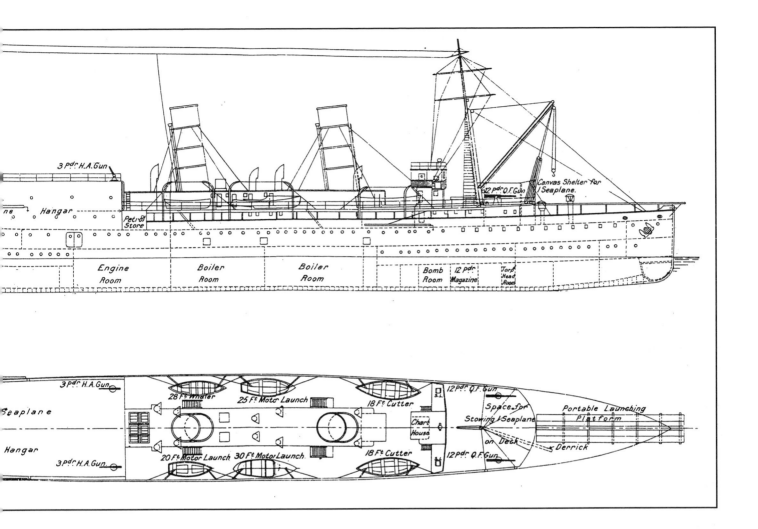

of all materials (especially steel which was in short supply) and labour. Those workers who remained were aware of their new industrial power, through shortages, and used strikes to raise their standard of living.

The Admiralty was under pressure to finish Fisher's building programme quickly to make good the Grand Fleet's shortages and to build more merchant ships. The situation was aggravated by a War Committee inquiry into why warship completion dates were not being met, inspired by Fisher and Churchill, themselves creators of the huge programme and unrealistic targets, as a means of securing their return to office.

One strategy (the Fourth Sea Lord's) was to return as many ships as possible to commerce. Another was to resist adding to the burden. Tudor opposed the building or conversion of any more ships including new carriers, although admittedly useful, which further strained the yards, took more ships away from the mercantile marine, or added to the DNC's workload. Even converting ferries meant six months' work. He advocated using existing carriers, rigids (being built) and flying boats until the need for new carriers had been proven.

It was the Naval Staff's task to counterbalance this material view with operational needs. The COWS (Oliver), though sympathetic to aviation, opposed the conversion of *Wahine*, earmarked as a minelayer, and impounding liners. He agreed to the transfer of *Engadine* and the new *Manxman* to the Grand Fleet, but gave anti-Zeppelin operations priority because he felt that fleet carriers (lacking suitable flying-decks) were under-employed. Jackson supported Tudor but like Oliver did not consult Jellicoe. He preferred to wait for *Campania*'s two-seater trials, hoping a better, flush deck design would be devised.

Jackson and Oliver failed to use the Naval Staff, which had only been created two years before the war, to study such issues in depth because of their lack of staff training. As a result they tried to do the staff work themselves, were overburdened with work and, in contrast to Churchill, were largely reactive to events rather than proactive.

The Air Department faced a struggle to get more carriers. Its prospects were hindered by poor staff work where Holmes' analysis of the Grand Fleet's carrier needs was not linked to a proper presentation of a full programme, with the benefits and savings outlined and the CinC's support made clear. Rather its *ad hoc* proposals were rejected piecemeal in March/April and months wasted. Four months later, on 10 August, Jackson agreed to build new seaplane carriers for a combination of reasons.

It soon became clear that Jellicoe required more carriers. Williamson visited the CinC on 17 April and gave him the Air Department plans. Jellicoe was primed to ask for *Wahine*'s conversion and the three new carriers. He also first suggested that the *Glorious* class (large cruisers) carry some seaplanes. Jellicoe wanted a seaplane carrier laid down at once since the only satisfactory fleet carriers were those which flew machines off and onto the deck. On 22 June, after Jutland, Jellicoe asked for two carriers because seaplanes had shown their value in a fleet action.

The operations of 1916 also showed that the fleet's aircraft had to improve. The attempts to intercept Zeppelins off the British coast had failed. In November 1915 the DAS suggested reverting to bombing the Zeppelin sheds, using 225hp Shorts, plus *Vindex*'s Bristol Scouts and a Deperdussin aeroplane on the cruiser *Aurora* to deal with snooping Zeppelins. The Grand Fleet was be in support because the new German CinC, Admiral Reinhard Scheer, was very aggressive. Again the Shorts and Sopwith Babies failed in their mission during operations in January and March 1916.

However, during Operation 'HRA' on 25 March Scheer sent out cruisers and an action was only averted by bad weather. By the winter of 1915/16 the Admiralty's reputation with the public, Parliament and government was low, having failed to stop the German fleet or bombardments (by ship or Zeppelin) of Great Britain. Jackson was therefore keen to force an action with the German fleet. Since an aerial torpedo attack on the German ports was still impossible (the Short 225s were under-powered and the 300hp version was still being developed) and Scheer had reacted to air raids Jackson wanted to use them as bait to the German fleet.

The development of the carrier (iv): HMS *Campania* (1915), a liner conversion and the first Grand Fleet carrier, shown as refitted with deck between funnels to fly-off large seaplanes. (Royal Navy)

So, on 4 May, Jellicoe's Grand Fleet waited in enemy waters for the German fleet to attack the carriers, *Engadine* and *Vindex*, after their eleven Sopwith Babies had bombed the Zeppelin sheds at Tondern (Operation 'XX'). However, only one Baby had managed to take-off and find the target and this proved insufficient to lure Scheer out. Seaplane carrier raids as bait were therefore abandoned and the next operation featured a cruiser attack on German merchantmen. When an action (Jutland) occurred, as Jellicoe and Beatty predicted, the German CinC took the initiative and sortied his fleet.

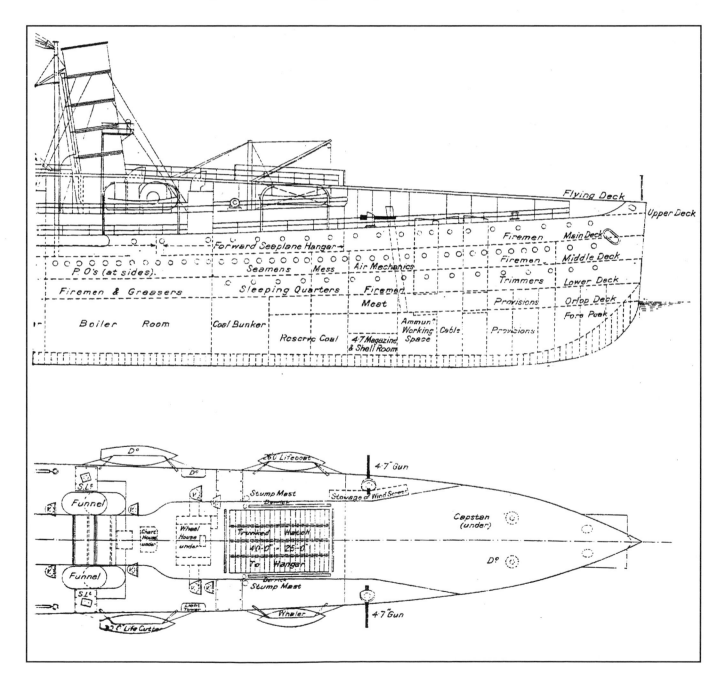

Meanwhile senior officers again focused on the seaplane failure. The Admiralty ordered two Courts of Inquiry. As in Operation 'G' (July 1915) the RNAS was heavily criticised for not testing the overloaded Babies at sea, not training inexperienced pilots in heavy swell and not using Shorts. However, the *Engadine* Inquiry, which included Commander R. H. Clark Hall (ex-CO *Ark Royal*) and Longmore, heard Flight Lieutenant F. J. Rutland (*Engadine*) testify that seaplane deck launches alone would make carrier operations independent of weather conditions. He suggested converting *Engadine* and *Vindex* but preferred the larger *Princess Margaret*, a converted minelayer.

The Inquiry therefore strongly recommended (11 May) that carriers deck-launch seaplanes so as to be independent of the weather and save time. As *Engadine* was too small, a larger more suitable vessel was required and all future ships had to fly seaplanes off the forecastle.

Schwann 'strongly' agreed and pointed out the need for more carriers as seaplanes could only fly singly off the deck at 15-minute intervals, whereas several could be hoisted out simultaneously. Jellicoe had already notified the Admiralty that the seaplanes' failure to get off the sea during Operation 'XX' confirmed that all must be deck-launched but he again failed to press for more carriers.

Jackson keenly awaited the Inquiry findings for an answer to the 'seaplane question', but the Air Department did not use this ammunition to gain Board approval for carrier building and Jackson never saw the findings because the former 'lost' them (May–September) possibly in an attempt to escape censure. By this time the findings had been overtaken by events, but it explains the failure to implement a carrier programme during the summer.

The Battle of Jutland on 31 May again demonstrated the fleet aircraft's problems, but also their great potential. Scheer decided to bombard Sunderland by which he hoped to trap and destroy an isolated British squadron to improve the relative fleet strengths. However, forewarned by the Admiralty's decrypting service, the Grand Fleet intercepted him. Jellicoe was denied a victory by the Admiralty's withholding of vital intelligence, the failure of his scouting forces and the skill of Scheer.

With his aircraft, except one seaplane, Jellicoe was also unlucky. *Vindex* was undergoing refit and *Campania* failed to notice the signal to leave port. She left later unescorted, but was sent back by Jellicoe, who feared losing his only, unprotected carrier to reported U-boats, for which he was later harshly criticised. From her new deck she had only flown-off single-seaters which Jellicoe had deployed to scout for minelayers, U-boats and Zeppelins. However, even these might have kept him informed during the day (especially about Scheer's movements) and her kite balloon likewise during the night.

Engadine was stationed with the battlecruisers and upon first contact with the German cruisers, Beatty (Battlecruiser Force) ordered her seaplanes up to scout. Rutland (SFO) and his observer (Assistant Paymaster G. S. Trewin) got off from the sea in a Short 184 within 28 minutes which was regarded as a record! Trewin made four signals before engine trouble forced them down. *Engadine* was unable to launch any more seaplanes because the fleet disappeared over the horizon while she was hoisting out the first seaplane.

This flight, however, did show Beatty and Jellicoe the potential value of seaplanes for scouting and gunnery spotting. British gunnery had been poor and post-battle committees identified it as an area that would benefit from the use of aircraft. The day after the battle Zeppelins were active over the fleet which resorted to its main armament to drive them off. Again aircraft were needed but everything depended on launching them quickly, hence Jellicoe's demand for two carriers with flight-decks referred to above.

On 19 August Scheer again tried to attack Sunderland and nearly caused another action. This time he made sure that Zeppelins were covering his advance and flank. *L13* spotted Tyrwhitt's Harwich Force which it wrongly identified as a squadron of battleships, and Scheer turned away from his collision course with the Grand Fleet (again warned by decrypts) to attack what seemed an isolated squadron. As Jellicoe came south from Scapa he ran into Zeppelins and U-boats, losing two light cruisers to the latter.

As before, he lacked carriers to protect the fleet. The old *Campania* was again missing, with engine trouble as the DNC had warned, and her kite balloon was being flown by the battleship *Hercules*. Tyrwhitt left *Vindex* behind because she was too slow. This left *Engadine* with the battlecruisers. Rutland intended to deploy his Sopwith Baby to attack two Zeppelins at 1,000 and 6,000 feet, but the sea was too rough for his seaplane whose potential was negated by being unable to launch.

Jellicoe made comparisons with the Zeppelins which he believed had scouted for the German CinC and enabled him to escape the Grand Fleet and direct U-boats on to Jellicoe's cruisers. He decided that the Grand Fleet, in view of this new U-boat/Zeppelin alliance, could not go to sea unless it had a full destroyer escort or seaplanes able to destroy the Zeppelins and signal the presence of U-boats. These conditions were not to be easily met; escorts were scarce because of the anti-submarine campaign and the seaplanes were unsuccessful. As a result the battleships were inactive.

The concept of useful fleet seaplanes came closer when Flight Commander V. S. Wilberforce successfully flew-off a two-seater seaplane (Short 225) from *Campania's* lengthened deck on 3 June, two days after Jutland. Holmes's 'Tail Directing Gear' and a wheeled axle, jettisoned into the sea, were used. Another four flights were made carrying weights and equipment. On 14 June a Short (with full load plus observer) and a Sopwith Baby (with a heavier load than during Operation 'XX') were flown-off. Jellicoe now had scouting and anti-Zeppelin aircraft while *Campania's* aircraft lasted.

Given his fear that seaplanes would take longer to fly-off than to hoist out, Schwann also experimented with flying-off in quick succession. On 22 June two Babies were placed one behind the other and flown-off in the space of a minute. Next day a Baby was placed behind a Short and both flew-off within a minute. Schwann concluded that the length of deck needed depended on the pilot's skill, but exceptionally long ones were no longer needed.

On 18–19 July, during fleet exercises, *Campania* showed what she might have achieved if seaplanes had flown-off her deck at Jutland. On the first day a slight Atlantic swell caused the ship to pitch 3° and the bow to rise 18 feet. To launch seaplanes from the sea was impossible, but they flew-off from her deck. However, *Campania* had left the fleet to turn into the wind, nullifying the argument that flying from the deck ended the need for speed to catch up the fleet and she was still obliged to stop to hoist in.

The second day the swell was less but the wind slight and the first seaplane to take-off crashed into the sea. A second Short was flown-off immediately and the first was salvaged (and her crew rescued) afterwards. In the afternoon visibility was too poor for flying. Seaplane scouting (full fuel, wireless and observer) was a great success, providing much information and unlike kite balloons they could reconnoitre behind smoke-screens.

Jellicoe's main problem – a perennial one – was the accurate reporting of the bearing, course and disposition of the enemy fleet which required experienced observers. He told the Admiralty that the seaplanes flown from *Campania*'s deck during the exercises had proved of great use, and on 20 July again asked for the *Glorious* class to be fitted with seaplanes. He did not press for more carriers, but possibly wanted these two ships converted because of their poor gunnery capabilities. From this time fleet interest in aviation increased rapidly. The Admiralty was encouraged and Schwann earned a letter of appreciation, some consolation for missing Jutland. On his advice Scapa Air Station was built up as a fleet training centre, the importance of preparation, especially for observers, now being fully appreciated. At this point *Campania*'s engines broke down and a new fleet carrier was clearly needed.

Meanwhile in response to Jellicoe's requests for Holmes's design to be built and the *Glorious* class to carry seaplanes, Tudor asked the DNC and DAS to report on Holmes's design. The delay (13 May–22 June) before the DNC replied was another factor in the lack of action on carrier design in the summer. The problem was that after Jutland the DNC was overworked, assessing battle damage and organising large numbers of repairs.

The DAS and DNC agreed that the *Glorious* class would be delayed by modifications to carry some seaplanes, but they could have been ready for operations in 1917. They were large ships with plenty of room, and if their air arrangements proved inadequate (probable) they could then have been converted in turn without depriving the fleet of carriers. No one asked Jellicoe whether the delay was acceptable, nor did he volunteer to sacrifice their gunnery potential (in *Furious*'s case very poor) as Beatty did in 1917. *Glorious* and *Courageous* were commissioned in October 1916 and changes so late required large and costly (in time and resources) alterations. *Furious* commissioned later, but Jellicoe did not realise she had only two 18-inch guns, of little value.

Despite shipyard congestion the DNC again stressed *Campania*'s poor state and the need of a replacement. With the Air Department's proposal to build a carrier refused

The development of the carrier (v): HMS *Furious* (1917), a converted large cruiser, showing the forward flight-deck on which Dunning proved that flying-on was possible. (Royal Navy)

and the COS's ruling against converting liners in service, the DNC for the first time suggested converting unfinished liners (12 months) on which work had ceased in August 1914. He recommended two Italian-owned liners: *Conte Rosso* (Beardmore No. 519) and *Guilio Cesare* (Swan Hunter No. 967).

Beardmore prompted the DNC by asking him in May to modify their liner to help ease the merchant shipping crisis. It is not known who made the connection, but the hunt was on for liners that could be converted to carriers. The DNC preferred No. 967 because she could stow more seaplanes and had larger flying-off and alighting decks. The main problem was the speed of only 20 knots, but the DAS accepted this because it reduced the time needed to meet Jellicoe's request for carriers.

Tudor reminded the Board that carrier building had been refused in March because of shipyard congestion and the CinC's request would affect either light cruiser or

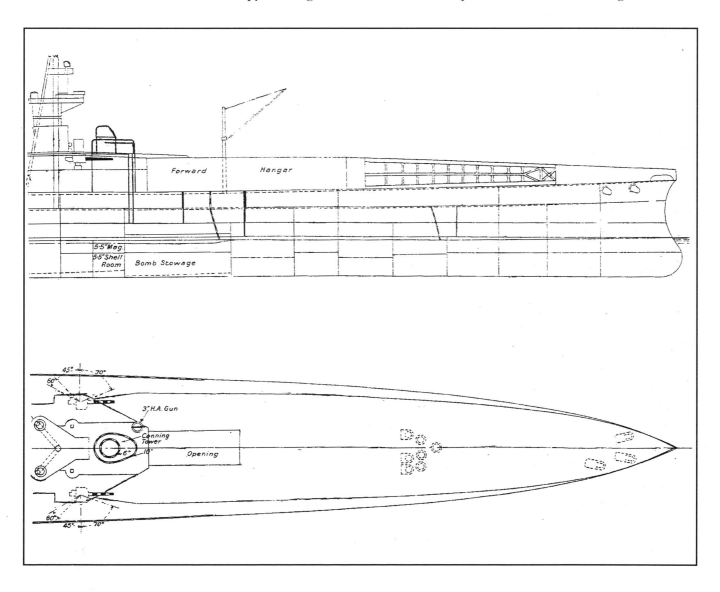

merchant construction. He also doubted if they could be completed in a year and wanted proof of their value which he found difficult to estimate.

He preferred to rely on rigid airships (the first expected in August), flying boats and kite balloons, while the DNC and DAS prepared a design for the future. Jackson agreed because he thought that a special 25-knot seaplane carrier would be superior to a converted liner and wanted an official design prepared for Board consideration.

Jellicoe was told that the *Glorious* class would carry a few seaplanes, but a carrier would only be considered when a design was ready and in the light of shipping resources. This was unpromising given the shipyard congestion and the Admiralty's not wanting to add to it. Tudor and Jackson also recognised that a conversion was not the best design and wished to build a carrier(s) after the immediate shipping crisis had passed. The problem was whether the fleet could wait and the Air Department and CinC required better carriers quickly.

Vaughan Lee (DAS) appointed an Air Department Committee of Sueter (chairman), Clark Hall, C. R. Randall (engineer), Seddon, Williamson, Edmonds and Holmes (secretary) to prepare carrier air requirements. There were two main issues: design and whether to build or convert.

Holmes argued that the Board was not fully informed of carrier experience and the consequent need of a new type. *Campania* had shown that his own design had too short a flight-deck to fly-off two-seaters, no 'shunting' facilities and was too small and narrow for flying-on. More controversially, he thought that a 21-knot converted liner would suffice since stopping to hoist out was eliminated (though he ignored the need to turn into the wind). This would save design time, require less material and labour and save on the parts already built.

On 29 July the Committee agreed that Jellicoe's requirements (flying scouts and fighters off the deck) plus torpedo-aircraft (added by Sueter) and a flight-deck aft for flying-on trials required a

The development of the carrier (vi): HMS *Argus*, the final concept of the aircraft carrier, with one long deck for flying-off and on but no island (though one was tried). (Royal Navy)

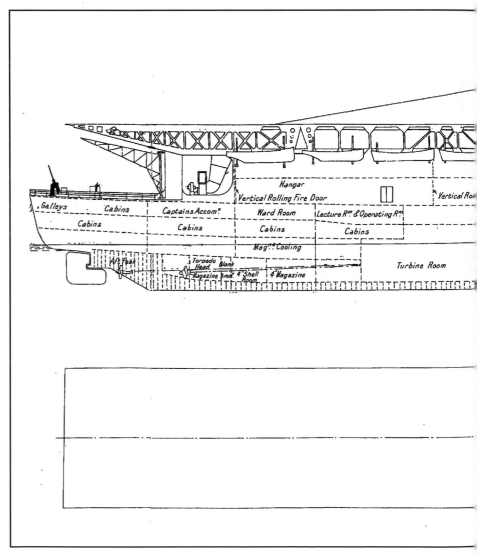

large ship. It also recommended converting liners, the Grand Fleet having confirmed that a 20-knot speed was sufficient, and asked the DNC to report on the time and resources saved. On the same day, surely not by coincidence, Beatty and Jellicoe recommended that the larger liner (No. 967), favoured by the Air Department and DNC, be converted. Their official requests allowed Sueter and the DNC to use her as the basis for the carrier design.

Meanwhile the DAS finally brought together the arguments (carrier experience and Jellicoe's requirements) for a programme of large, new carriers and asked for both liners to be converted. The DNC suggested undertaking a sketch design (an enlarged Holmes design with the flying-off and landing-decks linked between two islands). On 10 August Tudor and Jackson agreed to convert both liners, sacrificing the desired 25-knot speed for early delivery, dependent on the effect on other work and completion times.

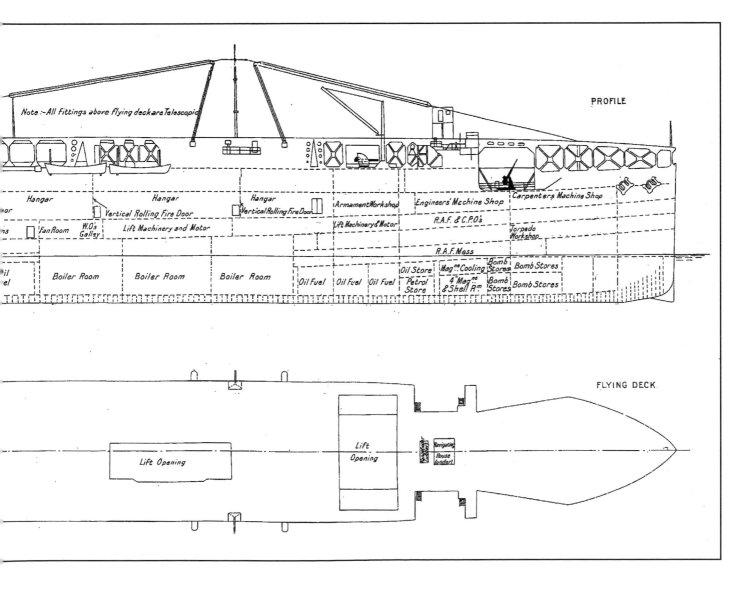

Tudor, having opposed carrier building since March, suddenly agreed to two. The need for a new carrier type (first called an aircraft carrier by Holmes in July) had been explained and supported by Jellicoe. Jutland had also shown the paucity of fleet aviation. Moreover, the rigid airships, his main hope for not building carriers, were delayed and *LZ85*'s capture at Salonika had shown their inferiority to the latest Zeppelins.

The Air Department opposed the deployment of land-based flying boats with the fleet because they required long flights to reach the fleet, refuelling was a problem and they were required for anti-submarine duties. Tudor now realised that new carriers would transform fleet air tactics, by flying-off and onto the deck and operating aeroplanes and add 'another string to our bow' if the rigids failed. However, he still had a get-out clause if the carriers affected other building.

Every effort was made to find another solution. The lists of liners were again searched but only two 20-knotters, needing lengthy conversion, were suitable. The question of 'extemporising' some carriers by spring was also explored. Holmes suggested converting the 23-knot cruisers *Cumberland* and *Suffolk*, due for refits, but they could only take a 140ft deck. At this stage no one gave consideration to warships still building, such as *Furious*. Further studies in October 1916 also proved fruitless.

On 16 September Jackson ordered a conference to consider the firms' plans and the shipbuilding consequences. He decided to complete only *Conte Rosso* (later *Argus*) by 1 November 1917 with precedence over the light cruiser *Raleigh* since Beardmore had men available and Swan Hunter had not.

The Admiralty was also encouraged by successful landing trials at Grain under Holmes and Aldwell. Three ropes with sandbags at each end, similar to Ely's gear in 1911, were used. Flight Lieutenant Wright (Avro) landed with engine off and taxied into the ropes, catching them with a hook. On 19 September four landings were made and Tudor authorised a mock deck to train pilots in ship landings. This system was simpler than Williamson's and took up less of the deck. Tudor, however, expected that Sueter's net would provide a final safety barrier. In fact Grain's arrester gear failed at sea as aircraft were blown over the side before catching the wires.

In the meantime fleet aircraft and carrier shortages were acute. At Scapa on 12 October Tudor discussed these needs with Jellicoe who asked bluntly about the Grand Fleet's lack of efficient carriers or scouting airships. Tudor stated that *Conte Rosso* would be converted in a year. He suggested relying on flying boats meanwhile, but Jellicoe thought that they lacked the range for fleet work. Tudor therefore agreed to repair *Campania* quickly. Back in London Jackson proposed relying on rigid airships, thought Jellicoe's request for carriers 'half-hearted' and did not circulate it.

However, the DAS and DNC took it up and in November suggested that *Guilio Cesare* be converted (slowly because of labour shortages) as a replacement for *Campania* and cover for *Argus*. The firm offered good terms, the DNC had a design and a slip would be cleared. Oliver (COWS), advised by Williamson on air matters since September, accepted that shore-based flying boats could not substitute for fleet carriers. Tudor, however, now opposed the second carrier conversion he had agreed to in September, being again optimistic about rigids. The new Zeppelin *L33* had been captured intact on 24 September and was to form the basis for mass production. Two rigids under construction, *R28* and *R30*, were cancelled because of their inferiority to the Zeppelin.

At this stage (December) Jellicoe, who as CinC had requested two carriers, became First Sea Lord but backed Tudor's decision on No. 967 despite the need to cover for the ageing *Campania* and the lone new carrier *Argus*. Jellicoe advocated her conversion but could see no prospect of finishing the vessel during the war. Moreover, a rigid airship supporter before the war, he exaggerated the Zeppelins' achievements and so agreed with Tudor's arguments.

By the end of 1916 considerable progress had been made in carrier design. The concept and designation of aircraft carrier had been accepted. Flying-off from and onto the deck were adopted after hard experience at sea. However, the Navy was still wedded to a mix of seaplanes and aeroplanes and the concept of the island carrier was still ignored.

The main obstacle to further progress was the lack of carriers. Only one new aircraft carrier with a long deck (*Argus*) had been agreed and she was not to arrive until November 1917 (optimistic). Meanwhile the Grand Fleet faced the Zeppelin, whose capabilities were over-estimated, with only the old *Campania* and the 'cross-Channel' carriers *Manxman*, *Vindex* and *Engadine* (the last with no deck at all).

Carrier Development in 1917

Within three weeks of Jellicoe's refusal to convert a second carrier, the new CinC Grand Fleet, Beatty, pointed out the fleet's inadequate provision of efficient carriers and scouting airships. The new 'cross-Channel' carrier *Manxman* had proved too slow, and intelligence reported that the Germans had six seaplane carriers as well as Zeppelins. These were harbour depot ships, but Beatty, not knowing this, as with Jellicoe and Zeppelins, believed the worst scenario. He therefore faced an even worse Grand Fleet carrier situation for 1917 than in 1916.

Up to December 1916 shipbuilding policy looked no further than to clear existing congestion. Asquith's government had been reluctant to intervene decisively in war planning. This was dramatically altered when Lloyd George became Prime Minister in December 1916. On 22 January 1917 the Admiralty was asked to submit to the War Cabinet a building programme for 1917, bearing in mind the U-boat crisis, and then to the end of 1918.

On the 31st Jellicoe presented a two-year programme to meet all needs, including probable losses to U-boats and German construction up to January 1919. The main priority was escorts plus the fleet's weak areas including four carriers for 1918. This programme was cut (it affected merchant building), but the carriers were designated a special case, essential to the fleet despite the length of construction time (15 months).

This programme embraced the short and long term and precipitated a debate on how best to meet fleet needs. Short-term replacements for *Ben-my-Chree* (lost to Turkish artillery on 11 January) and *Manxman* (too slow) plus two carriers for the East Indies and Western Approaches were needed. The DAS in one of his last acts requested six carriers, five 'cross-Channel' type (converting or completing ferries) and one large ocean-going (completing *Guilio Cesare*).

The War Cabinet decision to lay down four carriers was referred to the newly established Fifth Sea Lord (Commodore Godfrey Paine, the reorganised Air Board's new Admiralty representative). On 31 January the Board decided to separate the carrier question from the overall building programme despite Tudor's concern about the effect on merchant shipbuilding, a crucial factor given the rise in U-boat sinkings.

Paine's policy (15 February) was to build two ocean-going (24–25 knots, fourteen aircraft, flying off and on decks, slipway aft and 5-day range) and two 'Improved cross-Channel' (24–25 knots, 8 aircraft, flying off deck and 3-day range) carriers. As these four ships could not be completed for a considerable time, he proposed, while designing the ocean-going carrier, to convert two ferries (*Stockholm*, later *Pegasus*, and *Nairana*) on the slips for the fleet's immediate needs.

Jellicoe, despite Tudor's opposition, authorised the conversion of two ferries, instead of building two 'Improved cross-Channel' carriers, and the allocation of slips at Cammell Laird and Fairfield (the latter not available until August) for two ocean-going carriers. Fairfield was made the principal design firm (for economy, least duplication and speed of construction) because of their proximity to Beardmore who were converting *Argus*. However, Fairfield were building four urgently needed minesweepers and in early June their carrier was suspended and the design work handed over to Cammell Laird.

On 29 March the DNC completed the sketch design (9,000 tons, 540ft, 22 machines, flying off and landing on decks, two islands with funnels and linking bridge above the deck, lifts, stern slipway, light cruiser protection). Size was kept down to expedite construction. However, he felt that the new shipbuilding programme was impracticable and that only one new carrier could be built, the four minesweepers at Fairfield being completed instead.

On 31 May Rear-Admiral Lionel Halsey (ex-Grand Fleet and Fourth Sea Lord) replaced Tudor as Third Sea Lord. The latter had been in office since before the war and had opposed the Board's policy on building carriers. Halsey reviewed shipbuilding policy and got War Cabinet permission to lay down another carrier in addition to the Shipbuilding Programme of four carriers (Fairfield and Cammell Laird ships, *Pegasus* and *Nairana*). However, only one ocean carrier ('new *Argus*') was finally placed on 5 July with Armstrong because of the effect on Cammell Laird's light cruiser and minesweeper building.

Forced by the government to prepare a shipbuilding programme two years in advance, rather than on an ad hoc roll over basis, the Admiralty for the first time commit-

HMS *Argus* (1918). Converted from the uncompleted Italian liner *Conte Rosso* by William Beardmore, she was the first true aircraft carrier ever built and was completed with a flush deck. (FAAM)

ted itself to a carrier building policy for both short- and long-term needs. By July two ocean-going carriers (*Argus* and the 'new *Argus*', later *Hermes*) were being built for the long term, the former using a liner hull and the latter purpose built. Two more 'cross-Channel' carriers (*Pegasus* and *Nairana*) were being converted for short-term needs. All were to operate aeroplanes and seaplanes.

The problem still remained of how to provide large carriers for the fleet in 1917 from over-stretched shipyards when U-boats losses meant more merchant ships had to be built. Although the Board had a programme of four carriers, the DNC and Third Sea Lord considered it to be impracticable. It was early July before a slip and labour could be provided for an ocean-going carrier. It was the Grand Fleet itself which solved the problem of the short-term provision of large fleet carriers.

Beatty was badly affected by the Jutland failures and determined to take full advantage of any second chance. One Jutland lesson was the use of aircraft for scouting, spotting and eliminating enemy aircraft (the Zeppelins seemed to command the air). Within days of becoming CinC, Beatty instigated a review of fleet aviation. As a result he suggested converting *Furious* to replace *Campania* and develop Fleet aviation while waiting for *Argus*.

The first review was by Lieutenant Commander R. Seymour, Beatty's signals officer, whom he used as an additional staff officer. His was a controversial appointment as he was not a specialist, but his opinions were valued by Beatty, despite his having made crucial signal errors both at Dogger Bank and Jutland. On 10 December 1916

Seymour argued that aircraft had a big role in fleet operations, modern carriers were required for them and the matter was urgent if the Grand Fleet was to match the German fleet in a vital arm.

Schwann agreed and on the 15th recommended that the Grand Fleet deploy all 'cross-Channel' ferries; *Argus*; two more large carriers; and 80ft decks (for fighters) and catapults (for scouts) on cruisers to carry at least twenty scouts, twenty fighter escorts and thirty anti-Zeppelin fighters (all aeroplanes with better performance than seaplanes).

Beatty accepted this advice and asked the Admiralty to prepare for the coming operations season by laying down the fleet aircraft types and the functions that they would perform. He also set up (26 January) a Grand Fleet Committee under Rear-Admiral Sir Hugh Evan Thomas (5th Battle Squadron) to investigate urgently the fleet's needs for the summer. After consulting air officers this completed its report on 5 February which Beatty sent at once to the Admiralty.

The report assigned strategic fleet scouting of the North Sea to flying boats and rigid airships, tactical fleet scouting to seaplanes, spotting to kite balloons and destruction of Zeppelins to aeroplanes. For the last duty it recommended replacing Baby seaplanes with aeroplanes on the advice of Rutland (now SFO *Manxman*).

Its main problem was increasing the number of fleet aircraft. To keep two scouts and twelve fighters (against an expected six Zeppelins) constantly in the air during an action the fleet needed 20 scouts and 20 fighters to allow for wireless, engine and other failures. However, only twelve scouts and fourteen fighters were carried: eight in *Manxman* (16 knots) which could fly-off only four (aeroplanes), four in *Engadine* which could fly-off none and the rest in *Campania* (unreliable engines). *Argus* would not be ready until November 1917.

The Committee therefore considered ways to carry more aircraft. Alteration of old cruisers was considered impracticable. Re-boiling Manxman would take too long and only enable four aeroplanes to fly-off. The conversion of more 'cross-Channel' carriers was discarded because they were too short to support a long flight-deck. Large merchant ships were not an option; they were required to replace losses from U-boats. Thus they recommended *Furious*'s conversion. She had high speed, a wide deck and a long forecastle, and removal of the one 18-inch gun forward allowed a 200ft deck with hangar for eight fighters beneath it. Beatty accepted her conversion since she was of little gunnery value.

It is not known who suggested *Furious*, but it led to more warships, still building or lying unfinished, being converted. Warships had better protection, were more stable and faster than merchant ships. Surprisingly the DNC had not considered converting warships still building, only old cruisers (needing much work and unsuitable). He preferred to convert the liner, *Guilio Cesare*, which needed less material and labour.

The Evan Thomas Committee also revived the idea of using existing warships, specifically light cruisers, to carry aircraft. The Admiralty had looked at this in October

1916 but found it impossible with seaplanes. The Committee were the first naval officers, outside aviation circles, to decide to sacrifice gun power for aircraft (to attack Zeppelins). Beatty accepted the use of light cruisers but only if it did not decrease gun power.

This Grand Fleet air policy, which Beatty insisted must be implemented, had a great effect on the Admiralty. It produced for the first time a comprehensive policy statement for the CinC, emphasising that air development was limited by a shortage of fast carriers and high-powered engines for seaplanes. He was also given the details of *Argus* (eighteen aircraft), her date of completion and alighting trials at Grain, but was not told that *Argus*'s delivery in November was 'improbable'. Nor was he told about the War Cabinet's four-carrier programme.

The provision of fleet carriers, however, was reopened. Tudor strongly opposed the carrier conversion of *Furious*, a pet design of Lord Fisher's, since rigid airships would be

Squadron Commander Frederick J. Rutland (left). Commissioned from the lower deck, he flew the only seaplane launched at Jutland and pioneered aeroplanes with the Grand Fleet. (IWM)

ready more quickly. However, Paine (5SL), now on the Board, argued that the Grand Fleet Committee had shown serious fleet seaplane deficiencies which could be remedied in 1917 only by converting *Furious* as British airships could not match Zeppelins.

Jellicoe, unlike his predecessor, sought the CinC's opinion on removing *Furious*'s forward gun and the delay involved. A gunnery specialist, he thought little of *Furious*'s value with only two 18-inch guns. Beatty accepted the proposal and Jellicoe ordered the conversion on 14 March. She joined the fleet in July 1917 with Short seaplanes and Sopwith Pup aeroplanes. Her after 18-inch gun was not removed as this would have delayed her completion and that of the new fleet carrier which was due for the summer.

The problem, as Tudor pointed out, was the retrieval of her aircraft. Her seaplanes had to come down on the sea and her aeroplanes to ditch with flotation bags which was dangerous for the pilot and wasteful of planes. *Furious* was in effect a one-shot carrier in 1917 which affected her deployment. Any decision to fly-off was only taken if the risk of aircraft being unavailable later, when more urgently needed, could be accepted. For instance when German light cruisers raided the Scandinavian convoys, *Furious* did not launch her aircraft because the weather was too bad for her seaplanes, and her fighters were held back to counter Zeppelins.

On 16 June Halsey visited Beatty who complained at the lack of large, fast carriers and that new carriers would take 17–18 months to arrive. Halsey offered to convert the first *Raleigh* class light cruiser (*Cavendish*, later renamed *Vindictive*) which he hoped would not be delayed beyond her February 1918 completion date unless a flying-on deck were required. This was accepted as an addition to the Admiralty Shipbuilding Programme to provide another fast carrier for the Grand Fleet by early 1918.

HMS *Furious* (1917) as originally completed, with an 18-inch gun aft and flight-deck forward with hangar below. Note the massive superstructure, which affected attempts to land-on the deck aft later. (IWM)

In 1917 there were two main problems. The first was the recovery of the reconnaissance and anti-Zeppelin machines carried by *Furious* and light cruisers. The fleet and the Air Department still favoured the use of seaplanes, launched from the deck, for long flights over the sea. They could come down on the sea but their ship had to stop to hoist them in. There was no time to fit *Furious* with a stern recovery slipway as suggested for *Argus* and *Hermes*. The light cruisers, given their other duties, could not stop. As a result the anti-Zeppelin machines were one-shot weapons (usually wrecked on ditching in the sea) and their premature use would leave the fleet unprotected against Zeppelins.

If aeroplanes were used they could land on a ship as Holmes, Williamson and the Air Department planned, but *Argus* and *Hermes* would be unavailable for some time and *Furious* had not been modified to land aeroplanes on due to her short conversion

time before joining the fleet. Moreover, landing on a deck had been done only once, by the American Eugene Ely in 1910. It might be a 'stunt', impossible to achieve regularly at sea.

The other problem was that the Admiralty, despite many studies, had not found a way to fly-off from light cruisers without degrading their main armament; seaplanes needed a long run to get off, despite the cruisers' fast speed, and Beatty insisted that the gun armament remain unaffected.

The situation was transformed by two men. One proved that landing on ships was possible and the other that sufficient aircraft could be carried before the carriers now building and expected in 1918 arrived. This allowed the aeroplane's (i.e., as opposed to the seaplane's) adoption by the Grand Fleet on 1 September 1917. It is usually argued that this paved the way for the development of the aircraft carrier, but in fact the process was the other way round. The aeroplane was the final piece in the jigsaw puzzle whose completion showed that the aircraft carrier concept worked.

The fleet planners and thinkers could now develop a doctrine to take full benefit from the aircraft carrier concept. By the end of 1917 the Admiralty and the Grand Fleet had agreed that in 1918 the fleet's air capability could be revolutionised and make an important contribution to the war at sea.

It was Rutland who, in June 1917, overcame the problem of aircraft numbers by flying aeroplanes off very short turret platforms fitted in light cruisers (fighters) and capital ships (fighters and scouts). In December 1916 he had discovered that *Manxman* could not launch seaplanes from her forward flying deck and asked for Sopwith Pup aeroplanes which only arrived in March 1917 because of Western Front needs. Because of his pilots' reluctance to fly these over the sea, Rutland undertook flotation bag experiments. These showed that Pups floated better than seaplanes which capsized and sank, leaving only their floats visible.

Meanwhile Rear-Admiral W. C. Pakenham (Battlecruiser Force) asked Rear-Admiral R. F. Phillimore (1st Battlecruiser Squadron) to chair a committee to consider Lieutenant Commander C. H. B. Gowan's proposal to fit a flying-deck to the light cruiser *Yarmouth*. Gowan's planned 45ft deck would mask the forward gun while the plane was flown off. This was a problem given Beatty's ruling on light cruiser armament. Rutland, however, convinced the Committee that he could fly a Pup off a 20ft deck. On 27 June he flew off *Yarmouth*'s forecastle in only 14½ feet and the next day in 15½ feet while under way at 20 knots. Pakenham at once asked the Admiralty and Beatty to fit other light cruisers.

The Admiralty designed a deck that would not interfere with the armament, and canvas hangars for the aeroplanes. Beatty agreed that *Courageous*, *Glorious* and a light cruiser per squadron would carry fighters. On 21 August Flight Sub-Lieutenant B. A. Smart flew off *Yarmouth* in a Sopwith Pup and shot down Zeppelin *L23* at 8000 feet, after which he was picked up by a destroyer. The deployment of fighters in the light cruisers meant that the carriers could carry more scouts which they alone could fly off.

The platforms were fixed and the warship steamed into wind to launch the fighter. Light cruisers in the scouting screen could do this, but capital ships in the line could not, so Gowan designed a revolving platform which turned into the wind. On 1 October Rutland flew off a turret platform in the battlecruiser *Repulse*.

Now, neither capital ships nor light cruisers need leave their position to launch aeroplanes and on 23 October the Admiralty Operations Committee decided to fit them all with turret platforms. They carried two-seater Sopwith 1½-Strutters for gunnery spotting and large numbers of anti-Zeppelin fighters to compensate for the small number of carrier aircraft available.

At the same time the Admiralty was seeking to solve the problem of landing on a ship. Experiments at the Isle of Grain were re-started in late 1916 under Aldwell and then Squadron Commander H. R. Busteed. It was considered that Schneider seaplanes and flying boats too could land on. Since the experiments were conducted on land, aeroplanes (Avro and Sopwith Pup) were used. By 28 April 1917, twenty-eight landings had been made, twenty-five of them by Sopwith Pups. The arrangements were deemed promising though not yet 'absolutely satisfactory' by Busteed, and the experiments continued, using aeroplanes (two-seater Sopwith 1½-Strutters) and seaplanes.

Malone, now CO Isle of Grain, believed that they had solved the aeroplane landing problem and could tackle the seaplanes, but he knew that the fleet lacked a ship to carry out sea trials and the fleet's carriers could not carry out 'routine' work with aeroplanes because they lacked decks for them to land on.

Furious (Captain W. Nicholson) was not equipped with a landing deck, but was the best ship available, being fast and having a long, broad flying-off deck (228ft × 50ft). Commissioned on 26 June 1917, she joined the Grand Fleet on 4 July with three Short seaplane scouts and five Sopwith Pup fighters. Intensive trials were begun immediately under Squadron Commander E. H. Dunning (SFO). A brilliant pilot himself, he had been given the pick of the Navy's best pilots.

He estimated that, with *Furious* maintaining 31½ knots, he could land an aeroplane on her flight-deck at a very low speed. This would be a 'stunt' needing a very skilled pilot, but it would prove the feasibility of flying on to a deck. The procedure was for the Sopwith Pup, very manoeuvrable at low speed, to fly around the superstructure at its slowest speed into wind, and land with engine cut and a securing-party to keep the machine on the deck using hand toggles.

Dunning achieved this tricky manoeuvre on 2 August, only a month after Rutland had flown off *Yarmouth*, and now wanted to fly-on a Sopwith T.1 Cuckoo two-seater torpedo-aeroplane (the name Cuckoo was not assigned until after the war), for torpedo and reconnaissance work, after an obstructive derrick mast had been removed. Nicholson agreed that with improvement of landing space, all *Furious*'s fighter pilots could with practice land successfully. He understood that flying-on was vital for the carriers to maintain a continuous rather than one-off anti-Zeppelin and reconnaissance patrol in front of the cruiser line.

Beatty ordered *Furious* to remain at Scapa to train her pilots in landing on the deck
and requested a Sopwith 1½-Strutter to test its suitability. On the same day (7 August)
Dunning was killed repeating his feat for a third time. This ended attempts to land on
Furious until March 1918.

Between them Rutland and Dunning had solved the two major problems of aeroplanes with the fleet. Carriers could recover their aircraft while under way so they
could be deployed whenever required, though their numbers and usefulness depended
on the number of carriers available. Warships flying-off fast aeroplanes from a very
short platform meant that carrier aircraft could be boosted in numbers by one-shot
aircraft and could concentrate on their priority duties.

These exploits in the second half of 1917 led to an explosion of ideas concerning
aviation. The Flagship received many suggestions and papers from junior and senior
officers which led to a very radical and offensive aviation policy. This doctrine was
centred on the aircraft carrier and, with its building policy, placed the Royal Navy far
ahead of any other navy in the world.

Under Jellicoe the Grand Fleet Battle Orders (GFBO) had confined aircraft to
defensive duties against Zeppelins, mines and submarines. Kite balloons were relied
upon to give tactical reconnaissance and rigid airships long-range strategic scouting
and possibly to bomb ships. He had no seaplanes capable of carrying torpedoes, although an attack on the German Flagship during a fleet action was a Sueter priority, or
attacking Zeppelins.

Despite the Evan Thomas Committee's recommendations and the decision to build
Argus and *Hermes*, in practice the fleet's doctrine was incomplete and did not match the
aircraft carrier's potential until flying-on was available and warships could carry aircraft. After so little aid from aviation since August 1914, the fleet's officers suddenly

had the possibility of large numbers of fleet aircraft. The result, due to Beatty's openness to proposals, was to encourage the development of ideas for their use. His officers showed they were not conservative nor backward in suggesting aircraft roles, now that the technical problems were being overcome.

The lead was taken by the Battlecruiser Force since its admirals (Pakenham and Phillimore) were most involved with the scouting and Zeppelin problems and keen to use aircraft to overcome them. The advantages and dangers of fleet aircraft carriers and aeroplanes were brilliantly summed up for Beatty in the autumn of 1917, especially by Malone, *Lion* (BCF flagship), and Gowan, *Yarmouth*. They urged that aviation be developed 'unhampered by any considerations of finance or of tradition'.

There was frustration because, although everyone agreed that aircraft would be important in future naval battles, little use had been made of them so far. On land aircraft had developed into a weapon of great importance. At sea the same process had not yet happened, but the RNAS could become a decisive striking force. The worry was that the Germans had the advantage of Zeppelins and efficient carriers.

The Grand Fleet wanted to use its aircraft like the Army on the Western Front: to stop the enemy's aerial reconnaissance; provide tactical reconnaissance (reporting submarines, minelayers and the enemy's course); protect its own scouts with fighters; attack the enemy (bomb and torpedo the battle line) and spot for gunfire (fleet's battleships). Aeroplanes could increase the fleet's vision up to 100 miles (a constant airscreen 60 miles ahead of the light cruisers with a 40-mile vision).

On gaining contact with the enemy the light cruisers would launch fighters to blind him (destroying his Zeppelins before they reported the Grand Fleet's presence). The scouts could then provide information, harry the enemy with bomb or torpedo and spot for gunfire. Thus Gowan thought that given a second Jutland the Germans would not escape the Grand Fleet again.

Nicholson (*Furious*) advocated two air screens: a high-altitude fighter patrol (to destroy Zeppelins and protect the fleet's scouts) and a low-altitude scouting screen (to report enemy surface movements). The machines needed visual touch with the fleet since accurate reconnaissance was only possible by relative bearing and distance from their own ships. Inaccurate reporting of positions had been common at Jutland and during *Campania*'s seaplane experiments.

Freeing the carriers from fighters and scouts and the replacement of the seaplane by the aeroplane also made the 1914 plan of Churchill, Sueter and Malone to attack the German fleet in its harbours feasible. The new thinking stressed torpedo-aircraft operations to attack enemy capital ships whenever they were sighted by the fleet's aerial scouts and in their harbours.

Aircraft would return for more torpedoes to continue their attacks throughout the action and ensure that enemy 'lame ducks' did not get home. Malone also suggested attacking coastal merchantmen trading with the Baltic and Holland. Any success would be proportional to aircraft numbers. Malone, at Phillimore's request, planned an offensive in Germany, requiring 30–40 torpedo-seaplanes and eighteen fighters carried in *Campania*, *Furious* and six 'cross-Channel' carriers, and stressed a continuous offensive rather than isolated attacks (a major Admiralty stipulation later). Nicholson thought the slower, unarmoured *Argus* could be used to harass the enemy with successive torpedo attacks.

Moreover, there was a great danger from similar actions by German aircraft. The fleet had to stop German torpedo-seaplanes, which were already attacking merchant shipping from Flanders and were expected to participate in the next fleet action. Thus the fleet had to maintain command of the air using their fighters to restrict the enemy's use of aircraft. This was a recurrent theme of the papers sent to Beatty.

The key was the carrier since such continuous operations required ships with landing-decks and higher performance aircraft than seaplanes, flying boats (heavy floats or hulls) and land-based aircraft (heavy fuel loads for range). Given three or four carriers with aeroplanes, the fleet could maintain an advanced air screen from leaving port until anchoring again.

The carrier's design was evolving, but it had to be a fast, purpose-built ship (not a makeshift or a compromise) able to land-on machines to refuel and rearm with bombs and torpedoes. Speed was essential to keep in touch with the Scouting Forces, steam at full speed in poor weather, fly-off machines and escape enemy light craft. She had to carry the maximum aircraft and aviation stores which meant no heavy guns, torpedo tubes, mines or armour. The long alighting deck aft (200ft) and shorter flying-off deck forward needed to be joined as a continuous deck and ruled out any 'compromise with traditional naval forms'.

The problem was to provide three or four large, fast carriers operating scouts. Malone suggested converting *Courageous*, *Furious* and *Glorious* with landing decks for scouting aeroplanes. These would be stop-gaps until more carriers were built. Gowan devised a sketch for a 'Fleet Carrier' of 28–30 knots (25 aircraft, lifts and two islands) similar to the DNC's early design for *Hermes*. Nicholson agreed that everything depended on landing decks and fast carriers (30 knots) since they had to turn into wind for aircraft operations. He considered carriers needed sufficient armament to deal with light cruisers and also advocated converting *Courageous* and *Glorious* to carriers and giving *Furious* a landing-on deck.

Another key element in thinking on the use of aircraft was the provision of adequate advice for the high command. A recurring theme was the provision of more air staff officers. Malone advocated a small RNAS staff for the CinC and a Senior Air Officer for each squadron flagship to develop aviation. Nicholson also suggested appointing a Senior Naval Officer (SNO) to decide policy and command the carriers while the DAS provided the machines he required.

The 'new generation' of admirals such as Beatty, Pakenham and Phillimore encouraged junior officers' ideas about gaining maximum benefit from new weapons. They urged junior officers, whose views were very valuable 'on such new subjects' (Phillimore especially encouraged Gowan) to send in their unorthodox views which before were not always welcomed by senior officers and could damage their careers.

Pakenham (BCF) was sympathetic to the use of torpedo-aeroplanes since Sueter's torpedo-seaplane attack in September on Austrian submarines had been a fiasco due to weather, although there were still no flying-on decks.. Thus he sent Beatty a 'Suggested Air Policy' for two to four carriers with landing decks to provide an advanced aerial patrol (replacing half the light cruisers) and on contact to attack the enemy battle fleet with torpedoes. He thought torpedo-aeroplanes could get very close to their target, which would compensate for torpedo inaccuracy and slowness, in a way surface vessels, hampered by other duties and poor visibility, could not. He wanted to develop torpedo-aeroplanes and their carriers at once.

Beatty and his Chief of Staff (Rear-Admiral O. de B. Brock) thought Pakenham had ignored the need for anti-Zeppelin fighters and had underestimated the ability of light cruisers and other ships to attack with torpedoes. Brock was also worried about the vulnerability of heavy, slow torpedo-seaplanes when attacking the enemy at short range.

Pakenham was supported by Phillimore (9 August) who argued for more fleet aircraft and agreed the Grand Fleet was lagging behind developments on the Western Front and German naval aviation. He argued that the fleet needed to develop aircraft rapidly, even if they were not used on 'four days out of five' in the North Sea, since on a good day it might be defeated without them. The lack of aircraft at Jutland, and the exaggerated Zeppelins' role, reinforced this view. The theme of matching imagined German efforts was common.

Without British rigid airships similar to the Zeppelins, aeroplanes had to provide extended patrols but they needed carriers with landing decks. Without carriers the fleet had to rely on non-rigid airships and kite balloons because it could not risk its one-shot fighter and scouting aeroplanes from warships until the enemy's air scouts were sighted. Phillimore diagnosed the main problem as a lack of carriers. Only *Furious* had the speed to accompany the fleet's cruisers and the fleet could not wait while fast carriers were built. Thus *Courageous* and *Glorious* should be converted and like *Furious* and *Campania* must carry torpedo-aircraft.

Beatty's ideas developed considerably and he reacted very positively to this fleet debate and the aviation policies proposed. Whereas he had wanted to develop the fleet's aviation for 1917, he now agreed it was vital that the air requirements were provided for the 1918 operations. This was due to two stimuli – fear of what the German fleet might have and hope based on the promised contribution of fleet aircraft from new carriers.

The fleet's problems with aerial reconnaissance and Zeppelins could be solved rapidly if landing on carriers was developed and the Admiralty provided carriers and aircraft. Beatty was also attracted by the offensive potential of fleet aircraft. If they destroyed the German fleet, the fleet could turn its full attention to the U-boats. It was therefore essential that the Admiralty supply the Grand Fleet's air requirements for the summer of 1918.

These Beatty divided into two: the existing aircraft tasks and an air offensive. The first was essential to keep pace with German development and the Admiralty did everything to provide it. The second was more controversial, required large resources and was not met in full by the Admiralty.

To develop the Grand Fleet air requirements Beatty requested information on German Naval Aviation (converting seven slow merchant vessels without flying-decks to carry seaplanes), discussed the carrier question with Halsey and Paine, who visited on 17 August, and urged the formulation of a Naval Staff air policy to provide carrier construction, sufficient aircraft and 'air supremacy at sea' during 1918.

After their meeting Paine told Beatty that fleet aeroplanes would scout, attack enemy aircraft, torpedo enemy ships in harbour or during a fleet action, provide anti-submarine screens and search allotted areas for the enemy fleet. He stated that the sea state would not influence aircraft at sea since new carriers (*Cavendish* and *Argus*) would not hoist out but launch from and land on the deck superior scouting (Sopwith 1½-Strutter), fighter (Beardmore Pup WB.III) and torpedo- (Sopwith Cuckoo) aeroplanes, each with folding wings (except the 1½-Strutter) and flotation bags.

The Parnall Panther was specially developed for the new carriers to spot and scout for the Grand Fleet but did not arrive until 1919. Note the fore-and-aft arrester wires and aircraft arrester hooks. (FAAM)

Moreover, Beatty's comment to Halsey on 17 August that 'no air policy existed' spurred the Air Department to develop a comprehensive policy statement since Holmes (Carrier Section) wanted to advise the Board. On 22 August Holmes based the policy on four conclusions: hostile aerial reconnaissance threatened British sea power; the antidote was better British aircraft; high performance required shedding weight (floats and hulls); and no floats required flying off and on to decks. The fleet would have only scouting, fighter and torpedo-bomber aeroplanes and discard seaplanes, kite balloons and airships.

The problem was the lack of carriers and he wanted six large, fast, new carriers (*Furious*, *Hermes* and a sister and three *Raleigh* class cruiser conversions including *Cavendish*, later re-named *Vindictive*). The carriers would save their limited space for scouts, fighters being carried in cruisers and battleships. Holmes also agreed that torpedo-aeroplanes in large numbers had great potential for a fleet action or dawn attack on the German Fleet in harbour.

Argus would carry only torpedo-aeroplanes and recover fighters flown off warships since she was capacious but too slow for scouting. The *Engadine*s would ferry fighters from shore depots to the warships, *Ark Royal* would be a carrier tender and *Campania*, with a landing-on deck, would train 50–100 pilots for the carriers.

When the fleet put to sea Holmes envisaged the *Engadine*s taking fighters to every battleship and cruiser; the scouting carriers with the battlecruisers maintaining an aerial patrol 80–100 miles ahead of the fleet to report enemy aircraft before they spotted the fleet. All fighters would then fly-off to destroy enemy aircraft and remain up during the action, returning to *Argus* to refuel. During the battle scouts would patrol for submarines and spot for fleet gunfire. *Argus* would launch 12–24 torpedo-aeroplanes to attack the enemy's line and disabled vessels; they would return to their mother ship and land-on after dark, using lights.

Holmes, like his Grand Fleet colleagues, warned his superiors not only that was this policy possible, but that if the Germans adopted it, and the Royal Navy did not, disaster would follow. The Air Department accepted it although kite balloons and airships were kept on for fire control and scouting, *Nairana* and *Pegasus* would carry fighters and the *Engadine* class pick up aircraft that failed to land on carriers.

Meanwhile Beatty tackled Jellicoe at a conference on 24 August. He stated that to stop the enemy's aerial scouting and turn-away tactics and to harry him with bomb and torpedo attacks, the fleet required 30 scouts and 50 fighters plus torpedo-aeroplanes in four carriers (*Furious* and *Argus* and two new carriers) by March 1918. *Campania* was also to have a flying-on deck. *Nairana*, *Pegasus*, *Manxman* and *Engadine* and the light cruisers would carry the fighters. Jellicoe accepted aeroplanes, alterations to *Furious* and the provision of four carriers subject to detailed Admiralty examination.

Rear-Admiral G. Hope (DOD) aided by Williamson, his air adviser, reviewed the carrier programme: converting *Argus*, two 'cross-Channels' (*Nairana* and *Pegasus*), *Furious* and *Cavendish*; building one ocean-going carrier (*Hermes*); and fitting fighters and scouts in warships. Operations Division calculated that by the spring of 1918 the Grand Fleet scouting (25) and fighter (30) needs would be provided, assuming *Cavendish* and *Argus* were completed and no fleet operations took place within range of German land-based aeroplanes which would necessitate more fighters.

However, the building of the deferred second ocean-going and the conversion of two more *Cavendish* class carriers depended on shipbuilding priorities, the Grand Fleet's aircraft requirements and whether its operations would involve high-performance shore-based enemy aircraft. Paine pressed for more fleet carriers as the 'present makeshifts' except *Furious* were too slow.

Dunning's death had triggered a debate about landing-on decks. It was accepted that to land on *Furious*'s forward deck required exceptional skill, but trials with landing-on two-seater aeroplanes should go ahead. Debate therefore centred on whether it was possible to give *Furious* a landing deck aft for these trials given that she had great turbulence aft. Nicholson concluded that aeroplanes could land-on only in 'clean air' forward of superstructures and that pilots needed a means to judge their position relative to the deck.

The great potential of *Furious*, however, had been shown when she accompanied the fleet on sweeps, exercises and operations from early August to early November. On her second sweep, on 11 August, a Zeppelin was sighted and a Pup was flown-off but could not climb quickly enough before its quarry fled into cloud.

Furious's experience had shown that a flying-on deck was necessary, but there was little time before the 1918 operations season. On 13 September, therefore, Beatty asked her pilots to test the air turbulence over her stern. Most felt that the eddies made landing very tricky and preferred a flush deck (requiring a lot of work). The Admiralty advised a short deck with arrester gear and safety net in line with Williamson's ideas and the Grain trials. *Cavendish* was designed to have only a 200ft deck. The DAS considered that the Grand Fleet proposal, to fly on to *Furious*'s forward deck athwartships, too dangerous.

A conference chaired by Phillimore on 18 September decided to give her a 300ft deck aft and to streamline the superstructure in the hope of overcoming the eddy problem. This would allow another hangar and two lifts to be fitted. The alternative was to give *Glorious* a flying-off deck to relieve *Furious* during her refit. On 28 September Beatty agreed to convert *Furious* to pioneer landing-on for *Argus*, *Cavendish* and *Campania* and on 14 November she was ordered to Armstrong's Walker Yard to have her after 18-inch gun replaced with a landing deck and hangar.

On 24 September Beatty had asked the Admiralty for fifteen scouts, 30 torpedo-aeroplanes and 50 fighters (all aeroplanes, with flotation bags, flying-off and -on decks) by spring 1918, excluding his offensive plans, the fighters to be carried by warships, *Pegasus* and *Nairana*, the scouting and torpedo-aeroplanes by *Furious*, *Campania* and *Argus*, all with landing decks. If the carriers were unsuitable, new 22-knot carriers would be needed.

HMS *Furious* (1925) as rebuilt in the early 1920s to pioneer the large flush-deck carrier. She had the retractable charthouse of *Argus* and a lower flying-off deck for the rapid launch of fighters. (FAAM)

The Admiralty accepted (25 September) the carrying of fighters in warships plus *Nairana*, *Pegasus* and *Furious*; a flying-on deck in *Furious* or flying-off decks in *Glorious* and *Courageous* would accommodate the scouts and *Argus* would carry more than 20 torpedo-aeroplanes for fleet actions and a dawn or night raid on German harbours. However, *Glorious* and *Courageous* were due to commission in one month.

In mid October Hope (DOD) and Captain A. V. Vyvyan (ADAS) proposed that the Grand Fleet gradually replace seaplanes with aeroplanes in 1917, carry 15–20 scouts (Sopwith 1½-Strutters) in *Furious* and *Campania* (later replaced by *Cavendish*) and 20 torpedo-aeroplanes (Sopwith Cuckoos) in *Argus*. Grain's arrester gear would also be fitted to *Furious* in March, to *Cavendish* and *Argus* in May. *Argus* would carry fewer torpedo-planes than the 30 Beatty wanted for a fleet action, and an air offensive would require greater numbers to be successful.

To accommodate the CinC and Air Department's needs, the DNC sought more carriers, especially to supplement the torpedo-aeroplanes (*Argus*). There were few ships large enough to take a long flight-deck, with the speed and protection to operate with cruisers and which could be converted quickly. The DNC found the answer in Armstrong's Yard No. 858, the Chilean battleship *Almirante Cochrane* (28,000 tons, later *Eagle*), sister of *Almirante Latorre* taken over by the Royal Navy on the outbreak of war. She had been laid down in February 1913 and suspended in August 1914 with hull and machinery nearly complete but no armour, although this was in the yard. Her 14-inch guns had been diverted to monitors. The main obstacle was the Chilean protests at losing a second battleship, but the British Government promised to restore both to Chile at the end of hostilities.

The redesign of *Eagle* was completed by the DNC on 8 January 1918, along the lines of *Argus* and *Hermes* with a 640ft clear deck; 400ft hangar below; two lifts; two islands each with a funnel and mast plus a linking bridge above the deck and nine 6-inch and four 4-inch AA guns. By omitting weight it was hoped to increase her speed above 24/25 knots.

Beatty's requirements for 1918, took 3½ months (7 January) to reach Halsey, who was incensed and referred the matter urgently to the Operations Committee (set up by the new First Lord, Eric Geddes, to decide policy) for whom R. E. Wemyss, now First Sea Lord, summed up Beatty's fleet air requirements and the alternatives on 16 January. He proposed carrying fighters in warships plus *Pegasus* and *Nairana*; scouts in *Furious* and *Cavendish*; torpedo-aeroplanes in *Argus*; keeping *Campania* (with landing-on deck when perfected) for training; and converting *Almirante Cochrane* and the AMC *Alsatian* for more torpedo-aeroplanes.

On 21 January the Maintenance Committee, which decided *matériel* questions, reported on the shipbuilding implications. *Almirante Cochrane* would need nine months to complete and to join the fleet in the winter of 1918, and although at the same yard she

HMS *Eagle* (1924), converted from the Chilean battleship *Almirante Cochrane* beginning in 1918. Note the long island, wind barrier (down) and smoke jet (for wind bearing) forward, and the Flycatcher aircraft. (FAAM)

could be ready more quickly than *Hermes* (June 1919), delaying her by five months. However, *Alsatian* would cause great dislocation of work, require five months and up to 500 tons of steel to carry nineteen machines.

The Operations Committee therefore decided on 2 February to convert *Almirante Cochrane* but not *Alsatian*. Already, by 24 January, Beatty, Wemyss and Geddes had agreed the former's conversion, on which work was started at once, and on 14 February the DNC's design was approved. Thus the Admiralty met and often exceeded Beatty's proposals for fleet air duties by June 1918. The main shortage would be torpedo-aeroplanes but the arrival of *Eagle*, six months ahead of *Hermes*, would solve that.

However, the Admiralty still remained a bottle-neck, delaying vital decisions on which Beatty wanted swift action for the next summer. His plans took months to be approved by the Admiralty, which could never have happened under Churchill or Fisher. The new system of Operations and Maintenance Committees, instituted by Geddes, did however bring together all the arguments and the question was considered from both supply and policy sides before decisions were made. Once this new system got into its stride, Admiralty decision-making was greatly improved and speeded-up and Beatty got most of what he wanted.

The Admiralty's response to Beatty's proposed air offensive was far less satisfactory. On 17 August he raised the question of torpedo-aeroplanes with the visiting Paine who still thought in terms of seaplanes carrying a torpedo of value to the fleet. This was of immense significance for carrier policy and next day Beatty asked the Admiralty to supply him with torpedo-seaplane details to decide on their value for operations and asked about the policy concerning their use (20 August).

The Admiralty explained that the 320hp Short torpedo-seaplane (Sueter's replacement for the Short 225hp) was too large for carrier operations, but that Sopwith had developed an aeroplane (the T.1 Cuckoo ordered by Sueter in October 1916) suitable for flying-off the deck and proposed to test one in *Furious*. The scale of Beatty's plans became apparent when, on 31 August, he asked for a further 200, with personnel and torpedoes, for the fleet by spring and submitted a plan for an air offensive.

The key planner was Captain H. W. Richmond (*Conqueror*, 2BS), leader of the younger officers who wanted to modernise naval planning and more offensive policies. He had recently advised Lloyd George (Prime Minister), through Maurice Hankey (Secretary CID), and met him and Edward Carson (First Lord) in June to press for reform. His ideas and information had helped Lloyd George decide to appoint a new First Lord (Sir Eric Geddes) to re-organise the Admiralty for total war.

Beatty was aware of Richmond's role and himself proposed similar reforms. Richmond's contacts on Beatty's staff (Commander R. M. Bellairs and Lieutenant W. S. Chalmers) encouraged him to send in ideas for offensives. When Beatty's preferred scheme, to block the U-boats in with minefields, ran into trouble at the Admiralty he turned to Richmond on 11 August to prepare a plan, consulting experts, for Jellicoe's visit in mid August. After a meeting with Rutland, Richmond's plan included a significant change: a dawn attack on the High Seas Fleet by torpedo-aeroplanes.

Bellairs informed Beatty that Richmond had extended the plan into an offensive to destroy the German fleet in its harbours and urged him to tackle the question fearlessly to pre-empt German plans and regain the naval initiative. To ensure that Jellicoe accepted this offensive an agenda was produced and Beatty held a dress-rehearsal for the meeting.

Richmond's offensive plan was given to Jellicoe on 24 August. Jellicoe and Hope (DOD) questioned the capability of torpedoes to be dropped correctly and sink warships, whether the High Seas Fleet would be in the Schillig Roads, and the availability of *matériel*. Beatty and Richmond considered Jellicoe's reaction to be 'purely negative' and 'rubbish' respectively.

The Admiralty's official response was mixed. The Air Department, naturally, was keen on the offensive and was supported by Naval Staff Operations and Plans (Section XVI, Operations Division until September 1917). On 3 September Operations Division agreed that there would be few torpedo hits from aircraft in a fleet action though it was to be hoped much enemy confusion, but believed that an attack on enemy ships in harbour by moonlight or at dawn would have greater results.

However, carrying torpedo-aeroplanes in existing carriers would sacrifice scouts or fighters. Moreover, Beatty wanted 200 of them without disclosing how he would carry or deploy them. The Admiralty's plan was to provide, where possible, a sufficient number of carriers to work with the Grand Fleet. Its torpedo policy, from early 1917 when Sueter proposed an offensive against enemy ports, was to test torpedo-seaplanes against enemy bases in the Mediterranean before attacking German ports.

The Admiralty therefore decided to send only 100 because *Argus* was the only carrier available for them and the torpedo supply was limited. The Admiralty also supplied 180 torpedoes and provided pilot training schools at Lee-on-Solent (initially) and East Fortune, near Rosyth. Replacing the special air torpedo (18-inch Mark IX), designed in 1915 to weigh less than 1,000lb, with the 18-inch Mark VIII (double the explosives) was to improve their punch, but this shift was abandoned because the extra weight (500lb) required a new aeroplane design which would take a year. Later Keyes (DP) insisted on the new design to provide the larger torpedo for *Argus*.

Beatty's torpedo offensive was also limited by the Admiralty's preference for an air offensive developed by Plans Section, Naval Staff. Like his plan, the idea was to hinder the U-boat campaign. But in this case 100 Large America flying boats, carried by 58ft lighters, were to bomb the U-boats, building yards, torpedo and mine stores, crew accommodation, minesweepers and torpedo works. Only if the U-boat menace had been dealt with by the spring of 1918 would a torpedo attack on the German Fleet be the main objective.

The Grand Fleet's 100 torpedo-aeroplanes (carried by *Campania*, *Furious*, *Argus*, *Glorious* and *Courageous* and/or capital ships, the last one each) would launch an attack at night or dawn from within 120 miles of the German bases. *Argus* with either *Courageous* or *Glorious* (giving up their armament wholly or partly) would be available also during a fleet action to hinder the German 'turning away' tactics.

For torpedo operations the Admiralty had to provide aircraft and 18-inch Mark IX torpedoes, arrange torpedo trials, enlarge *Furious*'s hatches, hasten *Argus*, convert *Courageous* and *Glorious* and switch RNAS personnel from France. The main problem was the aircraft, since with the formation of an Air Ministry the Royal Navy no longer provided these and there was concern as to whether the Air Ministry would provide them for a 1918 offensive. Other problems were the reduction in numbers of scouts if carriers besides *Argus* had torpedo-aeroplanes; certain weather conditions would necessitate the retrieval of torpedo-aeroplanes by flying them on to decks or by other means; and the possibility of torpedoes freezing at high altitude.

Nevertheless by the end of August Beatty considered the Richmond/Rutland aerial torpedo attack essential to disable the High Seas Fleet before attempting to block up the U-boats in their harbours. He therefore visited Geddes at the Admiralty on 7 September to press its acceptance, claiming that careful preparations would ensure operations in the spring of 1918. He suggested that eight Armed Merchant Cruisers of the 10th Cruiser Squadron (10CS) be converted to carry seventeen torpedo-aeroplanes each.

The Admiralty, however, favoured a bombing offensive, as being more direct, more effective and involving fewer resources. Operations Division (Williamson) pointed out that, although warships were suitable targets for aerial torpedoes, it was easier to damage U-boats and dock gates with bombs since the slow and vulnerable torpedo-aeroplanes would have to attack by moonlight to avoid enemy fighters and AA guns. He also doubted whether converted AMCs, without extensive alterations, would be fast or large enough to carry and fly-off seventeen heavy torpedo-aeroplanes quickly. There were doubts about keeping the project secret, supplying the machines and torpedoes by summer 1918 and inflicting enough damage on the German fleet to enable blocking-up the U-boats in their harbours.

It was agreed that the fleet needed more fast carriers, whether warships or merchantmen, but Paine accepted Williamson's argument that merchant ships, even if labour for conversions were available, were unsuitable as carriers and not fast enough to launch torpedo-aeroplanes. He considered that *Argus* and *Furious* plus *Courageous* and *Glorious*, if converted, were the only suitable ships. These were not sufficient for Beatty's plan. On 19 September Oliver (DCNS) agreed that Beatty's requirements were 'far beyond' the *matériel* that could be obtained.

However, on 7 October Beatty again asked for eight AMC conversions for April 1918 to force the enemy onto the defensive or to fight fleet actions. Beatty got Clark Hall and Assistant Constructor Davies of his staff to inspect *Alsatian* (10CS). They reported that conversion would take only six to eight months. Beatty therefore suggested a conference on board. Wemyss explained to Beatty the Admiralty's offensive plans and rejection of merchant conversions, but his conference was accepted although Halsey warned that the AMCs would seriously delay other work. The experts, including Holmes, agreed conversions with flying-off and -on decks were feasible and produced plans. Beatty followed up with plans to convert *Orvieto* and *Teutonic*.

Paine wanted to approve the conversions, but they affected warship (cruisers, destroyers and submarines or *Cavendish*) and merchant ship building. Moreover, the Naval Staff (Hope, Oliver and Wemyss) questioned three-month conversions to carry only nineteen torpedo-aeroplanes and taking ships from the Iceland–Shetlands blockade and North Russia operations. Worse, Keyes reported to Wemyss in October that naval aircraft output was not keeping up with requirements or Air Board forecasts because of strikes, air raids and concentration on the Army and strategic bombing. The Board had little faith in Air Board promises, and would be proved right, but given the political support for the Air Board/Ministry, had to accept their optimistic forecasts.

Wemyss, Halsey and Jellicoe agreed to tell Beatty, ironically on the anniversary of the Christmas raid of 1914 which had aroused such optimism for torpedo-aeroplanes, that the three AMCs would not be altered. However, on 2 January Beatty visited the Admiralty and continued to press for his air offensive which was referred to the Operations and Maintenance Committees. On the 21st the latter reported that the conversion of *Alsatian* would cause great dislocation, take five months and require up to 500 tons of steel, now in short supply. The Operations Committee thought (16 January) that the results of bombing from Dunkirk had not been such as to encourage a carrier plane offensive against enemy bases and the decision not to convert *Alsatian* was confirmed on 2 February.

Keyes suggested using bombers from *Argus*, *Furious*, *Cavendish* and *Campania* against Kiel in 1918 and opening the torpedo offensive in the spring of 1919 against eleven major target areas. This required accelerating *Argus* for use in 1918, flying-on to carriers in 1918 and five or six carriers by 1919. However, Fremantle (DCNS) argued that the authorised flying boat offensive would be continuous, but the Grand Fleet carriers could not carry out offensive operations day and night with large numbers of machines and so the results would be ineffective.

Beatty was informed accordingly. Phillimore protested that, whereas bombing was ineffective if not continuous, torpedo attacks could produce 'great results' from only a few operations. Ships only needed to be sunk once. Beatty assured him that an air offensive was still of great importance.

The key to the Grand Fleet air offensive planned for 1918 was the provision of resources: personnel, aircraft and carriers. Personnel (except trained observers) presented few problems, but the embryonic Air Ministry's production of torpedo-aeroplanes was given a low priority behind strategic bombing and the Army. An even greater problem was that the Admiralty considered the conversion of eight AMCs to be beyond its shipbuilding capacity.

HMS *Hermes* (1923), the first ship designed as an aircraft carrier from the start and with an island (two in the original design). She started the small-carrier trend but her size limited her aircraft capacity. (FAAM)

The Admiralty Board had a problem of priorities and vision. By late 1917 the Admiralty and Grand Fleet had both produced offensive air plans for 1918 and 1919 requiring extra resources above those planned. The Board had the choice of cutting back existing priorities, finding extra resources or refusing further commitments. To produce the extra carriers meant putting back warships and merchant ships vital to the fleet and anti-submarine campaign. To provide torpedo-aeroplanes for 1918 operations the Air Ministry had to put them before its main priority, strategic bombing, which it showed no willingness to do. Anti-submarine aircraft, a main Admiralty priority, were already falling behind their production targets because of the low priority accorded them.

The First Lord (Geddes) had to persuade the Prime Minister and War Cabinet to provide resources (carriers and torpedo-aeroplanes) to attack the German fleet. With Lloyd George looking for ways to diminish the bloodshed of the Western Front (hence his support of strategic bombing and an Air Ministry) this might not have been difficult. To destroy the German fleet and U-boats bases would greatly improve the Allied supply situation and war effort. The problem was that the Admiralty had doubts that the torpedo-aeroplanes could sink enemy warships as their proponents claimed and so Lloyd George would not assign a higher priority to them. The Air Ministry argued that its strategic bombing would end the war quickly.

Beatty's plan to destroy the German fleet and to defeat the U-boats failed because the Admiralty did not believe the torpedo-aeroplanes could sink battleships and so justify the large resources required. This was partly in reaction to the many failed seaplane carrier operations, so it favoured an alternative offensive using flying boats which required fewer resources.

The Admiralty never formally asked itself these questions: Did the Grand Fleet really need more light cruisers or submarines if the German fleet was to be attacked in its harbours? What could be done if carriers were given the highest priority? How much would the defeat of the High Seas Fleet and U-boats relieve the merchant shipping and naval shipbuilding crises? How many torpedo hits could a mass attack achieve? If the torpedoes could not sink battleships, could the German fleet be neutralised by concentrating on its destroyers and cruisers? The Admiralty doubted the availability of resources for the Grand Fleet plan and its feasibility, but never seriously re-examined its priorities in the light of a possible naval air offensive.

Although the Admiralty provided only enough aircraft for a fleet action, the Grand Fleet still looked forward to using the air power of *Furious*, *Cavendish* and *Argus* in the summer of 1918 to great effect. The adoption of aeroplanes and the development of a fleet/air doctrine plus *Furious* had been a revelation and a great advance on the old *Campania* or the 'cross-Channel' ferries.

When Dunning 'proved' the concept of landing-on in August 1917 it suddenly appeared that aeroplanes could achieve their long-awaited promise. Grand Fleet officers envisaged offensive roles for fleet aircraft as well as auxiliary ones (scouting, spotting and anti-submarine). The plan for 1918 was to develop flying on to decks, aeroplanes operating from carriers and torpedo-aeroplanes deployed during fleet operations. In 1919, when the carriers with flying-on decks (*Furious*, *Argus*, *Eagle*, *Vindictive*, *Hermes*, *Courageous* and *Glorious*) were available, massive torpedo operations could be implemented.

Grand Fleet Carrier Aviation, 1918

The task in 1918 was to develop carrier operations to include flying-off and onto the deck. All the Air Department and Grand Fleet's plans depended on this. The designs of *Argus*, *Hermes* and *Eagle* all included flying-on decks, which concept had to be proven in operations. Moreover, the flying-on decks of *Campania* and *Vindictive* and possible conversion of *Glorious* and *Courageous* also awaited *Furious*'s trials. The full changeover from seaplanes to aeroplanes was also contingent on their success.

In the meantime only *Furious* of the carriers was to carry scouting aeroplanes (Sopwith 1½-Strutters) and fighter aeroplanes (Sopwith Pups and Camels) were to be carried in warships plus *Pegasus* and *Nairana*. In March a 1½-Strutter two-seater was flown off a platform on the battlecruiser *Australia*, and Phillimore, promoted in January to Admiral Aircraft Carriers (ACA), at once asked for every aeroplane of this type to be transferred to the Grand Fleet to fly from capital ships' platforms for gunnery spotting. In addition a reserve of fighter, scouting and torpedo-aeroplanes was needed at Smoogroo, Turnhouse and East Fortune airfields (near Scapa and Rosyth) to train pilots for the fleet's changeover to aeroplanes. Seaplanes were only to be kept for

HMS *Furious* (1939), in her final confirguration, with no lower flying-off deck and a small island added, which remained through-out the Second World War during the Norwegian, 'Torch' and *Tirpitz* operations. (FAAM)

exercises at sea too far from land, so as not to waste aeroplanes and endanger pilots, until flying-on decks were available.

Until more flying-on decks arrived *Furious* and later *Vindictive* would fly aeroplanes off and on to search before and during a fleet action. *Campania*, until fitted with a flying-on deck, would accompany the battle fleet but only launch her aeroplanes during an action, as they would have to ditch and would be lost. Fighter and spotting aeroplanes from warships would have to do the same.

On 15 March *Furious* returned from her second conversion with a 284ft flying-on deck, Rutland as SFO and flying the flag of Phillimore. In May twelve successful landings were made on her but there were far more crashes into the safety net at the end of the deck or over the side due to turbulence from the superstructure. It was therefore decided to continue her use as a one-shot carrier, mainly to provide fighters against enemy aircraft. The potential of the carrier however was shown by her operations.

On 17 June *Furious* launched two fighters against seaplanes, one of which was shot down. From this time the Zeppelins lost their command of the air and gave the Grand Fleet a wide berth. Seven Camels were flown off with 50lb bombs to attack the airship sheds at Tondern on 19 July 1918 and two Zeppelins (*L54* and *L60*) were destroyed. So the Admiralty's ambition to attack the Zeppelins at source was achieved by aeroplanes, but because of the lack of proper carriers losses in machines and pilots were high. For the remainder of the war *Furious* covered fleet operations, providing fighter cover and scouts.

THE ROYAL NAVY AND AIRCRAFT CARRIERS, 1908–1945

In the absence of carriers with large numbers of scouts and torpedo-aeroplanes, the Grand Fleet Battle Orders for aircraft remained essentially as they had been before Dunning's and Rutland's exploits. The fleet could only keep one scout on patrol during the hours of daylight, weather permitting, 40–50 miles ahead of the advanced light cruiser reconnaissance line. Fighters could not be scrambled to intercept enemy aircraft until they had been sighted, because they still had to ditch in the sea. During the approach scouts were to report the composition and distribution of the German fleet and during an action five were to keep watch on it. The carriers were to remain on the battle fleet's disengaged side to despatch, recover and refuel the seaplanes.

In practice, despite the great strides in policy and doctrine, the fleet's capabilities changed little until October 1918 when *Argus* and *Vindictive* arrived with flying-on decks. Not until November 1918, when the war was over, did the Grand Fleet Battle Instructions include a fleet air screen (limited numbers) and a torpedo attack on the enemy fleet by fifteen aeroplanes from *Argus*. The scouts and fighters carried by *Nairana*, *Pegasus* and warships were to deal with enemy aircraft and spot for the fleet's guns.

The failure of *Furious*'s flying-on deck also considerably affected the Admiralty's carrier policy and design. *Furious* was a hybrid because she could not recover her aircraft in the turbulence generated by her superstructure and funnels on the centreline. Unfortunately *Vindictive* was also converted with her superstructure intact and *Argus*, *Hermes* and *Eagle* had been designed, on the DNC's advice and ignoring the BIR's support of Williamson's single 'island' design, with two islands and a bridge athwartships, which might cause equal disturbance.

Wind tunnel tests confirmed that the problem was *Furious*'s mast and funnel. The DNC had the choice of fairing the superstructure, reducing it to light cruiser standard or adopting a flush deck or island. By June 1918 he had adopted Williamson's starboard island with funnel and a through deck for *Furious*, *Hermes* and *Eagle* but a flush deck for the smaller *Argus*. In July the Admiralty deferred the reconstruction of *Furious* and *Vindictive* as island carriers until trials aboard *Argus* with a mock island and funnel had been completed.

After many delays *Argus* was completed with *Furious*-type arrester gear. On 30 September R. B. Davies (SFO) tested the air flow during mock landings and on 1 October three successful landings were made, but her late arrival and the trials which followed meant that she had no chance to perform her designated role before the war ended. By 19 December thirty-six successful landings had been made by Sopwith Pups and 1½-Strutters which showed that flying-on was feasible, but the aircraft carrier's potential was never proven during the war and this slowed peacetime progress considerably. The question of whether flush deck or island carriers would prove best remained unresolved.

Even if the Grand Fleet was never able to deliver the *coup de grâce* to the High Seas Fleet, the Royal Navy's development of the aircraft carrier was to be the envy of its allies, especially the US and Japanese Navies. The team effort of the development of

The Fairey Flycatcher, a long-serving fleet fighter designed for easy disassembly to save space. Note the flaps for short take-off and landing, and the arrester gear hooks. (Ministry of Defence)

fleet air policy through aircraft carriers is striking. The work of Dunning and Rutland is well known, but that of Sueter, Williamson and Holmes and the enthusiasm for aviation of fleet officers, who realised the great possibilities opening up, is not.

Of special interest is the fleet's support for an air offensive against the German fleet in its harbours, made possible by the carrier concept which required, as Gowan and others recognised, the adoption of a new type of ship equipped with aeroplanes, unfettered by 'traditional' naval forms. The seaplane, had it prospered, was supposed to have avoided this necessity.

However, throughout the war the Royal Navy failed to launch a torpedo attack on the High Seas Fleet in its bases despite plans dating back to August 1914. The Air Ministry, whose establishment Beatty did not oppose, failed to provide the torpedo-aeroplanes (Sopwith Cuckoos) in time, and the shipyards delivered only one new carrier (*Argus*) in late 1918. Thus the war ended as it began, with the Admiralty's aviation plans still largely on the drawing-board. Although the Fleet had few operational successes to show from aircraft, it had developed the basic aircraft carrier and had several building. This gave it a large lead over its post-war rivals, the US and Japanese Navies, the importance of which was understood by all three.

Carrier Development, 1919–1939

In 1919 the Royal Navy had a potentially impressive fleet air capability. The first aircraft carrier in the world, *Argus*, had joined the fleet; two more (*Hermes* and *Eagle*) were building; another two 'hybrid' carriers (*Furious* and *Vindictive*) were earmarked for full conversion; and two more cruisers (*Courageous* and *Glorious*) could be converted. There were also the 'cross-Channel' carriers embarking more aeroplanes and fleet warships flying many more from their turrets. No other navy had such a vast air support.

This was enough to persuade the US General Board in June 1919 that it needed to develop naval aviation 'to the fullest extent' in order to meet the British fleet on equal terms. But the Royal Navy later fell behind its main rivals in the number, types and performance of its carriers and their aircraft. There were several reasons for this. The main one was the dual control of the Fleet Air Arm that persisted until the eve of the Second World War. This meant that the Admiralty consumed much energy in a slow, cumbersome system which its partner, the Air Ministry, wanted to perpetuate but had little interest in or incentive to develop.

The Admiralty also had a tendency to look back to and prepare for a rerun of the Battle of Jutland, which was much debated throughout the twenties, and to re-affirm its belief in the continuing dominance of the battleship. This attitude was aggravated by the main naval policy, after the Washington Treaty, of sending a battle fleet to Singapore in the event of any war with Japan. Replaced by the Atlantic (later Home) Fleet, the Mediterranean Fleet would go east for a set-piece fleet action against the Japanese.

Whereas in America by about 1929 naval officers were beginning to look forward to the offensive use of aircraft, the British were slower to do so. Most of their trained naval aviators had transferred to the RAF, leaving the Navy short of skilled and senior aviators to advise and campaign for more offensive use of aviation. Although by 1928 the Board recognised the importance of carrier strike aircraft, it was slow to find a new balance between battleships and carriers. It was handicapped by its many responsibilities, only one carrier with each fleet until the late 1920s, and few aircraft.

From war experience, however, the Royal Navy always considered carriers to be vital. In early 1919 Phillimore (ACA) sent the Admiralty far-sighted recommendations on the fleet's future air requirements and aircraft functions. Thus in March 1919 the

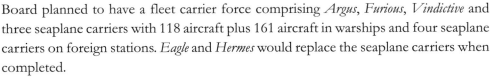

HMS *Glorious* (1930), sister of *Furious* but with an island. With *Courageous* she was the mainstay of the late pre-war fleet. She was sunk by German battlecruisers off Norway in June 1940. (FAAM)

Board planned to have a fleet carrier force comprising *Argus*, *Furious*, *Vindictive* and three seaplane carriers with 118 aircraft plus 161 aircraft in warships and four seaplane carriers on foreign stations. *Eagle* and *Hermes* would replace the seaplane carriers when completed.

However, this had to be scaled down by peacetime budgets. By early 1919 it was government policy that there would be no war for ten years and that there could be drastic cuts in defence spending. The 1919/20 Naval Estimates were sharply cut and in May 1919 it was decided to reconvert *Vindictive* to a cruiser, put *Furious* into reserve until fully converted as a carrier and dispose of the seaplane carriers. Further casualties were the three *Hood* class battlecruisers which had an indirect affect on carrier policy since, unlike the US Navy with the *Lexington*s, the Admiralty did not have comparable vessels for conversion to carriers and had to make do with the smaller *Courageous* and *Glorious*.

Admiral Sir Charles Madden, the new CinC Atlantic and Jellicoe's former Chief of Staff Grand Fleet, suggested in December 1919 a progressive air policy including carriers (eventually providing more than 230 aircraft in twelve carriers). The Naval Staff agreed and Admiral Brock (DCNS, February 1920) stated that aircraft carrier provision was urgent and the completion of *Eagle*, *Hermes* and *Furious* was given priority in the Royal Naval Dockyards. However, the carrier was still an auxiliary and the question became entwined with the controversy over the battleship's future. In a period of uncertainty about naval policy that of naval aviation drifted.

In mid 1919 a Post-War Questions Committee was formed to consider war experience and advise the Board on the value of warship types and the role of aircraft, both in attack and defence. The Chairman was Phillimore, former Admiral Commanding, Aircraft Carriers, but since it included four gunnery experts, only one engineer and no aviator (they were almost all in the RAF) or constructor, it concluded that aircraft would not render the capital ship obsolete in the near future or until the capabilities of aircraft increased.

Although in March 1920 it recommended the building of two types of carrier ('large and fast' for scouting, 'cheaper and slower' for the battle fleet), there was little provision for torpedo attack despite wartime plans to attack the German fleet and evidence from a recent torpedo-aircraft fleet exercise, where seven of eight torpedoes dropped had hit. Torpedo-aircraft could not yet carry torpedoes of sufficient size to worry battleships.

However, in November 1919 the Admiralty's official adviser, the head of RAF Coastal Area (Vyvyan), when considering the provision of fleet aircraft, not only stressed that 'modern efficient carriers' would be essential (recommending three with the Atlantic Fleet and two in the Mediterranean) for scouting, spotting and fleet defence, but also for a torpedo offensive which 'promised the best results' against enemy vessels.

Therefore the Admiralty's naval aircraft requirements, outlined to the Air Ministry in December 1919, were based mainly on Phillimore's recommendations from Grand

Fleet experience but with offensive roles. Their order of priority was spotting, carrier, torpedo and long-range land-based scouting aircraft. They also required a heavy armour-piercing bomb for use against warships and a full complement of air units. This was very similar to the priorities of the US Navy's General Board in June 1919.

The Admiralty responded to the Cabinet's proposed reduction of the 1920/21 Estimates, with a ten-year modernisation programme to match US naval building. When the latter did not cancel its massive building, the Admiralty won its case (mid 1920) for new capital ships and converting *Eagle* and *Furious* as the programme's first part.

As a result the Navy reviewed its carrier policy. In July 1920 Madden proposed eleven carriers (three scouting, four spotting, two torpedo, one bomber, one fighter) to provide 33 scouts, 32 spotters, 36 torpedo-bomber and 74 fighters plus fourteen scouts and 24 fighters on warships. This reflected the official view that carriers would be best operating one type of aircraft. E. C. Chatfield (ACNS, supervisor of the fledgling Naval Air Section, formed July 1920) stipulated that the fleet needed a minimum of 94 large aircraft plus fighters.

On 23 July 1920 Chatfield chaired a conference attended by representatives of the Fleet, Admiralty, Constructors and Air Ministry which decided that at least five carriers (including three spotter) were necessary. To provide this *Eagle* had to be completed and at least *Furious* and a sister (the only vessels fast enough to accompany the battlecruisers). The Board decided to convert *Glorious* since she was easily replaced as a Turret Drill Ship.

In November 1920 the Board approved the fleet's requirements for ship-based aircraft for the next two years. Their 'minimum needs' were stated to be 45 spotting, 22 scouting, twelve torpedo, plus as many fighters as possible. These would provide squadrons aboard *Argus*, *Eagle*, *Furious* and *Glorious*, of which only *Argus* had yet been completed as a true carrier. The high proportion of spotting aircraft compared with torpedo shows that the focus was still on the gun power of the battleship. In July 1921 the US General Board would give torpedo and bombing aircraft first priority, but their first carrier would not commission until March 1922.

When in March 1921 Chatfield circulated the Naval Air Section's review of naval aviation, including recent experience and development of catapults, arrester gear and aircraft with *Argus* and *Eagle*, the gun was still seen as the decisive weapon. However, naval aviation was seen as vital to its successful employment and its development as essential for the fleet.

In October, in preparation for the Washington Conference, Chatfield stressed that the number of aircraft carriers present would decide command of the air which would be vital in the next naval battle. He favourably compared Great Britain's position (*Argus* completed, *Eagle*, *Hermes* and *Furious* being completed and *Glorious* projected) with the Americans' (*Langley* converting) and the Japanese' (*Hosho* building). However, he also predicted that the Americans would convert unfinished capital ships, due for scrapping, to carriers. As a result the Naval Staff proposed for the Washington negotiations a carrier tonnage of 125,000 to provide the five carriers required by the July 1920 Conference at 25,000 tons each. This gave three carriers for the main fleet and one each for the Mediterranean and the Far East, but left little extra for refits or emergency.

At the Washington Conference the initial US proposals for carrier ratios were 5:5:3 (US, UK, Japan) but only 80,000:80,000:48,000 tons, based on two battlecruiser conversions of 40,000 tons each. As the British had or were building six experimental carriers which already totalled 81,000, and the US Navy wanted 135,000 tons, including the two battlecruiser conversions, the totals were greatly extended. Each nation was allowed to convert two capital ships building (up to 33,000 tons) which Japan and the USA did. Having scrapped the *Hood*s, Britain substituted the smaller *Furious* class. Pre-Treaty carriers were regarded as experimental and could be scrapped, but post-Treaty carriers had to be retained for 25 years.

As a result of the Treaty the Naval Staff in March 1924 developed a ten-year building programme (chiefly aimed at meeting the new threat posed by Japan). It assumed that *Argus* (15,750 tons), *Hermes* (10,850 tons) and *Eagle* (22,600 tons) would be joined by the fast, larger *Courageous*, *Furious* and *Glorious* (22,000 tons each) to provide 136 aircraft. Then the old, experimental and small carriers could be scrapped, to leave 69,000 tons of the 135,000-ton Washington quota for two large or four small carriers.

Thus the Naval Staff recommended, as part of the Ten Year Plan, to build up to the Washington Treaty limits by the time it expired by converting *Glorious* and *Courageous* and laying down four 30-knot, 17,000-ton carriers in 1926, 1933 (replacing *Argus*), 1933 (*Eagle*) and 1936 (*Hermes*) to give the fleet seven carriers with 275 aircraft. They also wanted carriers (under 10,000 tons) for commerce protection, unregulated by the Washington Treaty, but money was not available.

The Staff argued that experience had shown that large numbers of carriers were required, but that small carriers under 14,000 tons were inefficient. However, they underestimated the increase in size and weight of aircraft (the Air Ministry was not asked about the optimum size) and three carriers of 23,000 tons (*Eagle*'s size) would have agreed better with latter experience. The DNC therefore had two post-Treaty tasks: the conversion of *Furious*, *Glorious* and *Courageous* and preparing new carrier designs. The first part of the programme went according to plan, the four seaplane carriers being withdrawn into reserve, but the rest did not.

The Admiralty hoped to obtain the funds for the new carrier in a programme designed to relieve the post-war depression in the British shipbuilding industry. On 21 November 1923 the Board approved the programme (cruisers and smaller vessels) which went to the Cabinet. However, in mid January 1924 the Conservative government was followed by the first Labour administration which cancelled the new programme. A long-term policy, to give steady expansion at reasonable cost, was not accepted by the Cabinet until early 1925. Moreover, war with Japan was ruled to be unlikely for ten years and the operational aircraft total was reduced to 241 by 1935 which was low compared with both the USA and Japan.

The completion of the experimental carriers was also slower than anticipated due to targets being pushed back. *Eagle* was completed in September 1923, eighteen months later than planned, and *Hermes* in February 1924, two years late. The conversions of *Furious* (completed September 1925), *Courageous* (February 1928) and *Glorious* (January 1930) were put back between two and five years. New carrier building was put off altogether.

In May 1925 the laying-down of the first new carrier was put back from 1926 until 1928 and the second was cut. Then the carrier was put back again to 1929. As a result the ACNS (Dreyer) in April 1926 transferred aircraft intended for carriers to 90 warship catapults. The carrier aircraft would be provided by an increase of 105 aircraft later. In mid 1926 the Admiralty accepted a 100 per cent (and later only 50 per cent) rather than 200 per cent reserve to save a drastic cut, proposed by the Air Ministry, of its front-line aircraft from 241 to 144 by 1935. Although this allowed little room for heavy losses, the Admiralty knew that it must keep up with the US Navy which would have 283 fleet aircraft by 1928 and more than double that number by 1932.

Dreyer undertook another cuts review in June 1927 and proposed four carriers instead of five, with the new carrier accommodating more aircraft. However, this did not provide for refits and tactical needs, a larger number of smaller carriers being more flexible. Another alternative was to keep only four of the five carriers in commission. The Treasury, however, would not agree to a new carrier and the fleet had to continue with its experimental carriers. Finally in May 1928 Plans Division suggested that a new carrier was not an urgent priority, after comparison with US and Japanese building, in response to cuts to the Ten Year Plan. The new ACNS (Pound), who had already reduced the carrier aircraft total to 176, suggested a further postponement of the carrier until 1932–33 and keeping *Argus*, *Hermes* and *Eagle* a little longer. The Fleet Air Arm was to have 252 aircraft by 1938. This was accepted by Madden, who was now First Sea Lord, in November 1928, because the fleet had six carriers compared to three (USA). Bridgeman, the First Lord, announced its postponement to Parliament in March 1929, to obtain more experience with *Glorious* and *Courageous*. In June 1930 the First Lord (A. V. Alexander) pushed this back again until 1936 'unless foreign programmes rendered its earlier completion necessary'.

Thus the Admiralty was attempting to keep its Ten Year Programme (carriers and cruisers) in existence despite successive Conservative and Labour administrations calling for economy and disarmament. Madden and Alexander secured a new Four Year Plan in 1930, but it was clear that Treaty limits would not be reached until 1942–43. However, Madden's successor, Sir Frederick Field, was a poor one and in ill-health and Alexander took the opportunity to appoint an acquiescent Board.

One reason for the collapse of the British carrier programme was economic. Post-war trade and budget deficits led to a deteriorating economic situation, pre-Keynesian government economies and savage Treasury cuts. The Royal Navy had to face a rapid scaling down of its wartime effort in peacetime and a series of attacks on its estimates.

HMS *Courageous* (1928), the second of the cruisers converted to carriers. This gives an excellent view of her fighter flight-deck, the twin catapults forward and preparation to launch aft. (FAAM)

HMS *Ark Royal* (1938), the Royal Navy's 'new' aircraft carrier, which was designed within Treaty limitations and only arrived just before the war, equipped with Swordfish as shown here. (FAAM)

In early 1919 the Admiralty decided on the size of the post-war fleet (33 battleships, eight battlecruisers and seven carriers) and asked for £171 million for 1919. The Board cancelled three *Hood* class battlecruisers in December 1918 but only to build newer ships incorporating war lessons and matching more modern American vessels. However, the Cabinet ordered a return to peacetime conditions and the 1920/21 Estimates were kept to £60 million (August 1919). By cancelling new construction and reducing capital ships to 20 the Admiralty managed £84.5 million, but warned that this allowed the Americans a superior fleet.

In July the Board considered future policy and especially the huge American and Japanese capital ship programmes. Beatty, now First Sea Lord, proposed the laying-down of four capital ships in 1921 and four more in 1922 and to complete the carriers *Eagle*, *Hermes* and *Furious*. This provoked considerable controversy over the role of the battleship, mainly in the correspondence columns of *The Times*, and resulted in the establishment in December 1920 of the Naval Shipbuilding Sub-Committee of the CID (the Bonar Law Inquiry) headed by the future Prime Minister.

Lloyd George's government was worried by the prospect of another arms race and wanted to avoid exacerbating American rivalry. The committee, however, was divided (March 1921) between those who were doubtful about battleships but had little proof and those who stated that the 'One Power Standard' required the building of battleships to match American construction. Rather than an analysis of future naval warfare, the committee only reflected entrenched positions, the Admiralty defending the battleship's role and the RAF arguing that it was obsolete.

As a result capital ship replacement was postponed until the Standing Defence Sub-Committee of the CID reviewed the defence roles of the Navy and Air Force. The Cabinet thereby avoided any capital ship building announcement that would exacerbate the naval race. In August 1921 the Navy got a £12 million supplementary estimate (for four super-*Hood*s) through the House although there was opposition to battleships from Air Force proponents, such as Sueter, now an MP, and disarmament supporters.

However, a Cabinet Committee on National Expenditure (the Geddes Committee) recommended the forming of a Ministry of Defence and massive cuts in military spending (December 1921), but protests from the armed services led to a second Committee under Winston Churchill (Secretary of State for the Colonies).

The Washington Treaty, although it scrapped the proposed super-*Hood*s (postponed in October by the conference), allowed Great Britain to build two 35,000-ton battleships (later *Nelson* class) and 8-inch cruisers and convert *Courageous* and *Glorious* to carriers. The Treaty therefore resulted in more British construction than at any time since the war ended. Churchill accepted that the Treaty requirements, including ending the Japanese alliance, undermined Geddes' proposals to cut the naval estimates, but he still cut personnel, shore bases and auxiliary services (including airships sold off in 1922), and only allocated another £2 million more than Geddes (£62 million for the

1922/23 Estimates). The Navy finally got £65 million, a cut of £18 million compared with the previous year.

During the rest of the twenties the Estimates would stay at £55–60 million per year as both Conservative and Labour governments, using the treasury and different committees, sought to cut military spending. For instance 1925 was the first year that the cost of the FAA (Fleet Air Arm, as it was called from April 1924) was included in the Naval Estimates, but also saw a sustained attempt by the Chancellor (Churchill) to cut naval spending. The Admiralty finally won its case for a five-year programme (spread over seven years), but only at the expense of postponing as much as possible and introducing economies in the years 1925–26 and 1926-27. Later that year the Colwyn (Treasury) Committee again investigated the Naval Estimates.

Within these reduced sums the Admiralty sought to complete the two battleships; modernise older battleships (especially against torpedo and air attack); complete *Hermes*, *Eagle* and *Furious*; convert *Courageous* and *Glorious*; build the new carriers; provide modern cruisers, destroyers and submarines (which were not covered by Washington and therefore formed a mini arms race); and fortify Singapore as the Pacific Fleet base. This had to be done with reduced personnel (both Naval staff and technical departments) as well. In December 1923 the DNC (E. H. T. d'Eyncourt) complained that shortage of staff was hampering the design of ships and supervision of their construction. One way round the problem was to extend the design and construction over more years than had been planned.

Often the Treasury and Chancellors Churchill (Conservative) or Snowden (Labour) refused to countenance naval aviation proposals, arguing that there was no justification for new carriers and more aircraft when so many were in commission and the Americans and Japanese were far behind on a numerical basis in the 1920s. The proposal to scrap *Hermes* and *Eagle*, recently completed, to build four new carriers was also not a persuasive argument to the Treasury. The Ten Year Rule, introduced in 1919, renewed in 1925 and self-perpetuating in 1929, encouraged postponing new carriers because there was to be no war in the immediate future. The Treasury also refused increases in aircraft, for example in March 1928 and February 1930, arguing that the Royal Navy had a 'marked lead'.

Moreover, although US naval aviation overtook the FAA, this was not accepted as an argument for greater spending. The Cabinet and the Board acquiesced in the US lead since war with the USA was considered unthinkable. Also the Admiralty underestimated the US lead in the 1920s. For instance, Pound (ACNS) in 1928 accepted the Treasury's cut of the proposed aircraft expansion and to delay the new carrier since he estimated a low US carrier aircraft total. The Americans' ability to operate larger numbers of carrier aircraft was doubted by both the Admiralty and Air Staff. For instance the DNC (1928) contested an estimate of 50 aircraft for the *Lexington*s when in fact they carried 90 each. This was because the British carriers had no transverse arrester gear (invented by Constructor W. A. D. Forbes and sold to the US Navy) which pre-

HMS *Illustrious* (1940). The first 'armoured' carrier, she was saved by her flight deck in the Mediterranean. This photograph shows a hive of industry shortly after commissioning. (FAAM)

vented a deck park and meant that it took up to 40 minutes to land-on a strike of 24 aircraft in 1929. Also the lack of carriers meant that there was little attempt to concentrate large numbers of aircraft. In 1929 three large carriers (*Furious*, *Courageous* and *Eagle*) in the Mediterranean worked together for the first time.

It was not until Chatfield (1930) and W. W. Fisher (1932) were successively CinC Mediterranean that greater realism and modern tactics were introduced. With the help of the newly created Rear-Admiral, Aircraft Carriers, they introduced massed carrier strike forces in 1931 (one carrier), 1932 (two) and 1933 (three). Although using few aircraft compared to US exercises, they showed the great potential of air strikes (21 hits from 32 torpedoes in 1933) to the fleet and the Admiralty, showed the importance of numbers and were the foundation for the successful carrier operations of the Second World War.

The British tended to emphasise attacks on battleships rather than carriers and so were still behind the Americans and Japanese. As late as the 1937 Combined Fleet exercises, in which air power was given an important role, effort was concentrated on the attack and defence of the traditional battle fleet.

The Treasury's position was backed up by the government's pursuit of economy (although the Conservatives promised a steady programme to safeguard plant and skilled workers) and disarmament (especially the Labour administrations of Ramsey MacDonald who was personally committed to that cause) which pushed back and delayed programmes during negotiations to reduce Treaty limits. For the 1927 Geneva Conference the Admiralty in 1926 accepted a maximum tonnage reduction for carriers from 27,000, the original Washington figure, to 23,000 with a proportionate reduction in the total tonnage. This contrasted with its refusal to reduce battleship tonnage, but was in line with similar reductions for cruiser size. Design studies showed that a reasonable carrier was possible at 23,000 tons. The Conference, however, failed to reach agreement.

At the first London Conference (1930) the Admiralty refused to reduce the carrier tonnage total from 135,000 tons or 25,000 tons each (providing better protection than 23,000 tons) and wanted to make *Furious* an experimental carrier if the Americans got the *Lexington*s reclassified. However, the Cabinet was discussing a total as low as 100,000 tons. The Admiralty opposed this but considered that keeping carrier numbers down was in the British interest as it could not embark on a building race.

In 1932 the Admiralty would only reduce the carrier total tonnage (to 110,000 tons) if their size (22,000 tons) and not their number (five) were decreased (in line with the adoption of smaller 12-inch battleships). The Foreign Office was informed in January 1932 that the naval requirements were five 22,000-ton carriers and 400 aircraft. This was because the DNC had succeeded in developing a satisfactory design of 22,000 tons. At the second London Conference (1935) the British got a 23,000-ton limit accepted, but the total carrier limit was eliminated (due to Japan's withdrawal), which sparked off a carrier building race.

The Air Staff also allied with the Treasury to limit the growth of the FAA since they saw it as reducing the number of aircraft available to face first French and then German air expansion. Moreover, in 1932 it was proposed that each nation have a fixed total of aircraft including naval, leaving the RAF outnumbered by the French which had a very small naval air service. The Air Ministry at the same time supported Japanese proposals to ban carriers and sought smaller carriers than did the Admiralty. A British proposal to include carriers under 10,000 tons in carrier totals had been agreed in 1930, but, there being no general carrier agreement, the issue was left until 1935.

The Air Staff also aimed at a non-specialist cadre that could be rapidly expanded in wartime rather than the specialists needed by the FAA. Their alliance with the Treasury meant that FAA proposals were often cut (only eighteen aircraft were added to the FAA total between 1929 and 1934) and led to Admiralty pessimism in the late 1920s.

The lack of expert air advice also tended to allow the Admiralty to accept putting off its carrier construction and to prolong its faith in the battleship. For instance when modernising existing battleships the Naval Staff recognised the need for underwater protection through bulging and additional deck armour against bombs and plunging shell. However, both could not be afforded at the same time.

The Naval Staff decided to do the bulging first (which would include protection against aerial torpedoes) since it thought carrier aircraft could only carry 550lb bombs. This ignored land-based aircraft, which had carried 2,000lb bombs during the US trials of bombing warships, but also reflected the Admiralty's faith in AA gunnery when expert opinion agreed that passive protection was not the complete answer.

In August 1922 the CinC Atlantic Fleet (Madden) recommended fitting warships with fighters to intercept torpedo-aircraft, but the Admiralty preferred the development of multiple pom-pom and similar AA guns to defend against torpedo and bombing aircraft. This reflected the dominance of the gunnery specialists in the 1920s and a deliberate decision by Chatfield (ACNS), at a time of heavy commitments, to concentrate on carriers.

The problem was that the Board turned down the recommendation (a technically advanced long-range control system) of the Usborne Committee of gunnery experts in favour of a simpler system which proved greatly inferior to the German and American ones. At the same time the Admiralty sought to make the main armaments (16-inch and 8-inch) of warships dual purpose for use against aircraft, which required revolutionary new mounting and loading designs that never proved wholly satisfactory. When warships were given catapult aircraft these were only for scouting and spotting.

In March 1931 Chatfield (CinC Mediterranean), who as Third Sea Lord in 1925–28 had presided over the development of the new AA guns and fire control, thought air attack on ships would soon be ineffective although attacks on ships in harbour would give good results.

Another inhibiting factor on the carrier programme was the great technical problems of carrier design in the 1920s. The ideal arrangement of the carrier concept had still not been finalised. There were the issues of the island or flush deck, cruiser or just AA armament, many small or a few large carriers and one or two flight-decks. This caused delay because each development depended on the previous one and each carrier was different. The design of the new carrier depended on trials of *Furious* which depended on *Hermes*, which was affected by *Eagle* and which relied on *Argus*. They also offered ammunition, as did Air Staff opposition and other options (hybrid cruisers and battleships, airships, flying boats, long-range aeroplanes and catapult seaplanes on warships), to the Treasury which wanted to limit the expensive carrier programme.

With a clear lead in carriers, the Royal Navy wanted to develop the ultimate design and benefit from any US or Japanese experience before building its new carrier. This worked in that it adopted the island design, mixed armament and medium size (20,000 plus tons) quicker than the US and Japanese and resulted in the efficient *Ark Royal*, but surrendered the initiative. Its rivals, chasing the Royal Navy's lead, made bolder leaps to larger carriers and benefited from the operational lessons of modern carriers. There was also a sense that the Royal Navy, having established a lead, did not wish to expand it, unless forced to do so by rivals, so it could concentrate on other less adequately provided areas of the fleet.

The consequences were serious because the fleet had to retain the experimental *Argus*, *Hermes* and *Eagle*, taking up a third of the carrier tonnage and operating only 48 aircraft. If the Naval Staff had known they would last twenty years, they would not have been completed because the fleet was under grave disadvantage in carrying capacity (aggravated by using enclosed hangars against fire), large all-purpose aircraft and no athwartships arrester wires until 1931 (allowing no deck park or rapid landing interval). Aircraft capacity was not maximised as in US and Japanese carriers. Without the new carrier (deferred for ten years from 1926), the FAA was only aiming for 241 aircraft by 1939. Finally the lack of homogeneous carriers affected their use as a unit to develop advanced tactics.

Ironically the spur to re-evaluating the carrier situation was the Geneva Disarmament Conference's proposal to prevent any changes to the *status quo*, when it was realised that the FAA had fallen behind its rivals. Naval Air Division (Captain C. E. Turle, DNAD), backed by the Controller (Rear-Admiral R. R. C. Backhouse), proposed, in April 1931, a substantial increase in the projected FAA aircraft strength (502). The Naval Staff, wanting parity with the US, considered that 405–500 aircraft were required.

It was clear that the new carrier was required and a conference chaired by Backhouse specified 22,000 tons, more than 30 knots and 60 aircraft. Designs were prepared by the end of the year. In September 1932 Backhouse proposed building new carriers in 1933, 1936, 1939, 1945 and 1947. The Board (November 1933) included a new carrier and three new FAA flights, re-equipping eight others and modernising old battleships in the 1934 programme. This required the first increase in the Naval Estimates since 1931.

The Air Staff objected to this new total as diverting aircraft from their own expansion requirements. This was overcome, but it shows the struggle that was required for even limited expansion of the FAA. With the Geneva negotiations faltering, the First Lord (Viscount Monsell) took the FAA proposals and the new carrier (22,000 tons, 72 aircraft) to the Cabinet in December 1933, on the basis that Britain had six carriers but three were experimental whereas the USA would have six modern carriers and Japan five by 1935.

The new carrier (*Ark Royal*) was commissioned in 1938 and proved that the Royal Navy had not fallen behind in carrier design. Moreover, new features such as the first Royal Naval safety barrier and catapults ('accelerators') allowed the FAA to begin to catch up with rival operating methods.

By November 1933 it was clear to the CID that the worsening international situation required some action and they asked the Chiefs of Staff, Treasury and Foreign Office to prepare a programme to meet 'our worst deficiencies'. This resulted in the Defence Requirements Committee (DRC) which quickly decided on a five-year programme for each service and reported in February 1934.

HMS *Indomitable* (1941). The fourth of the *Illustrious* class, she was modified before completion to provide a second hangar and increase aircraft capacity to 48. (US Navy)

The DNAD (now Rawlings), when reviewing the FAA's requirements in November, argued for expansion because of Far Eastern weakness, one carrier (*Eagle*, 21 aircraft), compared with Japan's planned naval aviation of 590 shore-based aircraft and 329 (400) carrier aircraft by 1937 (1938). He predicted that if the FAA did not expand, the Japanese fleet would have air superiority with all its great advantages: continuous torpedo- and dive-bombing attacks, air spotting, day and night scouting of the fleet and night attacks. This was an accurate forecast of the situation in the Pacific from December 1941 to late 1943.

In view of US and Japanese plans to have 750 and 350 carrier aircraft respectively, the Admiralty decided in February 1934 to increase shipborne aircraft to 400 and to complete a 22,000-ton carrier in 1938 and 1940. The Naval Staff wanted as many carriers as possible with two-seater fighters for defence. However, because all warships with catapults and six carriers could not be sent, the Far Eastern Fleet would still only have 300 aircraft. The First Sea Lord, Chatfield, envisaged ten to twelve capital ships plus four carriers to provide 300 aircraft. There was 'serious concern' about aviation, especially defence against air attack. Chatfield now also stressed the need for defensive fighters.

The Admiralty thought that the FAA's main function was to defend the fleet against air attack, and that the ships' gunnery was decisive in an action. Moreover, Rear-Admiral, Aircraft Carriers Ramsay and the CinC did not challenge the big gun's dominance in favour of offensive aircraft or want to change the proportion of Torpedo-Spotter-Recce (TSR) and Fighter-Recce (F/R) aircraft. This was not surprising given the domi-

nance of gunnery officers (for example Chatfield and Fisher, CinCs Mediterranean) and the lack of naval airmen of flag rank.

Naval plans required £107 million for new building plus £4.5 million for the Singapore base (1934–40) and £6.5 million for the FAA (to 1941). Against a background of disarmament failures and German military resurgence, the Naval Staff appreciated (1933) that whereas they were matching the USA and Japan in carrier numbers, they had fallen behind in carrier aircraft and so needed more carriers. The DRC recommended £71 million for all services with the Navy getting £19 million (including £1.9 million for the FAA: 51-aircraft shortfall) plus £13.4 million for new building if the 1935 Naval Conference failed.

The Cabinet, however, would not commit itself to the Admiralty's long-term programme and missed the chance to negotiate with the dictators from a position of strength. By the end of 1934 the prospect of fighting Germany, Italy and Japan was real, but the Chancellor (Neville Chamberlain) insisted that the risk of financial collapse was higher. The Defence White Paper of March 1935 admitted that Great Britain must re-arm. From July the DRC aimed for reasonable re-armament by 1939, with financial considerations taking second place. This was accepted as not meaning a blank cheque for the services.

To achieve parity with Germany and Japan the Admiralty aimed for a long-term building programme of twelve battleships (plus modernisation of seven), four carriers, 23 cruisers and numerous smaller warships. The FAA would be increased from 190 aircraft in ships (1935) to 357 (1939) and then 504 (1942) compared to a projection of 374 (Japan) and 670 (USA) in 1938. The DRC accepted this programme in November, despite the enormous cost (£226 million), after so many years of economy because German and Italian expansionism required a new naval standard. However, the ability to send a fleet to Singapore was also less likely from 1935 because naval re-armament was delayed by persistent hopes of disarmament.

On a strategic level Great Britain was increasingly faced with the prospect of two or three enemies: Japan in the east, Fascist Italy and Nazi Germany. Thus the government wished to continue Treaty limitations of navies to avoid an expensive arms race, but at the same time could not allow Japan and Germany's combined navies to exceed the Royal Navy. Japan's claim to parity with the Royal Navy and US Navy was therefore unacceptable as was unrestricted German naval re-armament.

In devising the naval requirements for the London Naval Conference of 1935, Chatfield realised that Great Britain needed a Two Power Standard to provide for the Far East and Europe. The Admiralty therefore wished to retain size limits (to keep the price of disarmament low), but not limit the numbers of capital ships and carriers (needing two or three fleets), would not cede parity to Japan and agreed an Anglo–German agreement limiting the German fleet to 35 per cent of the British fleet. Politicians who favoured an agreement with Japan were defeated by her insistence on parity and the need for good relations with the USA.

Thus Chatfield sought to provide a fleet for Singapore and another equal to the strongest European fleet (Italy's). Under the Washington Treaty the British fleet was allowed a slight preponderance over the combined Italian and Japanese fleets. By limiting the tonnage of battleships (25–28,000) and aircraft carriers (22,000) in a new London Treaty (up to 1945), Chatfield hoped to be able to gain time to afford (given Great Britain's poor economic situation) the modernisation of the fleet. However, this also depended on limiting large submarines and therefore the bill for cruisers and escorts.

The conflicting requirements of the nations at the London Conference ensured no agreement on any class of warship. Japan insisted on parity with the USA and Great Britain, Germany insisted on re-armament, France faced Germany and Italy and refused submarine limits. The British did get limits on unit size, but battleships, cruisers and carriers (23,000 tons) all increased. So the new Treaty's aim was negated and Japan never signed it.

The significance of the Conference's failure for British carrier policy was two-fold. The limit on carrier tonnage and therefore numbers no longer existed, but there was less money available for carriers. The size of battleships and their price had increased and the abolition of submarines had failed which meant more escorts were needed. The Treaty also coincided with the Italian invasion of Ethiopia and the subsequent mobilisation of the Royal Navy in July 1935 revealed many deficiencies.

One need was for an aircraft depot ship and/or escort carrier to provide aircraft for the Mobile Naval Base and commerce protection. In October 1935 the Admiralty therefore changed its carrier programme from five fleet to three fleet and four escort carriers, a MNB depot ship (soon dropped) and an AA target tender (replaced by *Argus*) of which one escort carrier would be provided in 1936 (before the planned fleet carrier). If the Naval Conference failed more carriers would be added to provide a New Standard (eight fleet, five in the east and three in Europe, five escort and one training carrier).

The Naval Staff required a minimum of 360 front-line aircraft in eight modern, fleet carriers. This total was reduced since the TSR (Swordfish) combined the scouting and torpedo roles. The air capacity of each fleet carrier (including *Ark Royal* as the first) was now taken as 48 (with monoplanes) and each escort carrier only 36. Carrier capacity was now calculated in squadrons which meant multiples of twelve aircraft. Due to the pressure for fleet carriers and the armoured carrier design, the distinction between the two types was soon dropped.

The limited treaty of the Second London Conference signed in March 1936 showed the democracies that disarmament had ended. As a result the DRC proposed to the Cabinet in February 1936 a new building programme of twelve battleships (seven in 1937–42) and four carriers (1936–42) with 357 aircraft by 1937 and 504 by 1942 when it was ruled that war would break out. The preponderance of battleships reflected German and Japanese priorities as much as British. Four new carriers were to replace

Argus, Eagle, Hermes and *Furious* which, with *Courageous, Glorious* and *Ark Royal*, would give five modern ships out of seven.

By June 1936 the DRC had decided to accelerate the naval building programme. In the 1936/37 Estimates (plus Supplementary Estimates after the London Conference failure) the Admiralty included two battleships and two carriers. The 1935 programme of three fleet and four commerce protection carriers was dropped in favour of six carriers in the 1936–38 programmes to meet the Admiralty's 'New Standard' of eight large and five small carriers.

The 1937/38 Estimates benefited by the Loans Act which borrowed money for services' spending and another two carriers were provided. The 23,000-ton *Illustrious* class was therefore laid down in 1937 (*Illustrious* and *Victorious*) and 1938 (*Formidable* and *Indomitable*) with the *Unicorn* to support them.

In April 1937 the Admiralty also considered the 'New Standard of Naval Strength' to meet the DRC's strategic requirement of sending a fleet to the Far East against Japan and retaining a fleet to safeguard home waters against the strongest European fleet. The 'New Standard Fleet' was to have 20 capital ships, 100 cruisers, 198 destroyers and 82 submarines plus smaller vessels by 1946. The FAA would have 577 front-line aircraft and fifteen carriers (three in reserve) of which eight would be new (*Ark Royal* being the first). This would provide four carriers with the Home Fleet (one for training), two in the Mediterranean, two in the Far East, plus *Argus* for gunnery spotting, and three in reserve for commerce protection, plus a repair ship (*Unicorn*) and two for refits.

Fourteen of the carriers were to be built by 1943, but the DCNS (Admiral W. M. James) doubted if the aircrew shortage, which was acute, would allow the manning of such a large number. The Director of Plans pointed out that the number of carriers depended on whether there was war with Japan and Germany; if not three or four could be dropped. As the Staff would not allow any reduction in capital ships, any increase in carriers would have to be at the expense of cruisers, but no decision was made.

The Admiralty's faith in the capital ship was based on adequate defence by carrier-borne fighters and AA guns. At this time the 'bomb versus battleship' controversy had flared up again and the Vulnerability of Capital Ships (VCS) Sub-Committee of the CID under Inskip was set up to investigate in 1936. Due to the conflicting evidence it settled nothing, but nor did it invalidate the Admiralty's building plan.

However, Chatfield and Ellington (Chief of the Air Staff, RAF) agreed in October to an impartial scientific sub-committee, Assessors on Bomb v. Battleship Experiments (later Bombing and AA Gunfire Experiments) or the ABE Committee chaired by General Elles, to enquire into the effectiveness of bombing and AA guns. Although the trials did not reproduce battle conditions, they did show that no existing bomb could penetrate the 4in armour proposed for the *Illustrious* design. But the statistics on bombing also produced an unduly optimistic view of the effectiveness of AA guns as did the slow Queen Bee target aircraft, which was reflected in capital ship policy.

The Blackburn Skua, the Royal Navy's first all-metal, retractable landing-gear monoplane, which was an escort fighter/dive-bomber. After Norway it had to be withdrawn. (IWM)

By 1937, however, Chatfield came to realise the poor state of British AA gunnery when Fisher (CinC Mediterranean) pointed out that it was no defence against dive-bombers and that the Home Fleet had failed to shoot down a Queen Bee in two and half hours. At last it was decided to develop a tachymetric long-range control system, but British industry, which had fallen behind the Americans and Germans, could not deliver quickly. Part of the problem was that British gunnery specialists lacked scientific and engineering training, were slow to seek such advice and indulged in unfounded optimism. This affected the Admiralty's assessment of the relative merits of battle-ships and carriers.

The next phase was under consideration in the autumn of 1938. The 'Air Requirements in War' Committee under the ACNS (Rear-Admiral L. E. Holland), set up to create a naval air policy (whose development had been stunted under dual control) and FAA expansion, proposed another six new carriers with one every year from 1939. The total of 504 aircraft had proved hard to meet and a new target of 480 (300 in carriers) by 1942 was set. In October it was decided to authorise three carriers for 1939–42 but the other three were deferred for economic reasons. The first two Improved *Illustrious* class (*Indefatigable* and *Implacable*) were laid down, but the third was not because the war broke out.

In considering the design of the new carriers the easiest and most obvious thing would have been to order 'repeat' *Ark Royal*s but the Admiralty adopted a radical concept, the armoured carrier, largely at the insistence of Admiral Henderson (first RAA and then Controller), despite the fact that by foreign standards *Ark Royal* was well protected. His energy and unorthodox efforts produced a sketch design that was approved in the three months up to July 1936 (it usually took three years). As a consequence of her 3in deck and 4½in side armour, designed to withstand 500lb semi-armour-piercing bombs, *Illustrious* displaced 1,000 more tons than *Ark Royal* but embarked only half (36) the latter's complement of aircraft.

Henderson had realised in March 1936 that the Japanese and Americans carried far more aircraft (*Ranger* carried 75 aircraft on 14,500 tons), but accepted this inferiority for the sake of higher protection. The Naval Staff knew that the carriers would have to operate in narrow seas (Mediterranean and North Sea) in the teeth of opposition from shore-based aircraft and surface units, and launch and recover aircraft away from the protection of the battle line. There was also the problem of adequate fighter protection against land aircraft when there would be little in the way of early warning, radar having not yet been invented.

If the carrier could be defended by AA guns and armour, all its aircraft could be used for the offensive. The repair carrier *Unicorn* was also designed to support the armoured carriers and increase their effective aircraft operating capacity. Other operational and deck improvements pushed the number of aircraft up to more than 50 by the end of the war. The performance of the class in the Mediterranean and Pacific justified the design and ensured that armour protection was later adopted by the US and Japanese Navies.

In addition to fleet carriers the Naval Staff also recognised the need for commerce escort carriers. During the First World War the principle of air escort for convoys had been established and in October 1918 small carriers had been proposed for such purposes. This was reiterated throughout the 1920s and 1930s with a requirement for four to six carriers. In the mid 1930s War College games and exercises reinforced this need and in October 1935 the Naval Staff wanted sixteen in case of war with Germany and Japan but little was done.

In 1923 the DNC suggested 'Mercantile Aircraft Carriers' using grain ships and oil tankers. The Ten Year Programme of 1924 had recommended small 10,000-ton carriers for commerce protection (the emphasis was against air attack not submarines), but this was seen as 'a luxury'. The Admiralty intended to build four MAC ships and equip Armed Merchant Cruisers (AMC) with aircraft when war began, but the funds were not available. The old carriers were also expected to protect the ocean trade routes and the First Sea Lord (Backhouse) in October 1938 assigned them to this task once the new carriers arrived.

The Naval Staff also wanted to provide purpose-built escort carriers. One vessel was included in the 1936 programme and it was expected that seven would be built to

The MAC ship *Alexia* (1943), one of the tankers with more suitable hulls than the grain ships of the *Rapana* class. Note the primitive conditions for the aircraft: there was no hangar. (FAAM)

a 14,700-ton design with fifteen amphibious aircraft. However, this was dropped by Henderson for a larger, more cost-effective one which proved too expensive. The problem was that ASDIC, together with other developments, was thought to have defeated the U-boat and it was reckoned that the main threat would come from surface raiders against which armoured decks and armament were required. Anticipating major engagements between battle fleets that would be decisive for the sea war, the Admiralty not surprisingly gave priority to fleet carriers, but in April 1936 the Board decided to convert a carrier (*Argus*, 14,000 tons) for a commerce protection role and to carry Queen Bee target aircraft to train the fleet's AA guns. The dominance of the battle fleet concept over commerce protection ensured that there would have to be extempore expedients when war came. In May 1936 Chatfield thought that air attacks on merchant shipping were unlikely and that even one AA gun (in escorts or merchantmen) would keep the aircraft high enough to nullify their attack. Thus Catapult Aircraft Merchantmen (CAM) and Fighter Catapult Ships (FCS) had to be hurriedly converted early in the war.

When war began in 1939 the Royal Navy had fourteen carriers built or building compared to the US Navy's eight and the Japanese Navy's eleven. However, only half of them were operational, included four old carriers (*Argus*, *Eagle*, *Hermes* and *Furious*) which carried very few aircraft and were not homogeneous, and they had to be spread among three fleets (Home, Mediterranean and Far East). At the same time, the Royal Navy did not have a single escort carrier, built or building, although commerce protection had been seen as a major requirement for twenty years.

The Second World War

British carrier losses in the first years of the war were heavy (*Courageous*, September 1939, *Glorious*, June 1940, *Ark Royal* November 1941, *Hermes*, April 1942 and *Eagle*, August 1942). There were also absences caused by heavy damage requiring repair (*Formidable*, May 1941, *Illustrious*, June 1941, *Victorious*, mid 1942 and *Indomitable*, November 1941, August 1942 and July 1943).

The Royal Navy was stretched to the limit as it had to maintain three fleets: the Home Fleet against the German fleet, the Mediterranean Fleet against the Italians and an Eastern Fleet in case the Japanese joined the Axis. When the French capitulated in mid 1940, a fourth force (Force H) had to be formed at Gibraltar. Given these commitments, the Eastern Fleet was reduced to the old *Hermes* which was quickly sunk by Nagumo's élite carriers when Japan entered the war.

The more modern carriers also carried fewer aircraft than their US and Japanese counterparts. As regards aircraft carried with the fleet the FAA had fallen even more behind. By the winter of 1919/20 the number of fleet aircraft had fallen rapidly to only about 50. By 1924 this had risen to 105 and with *Courageous* and *Glorious* the total was 150. By 1939, with the expansion of the FAA still coming through, this had risen only to 230 front-line fleet aircraft. By comparison the US fleet was ahead by 1926 and as a result of the Morrow Board in 1930 had twice as many (300). The FAA (410 aircraft total) had surrendered, even by its own optimistic estimates, an early lead in naval aviation to both the US (811 with 3,000 voted by the 'Two Ocean Navy' Act) and Japanese (377 carrier in 1938 and 503 planned for 1942) Navies.

There was no consolation to be found in the shore-based aircraft element because the RAF's Coastal Command compared equally badly with its equivalents in the USA and Japan. This was a problem because the Naval Staff recognised in 1938 that it would probably have to fight both Japan and Germany. Moreover, the Fleet would face the large German and Italian air forces in Home and Mediterranean waters.

Like the US and Japanese Navies, the Royal Navy planned a large expansion in carrier numbers. The 'new carrier' (*Ark Royal*) had arrived in late 1938. The *Illustrious* class and their maintenance support ship (*Unicorn*) were on order. The first pair (*Illustrious* and *Formidable*) were commissioned in May and November 1940 and the second pair (*Victorious* and *Indomitable*) in May and October 1941.

Due to war experience *Indomitable* was modified while building to have a double hangar so that she could carry 48 aircraft. *Unicorn* was also modified with a double hangar so that she could operate as a carrier (24 knots, 36 aircraft) if necessary. The later carriers (*Indefatigable*, May 1944, *Implacable*, August 1944 and *Unicorn*, March 1943) suffered severe delays because of the huge burdens on the British shipbuilding industry which had contracted during the peace years.

With heavy losses likely and the need for a large Eastern Fleet against the Japanese, many more carriers were urgently required. The 1940 Supplementary Programme included a carrier which was to be ordered in the spring of 1941. It was to be a repeat *Implacable* with modifications from war experience: better protection, increased aircraft (and consequent stores and personnel) and larger flight-deck, lift and hangar height for larger aircraft. In February 1941 it was decided to order a repeat *Implacable* without these modifications so as to get a carrier quickly.

The shipbuilding situation meant that the order was not placed and war experience and losses (*Courageous* and *Glorious*) led to five new designs to improve underwater and flight-deck protection, and with double hangars. As a result in October 1941 the repeat *Implacable* was dropped for a 1942 Programme Aircraft Carrier (27,000 tons, 31½

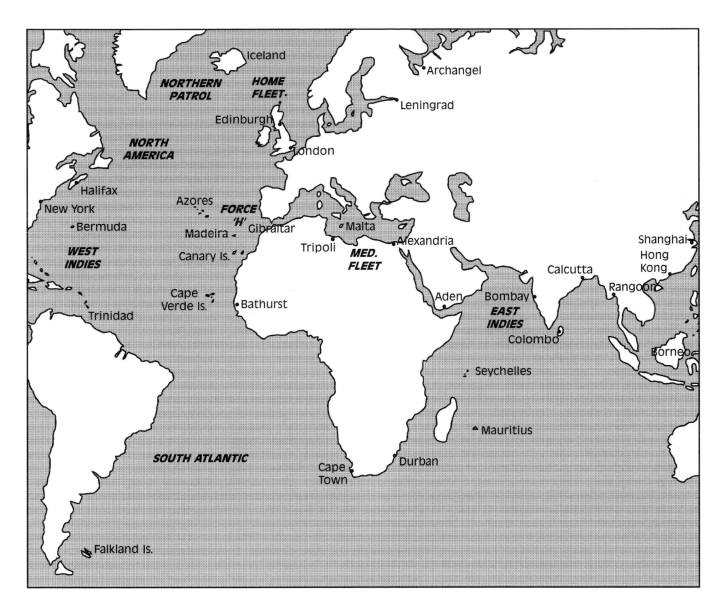

Worldwide overcommitment: the Royal Navy and its main commands, 1939–43. Except for vital missions, such as convoys to Malta, carriers could rarely be concentrated.

knots, 72 aircraft) whose detailed design the Board approved in September 1942. It incorporated the lessons learnt by the loss of *Ark Royal* (November 1941) through flooding.

Four carriers of the *Audacious* class were ordered. In the same month the design was again amended (31,600 tons, 31½ knots, 57–69 aircraft) due to the requirement to carry US and higher performance aircraft. Further delays were caused by annual reviews instituted by the ACNS (Air) to incorporate war experience. The fourth carrier (*Africa*) was quickly abandoned and the third (*Eagle*, Vickers-Armstrong), not laid down until April 1944, was cancelled in 1946. Neither *Audacious* (later *Eagle*, Harland & Wolff) nor *Ark Royal* (Cammell Laird) had been launched when the war ended, although laid down in October 1942 and May 1943.

To follow up the *Audacious* class for the 1943 Programme, the DNC first sought an improved, larger *Audacious* with double hangar. But later designs, influenced by US practice, had a single, open-sided hangar (allowing aircraft to warm-up below) with two deck-edge lifts as well as two centreline lifts incorporated. The hangar deck rather than the flight-deck gave the main structural strength. However, the armoured box, armoured bulkheads and armoured flight-deck (1in) were retained to protect the magazines, steering and machinery. Moreover, the bows would have been plated-up against the weather. The island was of a new, elongated design.

Four carriers of the *Gibraltar* or *Malta* class were ordered: *Malta* (John Brown), *New Zealand* (Harland & Wolff), *Gibraltar* (Vickers-Armstrong) and *Africa* (Fairfield) in mid 1943, but none had been laid down by the end of war, because of design revisions, and the last two were cancelled at once. The first pair were deleted in January 1946.

HMS *Glory* (1945), the second of the 'Intermediate' or 'Light Fleet' *Colossus* class carriers which were designed to produce large numbers quickly with reasonable air groups but arrived very late in the war. (IWM)

Given their lengthy build time, the problem, as it had been in 1914–18, was to get enough carriers before the war ended. By mid 1941 war experience had clearly shown that the fleet required great numbers especially to provide fighters. The DNC was asked to consider converting a warship (*Hawkins* class cruiser) or liner (*Winchester Castle*) or building a cheap, unprotected carrier like the 'Woolworth' escort carriers.

The DNC preferred the latter and was ordered to prepare designs (December 1941). He decided on low-cost merchantman-type hulls with cruiser machinery, little armament and no armour to allow rapid building (21 months) in merchant shipping yards. Due to overwork the DNC assigned the detail design ('Intermediate Carrier' or light fleet) to Vickers-Armstrong.

The final sketch design (14,000 tons, 25 knots, 41 aircraft) and three carriers were approved by the Board in February 1942. However, it was stipulated that the building time, which had crept up to 27 months, had to be kept down to 21 (later 24) months. Two carriers, *Colossus* (Vickers-Armstrong) and *Glory* (Harland & Wolff) were ordered in March, followed by more in August. Finally fourteen were ordered although only four were completed by war's end plus *Perseus* and *Pioneer* completed as maintenance carriers. In September 1945 the last six were updated as the *Majestic* class.

In March 1942 lengthening of the flight-deck was approved and in January 1944 a deck park to accommodate 24 Barracuda and 24 Seafires or eighteen Barracuda and 34 Seafires. The first three carriers commissioned between December 1944 and January 1945, but the 11th Aircraft Carrier Squadron (*Colossus*, *Glory*, *Venerable* and *Vengeance*) arrived in the Pacific too late for combat. *Glory* was equipped as a night-fighter carrier (32 Hellcats and Fireflies) and the others with Barracudas or Corsairs and Fireflies. These carriers were generally satisfactory, but living conditions and lack of storage were criticised.

The 1943 Programme included another eight light fleet carriers which were

to be an improved *Colossus* class. However, they would complete in early 1946 at the same time as the *Ark Royal* class fleet carriers and would have compatible aircraft (including US types). The result (June 1943) was a larger *Colossus* (18,310 tons, 29 knots 40–48 aircraft) which would take 33 months to complete. Because of the resources required, Board approval was not given until February 1944 and eight carriers of the *Hermes* class were ordered (*Albion*, *Bulwark*, *Centaur* and *Elephant*, later renamed *Hermes*, laid down in March, May, June 1944 and May 1945). Their low priority meant that progress was very slow and with the end of war the four not laid down were cancelled.

A feature of the later classes of carriers (*Ark Royal* and *Hermes*) was the introduction of bunks with kit lockers, rather than traditional hammocks, and centralised messing, along American lines, with separate dining-halls for CPOs, POs and junior ratings. This was to improve living standards (due to complaints from the *Colossus* class) and to rationalise space. Lagging for Arctic conditions and air-conditioning were fitted in all action stations and living-quarters as result of complaints from the *Illustrious* class about the heat in the Pacific. Arrangements for refuelling at sea and fuelling escorts were other lessons learnt from the Pacific. Welding was introduced to a greater extent. All in all, the final designs of the Second World War were excellent, the flight-decks, hangars, catapults, lifts, weapon, fuel and store stowage all catering for much larger, future aircraft plus lengthy operations. There were far higher standards for fire, flooding, weather, structure, armament, protection and living, developed from war experience.

Before the war, commerce protection carriers had featured in all the Naval Staff plans, but apart from the refit of *Argus* as a trade and AA training carrier, no funds had been forthcoming. The lack of fighter cover for the convoys in the 'mid-Atlantic gap' and down to Gibraltar was a major reason for the U-boat successes up to mid 1943. Thus the Admiralty had to resort to the one-shot Hurricanes launched from Catapult Aircraft Merchant (CAM) ships.

In 1931 the DNC was asked to consider fitting merchant ships with catapults and landing-decks for convoy duty. By 1934 an outline design for converting merchant ships (14–20,000 tons, 15-20 knots) in nine to twelve months was produced. Since this left the funnels and superstructure intact on the centreline, it was decided it was better to use diesel ships which were easier to convert to flush or island carriers. This led to a staff requirement in 1935 to convert Trade Protection Carriers (10–20,000 tons, diesel, AA guns, 12–18 aircraft), arrangements in 1936 for converting two typical ships (*Winchester Castle* and *Waipawa*) in twelve months, and permission to select ships and plan their conversions in 1937. Five ships were selected, but there were no staff available for conversion work.

In 1940 losses to U-boats and aircraft began to mount, the Staff Requirement was cut to the bare minimum and the German cargo liner *Hannover* (captured March 1940) was chosen for conversion. In January–June 1941 she was converted by Blyth Shipbuilders to a flush deck carrier (two arrester wires, safety barrier, no hangar or lift and her six Martlets were deck parked) and renamed *Audacity*. Meanwhile Staff Require-

The need for escort carriers on Atlantic convoys, 1942. Land-based air cover is shown; gaps are Greenland (A), the Azores (B), the Canaries (C) and the South Atlantic (D).

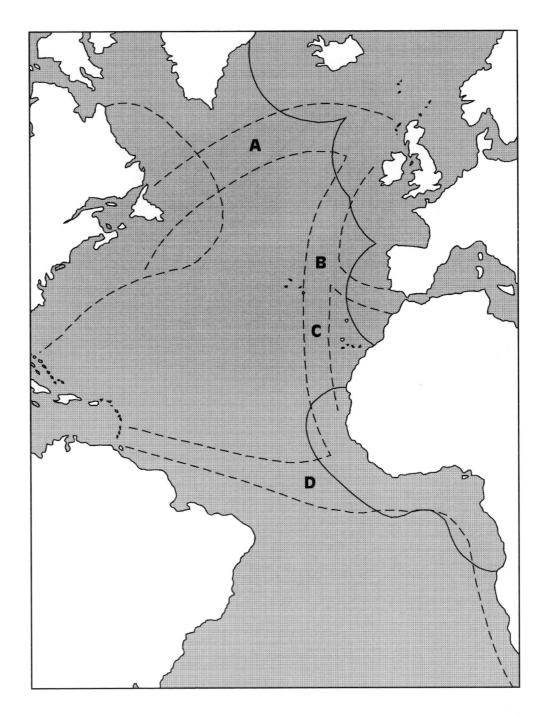

ments were produced for converting three types (A, B, C) of escort carrier (20, 18 and 16½ knots and 25, 15 and 10 aircraft) with hangars and lifts.

Five more carriers were then converted, mainly from ships not completed: *Activity* (18-knot liner, six aircraft, January–September 1942); *Pretoria Castle* (18-knot AMC, fifteen aircraft, July 1942– July 1943); *Nairana* and *Vindex* (16-knot cargo liners, fifteen aircraft, July/October 1942–December 1943); and *Campania* (18-knot cargo liner,

fifteen aircraft, August 1942–March 1944). As with the Japanese, most of the escort carriers were liners. War experience led to extra arrester wires and other modifications.

The problem, as with the fleet carriers, was producing enough escort carriers. In August/September 1940 Lend-Lease saw the exchange of British bases for US destroyers. This was followed in mid 1941 by negotiations with the Americans to procure escort carriers along the lines of *Audacity*. The US Navy was already converting USS *Long Island* and a sister from C-3 merchant hulls, with others in the pipeline. The sister (renamed *Archer*) and three others of the *Avenger* class (16½ knots, fifteen aircraft) were handed over to the Royal Navy. A fifth carrier (USS Charger) was retained by the US Navy to train Royal Navy pilots and crews. These were followed by the *Tracker* (11 ships) and *Smiter* (23 ships) classes, on the same hull.

Due to the loss of *Archer* from a single torpedo and war experience, the DNC made modifications to the US-built escort carriers: extending the flight-deck, round down aft, adding longitudinal bulkheads, larger hangars, bomb and fuel arrangements and ballast for stability, etc. Some improvements were incorporated in the *Tracker* and *Smiter* classes but speed of build was the priority and the Admiralty made arrangements for a six-weeks' modification programme at Vancouver, Canada, which handled three carriers at a time with one arriving every fortnight from Seattle. These improvements allowed the British to use their *Bogue* class carriers as small fleet carriers, which the Americans with their riches did not need to do. These escort carriers were completed between November 1941 and February 1944.

HMS *Nabob* (1943), one of the most numerous US-built class (*Smiter*), and crewed by the Royal Canadian Navy. She is seen here two months before she was torpedoed by *U 354* off Norway in August 1944. (FAAM)

HMS *Biter* (1942), an *Avenger* class escort carrier – the first US-built. She was deployed on convoy duty (except for Operation 'Torch'); note the anti-submarine Swordfish aircraft for the gaps in mid-Atlantic air cover. (FAAM)

In the interval before the arrival of the US-built escort carriers, it was decided in early 1942 to convert more merchant ships along the lines of *Audacity*, with a flight-deck and no hangar, but with four Swordfish for AS duties. These became known as MAC (Merchant Aircraft Carrier) ships and two types were converted: grain (six) and oil tanker (thirteen). The first, *Empire MacAlpine* (grain), was ordered in June 1942 and completed in April 1943. Conversions were completed in six months and the extra time to complete the tankers' building was only three months. All were delivered by February 1944.

The prolonged disputes with the Air Ministry, the unrelenting Treasury pressure for economy and an over-long adherence to the concept of an action between battle fleets had combined to postpone the expansion and modernisation of the FAA until it was almost too late. Thus in the early part of the war (1939–41) the fleet had to rely mainly on the old, 'experimental' carriers (*Argus*, *Hermes*, *Eagle*), conversions (*Furious* class) and the only 'new carrier' (*Ark Royal*) provided before the war.

In the latter part of the war and especially in the Pacific (1944–45) the Royal Navy relied solely on the *Illustrious* and *Implacable* classes which provided only six carriers, compared to the large numbers of the *Essex* and *Independence* classes which commissioned with the US fleet in 1943–45. It was largely due to Henderson's insistence on the provision of armoured carriers that the Royal Navy had even six carriers in the

Pacific, and it was largely through American assistance that there were enough escort carriers. Thus the Eastern Fleet in the Indian Ocean in 1945 was limited to using mostly escort carriers.

In 1941–42, because of the shortage of fleet carriers, the DNC considered some drastic alternatives. The production of battleship, cruiser and even destroyer hybrid carriers, similar to the Japanese *Ise* class, to carry twelve aircraft each was one (1941). The sketch design was heavily criticised and dropped. In 1942 the conversion of the liners *Queen Mary* and *Queen Elizabeth* was prepared with the help of builders John Brown. This was also dropped when they were required for trooping duties.

British industrial power, like that of the Japanese, could not match that of America, and British shipbuilding, concentrating on escorts and merchant ships, was unable to provide large numbers of carriers. Like the US Navy, the Admiralty concentrated its carrier building in a small number of yards: Harland and Wolff (ten), Vickers-Armstrong (eleven, Barrow and Tyne yards), Fairfield (three), Swan Hunter (three), John Brown (two) and Cammell Laird (two).

The brunt of the work was borne by Harland & Wolff and Vickers-Armstrong (Barrow) since in the early years the other firms were preoccupied with other warship building. In the 1936–1943 Programmes the Admiralty ordered five *King George V* (1936–37), four *Lion* (1938–39) and one *Vanguard* (1940) class battleships plus two *Southampton*, sixteen *Dido*, eleven *Fiji* and twelve *Minotaur* class cruisers and six *Abdiel* class minelayers, plus escorts and submarines as well as the carriers.

Although the light fleet carriers were to be built by merchant shipbuilders, in reality these were too busy as a result of losses to U-boats and the vast majority had to be built by firms who specialised in warships or could build both types. The congestion caused by these large shipbuilding programmes meant that the carriers planned after the *Illustrious* and 'improved' *Illustrious* classes were pushed back until the 1942 and 1943 programmes. Unlike the Americans, it was not possible to develop a large number of 'shadow' shipyards to mass produce certain types of ship and free the warship yards to build carriers. The only alternative was to cancel the four *Lion*s, which was done in 1940.

Due to the limited number of carriers that could be provided for the fleet during the Second World War, the number and quality of their aircraft and aircrew was crucial. However, the adoption of armoured carriers, to ensure their survivability in the face of large land-based air forces, limited the air group size. Moreover, as in modern carriers, the Royal Navy had fallen behind the US and Japanese Navies in modern aircraft in the 1920s and 1930s.

Carrier Aircraft, 1912–1918

Up to the end of the First World War, the best progress in developing carrier aircraft was made by the British. By August 1914 the Royal Navy had 93 aeroplanes and sea-planes of which many were obsolescent, mainly used for training, and some 50 standard types that were the new generation of front-line aircraft. By April 1918, when the RNAS was handed over to the RAF, there were 2,949 aeroplanes and seaplanes, the vast majority being land-based. This total was unsurpassed even at the height of the Second World War.

Progress before 1914 was mainly due to the development of seaplanes by Shorts whose main designer was the genius Horace Short. Their first naval seaplane (S.41, Naval No. 10) was developed from S.36 (70hp Gnome engine), a seaplane built for a private pilot, Frank McClean, which was based on their biplane tractor aeroplane. McClean lent the machine to the Navy and Longmore flew it 172 miles in four hours to win the Mortimer Singer prize (which gives some idea of the standard in the early days). S.41 had a 100hp Gnome (60mph) and was completed with wheels at the end of March 1912. After test flights by Samson she was given her floats (two plain pontoons) and streamlined flotation bags on wing tips and tail).

Shorts then completed a second seaplane (S.45 No. 5, 70hp) also with wheels (similar to S.36) in mid May. After tests one main float (no step) and three flotation bags were fitted. Two more of the S.41 type were then ordered, but S.45 was converted back to an aeroplane since her single float was difficult to handle on the water.

By the end of 1912 the seaplane was accepted as feasible and the Admiralty ordered 25 to test foreign types and encourage British manufacturers. Apart from the new firm of Tom Sopwith and Wights (an arm of Samuel White, the shipbuilder) Shorts had little home competition.

The Improved S.41s (Nos. 20 and 21) were completed in April 1913 and used for wireless experiments at Grain. Like S.41 they suffered from unreliability due to the use of two rows of cylinders. In February Shorts exhibited a private venture seaplane at Olympia which included all their latest features (alloy tube struts, improved floats, seats for two passengers, engine-starting gear, 80hp Gnome) and was purchased by the Navy (No. 42). Her floats proved insufficiently robust and she was converted to a landplane.

From No. 42 Horace Short developed a large patrol seaplane with a 14-cylinder 160hp Gnome, larger rubber sprung floats, steel tube struts, large ailerons, large front cockpit for observer and wireless and the pilot in the rear. The first of the type (S.63 or No. 81) was the first folding seaplane ever to go to sea, aboard *Hermes* during the 1913 manoeuvres. She had simple hinged wings, developed for S.41, which had to be man-handled and locked from outside. The second of the type (S.64 No. 82 completed March 1914) had a mechanical folding gear, operated from the cockpit, which again was developed and tested in S.41 (November 1913) and patented.

The standard Shorts' seaplanes at the start of the war were the Type 74 (Nos. 74–80, 180–3 production built non-folder 100hp Gnomes) sent to the air stations in January and February 1914, and the Improved Type 81 (Nos. 119–122, 186 folder, 160hp Gnomes) delivered in May and June. The Type 74 had a performance of 60mph, an endurance of three hours and a ceiling of 4,000 feet and carried two crewmen, a wireless, two 100lb bombs and a machine-gun. The Type 81 had a better performance (78mph, five hours) but still had engine trouble. These were to provide the first generation of two-seater scouts for the carriers that Churchill had specified in September 1913.

However, Sueter was aware of their lack of power and engine problems, and in that month ordered two Shorts prototypes (S87) with the new, more powerful Salmson engine. The first (No. 135 single row, 135hp) was delivered in July 1914 and the second (No. 136 double row, 200hp) in September. It was hoped that these would prove the basis of a new production type which would enable seaplanes to use torpedoes in the war at sea. Other seaplanes available were the Wight Pusher (folder, 200hp Salmson, eleven built) and the Sopwith Circuit or Type 807 (folder, 100hp Gnome, twelve built) which had been developed from the seaplane flown by Harry Hawker in the Circuit of Britain race in August 1913.

The comparison between these seaplanes and the latest airships shows how necessary a carrier was to enable them to perform the same scouting function. The latest German Zeppelin, *L3*, could cruise for 30 hours at 47½mph and carry 20 crew, three machine-guns, eight 100lb and ten 25lb bombs. Though slower than the seaplanes, the Zeppelin could climb to 9,300 feet. The rigid was comfortable for long cruises and able to defend itself. Hence the need for a fighter seaplane, as stipulated by Churchill in September 1913, but yet to emerge by the time of the war.

The standard Royal Naval Air Service seaplane of the First World War was the Short Type 184, originally ordered by Sueter in September 1914 for torpedo-carrying using the 225hp Sunbeam engine. Under powered for torpedo operations, it became the standard carrier and air station seaplane, later being upgraded with 240, 260 and 275hp Sunbeams and 240hp Renaults. The Type 184 had a maximum speed of 75 (later 88) mph and an endurance of 4½ hours.

Given the Type 184's insufficient power for torpedo operations, Sueter awaited the development of a 300hp engine or twin-engined seaplanes. A Blackburn twin 225hp was built but was too large for carriers. The Rolls-Royce 300hp engine was earmarked for bombers and flying boats and so the Sunbeam 310/20hp was used. The Short Type 320 was to carry an 18-inch aerial torpedo (1,000lb) for the first time.

The two prototypes were not ready until July/August 1916 and were rushed to Italy to attack the Austrian fleet. Both broke up in the air, delaying operations further. The problem was traced to the rear float attachment. An order for twenty-five was placed in January 1917 and 110 reached the RNAS. After the fiasco of the attack on the Austrian Fleet in September 1917 (a gale wrecked all the machines), the majority were used on long-range patrols (six hours' endurance, top speed 79mph, 72½ with torpedo). Production was halted when official policy turned to torpedo-aeroplanes.

On 9 October 1916 Sueter, Superintendent of Aircraft Construction (SAC) asked Tom Sopwith to produce a torpedo-aeroplane (Sopwith T1 Cuckoo) to be flown off *Argus* whose conversion to an aircraft carrier had been approved. Production aircraft

The Blackburn Dart torpedo-bomber, a single-seater which pioneered a long line built by Blackburn, one of the few British companies to specialise in naval aircraft after the formation of the RAF. (FAAM)

however were very slow to arrive. When Sueter left the Admiralty in January 1917 only the fuselage had been completed and the rest was re-started at the instigation of Longmore in February. It was not completed until June because Sopwith was preoccupied with the similar Sopwith B1 Bomber which also had a 200hp Hispano-Suiza.

After successful trials at Grain (100mph, 420 mile range) an order for 100 was placed with Fairfield Shipbuilding on 16 August. The prototype was then handed over to Blackburn to fit (because of engine shortages) a Sunbeam 200hp Arab engine (98mph, 4 hours), torpedo and aiming gear, engine silencing and torpedo warming for high altitudes. In February 1918, 230 more were ordered from Blackburn and 50 from Pegler & Co Ltd., another inexperienced aircraft manufacturer. Blackburn's deliveries began in May, but Fairfield and Pegler's not till September and October. Nor was the Arab engine a success. In November 1918 only about 90 of 350 ordered had been delivered. An operational squadron was formed at the Torpedo Aeroplane School, East Fortune, joined the fleet on 7 October and embarked in *Argus* on the 19th.

The main drawback of the Cuckoo was its inability to carry a larger torpedo than the 1,000lb Mk IX which was ineffective against large warships. The Admiralty therefore required (autumn 1917) an aeroplane to carry the 1,423lb Mark VIII 18-inch torpedo with a 50 per cent larger warhead. Air Board Specification N.1B called for deck landing plus ditching gear because of the delay to the new carriers. Blackburn and Shorts tendered using the 385hp Rolls-Royce Eagle VIII engine.

The prototypes were fitted with flotation bag, jettisonable axles and hydrovanes, and the Blackburn Blackburd and Short Shirl had operational trials in July at East Fortune. Both had higher power (Shirl 92mph), endurance (6½ hours normal 10 maximum) and weight lifting, but lacked the Cuckoo's agility for evasive action after dropping. A production order for 100 Shirls was placed, but cancelled when the war ended.

With the replacement of seaplanes by aeroplanes the fleet's scouting and spotting was assigned to the ship's Sopwith 1½-Strutter, a two-seater fighter (97mph) obsolescent on the Western Front and modified for warships with wireless, detachable wings, hydrovane, flotation gear and 140hp Clerget engine.

In late 1913 Churchill had envisaged carriers having scouting and fighter seaplanes. When the war started the RNAS did not have the single-seat seaplane fighter to attack Zeppelins and seaplanes. However, in November 1913 Sopwith had produced his fast Tabloid (80hp Gnome) which when fitted with two floats and a larger 100hp Gnome won the Schneider Cup in April 1914. With the outbreak of war this variant was developed as the Sopwith Schneider and put into production in November. It was designed to fly off the deck and climb quickly (top speed 87mph) to 8,000 feet to attack Zeppelins with bombs, darts and Lewis gun. In the absence of carriers with decks, it was found that her floats were too lightly constructed for sea use.

A more powerful version, the Sopwith Baby (92/100mph, 10,000 feet in thirty-five minutes), was therefore produced with 110 or 130hp Clerget engine and heavier floats. This however faired little better in operations off the sea or against Zeppelins. It also could not get off the small platform fitted in *Manxman* and was replaced in April 1917 at Rutland's instigation by the Sopwith Pup aeroplane (100hp Gnome, 111mph, 10,000 feet in 12½ minutes) adapted by Beardmore for folding, flotation gear and hydrovane and later with skids and hooks for landings. After pioneering flying from carriers and warships and landing-on, the Pup was replaced by the Sopwith 2F.1 Camel which could fold and carry bombs and had a 150hp Bentley (124mph, 15,000 feet in 25 minutes). It was highly successful against the Zeppelins.

From this review it is clear that the performance of carrier aircraft improved dramatically with the development of flight-decks and the abandoning of seaplanes. This led to a significant advantage over the German fleet's Zeppelins and seaplanes. In 1919 the British fleet would have been in a position to use air power to increase its ascendancy at sea. This was not lost on its allies who acquired British aircraft. The Americans had 1½-Strutters and Camels and the Japanese 1½-Strutters and Cuckoos.

Royal Navy Aircraft, 1919–1939

With the creation of the Air Ministry during the First World War, all control of the design and procurement of aircraft was transferred to the RAF. With adoption of the dual control of the FAA in the mid 1920s, the Admiralty was to stipulate its requirements which the Air Ministry would fulfil. In 1927 an Advisory Committee on aircraft for the FAA was set up by the two departments. This worked well if slowly. A Technical Sub-Committee of the FAA Advisory Committee was also formed in 1932 under an Air Commodore and included scientists and engineers. This became very active from 1936 with re-armament.

In 1925 the two departments also reached an agreement on the design and development of weapons for naval aircraft. Again the Admiralty specified the weapons needed, including bombs, and the Air Ministry designed and developed them. Torpedoes, however, were developed by the Admiralty. Every July an inter-departmental conference apportioned costs and the Air Ministry reported progress periodically. Under this system responsibility was divided and the impetus for new weapons development for naval aircraft was lacking. As a result air depth-charges were very slow in development and the anti-submarine bombs proved to be very poor during the early war years.

Because of the dual control of the FAA and the Air Ministry's preoccupation with strategic bombing and Home Defence, the FAA basically relied on modifications of RAF aircraft, especially fighters, or the products of two small firms who specialised in naval aircraft: Fairey and Blackburn (originally a subcontractor of Sopwith). Short, the mainstay pre 1919, concentrated on supplying flying boats for the RAF until about 1943. Sopwith, renamed Hawker, also concentrated on supplying the RAF.

This was a much smaller design base than that enjoyed by the US Navy or even the Japanese Navy, but the Air Ministry and Treasury ensured that there were not enough FAA orders to encourage more firms. By the time the RN regained control in 1936 it was too late to foster a larger production base before the war and it was still reliant on Air Ministry procurement. Moreover, the expansion of the RAF to meet the threat of the Luftwaffe in the late 1930s meant there was little left over for the FAA.

The British carriers finished the war with Sopwith Pup/Beardmore WB.IIIs and Camels (fighters), Sopwith 1½-Strutters (spotters/scouts) and Sopwith Cuckoos (torpedo-bombers). The Parnall Panther, which arrived in 1919, was already the designated replacement for the Strutter. In the early 1920s the Air Ministry developed its first generation of aircraft: a general-purpose fighter (Fairey Flycatcher), scout (Fairey IIID), spotter (Avro Bison) and torpedo-bomber (Blackburn Dart). For the large battlecruiser conversions of the *Furious* class the Air Ministry introduced a new generation of aircraft. There were two more generations in the early and late 1930s.

In the 1920s and early 30s Blackburn concentrated on the development of a succession of torpedo-aircraft: the T2 Dart (1923, 111mph, 285 miles at 95mph, 1,500lb torpedo); Ripon (1929, 132mph, 14 hours' endurance for scouting); Baffin (1934, 131mph); and Shark (1935, 157mph, 717 miles with torpedo or 1,260 miles scouting). These featured self-sealing tanks, wind-powered fuel pump, folding wings, low landing speed, strong metal frame and air-cooled engines, in line with US developments. They also produced the Blackburn Blackburd, a spotter/scout (1923, 127mph).

Fairey developed recce/spotter aircraft including the IIID (1920), the first three-seater naval aircraft, the IIIF (1928, 129mph 4 hours), with all metal structure and catapult strengthening, and the Seal (1933, 140mph), equivalent to the Gordon in the RAF. They also built the Fairey Flycatcher fighter (133mph, 310 miles) which went into production in 1923 and remained in service into the 1930s. It featured hydraulic brakes, floats and wheels, disassembly rather than folding and large flaps. It was replaced by the Hawker Osprey III (1932) and Nimrod fighters (1934, 195mph). The latter, a variant of the RAF's Hawker Fury, were still serving in *Glorious* in 1939.

Like the US Navy's BuAer, the FAA tried to reduce the number of aircraft types by the creation of new multi-role aircraft. In the early thirties the torpedo and recce/

spotter aircraft were combined in the Torpedo-Spotter-Reconnaissance (TSR) type. The Blackburn Shark (two- or three-seater) of 1935 was the first TSR aircraft and replaced both the Blackburn Baffin and the Fairey Seal. It was replaced from 1936 by the Fairey Swordfish (139mph, 1,030 miles), a mainstay during the Second World War.

In 1935, when it came to replace the Hawker Nimrod fighter, it was decided to develop a two-seater dive-bomber/fighter with an observer/navigator for long-range escort of the TSRs. The Blackburn Skua (225mph, 400 miles) was the FAA's first dive-bomber and all-metal low wing monoplane, but was mediocre in both roles. In service from 1938, it carried only a 500lb SAP bomb, lacked range and over Norway suffered heavy losses to German fighters. There was no high-performance fighter since it was believed that AA guns would prevent aerial attacks.

In 1937, with faith in AA waning and the RAF favouring the ill-fated Boulton-Paul powered turret for fighters, a variant of the Skua, the Blackburn Roc, was armed with a turret to provide a fleet fighter. It joined the fleet in February 1940 but had to be withdrawn from July. To provide a makeshift single-seater high-performance fleet fighter the Sea Gladiator (210mph, 415 miles), a navalised version of the RAF's obsolescent Gloster Gladiator biplane, was ordered in 1935 (production from 1937).

In September 1939 the FAA's aircraft were clearly inferior to those of the US and Japanese Navies and the large numbers of land-based aircraft of the German and Italian air forces. This was the result of the 20 years of dual control with the RAF which had caused an alarming, even apathetic, drift in naval air policy which affected aircraft procurement. The Air Staff gave a very low priority to Naval needs such as torpedo-bombers and was actively opposed to dive-bombers.

The Fairey IIIF spotter/scout – the mainstay of the Fleet Air Arm during the late 1920s and early 1930s. Fairey was another naval aircraft specialist. Note the Observer, a unique FAA branch manned by naval officers. (FAAM)

However, the Navy was responsible for its own requirements and persisted with two types of multi-role aircraft (TSR and two-seat fighters for escort and bombing), and wishful thinking on the aerial defence of the fleet. This reflected the low numbers of aircraft with the fleet and the lack of modern carriers and operating techniques. These were essentially a result of Treasury and RAF opposition. Another real problem was that of navigation over the sea by single-seaters. The Navy's expansion plans of the 1930s were given second place to the RAF and were put back until 1942. Thus in 1939 the FAA did not have the aircraft it needed.

Aircraft, 1939–1945

As in 1914, the war came when British naval aviation plans were still largely on the drawing-board. The fleet needed the most modern, high-performance aircraft to compensate for largely old carriers until 1940–41, the small air groups of the modern carriers, and to meet the large land-based air forces of Germany, Italy and Japan. What it had was a collection of obsolescent aircraft which were being replaced by modern successors far too slowly. The RAF was indifferent to the FAA and the British aviation industry was unable to provide for both. The FAA was equipped with modern aircraft only by recourse to American Lend-Lease.

In 1940–41 the fleet's greatest need was for a fighter when operating within reach of land-based aircraft. The planned replacement for the Skua was another two-seat fighter whose specification had been drawn up in 1938. A development of the RAF's Fairey Battle, the Fulmar, was adopted. The first production aircraft flew only in January 1940, but because of the crisis in fighters an emergency service trials programme saw the type operational in *Illustrious* by September.

The Fulmar (256mph, 830 miles) was heavily armed with eight machine-guns in the wings, but lacked the speed to take on single-seaters despite an upgrade of its engine (Fulmar II, 272mph). The Fulmar remained in service in escort and attack duties (and as a night-fighter until 1944), but was superseded as a day fighter by converted RAF types or US aircraft.

The replacement for the Fulmar, the Firefly, was conceived in 1940 as an advanced two-seat fleet fighter and remained in service into the 1950s. However, its design was much altered and because of production difficulties it did not enter operational service until July 1944. The Fairey design was approved in June 1940, the prototype first flew in December 1941 and production began in March 1943.

Designated a fleet fighter/recce, it carried four 20mm cannon and an ASH radar (in some versions), and although much heavier than the Fulmar its Griffon IIB engine gave it another 40mph. This still needed to be improved against single-seaters and a Griffon XII engine was installed. In the Pacific Fleet the Fireflies were largely used in the low-level attack role, and a night-fighter version was produced with improved radar to counter Japanese night tactics. A further upgrade (MK IV) did not reach the Pacific before the war ended.

As a result of the obsolescence of the Fulmar and the Firefly's slow production, the FAA depended on further emergency action to obtain fighters. The Royal Navy picked up (June 1940) a French order for 81 Wildcats (first known as the Martlet I in the FAA), which began delivery in July. However, the US Navy also had a crisis in modern single-seat fighters and most Wildcats and later Hellcats were required by them.

It was not until 1942–43, with production by General Motors' Eastern Aircraft Division, that 640 more Wildcats were delivered. Some Belgian Buffalos were also taken over by the FAA but were not used on carriers since they lacked arrester hooks. The FAA therefore turned to navalised versions of the famous Battle of Britain RAF monoplanes.

The Hawker Hurricane began to be delivered in October 1937. The first Sea Hurricanes were Mark Is without hooks and assigned to CAM ships to protect convoys. The Mark IIs had hooks and fittings for catapults and in 1941 reached the fleet. More than 800 were built or converted. The Sea Hurricane (340mph, 900 miles with drop tanks) was well suited to carrier operations, having a strong, wide undercarriage that retracted inward. However, it was by now becoming obsolescent.

The FAA therefore undertook trials of the later and superior Supermarine Spitfire (standard RAF Mark VB with catapult points and hook) on *Illustrious* in late 1941. As a result 166 similar conversions were ordered (Seafire I) which joined the first FAA squadron in mid 1942 plus 372 purpose-built aircraft (Seafire II). In 1943 the more powerful Seafire III (352mph, 465 miles, 725 with drop tank) with folding wings appeared. This was upgraded in May 1945 (Seafire XV) for the Pacific war and its squadrons were being trained when the war ended.

Fairey Fulmar two-seater fighter. The concept, pre-radar, was based on the need for an Observer for navigation. The aircraft reached the fleet in 1940 but lacked the speed for interception. (IWM)

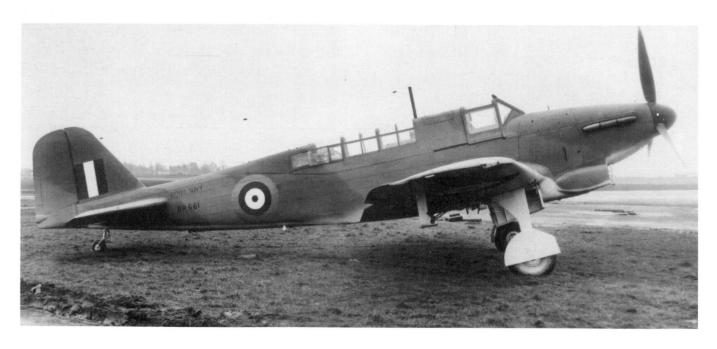

Fairey Swordfish Torpedo-Spotter-Reconnaissance (TSR) – the first of the type and a biplane, but a workhorse of the escort and MAC carriers up to 1945, armed with rockets and radar. (IWM)

The Seafire was an excellent interceptor (fast climb, high speed and manoeuvrable), capable of rapid take-off without catapult and recovery. However, it had a short range, and the long nose and low cockpit made for poor visibility in landing and forced a nose down approach which was also required to avoid the undercarriage 'bouncing' and missing the arrester wires. The undercarriage, which retracted outwards, was narrow and did not stand repeated hard landings. The Seafire 46/47, an improved version, arrived too late for action. The problem was that RAF needs meant there were few Hurricanes and Spitfires during 1940–42 when the FAA really needed them.

The FAA also needed a fighter of greater range for the Far East and the US Navy's rejection of the Corsair for carrier operations allowed the FAA, and the USMC, to benefit from the large General Motors output. In mid 1943 the FAA formed its first Corsair Wing with the modified Corsair II, with new undercarriage oleos, etc., which allowed successful carrier operation despite the long, turning approach necessitated by its long nose. Three Wings were deployed with great success in the Pacific.

The fleet entered the war with the Fairey Swordfish or 'Stringbag' still its principal TSR aircraft. This biplane was clearly obsolescent, partly because it had been designed to undertake so many roles. However, its low landing speed proved ideal for operation from escort carriers and MAC ships on convoy duty and it served until the end of the war. It was also used in the torpedo role with great success at Taranto.

Its planned successor was the Fairey Albacore, another biplane, designed to a 1936 specification and ordered in 1937. It first flew in December 1938 and was in production 1939–43. First deliveries were made in March 1940 and reached the carriers in 1941. The last FAA squadron was disbanded late 1943. The Albacores were then transferred to the Royal Canadian Navy for convoy duties. It was essentially a modernised Swordfish (enclosed cockpit, slightly faster, much greater range) and remained in service so long due to the delay of its successor.

The Fairey Barracuda was the first British monoplane carrier TSR. It was designed to a 1937 specification, but problems with the engine (Rolls-Royce Exe) meant that the prototype (with a Merlin 30) did not fly until December 1940. Production was further delayed by low priority and the first Barracuda I did not fly until May 1942. The Mark II (Merlin 32) was the main model, reaching the first operational squadron in January 1943. However, it was sluggish, heavy and a brute to fly. It served in both the Home and Pacific Fleets, used more often as a dive-bomber rather than a torpedo-bomber.

It was a controversial aircraft because of its ungainly appearance (high wings and tailplane designed to aid the observer's vision, large flaps, weapons, and radar antenna) while early performance problems raised doubts and concerns. Production delays caused the Royal Navy to order large numbers of the Grumman Avenger which was faster, carried more ordnance and had greater range.

The Barracuda was rugged and well liked by veteran crews, but caused losses of inexperienced crews and two carrier attack aircraft strained the Pacific Fleet's shaky logistics. Thus in September 1944 Avengers (also on escort carriers from 1943) replaced them in the Pacific Fleet, but they served in the Home Fleet and with the *Colossus* class. The Barracuda V (Griffon 37, ASV Mk 10 radar, two crew, much greater performance) was developed as a makeshift before the Spearfish was ready, but arrived too late for the war.

The FAA clearly needed a new generation of aircraft. The original replacement for the Barracuda was the two-seat Fairey Spearfish, designed and first flown in 1945. Changes of engine delayed production and only five prototypes were completed. The Blackburn Firebrand I was designed to a 1940 specification for a fighter and first flew in February 1942. However, its engine, the Napier Sabre III, was mainly assigned to RAF Typhoons and its development was protracted. The Seafire and US types filled the fighter gap until the Sea Fury was available. At the same time better navigational equipment and radar made a return to single-seat torpedo-aircraft (Cuckoo, Dart) feasible. The Firebrand IV was then developed with four 20mm cannon, to carry two 1,000lb bombs for dive-bombing or one 1,850lb torpedo. The first squadron was formed in 1945, too late for the Pacific.

In 1944 the Admiralty turned for the first time to twin-engined aircraft to increase performance. The de Havilland Sea Mosquito, and the Sea Hornet, developed from the

The Fairey Barracuda II, the belated monoplane TBR replacement for the Swordfish and Albacore. With an ungainly appearance and early problems, it proved too slow and of limited range. (FAAM)

former, two-seat fleet fighters were also too late for the war. Trials with a Sea Mosquito were undertaken in March (*Indefatigable*) and May 1944. Production began in 1945 and the first machine flew in November. The prototype Sea Hornet undertook trials on *Ocean* on 10 August 1945. The Short Sturgeon twin-engined reconnaissance-bomber was also being developed to provide a long-range strike and photo recce machine.

On 4 December 1945 the first navalised jet fighter, a de Havilland Sea Vampire, made landing trials on *Ocean*. This was developed from the RAF Vampire, designed in 1943. Single-seat fighters were also in the pipeline: the Hawker Sea Fury, developed via the Tempest and Fury and also tested on *Ocean* in August 1945, and Vickers-Armstrong Seafang, developed from the RAF Spiteful, a final version of the Spitfire.

The story of FAA carrier aircraft was basically one of rags to riches. By the end of the war it had a number of very promising designs coming into production. In 1944–45 it had an adequate mix of home- and US-produced aircraft. The problem was that during the years when the FAA was mainly dependent on older carriers, it also had obsolescent aircraft. There were no satisfactory aircraft designs in production before the war because re-armament meant that the RAF gave priority to Bomber and Fighter Commands, and the Royal Navy did not gain control of the FAA until 1939.

During the war the FAA gradually developed better designs, but getting adequate engine priority was a problem. As with the new light carriers, the new aircraft arrived just when the war finished. Once again the FAA was handicapped by a small production base: the Blackburn factory was at Brough, Yorkshire, and Fairey had two at Hayes, Middlesex (Firefly and Spearfish), and Stockport, Cheshire (Barracuda). The Sea Hornet was developed by the small Heston Aircraft Ltd., Middlesex.

In the second half of the war the larger aviation firms began to produce naval designs, but their main production was always for the RAF. For instance the, Sea Mosquito was produced by the Watford division of de Havilland which also developed the night-fighter version. Thus the FAA's achievements were almost entirely due to its personnel, especially in the early years when operating obsolescent aircraft from old carriers.

Lieutenant R. W. Salter RN landing on *Empire MacAlpine* (1943). This was the first landing on a MAC ship – a unique combination with the merchant marine brought about by the lack of escort carriers. (IWM)

Personnel and Training, 1908–1918

In the early days of naval aviation the first naval pilots relied on the pioneers and manufacturers for training. The first four pilots were trained by George Cockburn on aeroplanes lent by Frank McClean, and were given instruction in aeronautics by Horace Short. Other naval officers, for example Hugh Williamson, trained at their own expense at flying-schools which quickly proliferated and were reimbursed by the Navy.

Once the pilots had gained some experience, the Navy expected them to train others and carry out experimentation. Usually officers specialised in one or the other. Lieutenants Gerrard RMLI (Royal Marines Light Infantry) and Gregory trained more pilots, while Samson and Longmore concentrated on developing aeroplanes for the Navy. The Royal Navy quickly took over Eastchurch from the Royal Aero Club as its first air station and naval flying-school.

With the foundation of the Royal Flying Corps in May 1912, all elementary training for both services was to be undertaken by the Central Flying School at Upavon, Salisbury Plain, while Eastchurch performed advanced naval training. In practice Eastchurch continued to do elementary training, and most seaplane training was undertaken at nearby Isle of Grain. In 1913 torpedo-seaplane work was moved to Calshot Air Station on the Solent. One of Sueter's first priorities (August 1912) was to establish a chain of air stations for training with flotillas and air and coastal defence.

The early training syllabuses were very rudimentary and amounted to little more than a requirement to pass the Fédération Aéronautique Internationale's test with an official observer of the local Aero Club. This test consisted of flying figures of eight around pylons, cutting the engine to land near the marker and taking off again. Technical instruction was also emphasised. The Central Flying School and Eastchurch began to develop their own training for pilots, but little attention was given to training observers at this point.

One early problem for the naval air arm was to recruit sufficient personnel to train as pilots. Many officers were keen to volunteer (200 officers wanted the original four places in the Royal Navy). The snag was gaining permission to transfer trained officers from other branches since there were shortages of such officers due to financial restraints and rapid expansion during the naval arms race before the war.

Williamson, a qualified submariner, was given special permission to transfer to aviation despite the protests of the Inspecting Captain Submarines that he was losing a qualified submarine skipper. Lieutenant R. B. Davies was refused his first request to transfer because there was a shortage of qualified watch keepers in the Far East where he had been posted.

The Navy picked unmarried officers because it assumed that turnover would be high due to the risks and 'burn out' from stress. Another factor was the attitude of some senior officers who thought promising officers were ruining their careers. Longmore found his application blocked by his senior, Commodore Godfrey Paine. This attitude tended to change and Paine learned to fly in May 1912, became Commandant of the CFS and the first Fifth Sea Lord (naval aviation's representative on the Board).

From the RFC's foundation in early 1912, Churchill favoured the acceptance of suitable civilians on short-term commissions to make up the shortfall. It was thought that the strain of flying would entail short careers and the airmen would then transfer to other branches of the service or the reserve. In July 1912 the Admiralty circulated its requirements for regular officers (Lieutenant and below) and the RNR, RNVR and RFR (Royal Naval Reserve, Volunteer Reserve and Fleet Reserve, respectively) who had to be under 30 years of age and had a minimum of four years' service. Those who had learnt to fly would be refunded £75. Civilian fliers would be commissioned or attached to the First Reserve (regular flights every quarter) or the Second Reserve (service in wartime only). All but the Second Reserve had to qualify at the CFS.

Churchill also encouraged the training of ratings and Warrant Officers to fly. Specialist officers in gunnery, torpedo, navigation and engineering were seconded to develop these aspects of aviation. It was hoped that aviation officers would eventually attend specialist courses and fill these posts. In 1914 the RNAS had one specialist officer each for gunnery, wireless, navigation and torpedoes, and two engineers seconded.

When the RNAS was formed on 1 July 1914, it was deemed essential that regular officers and ratings have at least one year's sea service. Officers were not to spend more than four years away from the fleet and the aim was to return them to other duties without detriment to their careers and prospects. Officers could return to fleet duty or extend their service up to ten years. If not promoted or re-appointed, officers would return to the fleet or reserve.

RNAS seniority was according to RNAS and not naval rank, and officers could not take up a fleet command unless ordered by the Admiralty or SNO (Senior Naval Officer) in an emergency (when they reverted to naval rank). Civilian special entry officers ranked equally with regulars of the same grade and every year served sea time with the fleet. In 1914 there were two captains (Sueter, Paine) and seven commanders with the RNAS.

The Admiralty severed all links with the RFC on formation of the RNAS, although primary flying training continued at the CFS. The RNAS had its own ranks, wings (designed from Mrs Sueter's brooch), seniority and flight pay. At the outbreak of war the Admiralty took over some flying-schools such as the Bristol School at Hendon and Chingford, and racecourses such as Eastbourne and Redcar to train the flood of eager young men who wanted to become RNAS pilots.

Flying courses included theory of flight, aero engines, navigation and meteorology. Soon these were full and many applicants were sent to private flying-schools to gain their pilot's licence and then went to the CFS for further instruction. Pilots were then commissioned as Flight Sub-Lieutenants and posted to home stations for operational training including seaplanes which were very different from landplanes. They were then posted to carriers.

Later Crystal Palace and the White City, London, were taken over for preliminary three-weeks' courses of drill and 'traditions of the service' lectures for the probationary Flight Sub-Lieutenants. A gunnery and bombing school was also formed at Eastchurch. In November 1915 the Admiralty decided to establish a Central Training Depot and Instructional Establishment for the RNAS, HMS *Daedalus* (all RN shore bases are treated as 'ships' – 'stone frigates' – and given ships' names) at Cranwell under Paine, which took over advanced flight training from the CFS. Cranwell was the largest shore-based training station with two aerodromes and a bombing/gunnery school. Trainees usually started on box kites or Maurice Farmans and progressed to the Avro, American Curtiss JN4 'Jenny' and BE2c.

The initial training of pilots was only the first step in the production of experienced carrier pilots, especially in the days of seaplanes. It needed an experienced pilot to 'unstick' a seaplane from coastal waters let alone the open sea, to navigate out of sight of land and to recognise and report warships accurately. At the start of the war the carriers had very experienced pilots, but found it difficult to train new ones. Many of the experienced pilots were not with the fleet but in France or elsewhere, or at coastal stations.

In the summer of 1915 the Admiralty tried to provide training facilities by attaching the 'cross-Channel' carriers to air stations where pilots could be trained. However, the need to preserve front-line aircraft for operations and lack of facilities precluded any real sea training. As a result the operations in 1916, such as that on 4 May, suffered from pilot inexperience. In the Grand Fleet Schwann overcame this problem by developing the Scapa Air Station where pilots were trained for patrols, etc. As the Grand Fleet changed from seaplanes to aeroplanes, so airfields at Smoogroo, Turnhouse and East Fortune near the Scapa and Rosyth bases were developed to train the pilots.

From 1917 the Grand Fleet had the cream of the pilots, including many Canadians, posted to *Furious* and elsewhere, but many of them had little sea experience. Much depended on the experienced Dunning and Rutland until they were trained. The other great shortage was experienced observers. At first these were recruited from ships' officers, e.g., midshipmen, paymasters (such as Trewin, Rutland's observer at Jutland), Royal Naval Reserve and Volunteer Reserve officers and even Army officers, but many were lost to pilot training. As scouting and spotting with the fleet increased, so the importance of good observers experienced in navigation, ship recognition and wireless increased. The problem was finally overcome by recruiting signals ratings with the lure of a commission.

By the end of 1918, the Admiralty had trained and developed a large pool of experienced naval aviators, the élite of whom served with the Grand Fleet. However, with the end of the war, most former civilian pilots returned to civil life and the majority of the career officers and those given permanent commissions stayed with the RAF where they were no longer regarded as naval specialists. Basically the FAA had to start again.

Personnel and Training between the Wars

The Royal Navy's great efforts between the wars to provide naval officers as trained naval aviators shows that there were few doubts in British naval circles as to the importance of carrier aviation. Throughout its struggles with the Air Ministry the Admiralty insisted that the FAA was an essential part of the fleet and had to be manned by naval personnel.

There were two reasons for this. It was believed that to have such a vital branch of the fleet manned by another service would not work, even with the best will, and the Air Ministry gave the FAA a low priority. More importantly, FAA personnel needed advanced naval training and skills to be effective at sea, which a generalist RAF training and secondment for a few years to the FAA would not provide.

After the Armistice demobilisation reduced the fleet's RAF contingents to a skeleton, arousing many complaints from the fleet admirals (especially Phillimore and de Robeck) at the failure to meet naval needs. The First Sea Lord, Wemyss, accepting the creation of the RAF, was prepared to try to make the system work and proposed in January 1919 that naval personnel should be seconded to the RAF for training and service in the FAA. However, one month later he also suggested that all naval air personnel afloat should be naval officers or ratings trained by the RAF. This was regarded by the RAF as a restoration of the naval air service, and it only wanted a temporary secondment for three years to man the fleet's aircraft.

An impasse was reached because Wemyss would not fight to regain the RNAS, but could not get the Board to accept the Air Ministry's proposals. Despite the new First Sea Lord Beatty's truce with Trenchard (Chief of the Air Staff – CAS), the Air Ministry continued its policy, but the First Lord (Long) decided not to appeal as the Cabinet supported the RAF. Sir Oswyn Murray, Secretary to the Board, advised that the Admiralty had to accept the Air Ministry's proposed secondment of naval officers for three years, until the system was proved not to work.

Thus the Admiralty without enthusiasm issued a Fleet Order (July 1920) inviting volunteers, but elicited only nine of whom two were unfit and three retired under the 'Geddes Axe'. Most naval officers considered that service with the RAF, with lack of sea time, would damage their careers. Although one of the first pilots (Caspar John) became First Sea Lord in 1960, not one naval pilot had been promoted Flight Lieutenant by 1932.

Aware of these fears the Admiralty in 1921 asked that the conditions be improved to only a two-year secondment and purely for naval duties. Instead, in February the Air Ministry decided to lend RAF officers, but only for two years. Due to the lack of progress the Admiralty formed a specialist branch of Observers in July 1921 which, their role being wholly naval, were under the Admiralty's sole jurisdiction.

The RAF argued that General Service pilots could soon learn the necessary naval skills to become Observers and opposed any specialism. However, trials proved that specialist Observers were needed. They were trained by the RAF at Lee-on-Solent in

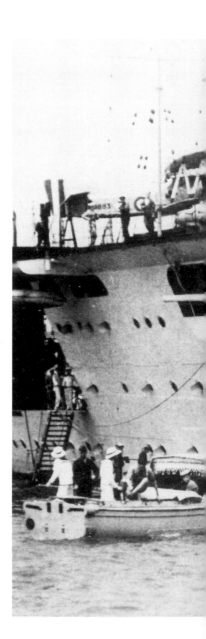

HMS *Hermes*, China, about 1926. The key to efficient flight operations is the close co-operation and flexibility of the air group and the ship's company, seen here in operating Flycatcher seaplanes. (FAAM)

airmanship, signals and wireless, but remained naval officers and performed shipboard harbour duties while the RAF officers went ashore.

The Observers played a decisive role in British aviation since they perpetuated the idea that the pilot was the 'chauffeur' and the Observer the expert. Moreover, the early establishment of their branch when few naval officers would volunteer as pilots meant they had seniority and early on dominated FAA commands. The first naval officer pilot did not command a flight until 1927. The first Observer was promoted commander in 1929, the first pilot in 1930. No further pilot promotions took place until 1932 (two) and 1933 (three). This meant that Observers had a decisive role in operational and procurement planning. The problem was that they became overqualified for

operational duties but had insufficient status for career development. The branch was not abolished because of the dual control and the needs of the 1930s expansion.

The third major component of the fleet's aircrew was the Telegraphist Air Gunner (TAG), trained in air gunnery and wireless telegraphy. These were recruited from experienced ratings, promoted in due course to Petty Officer and led by a Chief Petty Officer. They were developed from the Grand Fleet's experience in recruiting suitable experienced aircrew for spotting and as usual in the teeth of Air Ministry opposition. Like the Observers they were completely under Admiralty control.

Here matters rested until July 1923 when the Salisbury Committee decided that all Observers and 70 per cent of pilots should be naval officers in naval uniform, attached to the RAF rather than seconded. Naval ratings would gradually replace airmen aboard carriers. The Navy would also specify the training that was needed. The Admiralty promptly issued a Fleet Order calling for fifty-four naval officers for FAA pilot training, and was far more enthusiastic than in 1920, taking pains to re-assure naval officers of their status and prospects. The Board wanted to take advantage of a temporary surplus of junior officers to provide carrier personnel for the new *Glorious* and *Courageous*.

Despite high-level animosity, relations aboard the carriers were excellent with a very strong FAA *esprit de corps*. This sprang from enthusiasm for aviation, their anomalous position in the fleet and a dedication to high professional standards to convert sceptics. Naval pilots usually volunteered after five years' service. They did their initial training at No 1 Flying Training School, RAF Netheravon (Avro 504 and more advanced aircraft), going on to the Naval Flying Training School at Leuchars, Fife (eight months), and carrier landings on *Furious* in the Firth of Forth.

After four years with the FAA they did two years' general fleet service and could return to aviation for two further periods. The Admiralty was anxious that they be an integral part of the Navy, performing shipboard duties. While ashore the pilots were under RAF discipline and held RAF rank. The Admiralty was dissatisfied with FAA personnel disappearing into the RAF for training ashore when the carrier was in harbour because they were then unavailable for ship duties and not part of the fleet.

Moreover, most of the maintenance crews and ground staff remained RAF, under different customs and in different uniforms. The RAF would not let them perform naval duties; this meant an enlarged complement aboard which greatly increased accommodation layout problems in carriers. It also meant that FAA flight-deck crews were far smaller than their US counterparts which affected their ability to match US deck-operating procedures, especially deck parking and short deck landing intervals. As a result the FAA was sceptical of the US ability to operate the large numbers of aircraft their carriers had.

The main problem was the inability to recruit the necessary personnel, and there was little prospect of improvement by the mid 1930s when the Admiralty planned a major expansion of the FAA. The RAF could not fulfil its quota because of loss of privileges (e.g., marriage allowance), service under naval custom and few men wishing to specialise at sea. Moreover, most RAF officers only served two years, rather than the stipulated four, which meant that they left just as they had acquired the requisite specialised skills.

The Navy also had problems recruiting naval officers because of a general shortage and the faulty perception of junior officers that the FAA would affect their career prospects. Many FAA volunteers have testified that they were advised by their senior officers not to 'ruin' their careers. The feeling was that the dual control provided too little stability and that there was no organisation having the bureaucratic strength to protect the interests of FAA personnel. Junior officers disliked the divided allegiance and the dependence for promotion on two services (they held both a naval and an RAF rank).

As early as April 1925 the third training course was eight short when the naval staff knew it needed 190 pilots plus the expansion for the *Furious* class. In 1931 the Admiralty tried to improve pilot promotion in their RAF ranks to make the career more attractive, but again met Air Ministry opposition. The Royal Navy did not introduce naval aviation into the curriculum of the Royal Naval College, Dartmouth, as did the US Naval Academy, to encourage volunteers, but in 1932 it did introduce a compulsory three-weeks' course in flying for all junior officers.

The main problem was the Air Ministry, embittered by the dispute over the FAA, opposing the Admiralty's schemes to recruit personnel. Despite pressure on CinCs to encourage officers to volunteer and career prospect assurances, it became clear that 25 per cent of the Royal Navy's 70 per cent quota would have to be ratings. In May 1924 the Admiralty considered training RNR and RNVR officers and proposed training ratings (November 1926). The Air Ministry steadfastly opposed both schemes, as further navalising the FAA, and the Salisbury Committee (1928) ruled for the former and against the latter.

However, when in 1929 the Admiralty asked for funds to train 50 RNR officers, the Treasury refused. A 14-days' aviation course for RNR officers was no substitute. The Admiralty however introduced its own scheme to train ratings as Observers and after their success in 1934 again pressed the Air Ministry for a ratings pilot scheme. The Air Ministry finally agreed to train twelve!

The personnel problem was one of the main reasons that the Admiralty re-opened its campaign for the FAA. After gaining its victory the Admiralty insisted that it had the authority and air stations (six) for training, but it had enormous problems finding the personnel for 50 squadrons plus further expansion when the RAF was rapidly expanding as well.

Another problem was maintenance crews and the Air Ministry had to lend 1,460 men plus several hundred pilots. The Navy quickly moved to introduce ratings pilots, the first twenty starting their course in May 1938, and short-commission officers ('A' Branch, February 1938, seven-year appointments). The latter lacked the long naval

The Firey Firefly I two-seater operated during the attacks on *Tirpitz* and in the Pacific, where it proved sturdy and reliable and most effective at night and as a fighter-bomber. (IWM)

experience desired and at first ship duties were waived, but (like the US AvCads) made up for this with enthusiasm and by concentrating on flying duties.

They were quickly followed by RNVR(A) officers (A – Air) recruited from a list of amateurs, with sea experience, willing to serve as RNVR officers which had been started in 1936. This flood of new trainees affected the efficiency of the FAA during the Munich Crisis and the early part of the war because many experienced officers and carriers were involved in training. At the start of the war *Argus* was in the Mediterranean exclusively involved in flight-deck training, and the FAA's personnel were still very few in number.

Personnel and Training, 1939–1945

During the war, the lack of carriers and modern aircraft was exacerbated by chronic shortages of experienced personnel. As in the First World War civilian recruits tended to dominate and the RNVR(A) provided 97 per cent of aircrew. Thus the FAA's attempts to make a crucial impact in the years 1939–42 was greatly handicapped.

The demands of the RAF had priority and Churchill was reluctant to authorise an FAA expansion programme since the country lacked the manpower for both. Moreover, he and others of the high command failed to appreciate the full significance of the FAA's role. Thus it had to operate very rigorous manning levels, in direct contrast to the lavishness of the US Navy's air groups. Another problem was the provision of training away from the threat of enemy action.

The volunteers for aircrew undertook medicals at HMS *St Vincent*, the 'stone frigate' at Gosport (later at HMS *Daedalus*, FAA HQ at Lee-on-Solent). Then as Naval Airmen 2nd Class they were assigned to a numbered 'course' for pilots (two) or Observers (one) at *St Vincent* to learn to be seamen first through drill, elementary seamanship (in cutters) and navigation, naval history and organisation, ship recognition and Morse Code (two months). Passing the examinations meant promotion to Leading Naval Airman.

After this the Observers went to the Gunnery School, Whale Island, Portsmouth, for gunnery and spotting and then to the Signals School at Portsmouth for wireless telegraphy. On completion of the course the Observers were commissioned as Acting Sub-Lieutenants, had a brief officers' course at the RN College, Greenwich, and were sent to a Flying Training School at Arbroath, Scotland (753 Squadron) or Trinidad, West Indies.

The latter was set up in late 1941 but the first intake (43rd Observer) was lost en route, their transport being sunk by the pocket-battleship *Admiral Scheer*. Here practical navigation, including the use of smoke floats to judge wind strength and direction, and WT were learned in Swordfish. The Observers were then assigned to a fleet carrier squadron.

Pilots were sent to an Elementary Flying Training School (EFTS) such as No 14 at Elmdon, Birmingham, No 24 Luton (later Sealand, Cheshire) or Sydenham, Belfast, where they were joined by RN and RNR officers who had transferred to the FAA. Most of the instructors and maintenance crews were still RAF due to the late transfer to the Navy. The course was an intensive six weeks on Tiger Moth or Miles Magister trainers plus navigation, map reading, theory of flight, aerodynamics and engine theory. After about 35 hours' dual instruction the pupil went solo and then completed another 25–30 hours solo.

Then came the Intermediate or Service Flying Training School, such as No 7 at Peterborough, for another six weeks, again under the RAF. After conversion to a more advanced trainer (Hawker Hart), take-offs and landings, aerobatics, instrument flying, navigation and cross-country flying and some night flying were practised.

Advanced Flying Training School, at No 1 AFTS Netheravon, consisted of more cross-country, night and formation flying, dive-bombing and air to air combat (Hawker Hinds). After being awarded their wings, becoming Acting Sub-Lieutenant (A) RNVR and the officer course at Greenwich (two weeks) they were assigned to fighters or TBRs.

The fighter pilots were sent to NAS (Naval Air Station) Yeovilton (HMS *Heron*) and by late 1941 were being trained on Hurricanes. The TBRs went to the Operational Training Unit at Naval Air Station, Crail, Fife (HMS *Jackdaw*) for the Torpedo Training Course (786 Squadron, two months) which was mainly practising torpedo attacks on ships, day and night, using Swordfish and Albacores.

Both fighter and TBR trainees received (separate) advanced night training at Arbroath, one month at East Haven, near Arbroath (HMS *Peewit*, 767 Squadron) for day and night Dummy Deck Landings assisted by a Deck Landing Control Officer (DLCOs; it was also their training school) and then eight landings on a carrier (if available) in the Clyde. Later escort carriers, such as *Ravager*, from Greenock were used. As qualified fighter or TBR pilots they were assigned to operational squadrons, though some were held back for training squadrons. TAGs were trained at Worthy Down, Hampshire (HMS *Kestrel*, 757 Squadron), using obsolete Skuas.

Thus in 1939–41 pilot training took about one year and the qualified pilot emerged with about 200–250 flying hours and with about 150–160 hours solo. This was greatly inferior to the Japanese and less than US pilots, although training in Great Britain was handicapped by weather, enemy air activity and shortages of instructors and carriers. Gradually the UK element was phased out in 1941 and flight training was transferred to Canada and the USA.

After initial training at an EFTS, the pilots bound for Canada were shipped to Halifax, Nova Scotia, and entrained for 31 Service Flying Training School, Kingston, Ontario, which again was staffed by the RAF. Training was on the Fairey Battle and American AT6 Texan (Harvard II). Having completed the course, the pilots returned to England, attended conversion (on Miles Magisters for TBRs at RAF Errol) and officer courses at Greenwich plus an OTU at Yeovilton or Crail (now Barracudas for TBRs).

Given the war in Europe, the US Navy had accelerated the production of PBY Catalinas and agreed to assign some to the British. The agreement was that the US Navy would fly them to Bermuda and the RAF from there. However, this tied-up valuable US personnel and the RAF could not keep up with deliveries because of pilot shortages. Towers (Chief, BuAer) therefore proposed and Roosevelt agreed (June 1941) to train British pilots in the US who would fly the boats' ferry service. Towers extended this to include the US Navy training and working up all FAA carrier pilots using Lend-Lease combat aircraft. Thus the 'Towers Scheme' trained one-third of FAA pilots and worked up their squadrons in the US.

British pilots followed the US syllabus (see Chapter 2) but with some alterations, such as the Torpedo Attack Trainer, and had their own liaison officers, experienced

The flight-deck of HMS *Illustrious* (1940): a close-up view of the scene of flight operations which were the key to an effective carrier. Note the arrester wires and the waiting deck crews. (FAAM)

officers who passed on their combat experience. Throughout their training they also used British DLCOs since US and British methods were different. Most FAA pilots sent to America, undertook their Elementary Training at the US Naval Air Station, Pensacola, Florida, or the Naval Reserve Air Base, Grosse Ile, near Detroit. Basic Landplane Training was then undertaken at Pensacola and the pilots were awarded their wings and commissions. In the USA this took about fifteen months.

Advanced training for fighters and bombers was at Opa Locka near Miami. The pilots were trained for flying the Helldiver, Avenger and Corsair. However, problems with the Helldivers saw the dive-bomber pilots converted to Avengers (early 1943) and only one Helldiver squadron was formed. The last step was conversion and familiarisation with front-line aircraft: for instance Avengers at Fort Lauderdale, Miami. This included dummy landings (with a British DLCO or 'bats'), a Torpedo Attack Trainer (simulator, not used by the US Navy) and a live torpedo drop against a target ship.

The pilots then went to training squadrons for conversion to Fleet Air Arm methods: the Avengers at Lewiston, Maine (738 Squadron) and the Corsairs at the Naval Reserve air base at Quonset Point, Rhode Island. From 1943 squadrons from England were also re-equipped with American aircraft. Their pilots trained on Swordfish and Observers from Trinidad were converted to Avengers. By this stage bomber pilots trained in the US had achieved about 450 flying hours of which about 100 were in the Avenger.

In the US Navy the Avenger was designed to carry a pilot, gunner/radioman and turret gunner, the pilot assuming navigation duties. In the Royal Navy the Observer branch had been highly trained in navigation and Morse and took over the gunner/radio position and the TAG took over the turret. However, in American aircraft wire-

The Supermarine Seafire, the navalised version of the Spitfire. Note the narrow undercarriage track and the long nose, which meant that the aircraft was not ideal for carrier operations; moreover, it lacked sufficient range. (FAAM)

Grumman Avenger torpedo-bomber. This is a TBM, which was mass-produced (2,300) by General Motors. (IWM)

less was replaced by radio-telephony (RT). Thus the TAG took over the RT and bomb-release gear as well. Most TAGs were ratings and socially separated from the pilots and Observers.

Torpedo squadrons (two at a time) were then sent to Squantum near Boston with Observers and TAGs to work-up to combat readiness. From there the pilots flew down to Norfolk, Virginia, to undertake four landings on an escort carrier, USS *Charger*, in Chesapeake Bay. Squadrons were then assigned to carriers. The Corsair Squadrons worked-up at Brunswick, Maine, and also went down to Norfolk for carrier landings.

By 1943 Avenger squadrons flew to Vancouver (RCAF Station Sea Island) to join newly completed escort carriers and worked-up en route (San Diego–Panama Canal) to Norfolk before taking convoy to Britain, either on escort or transport carriers. Some squadrons joined their CVE at Norfolk. After NAS Machrihanish (working-up ASW techniques), squadrons were assigned an escort carrier which was worked-up under the Flag Officer Carrier Training (Lyster) and then went to convoys or a fleet. Corsair squadrons were sent to the UK by any available carrier, sometimes even US CVEs.

For the creation of the Pacific Fleet, NAS Katukurundu, Ceylon, was the centre for developing the carrier squadrons for the first operations against Sumatra and Java. In the Pacific the Royal Navy had largely to rely on US facilities and support. Indoctrination to US carrier methods in the Pacific was provided by the loan (April–May 1944) of the *Saratoga* which operated with *Illustrious*. British aircraft and new squadrons came through the Mobile Naval Air Station (MONAB) at Nowra near Sydney.

2. The US Navy and the Fast Carriers, 1910–1945

By August 1945 the US fleet had wrought an almost comprehensive destruction of the heavy units of the Imperial Japanese Navy (IJN), including its vaunted naval air service and the carriers which had swept through the Western Pacific three years earlier. This huge achievement was the result of a co-ordinated team effort, but it could not have been effected without the great defensive and offensive power of the fleet's fast carriers. The remaining obstacle to be overcome before the fleet reached the beaches of the Japanese mainland was posed by the massed attacks of the Kamikaze.

The rise of this carrier force had been very swift. In 1919 the US fleet had no carriers at all and looked with some envy and apprehension at the British Fleet which had a considerable lead in carrier aviation. Yet by 1942 the US carriers were first covering for the battleships lost at Pearl Harbor, then blunting the IJN's carrier offensive and finally spearheading the advance to Japan. This was achieved because resources had been committed to developing carriers, their aircraft and aircrew.

Compared to Great Britain and Japan, there was never any doubt that the USA had the resources to develop carrier warfare, and on looking back it seems inevitable that her great industrial might would produce the carriers and aircraft and train the aviators that victory required. However, these abundant resources had to be harnessed and in 1942 the margin between hanging on, until large number of carriers, aircraft and crews arrived, and disaster was perilously thin, as a consequence of the Americans' reluctance to re-arm before 1939.

The Development of Aircraft Carrier Policy, 1910–1945

The key to US defence policy up to 1945 was the decision taken during the Spanish–American War (1898) to attack Spain not only in the Caribbean, an area considered vital to US interests, but also in the Pacific. This resulted in the occupation of Cuba and Puerto Rico (greatly advantageous for the Panama Canal scheme) and of the Philippines and Guam plus the annexation of Hawaii. Thus America became a Far Eastern power, but, as the General Board persistently advised, lacked the naval power to defend her new possessions. Given the size of the fleet and American political realities, US naval planning before the First World War was essentially defensive and this was reflected in aviation.

Catapults and Flying Boats, 1910–1917

The work of Professor Samuel P. Langley and the Wrights inspired individual interest and suggestions for the use of aeroplanes in the US Navy as early as 1898. For instance in August 1909 the US Naval Attaché in Paris, Commander F. L. Chapin, was sent to the first International Aviation Meet at Rheims. The following month he suggested that the new *Connecticut* class battleships be fitted with the Wrights' catapults and aeroplanes and that auxiliaries have 'a floor over the deckhouses' for launching and recovering aeroplanes. Nothing was done since aircraft lacked control, range and seakeeping.

However, the 1910 Gordon Bennett Cup races at Belmont Park, New York, and Glenn Curtiss's 150-mile flight from Albany to New York in May inspired great popular interest in aviation. Curtiss predicted that aeroplanes would be launched from a battleship, and in July simulated a bombing attack on a battleship at Hammondsport, Lake Keuka.

This prompted Admiral George Dewey (Head, General Board) to suggest on 1 October that the Bureaux of Construction and Repair and of Steam Engineering investigate aviation's value to the Navy and that aircraft be provided in the new scouting vessels. On 13 October the Acting Secretary of the Navy (Beekman Winthrop) assigned Captain Washington I. Chambers, Assistant to the Secretary of the Navy's Aid for Material, with the help of two officers from the above Bureaux, to study these questions.

Chambers knew that the priorities were safe aircraft and proven feasibility at sea. He was concerned also to set up a framework of scientific research, recommended appropriating funds for experiments, a two-seater for every new scout cruiser, four training fields and establishing an office of aeronautics – all to no avail.

At this time the Hamburg Amerika Steamship Company and the New York *World* announced that a former Curtiss pilot, J. A. D. McCurdy, would fly-off from a platform on the liner *Kaiserin Augusta Victoria*. This experiment was designed to speed up the mail service, but many thought that the German Navy was involved. Bad weather and an accident meant that the liner sailed before a flight could take place and allowed Chambers to achieve a publicity *coup* by arranging the first flights in history to and from ships.

Because of lack of funds, Chambers had to adapt existing warships and do without any purpose-built equipment such as catapults. For the first flight off a ship he obtained a scout cruiser and the services of a Curtiss pilot, Eugene Ely, as a volunteer. Chambers relied on Norfolk Navy Yard labour supervised by Naval Constructor William McEntee to rig a temporary platform on *Birmingham*'s bow from available resources.

It was an 83ft long, 24ft wide wooden platform on uprights above the forecastle. It sloped 5 degrees towards the bow and gave the pilot a 57ft take-off run. Ely's aeroplane was fitted with a float under each wing and a crude hydrovane, and was hoisted aboard (without engine) from a tug. On 14 November 1910 Ely flew her off the deck in Hampton Roads, Virginia. It was planned for the cruiser to be under way but Ely did not wait for the ship to get up steam.

Chambers then progressed to a flying-on experiment for which he was limited to $500 and so again the deck was a simple wooden structure on uprights with diagonal bracing. The quarter deck allowed a longer run (119ft × 31½ft) for the more hazardous landing. The armoured cruiser *Pennsylvania*'s aft turret was completely masked by the platform's supports and bracing. An arrester gear of twenty-two ropes was fitted across the deck at 3ft intervals with 50lb sacks of sand to provide inertia. Three hooks were fitted to the aeroplane to catch these ropes. A deck awning at the end was to act as a crash barrier.

On 18 January 1911 Ely flew on to *Pennsylvania* anchored in San Francisco Bay using all the elements of modern landings (crude arrester wires and hook, deceleration device and a barrier). He caught the eleventh rope and stopped within fifty feet.

Although these were partly 'stunts', since they took part at anchor and not under way or at sea which was more challenging, Chambers had proved that with suitable equipment ships of the fleet could launch and recover aeroplanes. Later it was to prove very dangerous to land on a ship with a full superstructure because of turbulence. These achievements earned $25,000 from Congress to buy three aeroplanes from Curtiss and the Wrights plus the training of pilots (Lieutenants John H. Tower and John Rodgers) and enlisted men as mechanics.

However, like the British pioneer Samson, a year later, Chambers did not attempt any more development towards the modern carrier because any advantages of aeroplanes for warships were outweighed by the requisite bulky platform which masked the ships' guns. Secretary of the Navy Meyer told Curtiss that aeroplanes would only be of practical benefit to the Navy when they could take-off from and alight on the sea alongside battleships and could be hoisted aboard.

Chambers therefore encouraged Curtiss and Lieutenant T. G. 'Spuds' Ellyson, whom Curtiss had taught free of charge, to experiment with a seaplane on North Island, California. On 26 January Curtiss took off from San Diego Bay in the world's first successful seaplane flight. On 17 February he landed alongside *Pennsylvania* in San Diego harbour, the seaplane was hoisted aboard and out again, and then Curtiss took off from the sea.

Chambers immediately became a convert, first to the seaplane and later to flying boats. His view was strengthened by the failure of McCurdy to fly an aeroplane from Key West to Cuba; he had had to come down on the sea. Chambers stressed the favourable factors: no masking of ships' guns; an unlimited 'deck' provided by the sea; economy (few expensive facilities); and constant presence with the fleet in 'shipshape' fashion.

Safety, economy and flexibility were strong arguments, but there were heavy tactical penalties for a fleet which had to stop to hoist out its seaplanes. Chambers sought

USS *Langley* (CV-1, 1922), the original 'flat-top'. Note the bridge under the deck, the funnels (which could be lowered), the lift and the radio mast. (US Navy)

to minimise restrictions on ships and tactics by developing the means to launch seaplanes from the deck without restricting arcs of fire.

Curtiss, Ellyson and Towers tried many methods including overhead wires. These were not practical at sea and Chambers enlisted Lieutenant St. Clair Smith (Naval Gun Factory) and Naval Constructor Holden C. Richardson to work with Ellyson to develop a catapult. They already had the work of Chanute, Langley and the Wrights as a base, and Chambers as a torpedo specialist naturally used compressed air.

The first trial at Annapolis on 31 July 1912 wrecked the machine and put Ellyson in the river. The second trial at Washington Navy Yard in November quickly launched Ellyson's seaplane. In December the catapult successfully launched a flying boat after a limited run of 40 feet over a guided track. Richardson began work on an improved version, but for the next three years no warship was available for trials, and in its second appropriation Congress provided only $65,000 for various Bureaux.

The fitting of torpedoes to aeroplanes was another reason for the development of seaplanes. In April 1911 Captain (later Rear Admiral) Bradley A. Fiske (War Plans, General Board) suggested stationing at least 400 aeroplanes to defend the Philippines against the Japanese fleet. By July 1912 he was granted a patent for torpedo dropping which he conceived as a means to provide this aerial defence. However, an aeroplane carrying a 1,000lb torpedo could not take off from a warship's short deck or be catapulted (sway braces to hold the torpedo during sudden acceleration had not been invented). The only practical course was a seaplane taking off from the sea.

In June 1912 the General Board required further data on aircraft capabilities at sea and suggested that seaplanes join the fleet at Guantanamo. An aviation camp was set-up there (January–March 1913) using the colliers *Sterling* and *Vulcan* as transports. In 1913 Chambers reported to the General Board on the numbers of American naval aircraft as compared to foreign navies. By 31 August the Board had already admitted that aircraft should be the eyes of the fleet, should accompany it everywhere and that the state of naval aviation was deplorable.

It was also alarmed that airships and other aircraft might be transported to a Caribbean base to attack the US coast. It therefore proposed the organisation of an efficient naval air service. In December 1912 the General Board had already proposed an 80mph 'aeroplane destroyer', armed with a machine-gun and bombs, to defend naval bases from airship attack. Chambers and Richardson also prepared a specification for a two-seat 'pusher' amphibian flying boat capable of 55mph, a climb rate of 100 feet a minute and an endurance of four hours. During the summer Constructors Richardson and McEntee designed a flying boat with a 'V'-shaped hull which became the standard type.

The Bureau of Steam Engineering proposed using the cruiser *Columbia* as an 'aeroplane ship' for experiments and training. Chambers, however, opposed any special carrier and preferred to fit every warship with a seaplane which would be totally integrated into the fleet. Carriers were regarded as superfluous.

On 7 October 1913 Assistant Secretary of the Navy Franklin Roosevelt established a special board under Chambers to plan the organisation of a Naval Aeronautic Service. The Board proposed 50 aircraft for the fleet (one on each warship) and six more for an advanced base ashore. Auxiliary vessels would carry the mobile force and be fitted as 'special ships' to carry aircraft. Airships could wait until these needs were met. An air station at Pensacola would provide a flying school and training. The cost was nearly $1.3 million.

Captain Mark L. Bristol (Chambers' successor) secured the old battleship *Mississippi* in January 1914 as an experimental vessel at Pensacola, instituted an aircraft design competition and ordered foreign engines. However, before Richardson's second catapult could be finished and experiments undertaken, *Mississippi* was ordered to Vera Cruz (April) with a seaplane and a flying boat. After this she was sold to Greece. Her replacement, *North Carolina*, was commissioned on 28 July, but ordered to Europe on

6 August. So when the First World War began no catapult yet been installed in a US warship.

Chambers' policy seemed to be vindicated during the Vera Cruz expedition. The seaplane detachment scouted, under fire, for the fleet and Army, and impressed the naval hierarchy. Josephus Daniels (Secretary of the Navy) felt that they had been of great value in the Army and Navy combined operations. The seaplane was again favoured; the flying boat's take-off was poor in a seaway and its heavy hull affected performance.

Like those of the Royal Navy, the war found the US Navy's plans for fleet aviation unfulfilled. Both navies had decided to develop seaplanes, but the latter's adoption of the catapult as the main launching device was unique. Official US naval interest in carrier design was not to be aroused until British war experience showed its importance. US naval aviation was clearly behind that of Germany (rigids) and Great Britain (seaplane carriers) despite its early, promising start.

Under the Black War Plan of 1913, the US fleet based at Guantanamo, Cuba, with its advanced base at Culebra, Puerto Rico, was to intercept the German fleet before it could land a large army in the Caribbean or on the US coast. War Plan Orange of 1914 required the US fleet to advance via Panama–Pearl Harbor–Midway–Guam–Manila in 68 days. As the Japanese could reach the Philippines in eight days, this required the Army to hold out for 60 days which it could not.

Moreover, although Congress had approved a US battle fleet superior to that of the Japanese, it ignored the need of the requisite personnel and fleet train (transports, ammunition ships and colliers) for a 10,000-mile advance. Nor were the facilities of Pearl Harbor, Midway or Guam up to the task. In reality therefore the Philippines could not be defended and the Americans relied on *status quo* agreements made with the Japanese in 1905, 1908 and 1917. The Navy wanted to develop its main Pacific base at Pearl Harbor.

President Wilson and Secretary Daniels looked to avoid joining in the European war. The great building programme under the Naval Act of 1916 was designed not for possible participation but for post-war when the USA might again be threatened. Thus the construction was of battleships and auxiliary ships rather than escorts and the Navy was ill-prepared for anti-submarine warfare in April 1917.

The First World War, 1917–1918

Following on the work of Chambers, Rear Admiral W. S. Benson, the first Chief of Naval Operations (CNO, July 1915), and Secretary Daniels chose to concentrate on developing catapults in fleet warships. The success of catapult trials in *North Carolina* seemed to rule out any need for a carrier. In June 1916 the General Board also rejected aircraft as the striking force of the fleet because of their limited carrying power, and stated that their role would be auxiliary: scouting, anti-submarine and spotting duties. It favoured airships and coastal air stations.

Thus proposals to develop carriers got nowhere. In October 1915 Bristol recommended the purchase of a merchant vessel for conversion to an 'aircraft ship', as the British had done, to experiment with 'dirigibles, kite balloons and aeroplanes'. In March 1916 Commander H. C. Mustin, CO Pensacola, and the pilot in *North Carolina*, also recommended the acquisition of a carrier to the General Board.

In October 1916 Lieutenant John H. Towers, lately acting Naval Attaché in London and the new Aviation Assistant to the CNO, reported to the General Board that the British were adopting fighter aeroplanes with their fleet and tried to persuade it to adopt aeroplanes instead of seaplanes. He thought, erroneously, that carriers were out of favour with the British. In November, however, the General Board continued its policy of carrying seaplanes in warships, but did adopt fighter seaplanes.

With US intervention in the war the US Navy concentrated on the development of air stations for anti-submarine patrols on the US and European coasts and supple-

USS *Lexington* (CV-2; 1927) in 1939, showing the large deck park for fast flight-deck operations and large air strikes, which the British could not match and doubted were feasible. (US National Archives)

menting the Allies' plans for air offensives against the Imperial fleets and U-boat bases. Given the distances across the North Sea to the German bases, Admiral W. S. Sims (Commander US Naval Forces Europe) also quickly requested carriers.

In August 1917 Lieutenant K. Whiting, Commander of the first US naval air unit in France, proposed a bomber offensive from seaplane carriers against German ports. More than a year earlier he had suggested the conversion of a railway ferry. The problem was that carriers could not be provided before the war was likely to finish. The lack of carriers meant that attention was switched to towed lighters, for flying boats, designed by the Royal Navy. Mustin also suggested the use of sea sleds to launch bombers, but the war ended before any of these plans could come to fruition.

US carrier development was ultimately spurred into being by British achievements and the prospect of their establishing an aerial ascendancy. With *Vindictive* and *Argus* being converted for the Grand Fleet, Towers (ADNA, Assistant Director of Naval Aviation), now Lieutenant Commander, suggested converting a merchant ship as a carrier 'for experimental purposes'.

The Director of Naval Aviation, Captain N. E. Irwin (DNA, appointed May 1917), accepted this and on 24 June 1918 submitted a specification to the General Board for a 700ft, 80ft beam, 15,000-ton, 30-knot carrier with lift, folding aircraft, bridge amidships and above deck. This was based on the latest British designs brought over by the British Constructor Stanley Goodall, seconded to the Bureau of Construction and Repair. After the failure of *Furious*'s flying-on trials the design was altered in October to have a starboard island as in the British design for *Eagle*.

The General Board proposed construction of a fleet equal to that of the Royal Navy by 1925 and for the first time thought that high-speed carriers were required. On 10 September 1918 it recommended the building of six 35-knot carriers with 700ft decks and 45 aircraft over six years. Without any carrier experience, the General Board seems to have advocated this programme in order to keep up with British carrier provision.

The General Board's policy of developing fleet aviation was accepted, but there was no consensus on carrier development. Benson (CNO – Chief of Naval Operations) refused the request for a carrier in the 1920 Programme because, like the British in 1916, he could not see the vessel completing before the end of the war.

Moreover, he had set up a committee on fleet aircraft which had recommended installing none in capital ships and putting off a carrier to the future. Instead the Bureau of Ordnance was working in August on plans for a seaplane tender to provide the fleet's scouting and spotting aircraft. During the war the seaplane was continued with, supplemented by the airship and kite balloon.

From this point evidence quickly mounted of the importance of British carriers with aeroplanes as opposed to seaplanes. In October 1918 Sims, commenting on the arrival of HMS *Argus*, stressed that the British considered carriers so important that they had converted three warships (*Furious*, *Vindictive* and *Eagle*). Admiral H. T. Mayo,

CinC Atlantic Fleet, used British developments to justify asking in November for a carrier for scouting and torpedo-aircraft and able to accompany fast battleships. Rear Admiral H. Rodman, CO Battleship Squadron Grand Fleet since December 1917, also stated the necessity for several fleet carrier types.

Other officers (Commanders W. S. Pye, G. de C. Chevalier) with the Grand Fleet and the carriers *Vindictive* (H. E. Kimmel) and *Furious* (J. C. Hunsaker) reported that the Royal Navy stressed gaining control of the air before an action, through fleet carriers providing scouts and fighters whenever required. However, the war finished before Benson would agree to build any carriers.

Between the Wars, 1919–1941

After the war the US Navy had to face the same calls for an independent air force as the British, the administrative problem of incorporating aviation into the Navy Department and fleet, plus an adverse strategic position in the Pacific.

The Japanese occupation of the German Pacific territories (Carolines, Marshalls and Marianas) in October 1914 threatened US communications with the Philippines and were a major concern at the Versailles Conference. The safeguards against fortified bases in League of Nations mandates did not change the weakened US strategic position in the Central Pacific. At first the problem was seen in terms of submarine and logistical bases, but later the islands were viewed as 'unsinkable aircraft carriers' for Japan's naval aviation (initially trained by the Royal Navy).

In the first three post-war budgets the Navy Department did not succeed in getting any appropriations for new construction, and made only slow progress on the 1916 programme. President Wilson's main interest in the programme was as a lever with the British to attain the League of Nations. Moreover, the administration was then crippled by the President's illness and at the end of 1920 the Republicans returned to power with a mandate to cut spending.

In the summer of 1918 the Navy Department had recommended a large shipbuilding programme of 156 ships including ten battleships and six battlecruisers which was basically a repetition of the 1916 programme with completion again in three years. Congress cancelled this and in October 1919 a smaller programme of two battleships and one battlecruiser was recommended. In September 1920 the General Board rejected any arguments against the battleship's ascendancy and resurrected a three-year plan (1922–24) to build three battleships, one battlecruiser, four carriers for scouting and thirty cruisers. In July 1921 it repeated its call for a three-year programme (reduced to three carriers and eighteen cruisers).

While confirming the need of a navy 'second to none' and the primacy of battleships, the General Board gave carriers priority because they were essential to a modern fleet and the US Navy still had none. The British in their 1921 programme concentrated on capital ships because they had several carriers building but few modern battleships. The General Board also recommended three standardised types of aircraft,

USS *Saratoga* (CV-3; 1927), shown as a veteran in September 1944. Note the removal of the 8-inch guns and the enhanced anti-aircraft defence. (US Navy)

torpedo/bomber, scout/spotter and fighter, and were more aware of their offensive roles than the Admiralty which concentrated on scouting and spotting aircraft.

In 1919 the US fleet's air needs had highest priority in the Atlantic. Japanese naval aviation was still weak, but that of the British appeared very threatening, emerging from the war with a commanding carrier lead. The US and Royal Navies had taken divergent lines in shipboard aviation. Whereas the British had developed flying-off platforms and then decks, the Americans, under Chambers, had developed the catapult which had not necessitated the development of special ships.

At the end of the war, however, there were three basic points of view on fleet aviation. Having concentrated on the seaplane during the war, the first group sought to use these existing aircraft to provide scouting and spotting for the fleet. It was led by Benson (CNO) since little extra spending was required and he envisaged a minimal auxiliary role for aircraft. In December 1918 Benson opposed putting aeroplanes aboard the battleship *Texas*, which Sims had already done, despite the advice of observers in Europe that the British had adopted them over seaplanes (Chevalier), and that flying boats could not reach mid ocean (Captain E. J. King).

The second group (including Towers) favoured the use of rigid airships (using non-inflammable helium) for long-range reconnaissance, the record of the Zeppelin and British development encouraging this. Others pointed to their size and vulnerability.

The third group wanted aircraft carriers to launch the aeroplane fighters needed to gain air supremacy. The more advanced thinkers, especially Sims, foresaw that this would allow bombers and torpedo aircraft to attack capital ships and the carrier to revolutionise sea warfare. The majority, however, still considered aircraft too weak and warships' defensive capability too strong for this to come about.

From January to June 1919 the General Board undertook hearings to investigate fleet aviation and make recommendations. It soon became apparent that the carrier concept had much support. At the end of 1918 Admiral H. T. Mayo (CinC US Fleet), after reviewing British aeroplane and airship development, had recommended using warships to carry scouts while developing a naval air service to supply scouting, spotting, torpedo, anti-submarine and escort aircraft using airships and carriers (25 aircraft).

The case for a carrier was conclusively proven by Captain N. C. Twining's report on *Texas*'s main battery exercise in March 1919. This showed a great improvement in gunnery through using aerial spotting, and Twining recommended the conversion of two ex-German merchantmen as carriers; he felt that the fleet that neglected aviation development would be at an enormous disadvantage in an engagement with a modern enemy.

Battleships had to have aerial reconnaissance or face disaster at the hands of a more efficient fleet, and they must have command of the air both to protect their scouts and deter enemy reconnaissance. The British were already operating carrier aeroplanes and the Japanese had land bases in the Pacific. Carriers alone could provide similar fighters and keep them replenished during a battle. The Board therefore investigated a specification (500ft × 65ft deck, large holds and hatches, hoisting gear and small crew because of post-war personnel shortages) for a carrier converted from a merchant ship or fleet auxiliary since carrier building had been refused.

The Bureau of Construction & Repair suggested conversion of the collier *Jupiter*, and in an Interim Report to Daniels in April the General Board stated that a conversion was urgent to allow experimentation until a new carrier was authorised. Benson (shortage of colliers and no need for command of the air) and CinC Pacific Rodman (making a poor carrier) opposed the conversion but were overruled by Daniels.

In June 1919 the General Board submitted a naval aviation policy for Secretary of the Navy Daniels which stated that the US fleet had to meet any possible enemy on equal terms. This required air supremacy since aircraft had become an essential arm of the fleet. Thus fleet aviation had to be developed to accompany and operate with the fleet in all oceans which it was thought Great Britain had already accomplished. Their priority was fighter, spotting and scouting, torpedo and bombing and, lastly, long-range reconnaissance aircraft. In the USA this was to be achieved by developing carriers and rigid airships, but, as the British had found before the war, airship development ate into carrier funds.

In December 1920, however, the General Board agreed with the conclusions reached by the British Post-War Questions Committee that aviation was not yet effective against ships and was chiefly useful for scouting afloat and indirect attacks on an enemy fleet's base rather than at sea.

As in Great Britain, funds for naval spending were difficult to procure. During the war the naval aviation estimates for Fiscal Year 1920 had been $225 million. With peace Irwin (DNA) reduced this to $85.7 million including two ships converted to carriers, their aircraft, four 'Zeppelins' and 126 non-rigid airships. Congress reflected the country's mood for minimum military spending in the Act of 11 July 1919 for Fiscal Year 1920. This provided only $25 million for existing aircraft, six aeroplane bases and one airship base. It did however provide for converting *Jupiter* (renamed *Langley*) to a carrier, two merchant ships to be converted as seaplane tenders (not done), ten aeroplanes for battleships, one rigid and six non-rigid airships. The pattern was repeated the following year.

The US Navy Department and General Board were not pleased that the politicians ignored their advice as to the need for a navy 'second to none', and the General Board drew up a statement of US Naval Policy, issued in November 1922 and revised in 1928, 1931 and 1933, stressing this. The immediate aim was to complete the two battleships and ten light cruisers of the 1916 and 1917 programmes allowed by the Washington Treaty, plus the modernisation of existing battleships and the conversion of two battlecruisers (*Lexington* and *Saratoga*, scheduled for scrapping) to carriers.

The General Board was well aware that the Four Power Pact signed at Washington, which limited fortification of Pacific bases, and the Japanese League of Nations Mandate over the Central Pacific islands considerably strengthened the strategic position of Japan. The fleet was therefore redistributed towards the Pacific, like the British Fleet, and the General Board stated in April 1923 that any Pacific war would be with Japan.

On 12 July 1921 Congress created the first new bureau, of Aeronautics (BuAer), in sixty years, and Rear Admiral W. A. Moffett, who had become Director of Naval Aviation in March 1921, began his long term as Chief on 10 August. To equip the fleet the BuAer proposed a four-year plan (1922) to give every battleship and cruiser two fighters and two observation aircraft, each destroyer and submarine one of each, and aircraft tenders four observation and twelve patrol aircraft. There were also to be 30 fighters, 30 observation, fifteen scout and fifteen torpedo-aircraft for carriers. However, Moffett, unable to gain funding for this programme, extended it to five years in 1922, then saw it emasculated and finally reduced it to battleships only.

A five-year programme did not go to Congress until the Morrow Board's recommendations of 1926. The main problem was the reduction of the estimates by the Bureau of the Budget, guardian of the Federal Budget. It meant fleet aviation fell behind schedule and produced a vicious circle in the fleet where shortages or old material produced dissatisfaction, followed by resignations and more shortages. The fleet was unable to carry out the exercises required.

Before the Washington Treaty of February 1922, the General Board had been considering a 30-knot carrier for the Scouting Force and a 24-knot vessel for the Battle

Force. Afterwards it had three alternatives – 15-knot, 10,000-ton; 29½-knot, 20,000-ton; or 33/34-knot, 35,000-ton carriers – but opted for converting the two battlecruisers (*Lexington* and *Saratoga*) which were a special case under the Treaty.

Moffett quickly agreed because he realised that Congress would be reluctant to make appropriations with disarmament limitations in place, and he stressed the British lead and Japan's intention to build up to her full tonnage. It was a golden opportunity to gain carriers and still leave 63,000 tons for new carriers (*Langley* was classed as an experimental carrier under the Treaty and her tonnage was not included).

Like the British Naval Staff, the General Board reviewed policy in April 1924 (for Fiscal Year 1926). Unlike the British, the General Board was aiming to achieve a navy 'second to none', which meant parity with the Royal Navy rather than the Japanese

USS *Ranger* (CV-3; 1927) was based on *Langley* and designed flush-decked. However, she had a small island (for navigation) and three funnels either side, shown here in the vertical position. (US Navy)

Navy which posed the greater threat. The high cost of this programme ensured a pessimistic response.

They aimed to modernise the old battleships, build 10,000-ton cruisers and carriers up to the Treaty limit. This meant eight new cruisers and the modernisation of six battleships initially, but also further building under a 17-year plan (up to 1942) to achieve parity with Great Britain. This included a 23,000-ton carrier, followed by a 15,000-ton carrier once the new aircraft programme had got under way.

However, the grievances of the aircraft industry because of the Government's economy and strict application of competitive bidding led the House to appoint the Lampert Committee in March 1924 to investigate the organisation and procurement of aviation. Its lengthy deliberations resulted in recommendations for a ministry of defence, a separate air force and centralised procurement.

Seeking to cut the ground from under the committee, Secretary of the Navy Curtis D. Wilbur asked the General Board for an aviation policy. This led to the formation at the end of 1924 of the Eberle Board under Admiral E. W. Eberle (CNO) which included the Marine Commandant and six admirals – but no aviator. Although the Board believed in the battleship, confirmed by the poor results of simulated bombing attacks against the *Washington*, it was open-minded and listened to the views of numerous officers.

The Board concluded that naval aviation was 'highly important' and that its influence would increase, but contradicted predictions that it would assume paramount

importance in sea warfare, believing that the design of future battleships would be such as to prevent fatal damage from the air. However, it wished to encourage civilian flying and the aircraft industry and above all to bring the carriers, including personnel, up to full Treaty strength since they would show what fleet aviation could do. It urged expediting the *Lexington*s and completing a new 23,000-ton carrier.

President Coolidge had in mind a three-year naval programme and in January 1925 asked for the seven main Eberle recommendations to be given priority. Wilbur balanced his priorities between the fleet (modernising battleships, 1st and 3rd; building cruisers, 4th; and submarines, 6th) and aviation (*Lexington*s and their aircraft, 2nd; an aircraft programme, 5th; and a new carrier, 7th). Coolidge therefore asked Congress for funds (Fiscal Year 1926) to modernise three battleships, complete the *Lexington*s, build two cruisers and provide naval aircraft ($2 million).

Langley was the pioneer for carrier aviation. Before she joined the fleet a rotating turntable, like the British one at Grain (1916), which could be turned into the wind, was built at Hampton Roads. Lieutenant A. M. Pride used this to devise her arrester gear. He started with British-type fore and aft wires and added wires with weights athwartship, as used by Ely in 1911. Many more experiments followed with other types aboard *Langley*. The chief problem was to prevent the aircraft veering towards the ship's side. By 1923 *Langley* could land-on three machines in seven minutes, which was a great advance (during the Second World War the rate was three per minute).

Langley also received a compressed-air catapult, as developed from 1912. This allowed the testing of catapult launching but was not used in operations. It was not until the flush deck arrived in 1934 that a catapult operated by compressed-air became a dependable launching method. The turntable catapult made it possible to launch all types of aircraft in succession without having to change the gear for each type.

With the arrival of *Langley* in 1924 and Captain Joseph Reeves as Commander Aircraft Squadrons Battle Fleet (1925–31) the fleet was at last able to see what carriers

USS *Yorktown* (CV-5; 1937), shown in July 1937 at her builders, Newport News. Note the hangar openings and the light deck structure. (US National Archives)

could do. Reeves concentrated on carrying as many aircraft as possible to enhance strike power, and developing air tactics and dive-bombing (1926).

Unlike the Royal Navy with the RAF, he was not curtailed by the number of aircraft a unified air service would allocate to carriers. As early as 1921 Sims had envisaged a carrier with 80 aircraft aboard (which he increased to 100 in 1925) and Reeves, when experimenting with *Langley* and later the *Lexington*s, insisted on carrying as many aircraft as possible, despite the protests of the naval aviators. The result was that the US carriers were designed and operated to carry far more aircraft than their British counterparts.

In the exercises of 1925 *Langley* launched daily scouting flights plus a ten-aircraft strike. Reeves later launched two waves of eighteen aircraft to dive-bomb the battleship *California*, flagship of Admiral C. F. Hughes. *Langley* showed the potential of the *Lexington*s plus the need of air cover, better aircraft and equipment. In his 1926 report CinC Hughes sought the construction of smaller carriers as well as the *Lexington*s to free fleet aviation from the restrictions of land bases.

In the 1927 exercises (Fleet Problem VII, Caribbean) *Langley* showed the vulnerability of the Panama Canal and the need for carriers to provide air cover for convoys and the fleet. Changing weather and enemy fleet action also led to Reeves' recommendation of complete tactical discretion for the fleet's aircraft commander. Thus the basic lesson of the importance of mobility and freedom of action for carriers was quickly appreciated.

In April 1925 (for Fiscal Year 1927), despite discussions for a disarmament conference at Geneva, the General Board continued to press its programme which included modernising more battleships, the construction of eight cruisers, five submarines, a 23,000-ton carrier and more than 300 aircraft (including 99 fighters, 171 scout/torpedo) for the fleet. Although a start was made on this programme, the General Board still thought the US Navy was lagging behind the Royal Navy in carriers and again called for a 23,000-ton carrier in March 1926 (Fiscal Year 1928) plus more than 300 aircraft as the first part of the Morrow Board's five-year plan.

The loss of the airship *Shenandoah* on 2 September 1925 led President Coolidge to appoint Dwight W. Morrow to investigate every aspect of aviation. Admiral Moffett bluntly told his Board that scarce appropriations and the limitation of air stations in the USA to six was severely restricting naval aviation. He called for a five-year programme and the development of carriers and airships. Both services opposed a unified air force.

The Board's report of 30 November 1925 dismissed the supposed savings gained from a unified air force in favour of competition between the Army and Navy and suggested constructive, long-term plans for aviation. To achieve these it adjudicated on some long-term problems. In procurement, recommendations were made for standardisation of designs over three-year periods, provision for replacements and turnover of equipment at stated intervals.

As a result Congress passed an authorisation act on 24 June for a five-year pro-gramme (1,000 naval aircraft and three airships) and procurement by contracts to the lowest responsible bidder (subject to review by the President or courts only). How-ever, the funds had to come from the next Congressional appropriations. Moffet's $40 million for Fiscal Year 1927 was cut by the Bureau of Budget to under $20 million, but he persuaded Congress to add another $9.5 million. Each year as a result of the Mor-row Board, Moffett was able by his political skills to persuade Congress to allocate more funds to naval aviation.

Furthermore, the Morrow Board allowed the US Navy to overtake the Royal Navy in naval aircraft (638 in July 1926, 738 in 1927). In aviation training for Naval Academy graduates, post-graduate programmes to train technical officers in new specialist branches and the equality of engineers with line officers, US naval aviation had other great advantages over its British rival.

In order to develop the Morrow Board programme the Secretary of the Navy appointed the Taylor Board (Rear Admirals M. Taylor, Moffett and F. H. Schofield; Captains Reeves and H. C. Yarnell; and Lieutenant Commander M. Mitscher) in April 1927 to review the naval air policy of 1922. The most important issue was deployment of the *Lexington*s when commissioned (late 1927). It insisted on the carriers protecting the fleet, scouting and offensive operations at a distance from the battle line. It con-demned the design of hybrid, multi-purpose aircraft, in contrast to the Admiralty, and favoured fighters and dive-bombers. They also wanted two fleet rigids and non-rigids for patrol work.

Lexington and *Saratoga* commissioned in December and November 1927 respec-tively and carried out large-scale fleet exercises with aircraft to achieve these aims. Their conversion had been a problem since by the Treaty they were limited to 33,000 tons but exceeded this. However, another 3,000 tons was allowed for bulging capital ships. Because of the uncertain legal position of this they were always shown as 33,000 when nearer to 36,000. However, both the British and Japanese used similar ploys to circumvent the treaties.

Langley's longitudinal and athwartships arrester gear was fitted in *Lexington* and *Saratoga*, but in 1929 the longitudinal wires were removed. The introduction of hy-draulic arresting power, replacing weights, was the first development of the wartime system.

Not until the January 1929 fleet exercises (Fleet Problem IX) was it possible to test the theory and preparation of *Langley* with fleet carriers. Lieutenant A. M. Pride made the first landing on *Lexington* on 5 January and Mitscher on *Saratoga* on the 11th. After shake-down cruises both carriers joined the fleet and took part in the historic exer-cises.

Admiral W. V. Pratt, CO Black Fleet, had *Saratoga* and *Langley* (represented by *Aroostook* because of a refit) and 116 aircraft, and the defending Admiral M. Taylor *Lexington* and 145 aircraft. Numerically inferior, Pratt decided to avoid air attack on his

USS *Enterprise* (CV-6; 1938) with her sister *Yorktown* marked a return to larger carriers within Treaty limitations. Her heavy armament by August 1944 is evident in the numerous sponsons. (US Navy)

carriers and allow Reeves (Commander Aircraft – Battlefleet) to launch simultaneous attacks on both ends of the Panama Canal. Although the aircraft attacking the Pacific end lacked the range to return to their carrier, this bold move was brilliantly successful and established the principle of long-range carrier air strikes.

The CinC, Admiral H. Wiley, emphasised the need for a stronger air defence to repel air attacks on ships or bases, plus the need for small carriers to replace scouting cruisers. He also pointed out that when carriers were within range of gunnery they were sunk and concluded that the battleship was still dominant. Carriers were still regarded mainly as a replacement for cruisers as the eyes of the fleet. However, in 1930 the new CNO (Pratt), a convert to aviation, ruled that carriers were to be used offensively in war games and exercises.

USS *Wasp* (CV-7; 1940). Within Treaty limitations there was only enough tonnage for a carrier of *Ranger*'s size incorporating *Yorktown*'s features. The open hangar is visible. (US Navy)

In the 1930 exercises *Lexington*'s aircraft seized command of the air and dominated the outcome by attacking the defending battleships. These exercises also saw the first use of 'carrier groups' with a carrier, cruisers and destroyers as a tactical unit. The attacking commander, Rear Admiral F. Brumby, concluded that numerous carrier groups should be formed for independent attacks ahead of the battle fleet.

The simulated attack on the Panama Canal in 1931 against which the two carriers were defending showed the lack of effective methods to refuel the carriers (Admiral F. H. Schofield), their inability to stop the advance of battleships (Rear Admiral Reeves) and that their defensive value was less than expected (Admiral Pratt). However, the 'loss' of the rigid airship *Los Angeles* while scouting led the fleet to conclude that rigids should not be developed since their cost was out of proportion to their usefulness. With accidents to rigids *Akron* (3 April 1933) and *Macon* (11 February 1935), rigid airships were no longer a rival to carriers for scarce appropriations.

During the 1932 exercises Yarnell, the new CO Aircraft Battle Force, executed a successful surprise attack on Pearl Harbor, anticipating Yamamoto by ten years. He concluded that the fleet needed six to eight large carriers to advance across the Pacific and launch air attacks upon the enemy's (Japanese) bases and fight a decisive action. They would attack the enemy carriers, to gain command of the air, and the fleet with most carriers would have the advantage, though getting in the first strike was a matter of luck.

However, Vice Admiral A. L. Willard (CO Black Fleet) still thought the battleship was the backbone of the fleet. Even Reeves, the air enthusiast, Commander Aircraft Battle Fleet and now CinC US Fleet, in 1934 proposed large Pacific exercises along the traditional lines of a large fleet action with battle lines.

The main problem was the slow speed of the modernised pre-1922 battleships (21 knots). They could not keep up with the 25-knot *Langley* let alone the 33-knot *Lexington*s. However, if the carriers operated independently of the battle line it weakened both:

the carriers were open to surface attack (and had a weakened AA defence) and the battleships to air attack.

With the breakdown of the Geneva Naval Conference, the General Board devised a building programme to equal that of the Royal Navy. It included a new naval air policy (1927), based on the Taylor Board, by which BuAer was to build-up aviation for fleet operations at sea. For the five-year programme the General Board wanted a thousand aircraft plus one 13,800-ton carrier each year. This (69,000 tons) provided the 135,000 carrier tons allowed under Washington since 66,000 was taken up by the *Lexington*s (*Langley* was experimental and not included); 13,800 was deemed the minimum tonnage required to provide a stable landing platform.

However, first President Coolidge cut the battleships and destroyers and then Congress the cruisers and carriers. Even then the Cruiser Bill did not pass the Senate until 1929. Congress, even after the failure of the Geneva Disarmament Conference, would allow no more than one small carrier, *Ranger*. Nor would it improve equipment in the seaplane tenders or authorise the building of two new ones. This was fortunate, in one sense, as Moffett's preference for small carriers proved to be wrong.

Moffett's policy was based on the belief that the British *Hermes* (10,850 tons) and the Japanese *Hosho* (7,500 tons) showed small carriers to be effective, while having the fleet's aircraft in two large carriers was too risky. He, like the British, wanted many smaller carriers because he overestimated the number of aircraft smaller carriers could operate. In 1929 parity with British carrier numbers was the most urgent naval aviation priority. This was based on the view that the British possession of more carriers gave them a great advantage and over-estimation of British carrier aircraft capacities and performance.

The true measure of carrier effectiveness was the number and performance of her aircraft. The US Navy was well ahead of the FAA on both counts. Moffett failed to appreciate this superiority and regarded the *Lexington*s as a handicap since they took up half the allowable tonnage and the USA could not match the British carriers numbers (six) unless it built small carriers. In 1930 he even suggested making the *Lexington*s experimental and replacing them with two 10,000-ton carriers if carrier tonnage was reduced to 120,000 tons by the first London Conference.

The General Board, however, realised the great 'advantage' of size and speed and that the Washington Treaty would have to be altered to change their status. It therefore argued for a mix of large and small carriers. These arguments over the best size of carrier proved to be mainly academic since funds for new carriers were not forthcoming.

The new President (Herbert Hoover, March 1929) was determined to break the impasse with Great Britain over the limitation of navies, avoid an expensive naval arms race and foster world peace. To achieve this Hoover and Secretary of State H. L. Stimson sought to bypass the strong Navy advice and ignore the costly building programmes of Secretary of Navy C. F. Adams, Hughes (CNO) and the General Board.

So in September 1930 Hoover appointed Pratt, who was receptive to an agreement with Great Britain and arms limitation, to replace Hughes as CNO. The resulting London Treaty led most senior officers and the General Board to conclude that disarmament had weakened the Navy's ability to implement the country's defence, especially Plan Orange for the Pacific. On top of this came the effect on spending of the Depression. While the Board was concerned with the capabilities of Britain and Japan, Pratt considered war with them to be very unlikely and not inevitable respectively.

This led to open conflict since Pratt wished to diminish the General Board's influence on policy (its role was to advise on and not make policy as it increasingly sought). Pratt wanted alternative policies to be discussed whereas the General Board wanted the traditional united front to force Congress to spend. Pratt therefore resigned from the General Board to tender independent advice which the latter regarded as undermining its influence.

The General Board viewed the new London Treaty as the minimum for security and prepared a fifteen-year programme to build up to its limits. Hoover and Congress, however, viewed the Treaty as the maximum limit, allowing cutbacks not more expenditure. Hoover also believed that building only encouraged a naval race with Great Britain and Japan. Moreover, in 1930 the fleet had reached the limit in battleship tonnage and a cruiser programme was in place to reach their Treaty limit. Only in carriers was the fleet lagging.

Pratt therefore would not support a large General Board programme, which had no chance of being accepted, but was concerned to gain the Congress appropriations for battleship modernisation, carrier construction and completing the cruiser programme. He supported Hoover's approach to Great Britain because he considered Anglo-American co-operation worth concessions on the cruiser question.

Hoover in turn supported a bill to build a carrier and to continue cruiser construction, but Congress did not see the need for any building given the Treaty. A second Bill in 1932 also failed and naval appropriations declined steadily. Thus the carrier was not approved and most of the money voted went to battleship modernisation and the building of cruisers at a slow rate.

Caught between the unrealistic programmes of the General Board, a non-spending Congress and Hoover and Stimson bent on disarmament, Pratt was forced to cut personnel and ships in commission. This meant a smaller fleet and even less ability to execute Plan Orange. Some senior officers and the General Board felt betrayed by Hoover and Pratt, who agreed to the terms of the London Treaty and yet failed to build to its maximum. However, given the Congressional mood and Hoover's plans, Pratt's aim was to work within the administration's policies. Strident opposition, exemplified by the General Board, only ensured that their views were ignored and had a negligible naval influence on the administration.

Having failed to deal with the Depression, Hoover sought a place in history through achieving a lasting peace by moral sanctions and a 'holiday' in naval building. This

Top: USS *Hornet* (CV-8; 1941) was a repeat *Yorktown* with improvements, to provide another carrier quickly when the Second London Treaty terminated tonnage restrictions. (US Navy)

Above: USS *Essex* (CV-9; 1942), the first of the new carriers sent to the Pacific Fleet and deployed in the Gilberts to begin the Central Pacific offensive. (US National Archives)

coincided with the Far Eastern crisis after Japan invaded Manchuria in September 1931, but the only US naval reaction was to send the Scouting Force to the Pacific in mid 1932.

The problem was that the centrepiece of the Joint War Plan Orange, issued in 1929, was a rapid cross-Pacific offensive to a base in the Western Pacific and then an advance on the Japanese mainland. This could not be implemented with the existing fleet, but it remained the basic plan, though amended, until the far more defensive Plan Orange of 1938.

Pratt got on well with the Bureau chiefs, including Moffett who was an old friend, since he delegated responsibility to them. However, the most serious result of the appropriation cutbacks was the lack of funding for carriers. Pratt's plan was to have two 35,000 (*Lexington*s), two 20,000 and two 14,500-ton carriers for the total of 135,000 tons allowed under the London Treaty. This required building the 20,000-ton carriers and another *Ranger* (14,500 tons). After the *Lexingtons'* trials the fleet aviators under Yarnell (who succeeded Reeves as Commander Aircraft Battle Fleet) wanted large fast carriers, sacrificing armament. Although opposed to cutting 8-inch guns, Pratt accepted his aviators' advice.

During the 1930 London Conference, President Hoover, influenced by Moffett's advocacy of carrier aircraft as the primary offensive strike of the future, accepted the view that the dominance of the battleship was ending. He therefore suggested an end to new battleship building and the replacement of existing battleships when they became too old. This however was not a view shared by the General Board.

When Moffett attended the London Disarmament Conference his main interest was the flight-deck cruiser since he could not get carrier funding. After much argument he secured the right for the USA to build eight over and above the carrier tonnage. After the London Conference the General Board (October 1930) suggested building one small carrier per year from 1931 to 1935 to fill the 55,000 tons still in hand. The design of the carriers was left open because Moffett wanted to build flight-deck cruisers. In November the General Board reluctantly agreed to a design study, but when Moffett suggested in March 1931 that all 6-inch cruisers should have flight-decks, this was rejected.

These hybrids would probably have proven ineffective, but Moffett's aim was to provide large numbers of strike aircraft in as many hulls as possible because large carriers proved vulnerable during exercises. The General Board preferred laying down more small carriers. However, these were not funded by Congress so *Ranger*, finally laid down in 1931 and commissioned in 1934, was the only small carrier built. Because of her small size she had only two lifts which resulted in very slow launch and recovery operations. She was relegated to the Atlantic and *Wasp*'s second lift was shifted right aft and the *Essex* class were given a third deck-edge lift.

The 1932 exercises (surprise attack on Pearl Harbor) triggered continued debate on carrier size. The General Board continued to plan large numbers of small carriers since the loss of one or two would have less effect on the ability to command the air. BuAer, however, returned to the issue of flight-deck cruisers in February 1934. Moffet favoured building seven 30-knot cruisers with six 6-inch guns and 30–50 aircraft to get around the treaty obligations. He was again unsuccessful.

On 12 November 1929, after the Wall Street Crash, President Hoover had proposed government funds to relieve unemployment. Moffett at once submitted a $54 million plan for an airship base on the West Coast plus aircraft for *Ranger* and a new sister carrier (not yet authorised). However, the estimates for 1931, submitted in May 1930, for $53 million were cut by the Navy's budget officer to $35 million and Moffett, despite vigorous lobbying, only got another $3 million and no aircraft for *Ranger*, not included in the original 1,000-aircraft plan.

On 1 April 1931 a new Naval Air Operating Policy, focusing on fleet aviation, became effective. Admiral Pratt, CNO, had to reduce the fleet in line with the London

USS *Yorktown* (CV-10; 1943), the second of the *Essex* class; later sisters had longer bows. Note the 5-inch guns forward and aft of the island, the sponsoned AA armament and the hangar opening. (US Navy)

Disarmament Treaty and sought to end the controversy with the Army over responsibility for coastal defence. He thought that reduced strength made mobility essential and reorganised the fleet to place all units including aircraft under the CinC.

He also assigned the 'defensive' coastal defence role to the Army, thus allowing naval aviation to concentrate on developing the offensive power of the fleet and advanced base forces. Carriers and tenders would provide mobility for aircraft. Procurement of aircraft would be restricted to those for fleet operations, Marine expeditionary forces, patrol types for fleet scouting, airships in order to determine their military value, and training.

This new policy was still not supported by adequate funds. In 1932, under the new system of assigning a budget to each department, BuAer was given $32 million which was less than 1931 and again provided no aircraft for *Ranger* (found by cutting patrol aircraft) plus cuts in research (from 11 to 6 per cent of budget). Any Federal action to improve employment, which resulted in naval air stations, was offset by reductions in

regular appropriations which restricted anything above the completion of the 1,000-aircraft plan. At London Hoover's goal was disarmament and appropriations continued to decline until Moffet's last Fiscal Year, 1934, saw a total of $30 million.

Even with the inauguration of a new President (Franklin Roosevelt in March 1933) the naval appropriations did not increase. In July the outgoing CNO (Pratt) had asked for an eight-year programme, similar to the British plan, including 342 aircraft for the first three carriers. He also wanted nearly $14 million for aircraft in Fiscal Years 1938 to 1940.

Of the five larger (23,000-ton) and five smaller (13,800-ton) carriers planned by the General Board after the mid 1920s, only one small carrier (*Ranger*) had been authorised. It therefore recommended in May 1933 two carriers of 13,800 tons, a 6-inch cruiser with flight-deck and 390 carrier aircraft for Fiscal Year 1934 plus two more carriers in 1935 and another in 1936 in a large $400 million programme.

USS *San Jacinto* (CVL-30; 1943). The emergency *Independence* class clearly signalled their cruiser origins. Note the four funnels taken clear of the flight-deck and AA sponsons. (US Navy)

The new CNO (W. H. Standley, July 1933) expected Roosevelt, a 'big navy' man, to increase spending since the President promised him 10,000 extra men in 1934 and seemed to support the proposed legislation of Congressman Carl Vinson, chair of the House Naval Affairs Committee.

However, Roosevelt was committed to continue disarmament and had to be cautious in his dealing with Congress as many of Hoover's emergency employment measures were dropped. Then in 1935–36 he ran into trouble with both Congress and the Supreme Court over his New Deal legislation and had to be very careful in allocating funds for naval bases or new capital ships (due to the continuing strength of disarmament and isolationist views).

Roosevelt's new Secretary of the Navy, Claude Swanson, was opposed to reductions in capital ships, but was prepared to accept British proposals to reduce carrier tonnage. These attitudes were reflected in the programmes from 1933 onward which Roosevelt cut.

However, President Roosevelt ensured that naval appropriations were bolstered by $298 million under public works to foster employment (June 1933) and the two 13,800-ton carriers (*Yorktown* and *Enterprise*, eventually 20,000-ton carriers, laid down May and July 1934) became part of the 1934 programme. *Wasp* (14,700 tons, laid down January 1936) was also later added. However, as only 15,000 tons were left under the Treaty she was built to *Ranger*'s design with improvements from the *Yorktown* class.

This was a good example of the system making available *ad hoc* funds, which were taken advantage of when offered, rather than providing for properly prepared, long-term plans. Funds were provided by the Public Works Administration and $36 million up to 1939 was spent on improving air stations. This was followed in 1935 by Swanson pressing for the modernisation of older vessels including *Lexington* and *Saratoga* which were of 'great value'. Appropriations were gradually found for this work.

But because of his own party's opposition to re-armament, Roosevelt could only encourage Congress to establish the principle of building and maintaining a navy of modern, under-age warships and to end the practice of including over-age ships in the effective strength. However, public and Congressional support for shipbuilding to create jobs provided the main impetus for the replacement of an ageing fleet.

The Vinson-Trammell Act passed on 27 March 1934 allowed the Navy to build up to the provisions of the London Treaty of 1930 by 1941 and Standley to create the long-term programme consistently advocated by the Navy, using the funds of the National Industrial Recovery Act and annual appropriations for new construction. The annual funds were provided by the Emergency Appropriations Act of 9 June 1934.

This marked a radical departure from previous funding and brought parity with Great Britain within practical bounds since it committed the government to build to Treaty limits. It also authorised the extension of the 1,000-aircraft plan. No exact number (later fixed at 2,050) was specified so that modifications would not be needed later. It was now clear that Japan's policy was militaristic and the US position was weak. Whereas Japan had built up to 95 per cent of her Treaty limit, the USA had only 65 per cent of hers. The programme was needed to implement Plan Orange, revised again in 1934.

One of the main aims of Standley (CNO) and Leahy (BuNav) was to increase the Navy's personnel, sharply cut by Hoover, to man the ships and aircraft voted. In the event they only got an increase of 6,000 due to the President's inability to keep the promises he had liberally made. They also lobbied Congress to restore the 15 per cent pay cut which was required to retain key personnel and succeeded in regaining 10 per cent.

Personnel seconded to the Civilian Construction Corps were also returned and all graduates of the Naval Academy were commissioned (in 1933 only the upper half were commissioned). However, they failed to re-open closed training stations or to gain personnel for any new ships, although all existing ships could be manned.

Despite these increases Roosevelt was still restrained by public and party opinion against naval expansion and looked to the London Conference (October 1934–36) to prevent a naval arms race. Roosevelt hoped by compromise, but not conceding Japanese naval parity, to continue the Washington Treaty. Moreover, with elections due in November 1936 he was very cautious in regard to naval spending.

Thus he kept the 1935 appropriations to destroyers and submarines plus restoring the remaining 5 per cent pay cut and other allowances. In 1936 and 1937 the Navy's Budget Officer and the Bureau of the Budget continued to cut BuAer's estimates. For instance in 1936 the 468 aircraft asked for were cut by 84. Congress also opposed any non-rigids. The difference had to be made up by recourse to the New Deal agencies.

With only the USA, Great Britain and France signing the London Naval Treaty (March 1936) and Japan's withdrawal from the Treaties, Roosevelt agreed that more naval spending was needed, although action was delayed until after the elections. Thus Standley planned to re-start battleship building to match the British new construction (two) in 1937. None had been built since 1921. The General Board planned another two in 1938, but Standley preferred to evaluate the first two before ordering more. On the other hand, the Presidential Order for government departments to maintain reserves represented a 'cut' of $10 million in 1936 and $75 million in 1937–38, which, while not affecting shipbuilding, hampered the fleet's ability to operate ships of the new programme.

However, in January 1937 Standley was superseded by Leahy who was closer to the President and had greater political acumen. He was also greatly helped by the outbreak of the Sino-Japanese war in July 1937. At first Roosevelt refused to match British battleship building (another three), build auxiliaries and dry docks or rescind naval budget cuts. However, the China war, the Anti-Comintern Pact (Germany, Italy and Japan, November) and the sinking on 12 December of the US river gunboat *Panay* on the Yangtze by Japanese 'Susie' dive-bombers during the evacuation of Nanking, although resulting in no direct action or agreed co-operation with the British, led Roosevelt to order a revision of the Joint Plan Orange.

To implement the planned offensive against Japan the fleet needed more ships. Leahy (a member of the 'Gun Club') therefore added another two battleships and two cruisers to the two battleships, two cruisers, eight destroyers and eight submarines planned for Fiscal Year 1939. Under the Treaty the fleet had its quota of carriers (three and three building). However, the presidential advisers wanted to match Japanese building (which was undeclared).

In January 1938 President Roosevelt therefore called for a naval expansion act to increase naval combat tonnage by 20 per cent to maintain the Treaty ratios (5:5:3) with Great Britain and Japan. This meant an extra three battleships, two carriers, nine cruisers, 23 destroyers and nine submarines. Leahy successfully defended the increase, as the guarantor of US neutrality, in Congress against isolationist feeling. The Expansion Act became law in May 1938 and included a clause allowing the President to bring naval aircraft up to a total of 3,000. This would require more personnel and air stations and the Hepburn Board was to report on the bases needed. However, it was not until war was imminent that full funds were available.

At the same time the 1939 programme was also passed. It included four battleships and Vinson also secured disregard of the old treaty limit of 135,000 carrier tons in favour of 175,000 and authorisation of one carrier (*Hornet*, *Yorktown* class, laid down September 1939). BuAer and Vinson wanted more carriers, but Leahy opposed this while the new battleships had to be produced.

Under the BuAer/General Board plan *Saratoga* and *Lexington* were to be modernised also and when they reached the age for replacement, under the Washington Treaty, new ships of the same size built: one in 1941, two in 1945 and one in 1946. The designs however had not been completed nor had *Yorktown* (commissioned 30 September 1937) and *Enterprise* (12 May 1938) been sufficiently evaluated.

Early in 1939 Leahy was aware that the new Plan Orange faced the problem of a simultaneous Japanese (Pacific) and German (Atlantic) attack and that any diversion to the Atlantic would prevent its implementation. War Plans warned that the fleet could not undertake the offensive in both oceans and even the defensive in one would rule out an offensive in the other.

For an offensive in the Pacific and defensive in the Atlantic America required a Two-Ocean Navy. Thus Leahy preferred to concentrate on the Pacific and leave the Atlantic to the British and French navies. This was the basis of the US Navy staff talks with the British in the summer of 1939. However, Roosevelt planned, with continued German and Italian aggression, for an Atlantic Squadron to patrol and ensure the western hemisphere's neutrality in the event of war in Europe. Thus the fleet manoeuvres of 1939 were held in the Caribbean to develop the necessary techniques. On 30 June the Joint Board produced a new set of plans: Rainbow 1–5. Rainbow 2 was the Navy's favoured strategy: an offensive in the Pacific with the British and French covering the Atlantic.

Leahy's priority was to gain the naval bases, airfields (Pearl Harbor, Midway, Wake and Guam) and patrol aircraft for a Pacific offensive despite opposition from the State Department (in favour of appeasement) and US Army Air Forces (which wanted bomber production). Leahy also defended the battleship and the Naval Expansion Bill against the air power lobby. The Hepburn Board asked for $287 million for naval bases, but the bill was cut by the President, State Department and Congress to a tenth in April 1939.

After long negotiations with Vinson on how to implement the Navy's two-ocean capability, Admiral H. R. Stark (CNO from August 1939), with Roosevelt's approval, asked in November for a 25 per cent fleet expansion over five years plus refurbishment of old destroyers for the Atlantic Patrol to meet the increasing danger of an enemy coalition. Congress was not amenable and in January 1940 Vinson introduced a bill for only the first year of the programme (11 per cent). Part of the problem was that it was a presidential election year and Roosevelt was running for an unprecedented third term.

Before the Act was signed by the President, the fall of France left only the Royal Navy to face the German and Italian fleets and Stark formulated an even bigger programme and asked Congress for an increase of 70 per cent. Galvanised by events in Europe, Congress passed the Two-Ocean Navy Act which was signed within a month. The two acts of 1940 provided 326 ships including two capital ships and ten carriers. Construction awaited funding by appropriations, but a carrier authorised in 1938 was laid down, followed by four more of the class (two each in September and December) in 1941.

Under the Act of May 1938 Congress had authorised two carriers, but Leahy had only asked for one (*Hornet*) in the 1939 programme. In providing the sister, with Treaty limits abandoned, the General Board was able to plan an improved, larger *Yorktown* with better protection and more aircraft. The result, the *Essex* (27,200 tons, laid down April 1941), was the first of perhaps the finest carriers of the Second World War, a match for the Japanese *Shokaku* class and operating far more aircraft than the British *Illustrious* class.

Smaller than the *Lexington*s, the new class carried more aircraft and were more manoeuvrable. They were also larger than the *Yorktown*s which needed modernisation after combat experience, especially the addition of extra AA armament. The roomier *Essex* allowed the AA armament to be greatly improved and the fighters to be doubled for defence. Two more of the *Essex* class (*Lexington* and *Bunker Hill*) were laid down in September 1941 under the naval expansion.

However, until these carriers and the other ships of the programme arrived, the fleet was too weak for the growing danger. It was committed to an offensive in the Pacific but this relied on the Royal Navy holding the Atlantic. Moreover, the President, in an election year, tended to follow rather than lead public opinion.

After Roosevelt won the election in November, Stark recommended a defensive strategy in the Pacific and the offensive in the Atlantic to defeat Germany (the main

USS *Midway* (CVB-41; 1945), the first of the *Midway* class, which introduced armour to US carriers and commissioned days after the war. She carried 137 aircraft. (US National Archives)

threat) first. This was agreed with the British Staff (Washington, January 1941) and Rainbow 5 (Atlantic first) was beefed-up (Navy War Plan 46) and approved in May. Thus while the Pacific fleet remained a deterrent to the Japanese and efforts were made to improve its forward bases, the focus shifted to Lend-Lease (March), British co-operation (Argentia Conference, August) and escorting Atlantic convoys (September).

By the outbreak of war in Europe the General Board and BuShips had developed and designed an experimental carrier (*Langley*, later a transport), two converted *Lexington*s (modernised late 30s), a small carrier (*Ranger*, commissioned 1934), three *Yorktown*s (*Yorktown* 1937, *Enterprise* 1938, *Hornet* 1941) and an improved *Ranger* (*Wasp* 1940). This gave six fleet carriers and the smaller *Ranger* which compared favourably with the Japanese six. However, these were split between the Atlantic and Pacific because of the growing German threat and did not operate in a single task force like the Japanese carriers by 1941.

The main problem facing the commanders in the 1930s were the war plan (Orange) which called for an offensive across the Central Pacific involving amphibious opera-

tions against Japanese bases. These required offensive carrier operations but they were tied to defending the battle fleet. In the 1934 Fleet War Instructions the problem was still unresolved and it included only a general statement on carrier operations.

The exercises of the mid 1930s showed the inability of existing carriers to perform what was expected of them because their aircraft lacked the range and bomb load. At the same time a large number of small carriers was favoured because it was difficult for battleships and cruisers to handle aircraft while performing their other duties.

Fleet exercises of the late 1930s gave valuable experience of planning and executing fast carrier strikes against defended shore bases. For protection the carriers had a close screen of heavy cruisers for AA gun defence against air attack and an outer screen of light cruisers against surface attack. Destroyers provided anti-submarine defence. Visual signals were used so that radio silence could be maintained. However, radio bearings were also used over a 100-mile range to direct aircraft on to their targets. These exercises showed the need for larger fleet carriers.

Matters came to a head during the 1937 exercises when an amphibious operation was undertaken. Against the advice of the Commander Aircraft Battle Fleet (Vice Admiral F. J. Horne), who wanted mobility until the enemy carriers were destroyed, the Battle Fleet Commander (Bloch) confined the carriers to protecting the battleships and landing forces. As a result *Langley* was sunk from the air, the *Lexington*s bombed and *Saratoga* seriously damaged by a submarine. The landings were successful but at the cost of the carriers. This same problem was to recur during the landings of 1942–44 culminating at Saipan. For the aviators the key was maintenance of the carriers' mobility.

In the 1938 exercises (Fleet Problem XIX) *Saratoga* and *Lexington* under Vice Admiral E. J. King (Commander Aircraft) launched surprise attacks on Pearl Harbor and San Francisco and, aided by weather fronts as the Japanese would be in December 1941, evaded detection by the patrol planes and attack by defending forces.

USS *Long Island* (CVE-1; 1941), originally the C3 cargo vessel *Mormacmail*, converted as an auxiliary aircraft carrier (AVG) for ferrying and convoy escort. She was used mainly for ferrying and training. (US Navy)

Ranger (commissioned 1934), initially based in the Atlantic, replaced *Langley* (converted to seaplane tender, 1937) until the arrival of a second Carrier Division (Rear Admiral W. F. Halsey, the new *Enterprise* and *Yorktown*) in January 1939. With the increase to two divisions, a second carrier admiral and five carriers, King devised new carrier tactics in the 1939 exercises. Whereas the carriers had acted independently, they were now stationed three miles apart either in one group or in pairs, each with two destroyers (three at night) plus heavy cruisers. Each carrier was assigned a sector for her aircraft and launched them in the same type order to form squadrons for air strikes over the carrier and rendezvous with other air groups on the way to the target. In an emergency the aircraft would form up on the way to the target.

The main problem was that destroyers and cruisers were not assigned to carriers on a permanent basis, and senior commanders (such as E. C. Kalbfus, Commander Battle Fleet in the 1939 exercises) still tied the carriers to the battleships. Moreover, the new Atlantic Squadron was assigned *Ranger* and *Wasp* under Rear Admiral A. B. Cook, former Chief BuAer, which prevented carrier concentration in the Pacific.

In the 1939 exercises the carriers concentrated on destroying the 'enemy' carriers and seaplane tenders. The need for small carriers to escort troop transports, small operations and support landings was also shown. However, a 10,000-ton carrier had been suggested for twenty years without funding becoming available. In June 1939 *Saratoga* achieved the first refuelling at sea from a fleet tanker (two years ahead of the Japanese). This was a vital development for the logistical support of carriers across the Pacific.

The last peacetime fleet exercise in 1940 continued to develop both battle-line manoeuvres and independent carrier tactics. The naval aviators still argued that carrier operations required qualified commanders and freedom from the battle line. During this time Halsey also introduced common radio wavelengths for all carriers and radio telephony to speed up communications. His period as Commander Aircraft (beginning June 1940) also saw the introduction of radar which would revolutionise fighter tactics.

The Navy entered the war embodying the carrier doctrine issued by Halsey in March 1941. The carriers were still tied to the battleships until December 1941. Meanwhile the new CinC (H. E Kimmel) divided the fleet into three task forces (under W. S. Pye, Battle Force; Halsey, Carriers; and W. Brown, Cruisers) of which two were to be at sea always, except at weekends. As fighters needed to be transferred to Wake and Midway, Halsey's carriers were absent from Pearl Harbor on Sunday, 7 December.

The Second World War

Largely as a consequence of isolationist sentiments among the electorate, US re-armament was very tardy and carrier production was basically a race to provide a large number of carriers before the existing vessels were sunk. It was a very close-run thing, but by autumn 1943 the first of a huge armada of carriers began to reach the Pacific.

Shortly before the Japanese attack on Pearl Harbor two more *Essex* class (*Bon Homme Richard* and *Intrepid*) were laid down (1 December) under the naval expansion acts, followed by a sixth, *Oriskany*, in March 1942. Following the loss of *Yorktown* and *Wasp*, *Bon Homme Richard* and *Oriskany* assumed their respective names. To augment the *Essex* class, which would take time to complete, it was agreed in January 1942 to undertake a 'desperate experiment' and convert the light *Cleveland* class cruiser *Amsterdam* to a light carrier (*Independence*) with high speed (31 knots) and half the air group of an *Essex*. Eight more were ordered in February (two), March (three) and July (three).

In July Congress authorised another ten *Essex* class (one cancelled in January 1943, laid down August 1942 to March 1943), followed by three more in 1943 (May, September). To these were added two armoured carriers of the *Midway* class (45,000 tons, 33 knots, 120 aircraft) planned by the General Board (by March) because of the vulnerability of the existing carriers (*Saratoga* had been disabled by one torpedo). In addition 32 escort carriers were also planned.

Thus in the summer of 1942 the fleet could expect up to 40 fast carriers in due course. In contrast, the Navy had six new battleships, the first since 1923, which were to commission in 1941–42. However, the two *North Carolina*s and four *South Dakota*s (35,000 tons, nine 16-inch, 27 knots) were rather slow for the carriers. BuOrd therefore planned for six *Iowa*s (45,000 tons, nine 16-inch, 33 knots) and five *Montana*s (60,000-tons, twelve 16-inch). Given the low battleship losses and other, higher, priorities the *Montana*s, which had not been laid down, were cancelled in July 1943 and only four *Iowa*s were commissioned.

By July 1944 the fleet had in commission the pre-war *Saratoga*, *Ranger* and *Enterprise*, ten *Essex* class and nine *Independence* class light carriers, and another eight *Essex* and two *Midway*s were building. This would give 41 carriers (two battle, 20 heavy and nine light carriers) by January 1946, barring no losses. Four *Essex* class were begun in the first half of 1944 plus another three *Essex* class, a third *Midway* and two light carriers of the improved *Saipan* class in the second half of 1944. Finally the last *Essex* was laid down in January 1945. Another six (CV-50–55) were authorised but never laid down.

The 26 *Essex* class carriers laid down were assigned to only five yards in the interests of standardisation and rapidity of construction: Newport News (ten), Bethlehem (five), New York Navy Yard, (four), Philadelphia (four) and Norfolk (three). The *Independence* class, one of the *Midway*s and the two *Saipan*s were all assigned to New York Shipbuilding Corporation. One of the *Midway*s was built by New York Navy Yard, the other two by Newport News. The escort carriers were assigned mainly to mercantile shipyards (Sun, Federal, Seattle-Tacoma, Kaiser, Todd Pacific), often specially laid out for the purpose.

Despite the highest priority, these programmes clashed for resources with other high priorities especially escorts and landing-craft. Other problems were the many modifications made in the light of battle experience, especially in AA armament. For instance the *Essex* carriers laid down from 1943 onwards (except *Bon Homme Richard*

USS *Sangamon* (CVE-26; 1942).
To provide more escort carriers
quickly the US Navy converted
four T3 tankers, which could still
operate as oilers, deployed for
'Torch' and then in the Pacific.
(US Navy)

CV-31) were lengthened to give their forecastle 40mm guns better arcs of fire and the AA defence was massively reinforced up to 18 quadruple 40mm and 60 20mm guns.

The reliance on a few shipyards for the large carriers allowed a streamlining of design and construction effort. At first where possible the *Essex* class were built in pairs. However, the lead carriers were given priority over others, to ensure that they reached the fleet as fast as possible, and the second carriers lagged some four to six months behind. This method was therefore abandoned and a new keel was laid down on a free slip in sequence as workers were released from the slip ahead.

Thus the carriers were completed in as little as fourteen months and at most 22½ months or an average of 18½ months. This was a great achievement, and by comparison the Royal Navy only matched this for light carriers and took several years to build their heavy carriers. The same was true of aircraft.

The Development of Carrier Aircraft

The Shorts' main foreign rival in producing early naval aircraft was of course Glen Curtiss, who through his motor-cycle business had the advantage of building his own lightweight engines. His first seaplane was the A-1 (the Triad 50hp, later 75hp), accepted by the US Navy on 1 July 1911, which was used in unsuccessful experiments for wireless in December and a catapult (July 1912). Another three seaplanes were also built.

By August 1912 he had built his first successful flying boat, C-1, for the Navy, using a hull to give greater strength and seaworthiness. She was under powered and unstable but led to another four. In February 1914 Curtiss began a large flying boat, *America*

(two 90hp), to allow Lieutenant John C. Porte RN (Retd) to fly the Atlantic and claim the *Daily Mail*'s £10,000 prize. After trials at the end of June the flight was postponed by the need for more power (a third engine) and the war in Europe.

Porte returned home to persuade Churchill to purchase the flying boat and begin their development at Felixstowe. Although flying boats were not to be used aboard carriers, they were preferred by many naval officers and Curtiss began to develop larger types for the Royal Navy.

With the entry of the USA into the war in April 1917, the US Navy decided to concentrate on building improved flying boats for anti-submarine warfare, and large numbers of fighters and bombers (mainly to foreign designs) to launch a land-based offensive against the U-boats based in Belgium and Germany. These relied mainly on the mass-produced Liberty engine. The Navy also purchased British aircraft used by the Grand Fleet, for use off battleship turrets.

When the conversion of *Langley* was first authorised, designs for carrier aircraft were studied. In 1920 it was hoped to carry the Martin bomber, of which the Navy had purchased ten, but these proved to be too large, even when folded. BuAer decided to use existing Aeromarine (trainer) and Vought (VE-7 fighter) aeroplanes, with strengthened undercarriage and arrester hooks, until experiments in *Langley* with arrester gear identified the design requirements of carrier aircraft. Use was also made of numerous modifications of existing aircraft, such as the DH4, and a few new designs in the early 1920s.

BuAer also developed the torpedo-aeroplane, which had been advocated by Fiske as early as 1912 though little had been done at that time. At the end of 1918 an F-5 flying boat had a dummy torpedo fitted at the Naval Aircraft Factory, Philadelphia, and torpedoes were then dropped by a Curtiss R-6 aeroplane. Finally in 1920 Martin built the first aeroplane designed for torpedoes (the MBT). By May a torpedo squadron had been formed and practised attacks on the *Ostfriesland*, but they were discontinued because of Mitchell's antics. These were followed in 1923 and 1924 by the PT (Naval Aircraft Factory) and DT (Douglas) torpedo-bombers. In March 1924 a torpedo-bomber landed on *Langley*.

A little later the Navy developed dive-bombing. As early as 1919 USMC pilots had used the technique in Haiti and in 1925 Major R. E. Rowell made it commonplace in his Marine squadron at San Diego. Dive-bombers were usually used against enemy personnel, but in 1925 Captain J. M. Reeves, the new Commander Aircraft Battle Fleet, assembled his aircraft at San Diego to evolve new tactics and used F6F fighters to dive-bomb enemy landing-parties. By autumn 1926 this was extended to attack battleships.

BuAer rewrote the gunnery practice rules and improved the bomb racks and sights. Special trials were instituted in the winter of 1926/27 and a Board recommended the use of dive-bombing against personnel, light craft and carrier decks As a result the Martin XT5M-1 dive-bomber with a 1,000lb bomb was produced for trials in 1930. In dive-bombing the US achieved a much higher level of attainment than the FAA.

USS *Shipley* (CVE-85; 1944), an example of the *Casablanca* class produced in large numbers by Kaiser, and of the fleet's logistical support. She was used solely to ferry aircraft to the fleet. (US Navy)

During the 1920s new metal tubing began to replace wooden frames to eliminate the additional weight of waterlogging, and the use of metal spread to wings and tails. In 1925 metal propellers were introduced. With metal came special preparations to prevent corrosion by salt water. Eventually the corrosion of aluminium was virtually eliminated. Fire resistant dopes were also produced. BuAer issued manuals and specifications to ensure that fire and corrosion resistance were standardised. The other great advance in aviation design was the discarding of the water-cooled engine.

To produce a new generation of carrier aircraft, BuAer decided to encourage the use of air-cooled radial engines. This was a result of its Engine Section, staffed by qualified engineers, and the National Advisory Committee for Aeronautics (1920) advising, despite the available wartime surplus of liquid-cooled Liberty engines, that air cooling would give carrier aircraft engines less weight per horsepower (they required no water pump or radiator).

Just after the war the Lawrence Aero Engine Company designed a 220hp air-cooled engine that weighed 420 pounds. BuAer invested $100,000 in further design and production which culminated in a successful test in January 1922. Wright had backed water-cooled engines, but he purchased Lawrence and its J1 engine and developed the Cyclone engine. However, in 1924 their President, F. B. Rentschler, left for Pratt & Whitney, who in 1926 produced the Wasp air-cooled engine, which was more powerful for much the same fuel consumption.

From the mid 1920s to the early 1930s BuAer, aided by the Morrow Board which ruled that aircraft should be replaced every three years, relied on established manufacturers (Martin, Curtiss, Boeing, Vought and Douglas) to produce a series of biplanes based on the Wasp which continually improved the carriers' aircraft.

For instance Curtiss, which took over Wright, produced the F6C-2 fighter which was used in the first simulated dive-bombing of the fleet in 1926 and led to the F8C-4 Helldiver, F11C Goshawk, both fighter/dive-bombers, and SBC scout/dive-bomber. Vought specialised in the O2U and O3U observation/scout plus the SBU scout/dive-bomber. Martin built the SC-1 and designed the T3M and T4M torpedo-bombers. Boeing specialised in fighters (FB-1 to F4B). By the end of this period BuAer had sought to combine the scout and dive-bomber to reduce the number of carrier aircraft types. Aircraft with a wing span shorter than 36 feet did not have folding wings

During the reduced budgets of the late 1920s and early 1930s when research and aircraft numbers were cut, Moffett became worried that the fleet's aircraft were obsolete compared to foreign aircraft – especially British and Italian fighters. However, the new Grumman Company, founded by Leroy Grumman who had worked on Loening amphibians, extended the life of the biplane by introducing features of the monoplane. In late 1931 Grumman produced the FF-1 fighter, part of BuAer's attempt to produce a viable two-seat fighter, which although still a biplane had retractable undercarriage, closed canopy and all-metal stressed skin fuselage. This made it faster than

Naval Aircraft Factory SBN scout/bomber. Brewster designed the SBA for the first competition for US Navy monoplane scouts and the NAF undertook production. It was replaced by the Dauntless. (IWM)

Brewster SB2A-1 Buccaneer dive-bomber – a good example of the US Navy's policy of developing back-up designs. The aircraft did not become operational because of production difficulties. (IWM)

single seaters (207mph) with a range of 920 miles. From this he developed the single-seat F2F and F3F, the last US Navy biplane fighter.

In 1932–33 several designs and prototypes were produced for monoplane carrier fighters. With the Vinson-Trammell Act of 1934 it was possible to develop a new generation of aircraft with larger engines, higher speeds, high lift devices, improved take off/landing characteristics and longer range. For instance to improve the strike power of the carriers, the combined scout and dive-bomber carried a 500lb bomb.

The first US Navy monoplane was a torpedo-bomber. In 1934 BuAer initiated a new torpedo-bomber for the new generation of carriers beginning with *Ranger*. The design competition was between a biplane from Great Lakes and the Douglas TBD-1 Devastator all-metal low wing monoplane with powered wing folding which was put into production in early 1936. Deliveries began in June 1937. With a top speed of 206mph and a combat range of 716 miles (at 128mph) with torpedo, it compared very well with its rivals.

This was quickly followed by the first production monoplane scout/dive-bomber (specification of October 1934). The Vought SB2U Vindicator first flew in January 1936 and the Navy conducted comparative trials in the spring of 1936 against a biplane to determine the merits of monoplanes. The first contract was placed in October, deliveries began in December 1937 and it served with the *Lexington*s, *Ranger* and *Wasp*. Upgraded in production with larger fuel tanks, drop tanks, better armour and

heavier armament, it was capable of 243mph and had a 1,120-mile range at 152mph with 1,000lb bomb-load. It also had a special 500lb bomb mount to clear the propeller in dive-bombing.

With the success of the torpedo and scout/bomber monoplanes, BuAer in 1935 called for designs of fighters to replace the Grumman biplanes and match foreign high-performance fighters. The Seversky and Curtiss fighter-bombers were rejected. This left a monoplane from Brewster, primarily an aircraft subcontractor, and a Grumman biplane. BuAer ordered (November) design development by Brewster, but also by Grumman in reserve. In August 1936 the Grumman biplane was cancelled and the monoplane ordered.

From December 1939 the Brewster F2A-1 Buffalo (304mph 1,000-mile range) was assigned to *Saratoga* and *Lexington*. The upgraded F2A-2 (344mph 1,015 miles, 4 MGs) was a result of war experience in Finland and included armour protection; the F2A-3 (321mph, 965 miles) included increased fuel, armour and self-sealing tanks, to the detriment of performance.

The main defect of the Buffalo (the first naval aircraft to be given an official name) was its landing gear whose hydraulic retracting struts were weak. Brewster also proved unable to keep to their production promises while concentrating on newer designs, were charged with profiteering and eventually taken over by the government. Nevertheless in 1939 the Buffalo, an intermediate type, was the only US Navy fighter monoplane available.

Brewster F2A-1 Buffalo fighter – the US Navy's first monoplane, ordered in 1936, and the only one available in 1939. Landing gear and production problems led to its replacement by the Wildcat. (IWM)

In the late 1930s the aircraft building programme rose steadily to more than 700 per year. This was not without problems because in May 1934 the Comptroller General forbade 'negotiated' contracts whereby firms were given orders without competitive bidding, to cover their experimental expenses. The Secretary of the Navy therefore insisted on competitive bidding which remained in force until 1941 despite the protests of King (Chief BuAer 1933–36) and his successors. However, these programmes did ensure the support of the naval aircraft industry and a constant stream of designs to provide the next generations of carrier aircraft.

The first monoplanes were quickly followed by a second generation: the SBD-1 Douglas Dauntless (253mph 1,165 miles, 1,200lb bombs); the Grumman F4F Wildcat and the Grumman TBF-1 Avenger (271mph, 1,215 miles 2,000lb bombs). After initial engine problems Grumman had produced the F4F-3 (333mph) and F4F-4 (folding wings, 318mph) fighters which were less manoeuvrable and had half the Buffalo's range (770 miles).

However, the Wildcat's landing gear could withstand constant deck landings and Grumman had state of the art production facilities (first production fighter in February 1940) which quickly incorporated improvements. Thus *Lexington* exchanged its Buffalos for a Marine squadron's Wildcats, *Ranger* and *Wasp* following suit. *Saratoga*, *Enterprise* and *Hornet* re-equipped in early 1942. The Buffalo was relegated to the escort carrier *Long Island* and Marine squadrons who operated unsuitable carrier aircraft ashore.

The rugged Avenger torpedo-bomber was also delayed and the obsolescent Devastator was completely outclassed, suffering heavy losses at Coral Sea and Midway. However, after Midway the Avenger began to reach the carriers. Special rockets were developed for them to attack shore targets, but as they required a long glide they could not be used where AA gunfire was heavy.

These events proved the wisdom of BuAer's perseverance with back-up designs and fostering design and production facilities for the US Navy which were the envy of the British and Japanese. Indeed the British had to resort to buying Buffalos and Wildcats to make up for their own deficiencies. The Japanese of course had no such option.

Carrier Aircraft, 1941–1945

In December 1941 the fleet's aircraft were poorly matched against the Japanese aircraft. Each Air Group consisted of 72 aircraft: 36 scout/bombers, 18 torpedo-bombers and 18 fighter. The emphasis was on scouting for a massive air strike on the enemy carriers. However, the Wildcat was outmatched by the manoeuvrable Zero and did not have anything like the latter's range. Although excellent tactics enabled it to hold its own, it was not sufficient to dominate the skies. The Devastator torpedo bomber was obsolescent, old and slow and contracted for replacement. Only the Dauntless scout/dive-bomber matched the Japanese. Rugged and versatile, it acted as scout and fighter (without bombs).

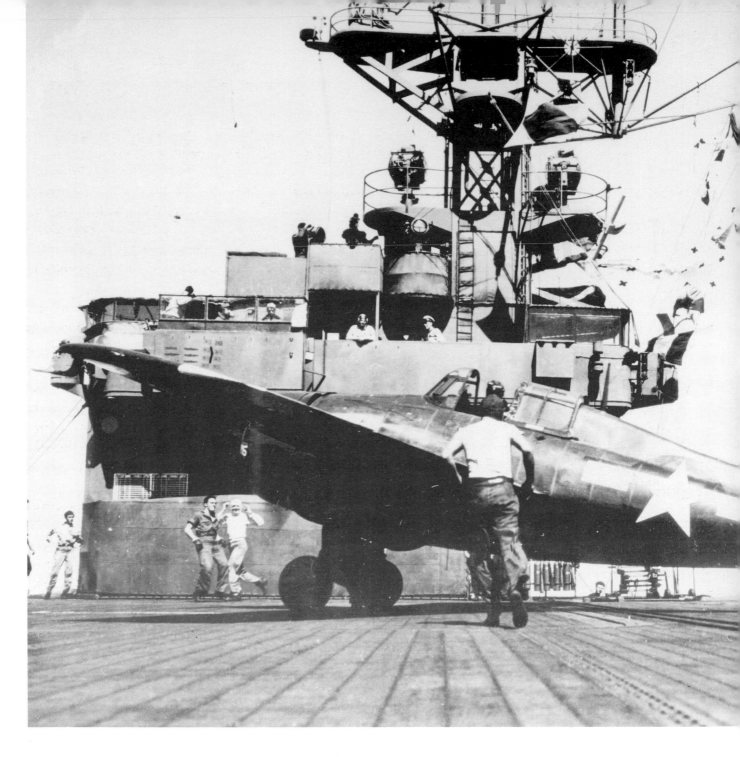

The superiority of Japanese aircraft required a third generation of monoplanes as quickly as possible. The Chance Vought F4U Corsair (415mph, 1.015 miles 6 MGs) was conceived before the war but experience forced design changes. Moreover, its low cowling, low cockpit, many bugs and weak undercarriage made it a poor carrier fighter. It too was passed to Marine land-based units where it quickly acquired a great reputation.

The Corsair did enter service (February 1943) with VF12 (*Hornet*) and VF17 (*Bunker Hill*). However, VF12 re-equipped with Hellcats, and although VF17 retained its Corsairs it was re-assigned to the Solomons on arrival at Pearl Harbor in October.

Eastern Aircraft FM-2 Wildcat fighter on board the CVE *Hoggart Bay*. The Wildcat represented modern fighter design and production and the General Motors plant built large numbers for Allied escort carriers. (US Navy)

162

With all Hellcats assigned to the US carriers, the Corsair was the only US fighter available for the FAA who developed the Corsair II into a great carrier fighter.

When a Zero was captured in the Aleutians during the Midway campaign, Grumman modified their Wildcat replacement (ordered June 1941) to produce in record time a superior fighter which joined its first carrier, *Essex*, in January 1943. The F6F-3 Hellcat (376mph 1,620 miles with drop tank, 6 MGs) was faster, had a greater ceiling, better armament, armour, self-sealing tanks, and could outclimb and outdive the Zero. The Navy also armed it with cannon and rockets for use against shore targets. Produced in huge numbers, the Hellcat proved a great Zero-killer.

The Hellcat also outranged the Dauntless and the Navy sought a faster bomber able to carry a greater payload. The Curtiss SB2C Helldiver (295mph 1,165 miles at 158mph, 2,500lb bomb-load) suffered from the production difficulties of a new factory, but in the spring of 1943 the first aircraft joined the carriers. The Helldiver was very rugged, heavily armed and carried a huge punch, but because of its great power coupled with aerodynamic problems it became known as 'The Beast' and defects in wing folding, arrester gear, tailwheel and other systems caused it to be recalled. However, it did later see wide-scale service, unlike the Brewster Buccaneer which proved a failure. Thus only the newly arrived *Bunker Hill* had Helldivers at the Gilberts and Marshalls.

The upgraded Dauntless (SBD-5, 2,250lb bomb-load, 4 MGs) therefore soldiered on into the autumn of 1943, being deployed in the scouting role for the last time at the Gilberts. After this torpedo- and fighter aircraft carried new radars for scouting. The Avenger, which had arrived just after Midway, was also improved (TBM-3 built by General Motors). The Hellcat, Corsair, Helldiver and Avenger (as a torpedo-strike aircraft) were all proven superior to their Japanese counterparts at Rabaul in November 1943.

BuAer also planned a successor to the Avenger and picked the Chance Vought TBU. This, however, was not a success and Consolidated Aircraft took over production of what became the TBY-2 Seawolf, because Chance Vought were concentrating on the Corsair. Other torpedo-bombers being developed were the twin-engined Grumman XTB2F and the Douglas XTB2D.

When J. S. McCain, the land-based air commander at Guadalcanal, became Chief BuAer he instituted studies on night-fighting. British experience favoured twin-engined aircraft so Grumman developed the twin-engined night fighter XF7F Tigercat with radar, the first production model of which flew in December 1943. In the meantime the Navy adopted the Corsair for land and carrier use.

The Hellcat, Helldiver and Avenger were the mainstay of the carriers from 1943 to 1945. They were equal or superior to their Japanese counterparts and were produced in far greater numbers. For instance the Hellcat, although less agile than the Zero, had the edge in speed, armour and above all fire power and by the end of 1943 2,555 had been produced. Moreover, the Hellcat was supplemented by the Corsair, superior to

163

the Zero in all respects, when it was finally approved for carriers by the Navy in late 1944.

The next-generation fighter posed a problem; although one was needed to counter new Japanese models, development of a totally new fighter would disrupt large-scale production. In April 1944 production of the improved F6F-5 Hellcat began as an interim measure. Meanwhile the F4U-4 Corsair was qualified for carriers and became available from October, the new XF7F Tigercat was assigned to the *Midway*s and after that the F8F Bearcat would come on stream.

However, the Corsairs had been assigned to Marine units and so the Tigercat was given to them to release the Corsairs for carriers in 1946. In January 1945 some Marine pilots were switched to carriers to fly them. The first F4U-4s reached the fleet in April 1945. Bearcat deliveries began in February 1945, the intention being to overtake Hellcat production by November and replace it from February 1946. In May 1945 VF–19 began to re-equip with the Bearcat, the first unit to receive the type.

With the Germans and British developing jets, the Navy also began development of the Ryan XFR-1 Fireball, piston-turbojet, and the McDonnell XFD-1 Phantom, pure jet, fighters. Production was beset by design and development difficulties though a few Fireballs had reached Pearl Harbor by mid 1945.

Grumman F6F Hellcat fighter. Rugged, well-armed and long-ranged, it allowed the US Navy to achieve superiority over the previously dominant Zero and pave the way for the bombers. (IWM)

As replacement for the Avenger and Helldiver, BuAer decided at the end of 1943 to develop one all-purpose type: the bomber-torpedo (VBT). This resulted in the re-design of the next-generation dive-bomber (Douglas SB2D Destroyer) as a single-seater (BTD Destroyer), and the development of the Curtiss XBTC and XBTC2C, Martin XBTM Mauler (ordnance in excess of 10,000lb), Grumman XTB2F (twin-engine), XTB3F Guardian, Douglas XBT2D Dauntless II (6,500lb) and XTB2D. BuAer decided to develop the Mauler and Dauntless II for carriers and cancelled the Seawolf and Destroyer contracts. The prototype XBT2D first flew in March 1945 and was put into production as the AD-1 Skyraider, but first deliveries did not reach Midway until December 1946. The first production Mauler, now designated AM-1, first flew in the same month.

All existing carrier aircraft were improved during production and the US Navy always had an abundance of design options, compared to Japan or Great Britain, in case any design failed. For instance the Brewster SB2A Buccaneer and Vought TBU Sea Wolf were produced (771 and 180 respectively) but never attained operational status. The alliance of BuAer and dedicated naval aircraft designers and production engineers allowed the US Navy's carrier arm to have enough strength to match the Japanese carriers in 1942 and rapidly switch to the offensive in 1943.

In December 1941 the main weaknesses of carrier aircraft were the lack of fighters (only 90 Buffalos and 148 Wildcats were available and half the units were in training) and the obsolescent torpedo-aircraft (Devastators). Fortunately the Navy led the world in naval dive-bombing and this was sufficient at Midway. However, US production radically altered the situation in 1943.

From 1943 to 1945 the Navy relied on improved models of the Avenger, Corsair, Hellcat and Helldiver. By 1946 the Bearcat was to replace the Hellcat, and the Skyraider would replace the Avenger and Helldiver; the Fireball and Mauler would also be available in small numbers. The Hellcat was no longer fast enough for high-altitude interception and was to be replaced by Corsairs in this role until the Bearcat arrived.

In July 1945 it was decided that new or reformed Air Groups would be re-equipped. The *Essex* class would have 32 fighters (Corsairs, four night Hellcats), 24 fighter-bombers (Corsairs), 24 dive-bombers (Helldivers) and 20 torpedo-aircraft (Avengers, mainly for scouting with early warning radar to replace picket destroyers), the *Saipan*s 48 fighters (Hellcats), the *Independence* class 32 fighters and the *Midway*s 73 fighters and 64 bombers. Moreover, the US Navy produced the aircrews to enable the use of these great aircraft to the fullest extent.

The Provision of Personnel and Training, 1910–1945

During the first days of naval aviation the pilots, usually officers, had to rely on the early pioneers and manufacturers for training. The first naval pilots were trained by Curtiss (Ellyson, Towers) and the Wrights (Rodgers). As in Great Britain the pilots then split between trials and training work. Ellyson and Towers did experimental work while Rodgers and later colleagues continued training programmes. The first air station established by the US Navy was at Annapolis.

One early problem for the naval air arm was to recruit sufficient personnel to train as pilots, there being a general shortage of officers and many senior officers regarding such activities as being the ruin of promising careers. For instance Towers found his application blocked by his senior officer. With better machines and clearer requirements, some navies began to carry out their own training, and in 1913 the US Navy introduced its own pilot certificate. Emphasis was placed on training with the fleet, but the lack of catapults delayed progress.

An aviation camp was established at Guantanamo in January–March 1913 to be the eyes of the fleet. In October the Chambers Board proposed that Pensacola provide a flying school and training, and the old battleship *Mississippi* was assigned as an experimental vessel in January 1914. However, she left with a seaplane detachment for scouting, under fire, for the fleet and Army at Vera Cruz in April 1914. Thus the lack of warships equipped with aircraft saw the US fleet fall behind the Royal Navy in training.

With the prospect of a war with Mexico, the Naval Appropriations Bill of August 1916 authorised the formation of a naval flying corps with a reserve to train civilians as pilots. However, although the Act remained on the statute books, its main provisions were not put into effect and naval aviation remained an integral part of the Navy. The CNO insisted that regular officers, trained in naval duties, would be required in the naval air service and would then return to line duties. The provisions for flying pay and a naval air reserve, however, were implemented. Some reservist units, such as one at Yale, were set up.

On 6 April 1917 the Navy had 48 qualified pilots, 239 enlisted men, one air station and 54 aircraft. During the First World War US naval aviation rapidly expanded by keeping regular officers in the fleet or in command posts and using reservists as new pilots. Most of the naval aviators after April 1917 were reservists rapidly recruited by Towers, the Assistant Director of Naval Aviation.

On 1 May a training programme and an 18-month syllabus to train pilots was approved with a course starting every three months. Another programme was to produce aviation mechanics and some enlisted pilots. Two Naval Militia stations were taken over at Squantum, Massachusetts, and Bay Shore, New York, for flight training while other stations (North Island; Moutchic, France; Hampton Roads) were built.

Ground School was set up at the Massachusetts School of Technology. Supplementary Ground Schools were later developed at Washington University, Seattle, and Dunwoody Institute, Minneapolis. Some US Navy trainees were taught to fly in France (Tours) and by the RFC in Canada (from July). The first units formed were from the universities such as Yale, Harvard and Princeton.

On 17 May Commander N. E Irwin (later Captain and Director of Naval Aviation) replaced Lieutenant Towers in the Aviation Section, CNO's office, so that the latter, as his deputy, could supervise the Naval Reserve Flying Corps. Towers, when Assistant

Naval Attaché in London, had seen the RNAS gear up for war in 1914–16, and so on 23 May 300 school machines were ordered.

On 10 July 1917 it was decided that training should be in three parts: Ground School (naval indoctrination, drill, aeronautical theory, eight weeks); Preliminary Flight School (flight training up to 5–10 hours solo) and Completion Flight School (advanced, award of wings and commission as Ensign USNRF).

Most of the trained pilots and mechanics served on coastal patrols from air stations in America, France, Italy or the United Kingdom or the Northern Bombing Group (organised to destroy the U-boats at Ostend, Zeebrugge and Bruges) in France rather than with the fleet.

With the end of the war and only about 50 regular officers in aviation, Congressional legislation was needed to transfer the war reservists to the regular service and provide the personnel needed. With the peacetime cutbacks more regulars were unlikely to be forthcoming from the fleet. The General Board, after its investigation into aviation in 1919, recommended that to man a vital fighting arm, all naval aviators had to be Naval Academy graduates, but in the meantime war or college reservists and enlisted men would make up shortages. The Board strongly urged Congressional action.

However, Congress in its July 1919 Act did not provide for the transfer of reservists and set the Navy's personnel at 170,000 of which officers provided only 4 per cent. This meant that naval aviation suffered from a lack of personnel, given the competition for officers. The continued cutting of the BuAer appropriations by the Naval Budget Officer soon brought about a real crisis in naval aviation personnel since there were no funds to transfer officers from the reserve or other branches, enlarge the Naval Academy intake, or train enlisted men.

It was also Navy Department policy to insist on full seaman qualifications, and trainees were periodically lost through rotation out of naval aviation for seagoing assignments. By 1924 it was clear that BuAer would not be able to man the *Lexington*s. Nor did Moffett have the funds to hire and then retain civilian experts. He therefore encouraged the development of the Naval Reserve.

Another problem was a lack of promotion policy for aviators whereby officers (e.g., Towers and Mustin) were passed over because they had no shipboard service. By the Act of 1921, 30 per cent of older officers seconded or transferred to naval aviation, including Moffett, had to qualify as observers within one year. Moffett thereafter insisted that all these officers qualify as aviators.

After receiving the Eberle Board's proposals to expand aviation in January 1925, Moffett quickly appointed another Board under his Assistant Chief, Captain A. W. Johnson, to recommend ways to increase the aviation personnel needed. Its proposals (April) to increase naval aviators fivefold over ten years, including naval ratings and the creation of a reserve (at about the same time as the Royal Navy made similar suggestions), led to a clash with the Bureau of Navigation which sought to limit aviation officer numbers which it considered of 'unproved value at sea'. So another Board was appointed under Rear Admiral M. Taylor.

It was overshadowed by the Morrow Board before which Moffett sought BuAer control over its personnel, enlarging the Naval Academy intake and the total numbers of the Navy. Other senior naval officers called as witnesses opposed a naval flying corps. To help solve the personnel and promotion problems the Morrow Board recommended that officers who specialised in aviation be promoted without affecting non-aviator promotions, and that command of carriers, tenders and air stations be reserved for qualified aviators.

Although the Morrow Board and the Act of 1926 made no provision for additional personnel to meet its five-year programme, Moffett had done very well considering the shortage of officers as a whole. In 1928 naval aviation officers represented 11 per cent of the total as against a mere 2 per cent in 1916, but a further 950 pilots would be needed during the next five years. To meet this demand the Secretary of the Navy got the number of midshipman appointments per senator and representative raised from three to four, but he failed to get the percentage of officers raised from 4 to 6 per cent of total personnel.

From 1925 the Naval Academy introduced aviation components into any related subject courses and flight training for all the midshipmen. This was designed to give all officers a general idea of naval aviation and to eliminate those unfit for flying. After a year of their two years' sea duty officers were also assigned to San Diego or Hampton Roads air stations for more experience. If they opted for naval aviation they went to Pensacola where regular and reserve officers were given training and refresher courses.

To meet the new demand two and then four classes a year were provided at Pensacola and the one training squadron expanded to three. Finally 50 trainees reported each month and there were five squadrons, two for elementary training and three for advanced training in large seaplanes, gunnery and bombing; spotting for ship's gunnery and air combat tactics.

By this time Observer training, introduced for older officers whom Moffett got transferred to naval aviation, fell into disfavour because senior officers were needed for carrier commands and had to be pilots. Moffett also had officers assigned straight from Naval Academy graduation to Pensacola, both to help the shortages and to maintain their enthusiasm. A brief trial in 1930 resulted in a doubling of volunteers for flying training.

Despite successes in the expansion of *matériel* due to the 1,000-plane programme, personnel shortages continued because the total number of officers allowed by law was kept so low. In 1933 this meant that only half of the class graduating from Annapolis could be commissioned, the rest being discharged. With every branch of the Navy short of officers it was harder than ever to get the number necessary for aviation.

Before his death Moffett suggested legislation for a whole Naval Academy class to transfer to aviation and increase Congressional appointments from four to five. Failing

Bird's-eye view: USS *Enterprise* (CV-6), clearly showing the wooden deck typical of US carriers, the elevator, and the increased armament at the deck-edge. (US Navy)

that, discharged midshipmen should transfer to the Aviation Reserve. Moffett also suggested the creation of Reserve cadets who could serve with the fleet for three years. The Vinson-Trammell Act authorised the recall of discharged ensigns of the class of 1933 and commissioning the whole class of 1934 to help the personnel shortage.

At the end of 1934 King secured President Roosevelt's support for a cadet scheme which was passed by Congress in 1935. These cadets (AvCads) were graduates, ranked between a warrant officer and an ensign, had twelve to fifteen months training (preflight and flight) and three years with the fleet. This was in strong contrast to the long-

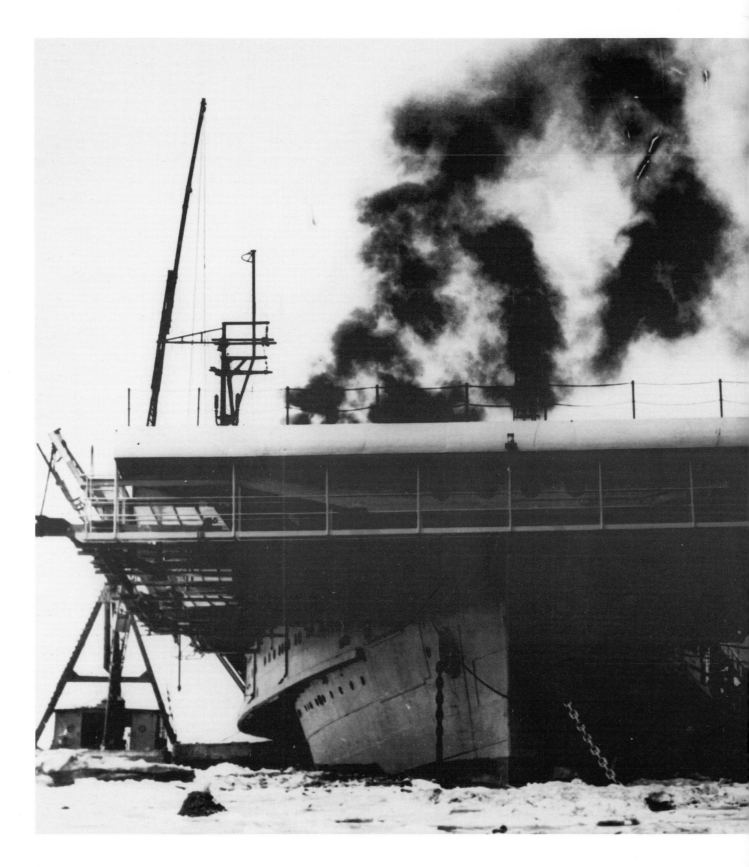

term training of Japanese naval pilots. Although lacking general sea training, which was made up by courses aboard ships, the cadets performed well as pilots. Within a year the BuAer cadets were a permanent source of recruitment and formed 45 per cent of naval aviators due to steady expansion and the paucity of regular service sources.

The early AvCads were of a very high standard because they were well-qualified college graduates and the physical qualifications were very stringent. They were highly motivated volunteers who accepted lower status (not being ranked as officers) and pay (no full officer's pay) to be fleet aviators. They reached the fleet from mid 1936, most signed up again after four years and by 1941, after extensive carrier duty, were beginning to take over training and squadron posts.

The number of fleet aviators required continued to mount (Admiral C. C. Bloch, CinC 1938–39, wanted 150 per annum) and this led to the Naval Aviation Reserve Act of 1939 which set the minimum strength at 6,000 officers, allowed reserve cadets to be commissioned after training and promoted after three years with the fleet and passing examinations, when they could serve another three years. This allowed the Navy to keep them on active duty, rather than returning to the Reserve, improved retention rates and gave more money for reserve training.

Funds remained totally inadequate to train the numbers needed, however, and the Civilian Pilot Training Program announced by the President in December 1938 with New Deal funding took up the slack. After 1939 the physical and college entrance standards were relaxed in order to churn out the large numbers of pilots required.

This programme was not regarded as ideal by senior officers who preferred experienced, sea-trained professional officers (Academy graduates had to serve two years at sea before flying training). However, because of the shortfall and the recognition by Plans Division, BuAer, that pilot production was the most vital requirement in any war, the only recourse was to the AvCads, Reserve (mainly graduates of College Reserve Officer Training Courses, ROTC) and the assignment of enlisted men (Naval Aviation Pilots, NAPs, mainly Warrant Officers). The last dwindled in favour of the first two.

The shortage of Academy officers for aviation meant that, as in the First World War, the Navy concentrated on producing large numbers of reserve pilots rather than a small, professional cadre with long-term training and assignment like the Japanese Navy. Naval career pilots provided the nucleus for both command and training. Low individual flying hours were compensated for by excellent tactics and a stream of trained pilots.

With the war in Europe, even greater efforts were made to increase the number of officers, including aviators, for the expanding Navy. The Chief of the Bureau of Navi-

Sable (IX-81; 1943). Flight-deck landing qualification was undertaken by fleet carriers, then escort carriers, and later two converted Great Lakes paddle-steamers, *Wolverine* and *Sable*, for U-boat-safe training. (US Navy)

gation (Nimitz) therefore introduced a number of schemes including enlarging the Naval Academy classes, increasing the NROTC units and rapidly training officers through the V-7 programme.

Most US Navy pilots before 1939 underwent their Elementary and Advanced Training at the US Naval Air Station, Pensacola, Florida (the 'Annapolis of the Air'), a huge air base with satellite airfields. Another training centre, NAS Jacksonville, Florida, was established as an aviation training complex from the spring of 1941, and with the rapid expansion of the fleet other training centres were set up. For instance in the autumn of 1941 a new elementary flight school at Corpus Christi, Texas, was created, and a cadre of veteran fleet pilots was trained to set up an advanced school there. The numbers of instructors and pupils were also steadily expanded at each centre.

At Pensacola or the other centres, the elementary course (N3N-3, two months) included thorough ground training and flight training in five stages: 12 hours' dual flying before the solo; dual and solo training in stalls, spins and touch-downs; aerobatics; inverted spin and elementary formation flying. AvCads had to enlist for four years as seamen 2nd class and pass evaluation of their suitability and elementary training (10 hours dual, one solo) at one of the sixteen Naval Reserve Air Bases such as Robertson, Missouri, or Grosse Ile, near Detroit. They then went to a training centre where after Navy indoctrination (two weeks) they passed to the next stage.

Primary Flight Training was handled by different squadrons teaching different elements plus ground school (aeronautical engineering and navigation). As well as emergency procedures and acrobatics on the NAF N3N or N25 Stearman Kaydet, and conversion courses, formation flying was taught on the O3U or SBBU (later SNV Vultee Valiant), instrument flying on the SNJ Harvard and the Link trainer, the inverted spin on the N25 Stearman Kaydet and advanced formation flying and aerial gunnery on the Harvard. After this pilots were divided between carrier, multi-engine/transport and warship training.

Advanced training for carrier fighters and bombers took place at NAS Miami (Opa Locka near Miami), Florida, which began operating in the spring and was officially opened in mid 1941. The early pilots were trained for flying the Dauntless, Devastator and Brewster Buffalo, but the shortage of front-line aircraft, especially torpedo-aircraft and fighters, meant biplanes (e.g., Boeing F4B and Grumman F2F and F3F) had to be used. Later training was on former front-line aircraft, on the Northrop BT1 for the Helldiver, the Devastator for the Avenger and the Brewster Buffalo for the Hellcat.

Ground school, elementary formations, dummy carrier landings, air to air gunnery on towed targets, dive-bombing and night-flying were included. Those students who failed the advanced school were invariably sent to the multi-engine school which was definitely second best to the élite carrier pilots.

The pilots were then awarded their wings and commissions (Ensign US Navy or Second Lieutenant USMC). In the USA this took about fifteen months. Later the last step was conversion and familiarisation with front-line aircraft at Fort Lauderdale,

USS *Long Island* (CVE-1) at Mare Island. The ship's company, as distinct from the air group, were responsible for seamanship and navigation – vital for operations and the ship's survival. (US Navy)

Miami, which included night-flying, dummy landings with a Landing Signal Officer (LSO), squadron tactics plus torpedo procedures and a live torpedo drop against a target ship (for bombers).

Instructors were experienced Academy or AvCad carrier pilots who were expected to pass on the high standard of their knowledge and skill. For instance the senior instructors of NAS Miami in March 1941 were Commander G. F. Bogan (CO and Director of Training) and Lieutenants J. 'Jumpin' Joe' Clifton (Academy 1930) and J. T. Blackburn (Academy 1933), all of whom were to have outstanding careers in the Pacific. They were assisted by AvCads and later the best graduates of their own courses. Until August 1941 the schools flew a five-day week and after Pearl Harbor a seven-day week, although instructors and pupils got one day off in seven.

There were no illusions that the pilots passed to the fleet were fully finished. Inevitably the pressure to produce as many pilots as possible meant that some elements, such as high-altitude flying, were not covered because of lack of time – and equipment. Few of the new pilots passed out with more than 150 hours (under the 1939 Act 300 flight hours was the aim for AvCads), but they were imbued with the *esprit de corps* of an élite service. Except for the Academy and Reserve officers few pilots had any fleet experience.

After Pensacola (Miami after 1940), carrier pilots were sent to one of two Advanced Carrier Training Groups (ACTG) at Norfolk, Virginia, or San Diego, Califor-

USS *Franklin* (CV-13; 1944), in her January 1944 paint scheme. She was hit by a 500lb Kamikaze bomb on 19 March 1945 off Japan, causing 989 casualties, and was saved only by heroic damage control. (US Navy)

nia, for further training, especially dummy carrier landings and qualification in carrier landing (three arrested landings on a carrier, CVEs from 1942). With U-boat activity on the East Coast confining the carriers to Chesapeake Bay, a move was made to the Great Lakes and two Lakes paddle-steamers were converted: *Wolverine* (commissioned August 1942) and *Sable* (March 1943). Later whole squadrons would take the course together.

Squadron training then passed on the latest tactics and above all more flying experience. Newly formed fighter, dive- and torpedo-bomber squadrons would then come together as an air group to co-ordinate training and weld together as a team. A mutu-

ally supported strike was essential to avoid heavy losses among the vulnerable bombers, so the air groups practised co-ordinated attacks on ships acting as targets.

The air group would then join its carrier for warm-up operations in the Chesapeake and a shakedown cruise to the Caribbean (Gulf of Paria, Trinidad). Intense drills and practice were needed to weld the air group and carrier's company into an operational team. The flight-deck and hangar officers and their plane handlers were key figures in achieving rapid spotting, launching and landing.

During the shakedown, flight operations were monitored by two pilots who ruthlessly sought to prune the time taken to launch and form-up strikes, so as to save invaluable minutes of air time which translated into increased range for the strike. The Fighter Direction Officer and Combat Information Center (CIC) also had to learn to co-ordinate the Combat Air Control (CAP) and interception of enemy attackers. In 1944 replacement air groups for carriers already in the combat area were qualified on *Ranger*, *Saratoga* or escort carriers at San Diego or Pearl Harbor.

USS *Hancock* (CV-19; 1944): a detailed view of the bow. Note the square flight-deck, the sponsons and the radio mast. (US National Archives)

During the first half of 1942 the US Navy carrier pilots had less than half the flight hours (305) logged by their Japanese counterparts (700). The Japanese pilots also had the edge in their fighters and torpedo-bombers. However, the American practice of rotating experienced pilots to shore training duties ensured that the latest tactics and skills were passed on to the new pilots. Above all this was essential in the fighter units where the correct tactics and skills were needed for Wildcats to match the Zero while escorting bombers or protecting the fleet.

By the time of the Central Pacific offensive in the autumn of 1943, the average Japanese pilot's flight hours had declined from 700 to 500, whereas the US figures had climbed from 305 to 500. However, whereas the US pilots had a fairly uniform standard, leavened by a few veterans, the Japanese tended to have some exceptionally experienced pilots with thousands of hours and under-trained newcomers with as little as 100 hours. When the latter met well-trained 'average' US pilots in Hellcats they were cut to pieces.

With the Gilberts and Marshalls landings plus the continued advance in the South West Pacific, the gap between the American and Japanese carrier pilots continued to widen. Thus by May 1944 on average the Japanese carrier pilots' flight training hours had fallen to 275, a near 50 per cent drop, compared to the US pilots' total which had again risen to 525 hours. Indeed by this time BuAer was producing a surplus of pilots and had to cut back training (March, and again in June 1944).

Given the large pool of pilots now available, the US Navy could systematically rotate tired, veteran air groups to rest and pass on their experience to trainees. At first this was undertaken by individual rotation, but in January 1944 ComAirPac decided that complete air groups would be rotated after six to nine months of combat. In April, because of the intensive Central Pacific operations, this was shortened to six months.

Thus in May 1944 six air groups, such as *Yorktown*'s Air Group 5, in action since August 1943, were sent home. In the spring of 1944 Nimitz requested 1.67 air groups per carrier to provide for this and reserves. Thus 32 air groups were needed by June 1945 and 39 by the end of the year. With the rise of the Kamikaze, which brought increasing pilot strain, King reversed the cutbacks of pilots (6,000 to 8,000) and required two air groups per carrier.

The Navy had estimated pilot numbers on casualties alone, and underestimated the factor of strain and fatigue under constant operations. Thus some air groups had to be replaced before their six-month tour ended. This required emergency action and the cutting of combat tours to four months. USMC pilots with their Corsairs were also added to the fast carriers for the first time to beef-up the CAPs.

The Americans' production of experienced, well-trained pilots led by veterans was a remarkable contrast to the British and Japanese lack of pilots, especially given that the fast carriers were deploying more than 1,000 aircraft by mid 1945, and these brought victory after the dark, defeated days of 1942.

3. The Imperial Japanese Navy, 1900–1945

By the end of the First World War Japanese modernisation had been so successful that she was recognised as the third greatest naval power after the USA and Great Britain. The preparation for and the bulk of the fighting in the Pacific from 1941 was left to the Navy while the Army pursued its own ambitions in China. Traditionally a defensive force protecting the homeland, the Navy realised that it could not defend successfully against the full British or American fleets let alone a coalition of the two.

The greatest fear, however, was of the great industrial power of the USA (not appreciated by the Army) which led to the adoption of a risky, offensive strategy. As in previous wars with China and Russia, Japan sought to defeat its opponent in a short war. The problem was to find a way to maximise Japan's limited resources just long enough to defeat a potentially far stronger opponent(s).

Japanese Naval Policy and Strategy, 1900–1945

With modernisation from 1868 Great Power status was achieved in 1906, but equality with the strongest Western Powers was still a long way off. Because of the traditional dominance of the Army, the Navy's part was limited by its traditional roles (defence of the homeland and transportation of troops) and its small size. With local naval supremacy and the steady increase in the size of the fleet, the Navy gradually began to see itself as an equal rather than a subordinate of the Army.

Moreover, a large fleet, based on the technically advanced dreadnoughts, and the development of an indigenous shipbuilding industry required a larger (even equal) share of the national budget. Also modern naval doctrine required 'offensive' naval operations with a view to a decisive fleet action, as opposed to those designed solely to support the Army's operations. Yalu and particularly Tsushima established fleet operations centered on the battle fleet, rather than amphibious operations, as the way for the Navy, in line with Mahan's doctrine, to establish and maintain Japan as a naval power.

During the first fifty years of the Meiji era the pursuit of the modernisation of the Navy largely meant the adoption of the best training, methods and technology available because the Japanese were starting from virtually nothing. Thus it modelled itself on the most successful navy, the Royal Navy, and received from them great assistance in training and equipment. However, unlike the Royal and US Navies where there was strong resistance to the introduction of a naval staff, the Japanese quickly adopted the German model of a naval staff for planning. This allowed the Navy systematically to develop a modern fleet and to use it to the maximum effect against the Chinese and Russian fleets.

After the First World War Japanese naval policy, her carrier policy, and eventually the whole course of the war in the Pacific was shaped by two, related issues. The naval administration had to grapple with the problem of a fleet inferior to those of its potential enemies and the Army's expansionist policy in China. There were two completely different approaches to the problem which in effect polarised and divided the top echelons of the Navy.

The problem was that the weakness of the Japanese constitution was exploited by the extreme militarists of the Army who gradually took control of government policy. Any idea of civilian control over policy was lost after the mid 1930s when US and British trade protection, the failure to gain naval parity at the London Conference and the Depression lent impetus to the rise of militarism.

The Prime Minister was increasingly either a civilian controlled by the services, or a senior officer. Moderate civilians and senior officers were under great pressure from ultra nationalists and middle- and junior-ranking Army officers who did not hesitate to 'meddle' in politics or to use assassination to get their way. Junior naval officers were also steadily politicised, but it was naval tradition that naval officers did not interfere in politics but followed Navy Ministry policy. Therefore junior naval officers increasingly pressurised senior officers to change that policy. This was aided by the Japanese tradition of reaching consensus and allowing junior officers considerable freedom of expression until a decision had been made.

The Army was the prime mover in masterminding the provocations which from 1931 led to the 'China Incident' and outright war with China by 1937. Its main fear was an intervention by the Soviet Union so an alliance with Germany was seen as necessary to prevent this. The Army, after initial foreign influence, remained imbued with traditional Samurai values, indoctrinated in early education, and was far less technical, more insular and authoritarian than its German model. It did not fear the small British and American armies and underestimated the great resources of the latter. In fact it blamed the Western Powers for its failure to conclude the 'China Incident' quickly.

The main obstacle to the Army's policies was the Navy and not the civilians. Bitter inter-service rivalry prevented any co-operation. The Navy could not prevent the War Ministry pursuing its China policy because the Army was independent and gained the majority of resources while bearing the brunt of the Chinese war. However, the Navy could refuse a German alliance which might lead to a premature war with Great Britain and the USA.

The Navy's senior officers appreciated far more than the leaders of the Army the importance of industrial power and Japan's continual relative inferiority in that respect.

The Navy was a technical service, its education encouraged foreign study and languages, officers were often sent abroad (more than half its senior officers had served or trained abroad, mostly in the USA or the UK) and service included far more contact with foreign officers and visits to their countries.

The Navy did not oppose Japanese imperialism in China or even in South East Asia (the 'Southern Area'), had no qualms about operations in China and gained important operational experience. But it favoured more diplomatic means at least until it was ready. Moreover, in a technical service, key senior officers realised that any naval war against Great Britain or the USA, and especially both, would be premature until the fleet and above all the economy had moved closer to parity.

They thought that Japan had reached the same stage as Germany in 1914 when, if she had exercised forbearance for another five to ten years, she could have dominated Europe. Thus they did not wish to embark on a premature war and risk defeat when patience would allow time to overhaul her rivals economically.

The opposition to the Army was championed by the Navy Ministry staffed mainly by the 'Tokyo warriors' or 'Treaty Faction' led by Admirals T. Kato, Taniguchi, Sakonji, Yamanashi and Yonai, and followed by a second generation of Hori, Yamamoto, Koga and Inoue. The officers of the Treaty Faction (most of whom, such as Yamamoto when Naval Attaché 1926–28, had served in USA) were aware of the greater US resources and the impossibility of winning any war at that time.

If Japan built up its strength, it too could be equal to or stronger than the Western Powers. But if Japan challenged too quickly it would be easily outbuilt by the USA and its challenge would have been premature. They therefore viewed the limitations treaties as not holding Japan to 60 or 70 per cent of the USN, but keeping the USA to 100 per cent at a stage when it could quite easily leave them behind.

The Navy Minister, Admiral Baron T. Kato, who attended the Washington Conference, was therefore prepared to accept an inferior naval status to that of Great Britain and the USA. Kato had been behind the planned eight battleship and eight battlecruiser fleet, designed during the Great War with the US in mind. However, he knew by 1921 that the Naval Estimates would be one-third of the total budget (against the Army's 60 per cent) which was beyond what Japan could afford. The resources were not yet there to complete the 8-8 fleet let alone compete in an arms race with the USA and Great Britain which was rapidly developing.

He and Prime Minister K. Hara decided to abandon the 8-8 fleet if a disarmament agreement could be made. They recognised that Japan could not yet compete in an arms race or war and furthermore would need US loans to afford war with any other major naval power. Japan's best policy was therefore to increase its fleet within national resources and avoid war by diplomatic means.

Kato therefore accepted the 5:5:3 ratio of the Washington Treaty (1922) with the price of limiting US fortifications in the Pacific. Kato had to accept 60 per cent of the US total, rather than the 70 per cent deemed necessary by the Naval Staff for success-

IJNS *Kaga* (1928). After the loss of *Amagi* in the 1923 earthquake, this battleship was converted; she is shown after her modernisation in the mid 1930s. Note the downturn of the funnel. (IWM)

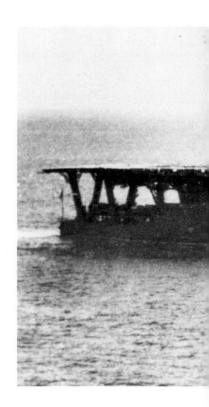

ful defence, because the Americans had broken the Japanese diplomatic codes and knew that he would accept the lesser figure.

The problem for the Treaty faction, as its name suggests, was that it was closely associated with the disarmament treaties between the wars. Alone of the nations, due to its constitution, Japan sent senior naval officers, Navy Ministers and their advisers, as delegates to the disarmament conferences. T. Kato had supported the liberalisation of Japan and the idea that the Navy Minister should be a civilian along British lines, to ensure that navalism was counter-balanced by consideration of other factors such as the economy. However, this was never implemented and there being no civilian responsibility for naval policy the full accountability fell to senior naval officers.

This led to a rift in the Navy because the Washington Treaty was not accepted by all its senior officers. The Navy Ministry policy was opposed by the 'Fleet Faction' led by K. Kato (a naval adviser at Washington), S. Takahashi and N. Suetsugu. Although they realised that the Navy would have to fight a defensive war, they regarded 70 per cent of the US fleet as the minimum required for success. Moreover, in an atmosphere of great nationalism and pride in the 'invincible' Japanese fleet, they were incensed when the new battleship *Tosa* was scrapped under the Washington Treaty and felt that the Treaty Faction had given in too easily to US and British pressure.

In early 1925 K. Kato became Vice Chief of the Naval General Staff and advocated more hawkish policies. He and his disciples, holding key posts in the Naval General Staff, were a focus for those who insisted on early parity with the British and

Americans. Even so the Fleet Faction in the 1920s knew that it could not take on the British or US fleets. They failed to alter Naval Ministry policy, but Kato (as a Military Councillor) remained the key influence behind the Fleet Faction throughout the 1930s.

The problems of the Treaty Faction really began with the London Conference of 1930. The Japanese naval delegation, led by Admiral T. Takarabe and including Rear-Admiral I. Yamamoto, agreed to the extending of the Washington Treaty rather than gaining parity with Great Britain and the USA. This caused great bitterness in naval circles and public protests that Japan was not being treated equally. Part of the problem was that, outside the Navy, few Japanese knew anything about Great Britain or the USA (particularly the latter's mighty resources) at first hand. There was a tendency to belittle Anglo–American strength. The Navy's acceptance of naval inferiority contrasted strongly with the Army's militancy in China.

IJNS *Ryujo* (1933) – an attempt to produce a small carrier design to be built in numbers. To carry 48 aircraft a second hangar was added, creating stability problems. Note the bridge under the flight-deck. (IWM)

One result was that the new Naval Minister, Admiral M. Osumi from January 1933 to February 1936, allied himself with the Fleet Faction and appointed its leader Suetsugu CinC, Combined Fleet in 1933. Suetsugu's ally and successor as CinC, Admiral S. Takahashi (Vice-Chief of the Naval General Staff), introduced subtle administrative changes to increase the Naval Staff's independence, along Army lines, at the expense of the Navy Ministry. This undermined the Minister's ability to control the Fleet Faction who demanded an unattainable goal of parity with the USA and Great Britain in the arms limitation talks. With Osumi's agreement Japan withdrew from the League of Nations in March 1933 because of criticism of her aggression in China. After great

pressure on the Prime Minister, Admiral K. Okada, by the militant Fleet Faction Japan also opposed the continuation of the 5:5:3 ratio and gave her statutory two years' notice to end the Washington and London Treaties (August 1934).

The twin aims of Japanese naval arms limitation negotiations in the mid 1930s, under Naval Minister Osumi, were to win parity with the US and British fleets and to limit the threat of the US fleet. Thus they sought a continued decrease in ship type sizes and main armaments which would entail less strain on the Japanese economy when matching US shipbuilding.

The Navy was also aware that US plans to advance across the Pacific and her ability to mount air attacks on vulnerable Japanese cities depended to a large extent on her carrier aviation, hence the determination to match US carrier building. At the Geneva Naval Conference of 1932, the Japanese delegation even proposed that 'offensive' naval warships (battleships and carriers) be scrapped, and suggested abolishing or limiting the numbers and sizes of warships essential to any advance by the US and/or Royal Navies across the Pacific.

At the second London Conference in 1934 the same bargaining point, the abolition of 'offensive' weapons, which it was now clear would not be accepted, was again posed in an attempt to split the British and Americans. The problem was that neither the British nor the Americans, with commitments in the Atlantic and elsewhere that Japan did not have, felt that they could concede the naval parity that the Japanese desired. However, the increasing Japanese militarism at this time also put great pressure on the Navy Minister not to accept continuing naval inferiority under the Naval Treaties even if that meant the end of continuing limitation of US building.

Matters came to a head at the second London Conference. The leader (Yamamoto, a member of the Treaty Faction) of the Japanese delegation in the negotiating phase, within his instructions imposed by the Fleet Faction, sought some compromise (on common limits) to prevent a naval race which Japan could not win, but his orders to insist on parity with Great Britain and the USA prevented any deal.

Given their own economic and international situation, the British were sympathetic to limiting construction, but they were facing a resurgent Germany and Italy and could not allow any further erosion of their already inadequate margin of safety in the east. With their greater resources, the Americans could afford to refuse parity to the Japanese and were very aware of their already inferior strategic position in the Western Pacific.

The Japanese delegation (under Admiral O. Nagano) continued to insist on parity and to try to split the British and Americans. They hoped to achieve parity by the reduction of all type totals down to Japanese tonnage levels on the basis of the abolition or limitation of 'offensive' naval weapons (capital ships, carriers and heavy cruisers), while submarine tonnage ('defensive') would remain the same, allowing a Japanese increase of 50 per cent. When this was rejected Nagano and his delegation, under Osumi's orders, withdrew.

A new Treaty was signed by Great Britain, France and the USA, with Germany, the USSR and Italy eventually joining, to continue building limitations until 1942. However, there were let-out clauses in case Japan did not join, and she, although given the chance, did not agree to a further extension of the Washington Treaty. The clauses were invoked in March 1938 as a consequence of suspected secret Japanese naval programmes. The Japanese insistence on parity merely undermined the limitation process and, because of distrust of their plans and building, started the very naval arms race the Treaty Faction knew Japan could not win. Thus war was brought closer.

From the summer of 1934 Navy Minister Osumi also began a purge, from their posts and the Navy, of members of the Treaty Faction, including Admirals Sakonji (former Vice-Minister) and Hori (former Chief Naval Affairs) who were deemed responsible for the London Treaty fiasco. This was very significant because many of the ablest, more moderate, Western-oriented senior officers were retired and were not available for the key posts of Naval Minister, Vice-Minister and Naval Affairs in the crucial years of 1939 to 1941 when pressure for an alliance with Germany was at its height.

Thus the Navy's stand against an Axis alliance, which would provoke further Anglo–American rearmament, co-operation and trade embargoes (affecting 80 per cent of the raw materials so vital to naval armament), was critically undermined by lack of moderate leadship. By the mid 1930s the Fleet Faction began to find allies in middle-ranking officers who were pro-German since Japan, after the end of the Anglo–Japanese Treaty of 1922, had turned to Germany for technical and training assistance and many of these officers trained there.

At the same time the Army was increasingly dominating national politics. On 26 February 1936 an attempted *coup* by young Army officers, although suppressed, saw the end of the government of naval veteran Prime Minister Okada and a succession of governments coerced or dominated by the Army. By refusing to accept appointments as War Minister it prevented the formation of Cabinets it did not like. Assassination was also a constant threat for its opponents.

Ironically, in line with protocol, Osumi resigned with the Okada government. His successor as Navy Minister, the weak Nagano, only lasted a year due to the fall of the new Hirota Cabinet in May 1937. This brought together the team of Admirals M. Yonai (Navy Minister), Yamamoto (Vice-Minister appointed by Nagano) and S. Inoue (Naval Affairs) who sought to unite the Navy. They were staunch in their opposition to the Army's plans for a Tripartite Pact with Germany and Italy which they considered would merely antagonise the Americans and British, while gaining minimal naval help in the Pacific. They resisted any such moves until the Navy's building programmes were ready.

Yonai had to resign as Minister in August 1939 together with the extremist Premier Baron Hiranuma whose pro-German policy was discredited by the Molotov–Ribbentrop Pact. This pact and Yonai's short term as Prime Minister (January–July 1940) briefly halted all thoughts of an alliance with Germany, but his administration was soon brought down by the Army. Moreover, in August 1939, rather than propose Yamamoto as his successor, Yonai appointed him CinC Combined Fleets since he was the militarists' Number One Enemy and his life was in great danger. Also Yonai went on the retired list when he became Prime Minister. Thus the Treaty Faction's staunchest leaders had quit the Navy Ministry.

Yonai's successor as Navy Minister was Admiral Z. Yoshida, lately CinC, who continued his policy. But Yoshida, like Roger Backhouse, the British First Sea Lord, was an arch centraliser and over-worked. At the same time pressure for an alliance with Germany increased steadily with the German victories in Europe and the collapse of British and French naval power in the Far East which persuaded the Army that a strike in the Southern Area against European colonies would solve the pressing problem of raw materials and dependence on the British and Americans for them.

Navy Minister Yoshida continued to want no confrontation with the Western Powers until the Navy's Third Replenishment Plan was completed in 1942, but he became virtually a lone figure fighting the Pact. The new Government of Prince Konoe was dominated by the War Minister (General H. Tojo) and nationalist Foreign Minister (M. Yosuke) who argued that the Axis alliance would restrain the USA from intervening in Europe and thus prevent war with Japan.

As a consequence of the Osumi purges and the absence of Yonai (retired) and Yamamoto (with the fleet), Yoshida had second-rate officers in key posts such as Vice-Minister T. Sumiyama who was not a fighter or master of the press like Yamamoto. Moreover, many of the pro-German middle rank officers were now reaching influential positions in the Ministry and Staff. Stressed and overworked, Yoshida suffered a nervous breakdown on 3 September 1940 and was replaced on the 6th.

Within days the Navy had agreed to the Tripartite Pact with Germany and Italy which was signed on 27 September

IJNS *Soryu* (1937), the first of the second-generation Japanese carriers, designed under Washington Treaty rules with double hangars to accommodate a large air group of about 70 aircraft. (IWM)

1940, although with a clause which allowed Japan to avoid war with the USA if possible. This was due partly to the growing influence of middle rank officers who had trained or served in Germany, but in the main it reflected the collapse of Navy Ministry opposition.

The new Navy Minister, Admiral K. Oikawa, was a scholarly, non-political officer who had not served in the senior posts of the Ministry. A weak character, he was willing to co-operate with the Army. However, as a former Chief of the Aeronautics Department he did represent an increase in air influence. He thought that continued naval opposition would only lead to a confrontation with the Army.

His Vice-Minister, T. Toyoda, though very pro-Royal Navy, was also ambitious and thus allied with the prevailing opinion. Admiral K. Abe (Naval Affairs Bureau) also lacked political skills and was pro-German. These men were not strong enough to stand up to the prevailing pro-German mood conditioned by co-operation with the

German Navy since the 1920s and the German victories in Europe. Other factors were the Foreign Ministry's assurance that the Pact would restrain the Americans and allow Japan to pick its moment; fear of missing the 'window of opportunity' to acquire Western possessions in the Southern Area (South East Asia); and fear that continued confrontation with the Army would result in civil war or a reduction of resources for naval programmes if the Navy did not support the Army's priorities.

For the Army the Tripartite Pact was just the preliminary to a move south to gain the raw materials required for its war machine in China. This meant operations to seize Malaya (rubber, etc.) and the Dutch East Indies (oil). For the Navy, however, this would mean war with the USA as well as with Great Britain for which it was not ready. Moreover, US oil supplies would be cut off. The Navy knew that it had to reduce its dependence on US oil supplies and sought to do so in the winter of 1940/41 by negotiating an oil agreement with the Dutch East Indies.

The Navy Minister therefore held out against any operations in the south that would provoke the British and Americans. In the meantime the Army negotiated a neutrality pact with the Soviet Union (April 1941) to protect its Manchurian frontier during the

IJNS *Hiryu* (1939) was the second of the *Soryu* class but improved and larger. Her freeboard was also increased following the fleet's experience with storms in 1935. She was sunk at Midway. (IWM)

southern advance. In the same month negotiations were opened with the USA through the new Ambassador, Admiral K. Nomura, to avert war with her.

Events came to a head in June when negotiations with the Dutch and Americans broke down, the US cut back oil exports because of home shortages and Germany invaded Russia. The Army, still embroiled in China, was in no position to take advantage of the opportunity to strike at the Soviet menace. Moreover, the foundations of the services' ability to continue the war in China or even defend the nation was being undermined by failure to provide a safe supply of raw materials especially oil. The southern advance, whether by negotiation or war, was now seen as crucial to national defence.

In order to pre-empt the Free French, acquire bases and coerce the Dutch, it was decided to occupy French Indo-China in July. The result was to provoke the American, British and Dutch trade embargo so greatly feared. The Army now argued that unless the negotiations succeeded war was inevitable because Japan must seize the necessary raw materials before its stocks (18 months at most for oil) ran out.

The Navy, although wishing to avoid war, was now also preparing for it. The embargoes on raw materials also affected its operations and shipbuilding programme (Fifth Replenishment Plan) designed to maintain 70 per cent of the US Fleet which was expanding under the Third Vinson Act and the Stark Plan. Agreement had to be reached with the Dutch and Americans or Japan must go to war before its raw material stockpiles ran out. Contingency plans were therefore put in place. November and December were the most favourable months for war in the Pacific, and extensive preparations, including the requisitioning of 265 merchant ships, were made.

In September the Cabinet and Imperial Conference agreed on war unless negotiations with USA succeeded. Premier Konoe and Foreign Minister Admiral T. Toyoda favoured continuing diplomatic negotiations and a withdrawal from China to achieve agreement with the Americans. Navy Minister Oikawa decided to support them because he felt that China was not worth a war with the USA. However, at a crucial meeting on 12 October he was equivocal and failed to support Konoe whole-heartedly.

Firm naval support, backed by the threat of resignation from the Cabinet, might have stopped the slide into war. However, Oikawa thought Konoe too weak to control the Army and feared an Army *coup d'état*. Above all the Navy itself was deeply divided. The new (April 1941) Chief of the Naval Staff, Nagano, was not a strong character and was soon under the influence of middle-ranking officers who were pro-Pact, prowar and pro co-operation with the Army. He thought war inevitable and that Japan must move while raw materials lasted and the US, British and Dutch Navies were relatively weak.

Pro-war officers were steadily taking over the key posts in the Navy Ministry and Naval Staff. Moreover, in December 1940, with the growing crisis, the Naval National Defence Policy Committee was created to liaise between the staff and Ministry to expedite mobilisation and readiness in case of war. It in turn created four committees of which the First Committee was responsible for planning and liaison with all departments and the Army.

This First Committee came to be dominated by officers who thought war was inevitable and that Japan should strike when her building programmes were almost complete (giving 75 per cent of the US fleet) and before the USA could complete the Vinson re-armament programme and draw out of sight again. The influence of the First Committee spread to the Section Chiefs' Conferences, of the Navy Ministry and Naval Staff which often met together, and by the summer of 1941 they were in favour of war.

Konoe's support for withdrawal from China caused Tojo (War Minister) to bring down the government and he headed the next Cabinet (17 October) as both Premier and War Minister. Because of Oikawa's lack of support for him, Tojo stated that the former's choice for Navy Minister (the able S. Toyoda who thought war with the USA was unrealistic and had little time for the Army) was not acceptable. Instead Admiral S. Shimada, a weak man who favoured co-operation with the Army, was appointed. He co-operated so closely with the Army that he was often referred to as 'Tojo's lackey'. Under Shimada and Nagano the pro-war faction took complete control, most naval officers now saw war as being inevitable and the focus was on preparation.

The significance of Tojo's appointment was not lost on the British and Americans. It led the British in October to despatch Force Z (*Prince of Wales* and *Repulse*) to Singapore as a deterrent, and Secretary of State Cordell Hull to insist on 26 November, during the continuing negotiations, that Japan withdraw from China and Indo-China and revoke the Tripartite Pact.

This ended any last hopes of negotiation, chiefly continued due to the Emperor's request to explore every avenue, and the Army and Navy (Shimada and Nagano) agreed that there was no alternative to war except complete withdrawal from China. The Army would not contemplate this and on 2 December it was agreed that war should begin on the 8th.

At face value the Fleet Faction had won and forced a hard-line response to American and British demands. Naval Ministers Oikawa and Shimada lacked the strength of character to oppose the Army and the general war mood in the nation and the Navy's middle ranks. They also feared that the Army's will would be imposed by a *coup* anyway and that the Navy would lose its influence.

The problem was that most senior naval officers knew that the Navy could only fight a short war because of superior American resources and the paucity of Japan's reserves of raw materials. The widespread confidence of victory was based on the German defeat of the British Army in France and successes in Russia, wishful thinking about the Americans becoming tired of a war and belief in the superiority of the tactics, strategy, *matériel* and personnel of the Japanese fleet.

Yamamoto, as CinC Combined Fleet from August 1939, had to devise a viable strategy against the US fleet despite having sought to avoid war with the USA which he knew, from three visits in the 1920s, Japan could not win. Moreover, after the signing of the Tripartite Pact in September 1940, he had little faith that the politicians could prevent war. He calculated that the Navy would prevail for six months to a year, but that the US Navy would win in the second and third years because of massive industrial strength.

Traditionally Japan's Navy pursued a defensive strategy whereby it covered the Army's operations and defended the homeland, but because of the relative weakness of the fleet this strategy could only be pursued through offensive tactics. Thus Japan won the Sino–Japanese War (1894–95) chiefly as a result of the decisive battle off the Yalu River. Under the Treaty of Shimonosiki Japan was to have received Korea, Formosa, Shantung, Liaotung and other areas. However, the Western Powers refused to agree and under the guise of long-term leases robbed Japan, whose navy was still inferior to theirs, of its territorial rewards. The Europeans took the coastal enclaves with their trade and strategic positions. Russia had Liaotung (Dairen), Great Britain Shantung, Portugal Macao and France Kwangchowan. It was clear that to ensure its own defence and place in China, Japan had to have military power and especially a fleet able to hold its own with the Western Powers.

Japan had looked to Great Britain to modernise the Navy in the 1870s and the British were the major suppliers of the warships which allowed the Navy to take on the Chinese and Russians. The Anglo–Japanese alliance of 1902, renewed in 1905 and 1911, gave the Japanese great technical and other assistance, plus an ally which ensured that it need not expect to be faced by two hostile Western navies at the same time. The defeat of Russia (again, mainly as a result of a single decisive battle – Tsushima) saw the Japanese recognised as a major naval power, although still some way from being a premier power.

The preoccupation of the Western Powers during the Great War, especially that of Japan's main ally Great Britain with the German threat, created a vacuum in the Far East which Japan filled. In 1914 it took the chance to seize the German possessions in China and the Central Pacific. At the same time Japan did little to help Great Britain in Europe until 1917 when it agreed to send destroyers to the Mediterranean to escort convoys. The demise of the German fleet left Japan, which had been building up its maritime strength, with the third largest fleet. Parity with the Royal Navy and the US Navy would ensure that its ambitions in the Far East could not again be interfered with.

However, as long as the Japanese Navy was allowed only 60 per cent of these navies under the Washington and London Treaties, there was the problem of how to defend Japan with a weaker fleet when the USA was usually considered to be the likely enemy. Given the US Navy's need to despatch a fleet to the Western Pacific, to defend the Philippines and attack Japan, the Navy again planned an essentially defensive strategy combined with very offensive tactics.

Light forces and aircraft would undertake a steady attrition of the US fleet until the two fleets were approximately equal in capital ships, and the cruisers would then encircle and ambush the enemy in a decisive battle. As with Royal Navy (fleet to Singapore) and US Navy (fleet to the Pacific) planning, this strategic plan was modified and simulated in exercises over a long period and became almost gospel to the planners, however unlikely it was that it could be executed.

The difficulty was that with the adoption of the policy to secure the raw materials of the Southern Area (Dutch East Indies, Malaya, Philippines and Indo-China) the fleet also had to transport and cover the forces for these operations. Yamamoto feared that the US fleet would advance to the relief of the Philippines and both cut the lines of supply to the Japanese forces in the Southern Area and attack his covering forces in their flank. He thought it unlikely that the US fleet would follow the Naval Staff's wishful thinking and over-optimistic planning and advance into a trap off the Japanese coast.

Initially Yamamoto decided to advance the proposed area for the decisive battle from the Bonins–Marianas, to the Carolines–Marshalls and then to the Hawaii area (where the US fleet moved from San Diego in 1940). This was to keep the US fleet busy and bar it from the Southern Area during operations there. However, in November 1940 Yamamoto decided to carry the war to the US fleet in or outside Pearl Harbor.

His plan, which he had been considering since spring, was for a pre-emptive carrier strike on the US fleet at night or dawn to cripple it at the start of any war; to keep it busy during the Japanese advance into the Southern Area; to ensure that it did not have the heavy units necessary for an advance across the Pacific; and to undermine the Americans' will to continue the war. This required a refocus from the traditional defensive strategy and tactics which relied on attrition to overtly offensive ones which sought to knock the enemy fleet out right at the start.

Fleet Strategy and Tactics, 1900–1945

From medieval experience, British naval tradition and the successes at the Yalu and Tsushima, the Japanese Navy embraced whole-heartedly the concepts of taking the offensive whenever possible and the decisive fleet battle. These suited the Japanese temperament. Their fleet made every effort to prepare for offensive operations designed to lead to a decisive battle with the enemy, despite his superiority in numbers, which would end the naval war quickly. Thus in the modern era careful preparation and rigorous training was emphasised.

As in the Royal and US Navies, the battleship was seen as the key to winning a decisive battle and the majority of senior Japanese naval officers continued to believe in the primacy of the battleship; aircraft were seen as essentially an auxiliary weapon. This classic concept was reflected in the formation of the Combined Fleet which centred on battleships. The idea that they would be replaced by the Naval Air Corps was regarded by many as blasphemy. One Japanese admiral, Z. Yoshida (CinC as late as 1937–39), even refused to fly in aircraft.

IJNS *Zuiho* (1940), a good example of the Imperial Japanese Navy's 'shadow' programme (she was laid down as a depot ship but converted before being finished). Note the absence of an island and the downward funnel. (IWM)

However, with their fleet still expanding and inferior in numbers to those of the Western Powers, the Navy developed two methods to implement the 'ambush' strategy. The first was attritional warfare by light forces to whittle down a superior enemy fleet before the decisive battle. For this the Navy developed the Long Lance long-range, high-speed 24-inch torpedo (Type 93), submarines, midget submarines and naval aircraft for the land bases in the Central Pacific.

In the Russo–Japanese War Togo's staff before Tsushima planned night attacks by torpedo-craft before the fleet action. After the Washington Treaty (which established the 5:5:3 fleet ratios) the Navy expected to meet either the British or US fleets advancing towards Japan from Singapore or Pearl Harbor. The strategy was therefore to hold the perimeter until night torpedo attacks by cruisers and destroyers, supplemented by submarines and aircraft, had given the Japanese fleet near parity for a decisive battle.

In the strategy to whittle down the enemy, fleet aircraft were to play their part, but as the Navy had the same ratio disadvantage in carriers as in battleships, it looked to land-based aircraft to overwhelm the enemy carriers. Command of the air would then give the fleet a key advantage in the action. The idea was to use the Central Pacific

Mandate islands as 'unsinkable carriers' with the land-based aircraft flying between them to locate and mount a pre-emptive strike.

Thus the Navy, while, like its rivals, placing the main emphasis on battleships, sought to develop aviation and to assimilate carriers into fleet tactics to ensure air command for scouting and spotting. However, it also saw aviation as another means, with torpedoes and submarines, to whittle down superior battle lines.

In order to make these plans effective the fleet placed great emphasis on out-ranging the enemy. Thus it steadily developed torpedoes culminating in the 1930s with the long-range oxygen torpedo which gave its submarines and destroyers' night attacks greater punch. This concept was also adopted to give it the edge in the decisive gunnery duel. The Navy therefore consistently developed the largest guns in the world, starting with the 14-inch of the *Kongo* in 1914, through the 16-inch of the *Nagato* class in 1921 to the 18-inch of the *Yamato*. This allowed them to push the range of their opening salvoes from 38,000 yards (1938) to 45,000 yards (1941).

Despite these preparations the Navy realised it might still enter the decisive battle with inferior forces. It therefore sought to give itself the edge not only in the quality and range of its equipment but also in the superior training of its personnel. Thus during the inter-war period the Combined Fleet conducted unremitting training in all weathers and under war conditions, aiming at the highest proficiency.

From February to April the Fleet engaged in ship and squadron training and from June to October it came together for training. Both periods culminated in war games at the Naval War College and manoeuvres with opposing fleets. The 'China Incident' cut this to only one period (November–December) but gave invaluable combat experience. From 1929 great emphasis was placed on night actions, especially of torpedo-craft, including aircraft, to whittle the enemy down and after the mid 1930s even for a fleet action. In 1939 Yamamoto intensified training, and gunnery efficiency increased from a 12 per cent hitting rate to an unprecedented 20–25 per cent. In 1941 the fleet was actively preparing for a possible war.

Naval aviation was expected to provide cover for the fleet plus scouting and spotting (from carriers) and to help 'equalise' the two fleets (from land bases). For the latter role torpedo attacks and high-level bombing were emphasised, but dive-bombing was ignored until quite late. In the manoeuvres of the 1930s the carriers were dispersed among the fleet units primarily to provide air cover and, like the US fleet, to prevent the carriers being lost to one enemy strike. However, this meant that it was difficult to mount effective mass air strikes on enemy targets and the battleships were still expected to be the main strike power in the decisive battle.

For air striking power to help whittle down the enemy fleet the emphasis was placed on land-based naval aviation. Great advances were made on this front when Yamamoto was Head of Technical Division (1930–33) and Chief of Naval Aeronautics (1935–36). His policy was based on producing the long-range aircraft vital to the Navy's plans to use Formosa and the Pacific islands as bases for air strikes against the advancing US fleet. From Lindberg's solo flight of 1927, while he was Naval Attaché in Washington, Yamamoto realised that long flights between islands (to mass aircraft at the crucial point) and air strikes were now possible.

His policy, plus the deficiencies shown at Shanghai, led to a determined effort to upgrade naval aviation by 1937 under the First Replenishment Programme. Further programmes meant that by 1941 the Japanese Naval Air Arm was a match for that of her Western rivals. For land-based operations the Navy had put into production a team of long-range aircraft: the Mitsubishi G3M 'Nell' torpedo-bomber (1936); Mitsubishi G4M 'Betty' medium bomber (1941); Kawanishi H6K4 'Mavis' long-range maritime reconnaissance flying boat (1938); and Mitsubishi A6M Zero ('Zeke') fighter escort (1940).

Even at the start of the 'China Incident' the First Combined Air Force, based on Taiwan, could launch a 1,200-mile strike across the East China Sea to destroy most of the Chinese air force in August 1937. In 1941 all land-based aircraft were concentrated under the Eleventh Air Fleet (Admiral N. Tsukahara) and assigned the important roles of the attrition of any British (from Singapore) or US (San Diego) advance in the Pacific and in securing the Southern Area. Carrier aviation until that year was still tied to the battle line. However, the prospect of war by the end of the year rapidly changed this.

In 1939 the Naval Staff's plans (tested during the Naval War College war games) still followed the formalised, defensive policy whereby Japan would seize the Southern Area and the enemy fleet (American) would advance into the Western Pacific to the rescue and even up to Japanese waters where inner lines of communications would give the Japanese Navy the advantage in a decisive battle. During the enemy's advance, light forces, submarines and land-based aviation would effect the attritional phase of the plan to ensure that the Japanese entered the battle on equal terms. The fleet's carriers were to cover the battle fleet, knock out the enemy carriers and spot for the fleet's guns.

When considering an offensive strategy against the US fleet off Hawaii, Yamamoto saw carrier air power as the main means of eliminating the US strike power which it would need in order to advance across the Pacific. In this he was encouraged by the intensive training of his carrier-based aviation culminating in very successful air strikes, especially with torpedoes, during the manoeuvres of autumn 1940.

Also on 11 November British carrier aircraft had successfully attacked the Italian Fleet at Taranto where the shallow anchorages, similar to those at Pearl Harbor, posed a problem for torpedo attacks. Commander M. Genda, the new Air Staff Officer CarDiv1, also realised in late 1940 that the concentration of the carriers into one unit would require fewer defensive fighters and allow the launch of massive air strikes. Yamamoto therefore decided to continue fleet training and exercises with the carriers, on the centralisation of the carriers under the First Air Fleet (December 1940), and ordered preliminary planning for an air attack on the US fleet (January 1941).

The Development of Japanese Carriers

Given the explosion of Japanese carrier air power up to mid 1942, and Japanese industrial might post-war, it is easy to forget that Japanese industrial and maritime power was still a very recent growth in 1941. Naval aviation was even younger. The Treaty Faction were correct to assume that Japan did not have the breadth and above all the depth of industrial power to meet the US Navy on equal terms.

By securing foreign technical and training assistance the IJN was able to develop its air arm rapidly and by 1941 was the equal of the Americans and ahead of the British. However, this was achieved by specialisation and maximising its resources. As Yamamoto well knew, the carrier force of 1942 represented almost the peak of Japanese armament whereas the Americans had only just begun to re-arm. The Navy was an élite force designed to win a short war because the Japanese economy could not sustain a long war. Also, unlike the British, who received US escort carriers, aircraft and personnel training, the Navy could not rely on any assistance from its German or Italian allies both of whom had neglected carrier aviation.

In line with their determination to match the Western Powers in military capabilities, the Japanese were not slow to develop aircraft. The first interest in aviation had been in balloons. In 1876 the Navy's first hot air balloon was built at the Naval Training College and two larger balloons were built the following year, though not deployed, for use against the Satsuma rebels.

The Army continued its balloon development and at the start of the war with Russia ordered two kite balloons, designed by Isaburo Yamada. These were sent to the siege of Port Arthur and on 9 August 1904 the commander of the naval siege guns (T. Kuroi) went up in a balloon to spot for his 4.7-inch guns against the Russian battleships. *Peresviet* and *Retvizan* were both hit and the latter's speed reduced during the Battle of Tsushima. This was the first damage inflicted on a warship by aerial means, albeit indirectly.

The severe strain placed on the economy by the war with Russia prevented further developments until, encouraged by the use of these limited balloons, the Provisional Military Balloon Research Society in 1910 sent Army officers (they made the first aircraft flights in Japan in December), and in 1911 the first naval officer (Lieutenant Yozo Kaneko to France), to Europe for pilot training.

Senior naval officers also watched an exhibition (May 1911) of a Curtiss seaplane, flown by stunt pilot William Attwater. As a result in June 1912 the Navy formed a research committee, authorised construction of an airfield at Tokyo Bay and officially sent three lieutenants to France and another two to Glen Curtiss's school for training. One of the latter was Lieutenant Chikuhei Nakajima, the founder of Nakajima Aircraft.

The influence of France, which had invested heavily in aviation, was very strong. The Navy purchased two Maurice Farmans and an American Curtiss seaplane. In November 1912 the pilots began flights in Japan, from a field near the Yokosuka naval

Members of the British Naval Air Mission to Japan with Parnall Panthers. They helped Japan's rapid progress in the 1920s, although opposed by the Royal and US Navies. (IWM)

base, and flew over a fleet review at Yokohama. The Farmans were preferred and indigenous manufacture was begun.

As early as the end of 1911 the French had fitted-out a vessel to operate seaplanes and the British followed suit in 1913. The Japanese were at a comparable stage to the British. In the autumn of 1913 the naval transport *Wakamiya Maru* (launched 1901) was fitted with two seaplanes to accompany the attacking fleet on manoeuvres (October–November). Like the British *Hermes* in July 1913, she was fitted with canvas hangars forward and aft and booms to lift out the seaplanes. The defending fleet had a shore-based seaplane. After the exercises the ship returned to her normal duties.

With the outbreak of war in 1914, the Japanese, acting as Great Britain's allies, seized the chance to occupy German territories in the Far East. On 1 September operations began against Kiaochow in China, and *Wakamiya Maru* joined the 2nd Squadron. On 17 August she was refitted as a seaplane tender with improved Maurice Farman seaplanes (four, two dismantled). The first flight was made on 5 September followed by scouting flights and an unsuccessful attempt to bomb German and Austrian warships on 27 November. However, a minelayer was sunk with bombs made from shells. There was also an inconclusive fight with a German aircraft.

On 30 September the carrier was damaged by a mine and had to return to Sasebo for repair, her aircraft being transferred to a beach base. In December 1914 the naval air arm returned home in the carrier. On 1 June 1915 she was re-rated as an aircraft depot ship, attached to Yokosuka naval air station, and renamed *Wakamiya*.

For the remainder of the war the Navy was mainly employed on escort duties. Thus the only other Japanese vessel to carry aircraft during the war was the auxiliary cruiser *Chikezen Maru*, which carried two seaplanes during a search for a German commerce raider in the Indian Ocean in October 1917.

However, the Navy continued to keep abreast of British naval aviation and, like the US Navy, sent several observers, one of them aboard the carrier *Furious*. Experiments were then made in flying from gun turret platforms on capital ships as in the Grand Fleet. Through experience with the seaplane carrier *Wakamiya Maru* and information from the British about their carrier design, the Navy quickly perceived the importance of aircraft carriers. One of the lessons of war had been that a modern fleet had to include naval aviation. Thus the building of two carriers to operate aeroplanes was authorised in the 8–6 Fleet Completion Programme of 1918.

By the end of the war Japan had twenty capital ships plus four *Kaga* battleships and four *Akagi* battlecruisers under construction. Post-war the main goal was equality with the greatest powers which, after the demise of the German fleet, meant parity with Great Britain and the USA, and throughout the inter-war years the Navy was determined to match them.

As a result of British and American building programmes the Japanese Diet in 1920 accepted a plan to provide 27 modern capital ships by 1927. The '8–8' Fleet Replenishment Programme of 1920 was to provide eight new battleships and eight new battlecruisers, plus two aircraft carriers of 12,500 tons. This would give the Navy three carriers of 34,500 tons in total. Like the US Navy, the IJN was also impressed by the British lead in naval aviation and they asked their allies for technical assistance in 1920.

The Admiralty, led by First Sea Lord Beatty, was opposed to any aid to Japan which 'might become a considerable menace in the Far East', but the Foreign Office and Air Ministry disagreed. The semi-official mission, of some thirty ex-RNAS officers under Colonel Sir William Sempill RAF, was therefore sent to Japan from 1921 to 1923 to train the earliest Japanese naval aviators, Sempill being given the rank of Captain in the IJN.

Other British naval aviators, such as F. J. Rutland, who had flown at Jutland, and design teams from Shorts and Sopwith, were also employed by Japanese companies, especially Mitsubishi, to develop successful naval and carrier aircraft. This aid to Japan while doing nothing to improve Anglo–US relations saved the Japanese much time and effort in their endeavours to catch up the Americans and the British. Rutland was imprisoned by the British authorities throughout the Second World War because of his Japanese connections.

Assistance was given to the Japanese in every area, from training to design details for their first carrier. As with the American *Langley*, it was decided to convert a trials carrier before building the two projected carriers. On 19 December 1919, *Hosho* (7,470 tons) had been laid down as (contrary to many reports) a tanker.

Launched in November 1921 and fitted out with British aid on the lines of *Hermes*, she was in fact completed first (December 1922), but was not, as often claimed, designed from the start as an aircraft carrier. *Hosho*, flew off and landed her first aircraft on 22 February 1923, only a few months after the Americans' first landing on *Langley*. Her role was to pioneer flying off and on to decks and deck training, and her equipment included British-type longitudinal arrester gear.

The Sempill Mission reported that the Japanese naval aviation officers were technically and operationally backward and reliant on Western technology and their senior officers were ignorant of aviation. The IJN at this time would order single items of equipment or acquire drawings and then produce copies from them, as well as sending large inspection staffs to shipyards and factories to learn as much as possible about the latest techniques and designs. This caused the Royal Navy to go to some lengths to ensure that their latest carrier, *Furious*, undergoing conversion as a flush deck carrier, was not seen by Japanese officers.

The British and Americans persisted in the view that the Japanese were merely poor copyists of Western technology well into the 1930s, and this underestimation, exacerbated by Japanese secrecy, would cost them dear in Malaya and at Pearl Harbor. In fact the Japanese naval air arm, building rapidly on the foundations of the Sempill Mission, was making great strides.

The development of the air arm as an integral part of the Navy was never in doubt, but as in the Royal and US Navies there was considerable debate as to whether aviation could develop from an auxiliary to an offensive role. Such was the influence of the 'battleship school' upon the IJN and its construction programmes, that Japan was the only naval power to build large battleships with 18-inch guns.

As a result of the Washington Treaty limitations the IJN knew that it was allowed (if it built up to the full Treaty tonnage and totals) a maximum naval strength for Japan's defence of nine battleships, three carriers, 40 cruisers, 144 destroyers and 70 submarines plus aircraft groups which were counted as front-line ships. Thus the Auxiliary Replenishment Programme of 1924 proposed building one aircraft carrier (27,000 tons) and three aircraft supply ships (10,000 tons each). This programme was not carried out because of the great cost and budgetary restraints.

However, under the Treaty's provisions those nations which had to scrap capital ships could convert two of them to carriers. The Japanese, like the Americans, chose to convert two fast battlecruisers (30-knot *Amagi* class) of which *Akagi* and *Amagi*, both laid down on 6 December 1920, were the most complete. They were of similar size (41,200 tons, ten 16-inch) to the *Lexington*s (ordered for conversion in November 1922). Work began in late 1923. *Akagi* (26,900 tons, 60 aircraft) was commissioned in March 1927, but *Amagi* was scrapped after incurring severe damage in the earthquake of September 1923.

Rather than convert another sister, of which two more were available, she was replaced (because the sisters were less complete and on grounds of economy) by the battleship *Kaga* (39,900 tons) which was completed to the same design. Officially commissioned in March 1928, she was not fully operational until 1930.

Despite the efforts of the British to keep her design secret, the Japanese had followed closely *Furious*'s flush deck design (with three rather than two flight decks). However, *Kaga* was first installed with a French-designed athwartship arrester gear which was also fitted in *Akagi* in 1931. This brought Japanese operating methods ahead of those of the British and on a par with the Americans' especially as the displacement of *Amagi* and *Akagi* was greater than that declared.

Carrier policy was for a steady construction programme which would build up to the Treaty limits but not develop a naval race with the USA. In March 1928 the Naval General Staff decided that the IJN needed four front-line carriers to match proposed US Navy carrier building. At that time the fleet had the *Wakamiya* (re-rated as an aircraft carrier in April 1920 and fitted with a forward flight deck for fighters), *Hosho*, *Akagi* and *Kaga*. But *Wakamiya* was clearly not a modern carrier and was to be replaced. The problem was what type of carrier to build.

As the most likely hypothetical enemy was the USA, it was decided that the Navy should have the same number of carriers as the US Navy, despite its having a larger

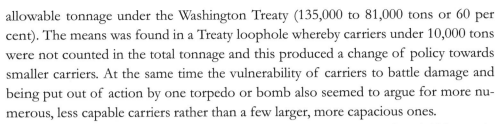

IJNS *Shokaku* (1941), the best of the Japanese carriers. She had enclosed hangars, following British practice, which allowed a build-up of avgas vapour which was disastrous when she was hit. (IWM)

allowable tonnage under the Washington Treaty (135,000 to 81,000 tons or 60 per cent). The means was found in a Treaty loophole whereby carriers under 10,000 tons were not counted in the total tonnage and this produced a change of policy towards smaller carriers. At the same time the vulnerability of carriers to battle damage and being put out of action by one torpedo or bomb also seemed to argue for more numerous, less capable carriers rather than a few larger, more capacious ones.

It was believed, erroneously in retrospect, that small carriers under 10,000 tons, in the trend set by the British *Hermes*, could operate with the fleet carrier and enable the US carrier numbers to be matched. This led to the building of the light carrier *Ryujo* (7,100 tons, 36 aircraft), classed by the Treaty as a seaplane carrier, under the New Shipbuilding Replenishment Programme of 1927. She was laid down in 1929 and completed in 1933.

The original *Ryujo* design had one hangar which could only accommodate 30 aircraft, so a second hangar was added above (48 aircraft). This allowed no protection or armour and affected stability. Thus in 1934–36 she was lengthened and bulged and her displacement increased to 10,800 tons. This in turn increased her draught and she had to have further modifications to raise her forecastle.

Another way to circumvent the Treaty limitation on carrier tonnage was to build flight-deck cruisers because these were not classed as carriers. Under the Washington Treaty only vessels laid down before November 1921 could be replaced before the obligatory replacement age. This meant that *Wakamiya* and *Hosho* could be scrapped and 20,100 tons was available for more carriers. Under the 1931/32 First Naval Armament Replenishment Programme, which consisted of cruisers and smaller vessels to be built between 1931 and 1935, one carrier (9,800 tons) was included and plans were drawn up for a flight-deck cruiser (designed with six 8-inch guns).

However, the US Navy under Moffett was also planning to build flight-deck cruisers, to circumvent the Treaty, and this threatened to more than annul any Japanese advantage in building many of these, given the United States' greater resources. The US delegation at the London Conference of 1930 stressed their legality. As a result Japan suggested that carriers of less than 10,000 tons and flight-deck cruisers should be included in carrier tonnage which was agreed. This Conference also extended the Washington Treaty, with Japan's reluctant agreement, to heavy cruisers (60 per cent of US and British totals), light cruisers and destroyers (both 70 per cent) and submarines (parity).

Thus the flight-deck cruiser of the First Naval Armament Replenishment Programme was cancelled, but Japan still had the problem of providing the same number of carriers as the Americans on a smaller tonnage. In 1934, before the First was completed, the larger Second Naval Armament Replenishment Programme was instituted. It added a second carrier and three seaplane carriers (designed for rapid conversion to light carriers within three months). Thus Japan sought to provide for fast carrier expansion when war seemed imminent.

The *Soryu* class (*Soryu* 15,900 tons, 71 aircraft and *Hiryu* 17,300 tons, 73 aircraft) were laid down (1934 and 1936) and completed (January 1937 and July 1939) as a result of the Naval Armament Replenishment Programmes. The flight-deck cruiser (17,500 tons, six 8-inch guns in three turrets forward, flight-deck) became the basis of a complete re-design for the first modern Japanese carriers, because by now it was clear that the smaller carrier of the *Ryujo* type was not a success. They had an island, one flight-deck, double hangar, light structure and armour with cruiser machinery for speed and the cruiser armament replaced by 5in and 25mm dual-purpose AA guns.

The new design also meant that the two carriers exceeded the remaining carrier tonnage. However, *Soryu* alone did not infringe the Treaty and by the time *Hiryu* was completed it was planned that Japan would either have achieved parity with the USA at the second Conference of London (1936) or abrogated the Washington Treaty. *Hiryu* was an improved version, being lengthened and with better armour and oil bunkerage, and her forecastle was heightened because of storm experience in 1935.

At Geneva (1928) and London (1930, 1934–36) the Japanese delegations proposed to abolish carriers or severely limit their size. They knew of their importance to the US and Royal Navies for any advance into a Western Pacific dominated by Japanese land-based air power. Later, knowing that the abolition would not be accepted, they hoped to keep a limit on US carrier building.

Up to the end of 1936 these disarmament conferences produced profound problems for the IJN where they sought to attain a numerical equality in carriers with the US Navy on a smaller tonnage since parity was not agreed by the Americans or British. A plan was therefore adopted to convert merchant vessels rapidly on the outbreak of war to make up for the numerical disadvantage of the fleet. For carriers this meant the conversion of liners. This policy was based on that of the Royal Navy during the First World War which had developed the aircraft carrier by converting merchant ships including the old Cunard liner *Campania* and the unfinished Italian liner *Conte Rosso* (later *Argus*). It also followed a long Japanese tradition in other types.

During the Sino–Japanese (1894), Russo–Japanese (1905–06) and First World Wars the Japanese Government subsidised and encouraged the weak and inferior Japanese shipbuilding industry and the merchant marine to provide ships for national defence. The merchant marine grew rapidly from 160,000 tons in 1894 to 3,350,000 tons in 1921.

This was achieved mainly by the rapid development of Japanese shipbuilding, the expansion of the Navy and two laws passed by the Diet in 1896. The first subsidised Japanese owners to build ships in Japan and the second gave operating subsidies only for Japanese-built ships. With Japanese expansion into China it was part of the defence policy to have shipping available in an emergency for transporting and supplying troops, medium and large cargo ships and liners being the most suitable vessels. Furthermore, the largest and fastest liners would make the best carriers.

From 1926 the IJN demanded a speed of more than 20 knots and at least 15,000 tons for conversion to auxiliary carriers. The first liners so designated were the *Asama*

IJNS *Shoho* (1942), another product of the 'shadow' building programme and converted from the submarine depot ship *Tsurugisaki*. With one hangar her air group was small. She was sunk at Coral Sea. (IWM)

Maru class (*Asama Maru, Tatsuta* and *Titibu Maru,* later *Kamakura Maru,* 20.7 knots, 16,975 tons) subsidised by the Ministry of Transportation and commissioned in 1929 and 1930 for the San Francisco service. With war in December 1941 the Navy wanted to convert these vessels to carriers, but the shipyards were full of more modern conversions for the first year of war and by then all three had been sunk.

When the USA began the construction of large merchant ships, Japan responded with a law to subsidise first class merchant ships. In its first phase twelve liners were built of which five were designed for conversion to carriers. The *Nitta Maru* class (17,000 tons, 21 knots) were subsidised in 1931 for the Japanese Mail Steamship Company's (NYK) European service, and the *Argentina Maru* class (13,000 tons, 21 knots) for the Osaka Merchant Ship Company's (OSK) South American service in 1932.

All were designed to convert as carriers, although there were no visible special characteristics. Shortly before and after Pearl Harbor these vessels were converted as escort carriers: the *Nitta Maru*s as *Taiyo, Unyo* and *Chuyo* and the *Argentina Maru* as *Kaiyo.* The latter's only sister, *Brazil Maru,* was sunk before conversion could take place.

In 1933 the Navy worked with the NYK and the OSK to develop first class 24-knot liners for the North American service which could be converted to auxiliary carriers, but the project failed through lack of money. In 1935 the Navy and NYK

again collaborated on a plan to build three 24-knot cargo/passenger ships (carrier conversions) for the European route, but again money for the project was unavailable.

This was the time of great spending on a Shipping Improvement Programme (1932) which was a scrap and build policy designed to replace old, slow First World War shipping and improve military transport. Moreover, there was a glut of shipping during the Great Depression.

In 1934 the Navy decided to reconstruct *Kaga*, followed by *Akagi* in October 1935 on the lines of the *Soryu* design. They were given one, long flight-deck and lengthened hangars to take more than 90 aircraft. These conversions and the new carriers were part of an ambitious plan to operate modern aircraft and modernise carrier operational practice. As a result *Kaga* and *Akagi* developed new carrier tactics in fleet exercises and in China after 1937.

After the failure of the second London Naval Conference Japan embarked on an enormous covert naval building programme to match the First Vinson Act (1934) which expanded the US fleet. This was undertaken in the utmost secrecy, for completion in 1942. The front-line fleet was to comprise twelve battleships, ten carriers, 28 cruisers, 109 destroyers, 70 submarines and 65 naval aircraft groups. The first part, the Third Naval Armament Replenishment Programme, proposed in June 1936 and funded in 1937, included two battleships, two carriers, eighteen destroyers, fourteen submarines and 34 auxiliaries.

However, the intensive planning for the second London Conference had shown that Japan did not have the facilities, material or finance to compete with the USA in a naval race. With the First Vinson Act the Navy realised that the gap in battleships compared to the US Navy would begin to widen again, and decided that the difference would have to be made up in quality. From October 1934, contrary to the terms of the Treaties, the Navy stockpiled *matériel* and prepared designs for fast super-battleships able to outrange any US battleships.

In the same month the Technical Department was asked by the Naval General Staff to study a new design for battleships with quality (including the largest guns available) compensating for quantitative inferiority. Moreover, the ships (72,000 tons full load) would be too large to pass through the Panama Canal and thereby would put the Americans, who needed battleships in both the Atlantic and the Pacific, at a disadvantage if they attempted to match them. By 1936 it was time to decide whether to go ahead with building the super battleship design, and this therefore sparked off a major debate on shipbuilding policy.

Yamamoto (Chief of Naval Aeronautics 1935–36) wanted to abandon battleship construction. He argued that the money and material applied to naval aviation and especially carriers would improve the Navy's fighting power far more. He also argued that super-battleships, however large, could not be made unsinkable and the strike power of aircraft, increasing rapidly, would sink them before the fleets even saw each other.

He was opposed by Admiral R. Nakamura, Chief of the Naval Technical Department. He and Nakamura repeatedly clashed over the issue until it was decided to build the battleships. The problem was that Yamamoto had little concrete proof of his position since not a single battleship had yet been sunk in battle and aviation lacked funds to make any impact on the fleet.

His supporters were senior naval aviators, but most of them, such as Onishi, were still junior captains. In contrast Nakamura was supported by the Vice Chief of Staff and leader of the Fleet Faction, Suetsugu, and the senior battleship admirals. Navy Minister Nagano was not a strong character and would go along with prevailing opinion.

Moreover, the constructors had devised a new, light honeycomb armour, difficult to pierce with bombs from high altitudes, of which the new battleships were to have 11.7in plates. Although this did not allow for the torpedo threat, it was decided in July 1936 to lay down the first two super-battleships. In March 1937 the Technical Department's plans for the battleships were ready. The *Yamato* class was the largest in the world (64,000 tons, nine 18.1-inch guns, 27 knots, 16in belt armour, deck armour to withstand 1,000lb bombs, full compartmentalisation). It was planned to build four, giving twelve battleships in total.

After the expiration of the Disarmament Treaties Japan therefore laid down two super-battleships, *Yamato* (November 1937, completed December 1941) and *Musashi* (March 1938, August 1942), under the Third Replenishment Programme. No. 110 (May 1940) and No. 111 (November 1940) followed under the Fourth Replenishment Programme of 1939.

After Midway in June 1942, No. 110 was converted to the armoured carrier *Shinano* (completed November 1944) and work was stopped on No. 111 in March 1942 (she was dismantled in 1943) and her material diverted to carrier construction. As Yamamoto predicted, the two super-battleships hardly fired a shot in anger and were sunk by carrier aircraft in 1944. *Shinano* was also sunk, by a submarine, on her maiden voyage. These costly ships therefore provided very little return.

If Yamamoto had had his way there might have been another two carriers available in late 1941 and two more in 1944. However, this presupposes that the Japanese shipbuilding industry could have managed to complete these to time given the labour shortages and other work such as carrier conversions. The *Shokaku*s were successfully accelerated for completion before December 1941. Of course another two carriers of the class might have made all the difference at Midway, if they could have been provided with aircraft and crews.

With the expiry of the Washington and London Treaties on 31 December 1936, maximum naval re-armament was the goal and, despite going ahead with the *Yamato* class, the IJN continued to seek parity with the US Navy in carrier numbers. The problem was whether it had the resources for both. The Third Replenishment Programme included two carriers (25,675 tons), *Shokaku* (completed August 1941) and

Zuikaku (September 1941), to match US carrier building of the first Vinson-Trammell Act.

These were excellent designs, on the lines of the *Soryu*s, and the most successful the IJN produced. Being considerably larger, they combined high speed (34½ knots), good defence (sixteen 5in and 36 25mm AA guns, 8½in belt) and a large air group (84 aircraft). However, like the US carriers, they had a light, wooden flight-deck and un-protected (double) hangars which, unlike the American ones, were completely enclosed.

The other major defect, as with all Japanese carriers, was the poor system of petrol storage and supply lines. *Zuikaku* narrowly escaped being consumed by fire, at the Battle of the Philippine Sea, like the other carriers at Midway. The Japanese emphasis on the offensive and lack of modern battle experience led to neglect of this aspect.

In reply to the US Naval Expansion Bill (second Vinson-Trammell Act) of June 1938, the IJN decided on the Fourth Naval Armament Replenishment Programme in September 1939. This meant another two *Yamato* class battleships, just one purpose-built carrier, *Taiho* (March 1944, 75 aircraft) but also the conversion of the submarine depot ships (*Takasaki* and *Tsurugizaki*) to carriers *Zuiho* (completed December 1940) and *Shoho* (January 1942). The former was converted before and the latter after com-pletion as depot ships.

Taiho began as an improved *Shokaku*, but after war experience was completed with a 3in armoured flight-deck designed against 1,000lb bombs. Unlike the British *Illustri-ous* class, she did not have armoured sides to the hangars but had a heavily protected belt. She also pioneered new 3.9in AA guns and was designed for the new Aichi B7A 'Grace' torpedo/dive-bomber (never carried). *Zuiho* and *Shoho* were converted to flush deck carriers with only a single hangar (30 aircraft), new machinery to achieve 28 knots and increased armament. As such they were no substitute for a fleet carrier.

With the curtailment of carrier construction in favour of battleships, Japanese ship-building could not match increased US carrier building. The IJN's Fourth Naval Arma-ment Replenishment Programme did match the second Vinson-Trammell Act (*Hornet* only). However, the Americans continued to expand their programmes with the Naval Act (third Vinson-Trammell Act), signed on 14 June 1940, which provided for an 11 per cent expansion and the Stark Plan (Two Ocean Navy), signed only a month later on 19 July 1940, for a 70 per cent increase and 15,000 naval aircraft. Together the two programmes provided ten carriers.

To meet this the IJN implemented the Fifth and Sixth Naval Armament Replenish-ment Programmes neither of which could be completed because the Japanese ship-building industry had reached its limits. It was therefore planned to maintain parity with US carrier numbers by including the merchant fleet in its calculations and con-verting first class merchant ships as well as naval auxiliaries. IJN policy under the re-plenishment programmes had been to develop a 'shadow' fleet by subsidising the build-ing of large, fast liners and constructing naval auxiliaries. In both cases they were designed for easy, speedy conversion to auxiliaries or carriers.

In 1936 NYK planned to build two super liners for service between Japan and North America to challenge the Dollar, Canadian Pacific and North German Lloyd Lines and to provide for the Tokyo Olympics in 1940. Such a plan needed subsidies and, since similar plans had already failed in 1933 and 1935, the Navy Ministry took a special interest and suggested two designs (720ft, 24 knots, or 656ft, 24 knots) to the Ministry of Transportation, which agreed to an 80 per cent subsidy in 1937. However, the Ministry of Finance would only pay 50 per cent, requiring the Navy to intervene, and a compromise of 60 per cent was agreed. The Diet passed a law in 1938 to build two super liners.

As a result the Naval Technical Department, Transportation and NYK collaborated on the designs. The Navy required conversion to carriers in three months plus a 25½–26-knot speed (24 knots was more economical for NYK). As a compromise turbines and special high-pressure, high-temperature boilers were fitted for 25½ knots, but the liner would only use 80 per cent (24 knots).

In late 1938 NYK ordered *Kashiwara Maru* from Mitsubishi's Nagasaki Yard and *Izumo Maru* from Kawasaki's Kobe Yard. The former was laid down in March 1939 and the latter in September after the launch of the carrier *Zuikaku*. The German liner *Bremen* was taken as a model and the leading naval architect (Technical Vice-Admiral Y. Hiraga) advised Mitsubishi. These were the largest liners Japan had built.

The subsidising of merchant vessels designed secretly in peacetime to strengthen the Navy was formalised as the War Armament Preparation Programme. The owners of these vessels would have their ships requisitioned and converted in wartime, so they had to incorporate extra fuel capacity, aviation fuel tanks, a strengthened main deck, additional space for extra cabling, extra deck height and a layout that would allow the speedy installation of lifts and hangars. There was little provision for damage control until 1932, when double hulls were incorporated. In 1938 provision was made to fit extra transverse and longitudinal bulkheads, including separating the turbines, and bulbous bows.

Even before December 1941 a large number of merchant ships were requisitioned (519 for the Army, 482 for the Navy). These included fast tankers for the fleet train and auxiliary cruisers, seaplane carriers, patrol boats and minesweepers, etc. Of the ten liners specially designed for alteration to carriers, four were sunk before conversion, four were converted to escort carriers and only two, the *Kashiwara Maru*s, were converted to fleet carriers (*Hiyo* and *Junyo*, 53 aircraft each).

These were part of the first round of requisitions under the War Preparation Programme (November 1940) designed to counter the third Vinson-Trammell Act. The yards were informed unofficially in October 1940 and officially by the Ministry of Transportation in February 1941 after the Diet had voted funds under the Special War Budget. Despite alterations and the dismantling of some of the completed work, *Junyo* was completed in eleven months on 3 May 1942 and *Hiyo* on 31 July. In July both were classified as fleet aircraft carriers.

With large island and deck and heavy AA armament, the *Hiyo*s looked like fleet carriers, but despite 24,150 tons had the short length of a liner and lacked the speed, armament and air group of purpose-built carriers. The air group was only 48 compared to *Hiryu*'s 71 (on 8,000 less tonnage) and *Shokaku*'s 84 (1,500 more). However, the Japanese constructors did a fine job within the limitations of a liner hull. The Italian *Aquila*, also converted from a liner, was only 800 tons lighter, but was designed for only 36 aircraft.

The difference was a double hangar in the *Hiyo*s, but at the expense of a hangar height of only sixteen feet. After the loss of four fleet carriers at Midway the *Hiyo*s became one of the mainstays of the carrier fleet and the only merchant conversions in the world to be regularly used as fleet carriers. The difficulties of their conversion and operations makes it clear why no other navy did the same, but the IJN had little option when trying to match the vast US resources.

From 1938 until December 1941 the Navy greatly expanded its carrier force from four to ten, and added five seaplane carriers, compared with the US Navy's seven and the Royal Navy's eleven. However, by the latter date three of the RN's carriers had been lost and it could only deploy the obsolete *Hermes* with the Eastern Fleet. Only six of the Japanese carriers (*Akagi, Kaga, Soryu, Hiryu, Shokaku* and *Zuikaku*) were fleet carriers with more than 50 aircraft. *Hosho* (26 aircraft) and *Ryujo* (48 aircraft) were experimental and small, while *Zuiho* and *Shoho* (30 aircraft each) were light carriers converted from submarine depot ships.

The main problem for the IJN during the war was to replace the heavy losses of carriers during the Coral Sea and Midway battles and to match the rapid expansion of the US carrier fleet. Massive US shipbuilding resources soon produced a stream of *Essex* class fleet, *Independence* light fleet and escort carriers. Japan relied in the first instance on her 'shadow' programme to provide hulls to be quickly converted to carriers, some of which were taken over before the war began.

Thus, as has been explained, liners were converted to the *Hiyo* (July 1942, 53 aircraft), *Junyo* (May 1942, 53) and *Shinyo* (December 1943, 33). Several liners, however, were sunk before they could be converted. Naval auxiliaries were also converted: the submarine depot ship *Ryuho* (November 1942, 31), similar to the *Shoho*s, in early 1942 and the seaplane carriers *Chitose* (January 1944, 30) and *Chiyoda* (October 1943, 30) in late 1942. The *Chitose* class near-sisters *Mizuho* and *Nisshin*, however, were also sunk (May 1942 and July 1943) before conversion.

After the heavy losses at Midway the Navy, like the British in the First World War, resorted to converting uncompleted or elderly warships. Many of these schemes were not realised, including *Ibuki* (27 aircraft), a heavy cruiser suspended after launching in May 1943, whose conversion was begun in November of that year. Two old battleships, *Ise* and *Hyuga*, had their after turrets removed for short flight-decks. The third vessel of the *Yamato* class was completed as *Shinano* (64,800 tons, 50 aircraft), but she was sunk on 29 November 1944 on her way to Kure to complete fitting-out.

IJNS *Kaiyo* (1943) was yet another product of the 'shadow' programme, converted from the liner *Argentina Maru*. She was disabled by British carrier aircraft and beached.

In order to match the Americans the Navy also had ambitious building plans. After Midway the Modified Fleet Replenishment Programme of 1942 planned two modified, and then another five enlarged, sisters of *Taiho* (29,000 tons) and fifteen modified *Hiryu* class. The Navy had ordered an improved *Hiryu* and a sister in the 1941 programme. This programme was comparable to the American carrier building, but because of a weak industrial base, shipyard congestion and shortages of *matériel*, proved unrealistic.

Unryu (17,150 tons, 65 aircraft) was laid down in August 1942. She was one of a projected batch of six, to be followed by another ten. But only six were laid down and of these only three were completed, work on the others ceasing in 1945: the ten 1942 ships were cancelled. Although *Unryu*, *Amagi* and *Katsuragi* commissioned in August and November 1944, they were never operational because of lack of aircraft and oil.

In short, the fears of the Treaty Faction were entirely justified. Japanese resources proved woefully inadequate to equip the Navy during a long war with the USA. Moreover, the Navy had not helped itself by continuing to build battleships, and of enormous size, instead of concentrating on carrier construction. Their problems were exacerbated by faulty avgas arrangements and poor carrier formations which ensured heavy losses. At the same time it neglected anti-submarine warfare and produced only a handful of escort carriers. Thus US submarines were able to cut the supply lines of raw materials and oil to Japan which decimated her industry including shipbuilding. The root cause was the IJN's obsession with offence and the decisive battle as the best defence, which led to the neglect of merchant shipping protection.

In addition to *Hiyo* and *Junyo* the IJN converted another five liners (*Kasuga Maru* class and *Argentina Maru*) as the escort carriers *Taiyo* (September 1941, 27 aircraft), *Unyo* (May 1942) and *Chuyo* (November 1942), plus *Kaiyo* (November 1943, 24 aircraft). However, in contrast to the Allied escort carriers, these were used mostly for transporting aircraft and to a lesser extent for training pilots, because of the desperate shortage of carriers, rather than anti-submarine, fighter cover and combined operations. This was partly due to the large size of the IJN escorts, converted from liners, but also to its neglect of the protection of trade.

It was not until late 1944 that two tankers (*Shimane Maru* and *Otakisan Maru*) were taken over as convoy escorts, but by then it was too late and the former was not used operationally and the latter not completed. In the end, not only was Japan unable to match the US carrier building programme, but she also was unable to compete with US aircraft production.

Fleet Aircraft

For the carriers the IJN had to provide efficient aircraft on a scale commensurate with the mighty industrial power of the USA. In the beginning, Japanese industry was groping towards modernisation and foreign expertise was essential. Before the First World War the Navy had sought aid and aircraft from the French; in the 1920s from the British; and by the 1930s had turned to Germany.

On Yamamoto's recommendation Captain T. Sakurai, a graduate of the Engineering College, was sent to New York as a naval inspector to make a survey of US aviation in the mid 1930s. As with naval equipment, the Aeronautical Department would purchase one example of an interesting aircraft and dismantle it for study and copying. However, in the late 1930s Japanese industry began to produce excellent, indigenous designs, based on extreme range.

Before 1914 the Navy relied mainly on Maurice Farman seaplanes. With the arrival of the Sempill Mission, which could place orders for 200 aircraft, the Navy purchased Sopwith Pup fighters, Sopwith T1 Cuckoo torpedo-aircraft and Parnall Panther scout/spotters from Great Britain. To replace the ageing Pups, the Gloster Mars (renamed Sparrowhawk) was also purchased.

The designer Herbert Smith, from Sopwiths, and seven engineers of the Sempill Mission helped Mitsubishi design a fighter (Mitsubishi 1MFI Type 10, 140mph, 2½ hours' endurance, prototype October 1922) and a torpedo/bomber/scout (B1M Type 13, 130mph, 2½ hours' endurance, prototype January 1923). These aircraft stayed in service until the late 1920s because of low funding for naval aviation.

The next generations of aircraft continued to rely on foreign designers or inspiration. For instance in 1930, when the IJN required a new torpedo-bomber Mitsubishi hired British design teams (from Handley Page and Blackburn with the assistance of Herbert Smith) to prepare several designs. Blackburn's design won and the first prototype was built in the UK and delivered in 1930. Blackburn's chief engineer then supervised the construction of more prototypes. The three-seater Mitsubishi B2M1 Type 89 went into production in 1932.

In the mid 1930s Yamamoto, as Head of the Technical Division and then Chief of the Aeronautical Department, began the policy of encouraging the manufacturers to produce their own designs, albeit based on foreign technology, and to concentrate on long-range aircraft for the Pacific. To foster this endeavour a Naval Air Arsenal was set up at Yokosuka (1932) as a combined organisation of aircraft manufacturers for research, development, testing and co-ordination of the requirements of new aircraft.

Using the work of Junkers and other foreign firms, Mitsubishi in 1933 produced an experimental scout from which in 1934 it developed a land-based torpedo-bomber. In 1936, while Yamamoto was Chief of the Aeronautics Department, this was put into production as the Mitsubishi G3M2 Type 96 'Nell' land-based bomber.

This was the first Japanese military aircraft to have twin engines, retractable undercarriage and all-metal monocoque fuselage. However, it also surpassed all its contemporaries in its long range. World experts were astonished that the Japanese aircraft industry had produced an aircraft in large numbers that could strike 1,200 miles across the ocean.

This was followed by an even better land-based strike aircraft, the Mitsubishi G4M1 Type 1 'Betty' torpedo-bomber which was produced in 1937 and operational in 1941. A long-range reconnaissance flying boat (the Kawanishi H6K 'Mavis', later replaced by the H8K 'Emily') was also developed to locate an enemy fleet.

Yamamoto's ambitions were helped by the emergence of a world class designer of fighters at Mitsubishi, Jiro Horikoshi, who had joined the Nagoya Aircraft Works of Mitsubishi in 1927. A requirement was issued in 1934 for a naval monoplane fighter, which no country had yet developed so one could not be copied. Horikoshi designed the single-seat all-metal monoplane Mitsubishi A5M Type 96 'Claude' which first flew in February 1935 and went into production in 1936.

This all-metal single-seater was the first Japanese aircraft with flush riveting and allowed the Japanese Carrier Striking Force to establish air superiority over their beleaguered garrison in Shanghai in September 1937 despite the Chinese Air Force being equipped with British, US and Soviet fighters. However, the Claude's range of 460 miles was insufficient for operations in the Pacific.

The Navy therefore issued in May 1937 an exacting specification for a fast (311mph), light, long-range carrier fighter. Nakajima thought this specification too rigid and did not bid, but Horikoshi produced a design for a low wing, all-metal monoplane with retractable undercarriage. He concentrated on saving weight to give manoeuvrability and long range.

This new carrier fighter, the Mitsubishi A6M2 Type 0 (Zero), was put into production in July 1940 and fifteen pre-production examples were sent to China the same month; by the end of the year they had shot down 59 Chinese fighters for no losses. Although the Allies had been informed about the Zero by Claire Chennault, leader of the Flying Tigers, it still came as an unpleasant surprise to them. The Zero's chief weakness was its lack of armour and self-sealing fuel tanks which had been accepted because of its amazing range of 1,600 miles.

Like the British, the IJN put its main faith in torpedo-aircraft and was slow to develop the dive-bomber. In early 1936 the Aeronautics Department issued a specification for a carrier monoplane torpedo-bomber. The Nakajima B5N 'Kate' (235mph, 684 miles range, 1,756lb torpedo) first flew in January and production began at the end of the year. It was all-metal with retractable undercarriage and mechanically folding wings. It continued to serve into 1944.

In 1933, the Navy invited designs for the first Japanese aircraft specifically built as a dive-bomber. It granted permission for Aichi, who had been building Heinkel aircraft under licence, to adapt the Heinkel He 50 with an air-cooled engine. The Aichi D1A2 Type 94 'Susie' (174mph later improved to 195mph, 660 miles range) was put into production in late 1933 and a flight of them became notorious for sinking the US gunboat *Panay* in 1937.

An agreement with Heinkel brought a further exchange of technical and design information and led (1936) to the first Japanese all-metal low wing monoplane dive-bomber, the Aichi D3A Type 99 'Val' (242mph, 915 miles range), which went into production in December 1937. It was similar to the Heinkel He 70 and He 170. It continued in production, with a more powerful engine, until January 1944 and was the Navy's mainstay in the role, but obsolescence and lack of experienced crews greatly reduced its strike power.

By the late 1930s Japanese naval aviation was keeping pace with that of the USA and was ahead of the Fleet Air Arm in carrier aircraft design and numbers. The original Japanese building programmes resulted in seventeen shore-based squadrons by 1932. The First Replenishment Plan included fourteen more squadrons (472 aircraft by 1937). Their 1934–35 programme also provided eight new squadrons for the two new carriers and cruisers. This gave a total of 590 shore-based aircraft by April 1937 and 400 shipborne aircraft by 1938.

Although the big ships continued to dominate, increasing funds were allocated to building carriers and their aircraft. Although the Americans and the British knew of this expansion, they underestimated its extent and the advances being made in carriers, aircraft and personnel. In comparison with British and American carrier aircraft, the Japanese in 1941 were ahead of the former and keeping pace with the latter. Japanese naval aircraft had a distinct advantage in their long range. The Zero had the range to escort the bombers all the way to their target. The torpedo-bombers did not carry the Long Lance torpedo, with its unsurpassed speed and range, but they too had very long range. The weak area was in dive-bombers which had only been added to the Japanese carrier arsenal in the early 1930s.

However, the emphasis on long range had been at the expense of being able to absorb punishment, the aircraft being built without armour or self-sealing fuel tanks.

The Mitsubishi A6M Type 0 (Zero) fighter surprised the Allies, despite intelligence reports, and allowed early Japanese victories. However, armour and fire power were sacrificed for its range. (IWM)

The Zero was very vulnerable to battle damage compared to the rugged American fighters, and the 'Betty' was known by its pilots as the 'Lighter' because it caught fire so easily. The 'Val' and 'Kate' were also very vulnerable.

The Americans were beginning to gear up to produce large numbers of existing designs and of much improved designs. As early as July 1941 the Chief of Naval Aeronautics (Admiral S. Inoue 1940–41) warned that Japanese production was not meeting requirements for carrier- or land-based aircraft and flying boats. The target for 1941–42 was 7,000 aircraft, but production was a mere 162 per month and only expected to rise to 196 per month by the year's end. Lack of skilled labour, machine tools and raw materials meant that there were shortages of machine-guns, ammunition, bombs, torpedoes and instruments.

By great efforts the monthly production reached an average of 245 at the end of the year, still well short of the target. Thus there were only 150 Zeros available by October 1941 and these had to be split between the carriers and the land-based 11th Air Fleet. Priority was given to units mounting the attack on Pearl Harbor (1st, 2nd and 5th Carrier Squadrons), then 11th Air Fleet and finally Southern Area carriers (3rd and 4th Carrier Squadrons). There was an even greater shortage of 20mm machine-guns for the Zeros. This was another reason why the Navy Staff were reluctant to undertake the Pearl Harbor operation in addition to the Southern Area advance.

The Japanese naval aircraft industry was very dependent on Mitsubishi (which also built Army aircraft), Nakajima (Handa, Fukushima and Koizumi factories), Kawanishi and Aichi plus the Yokosuka Naval Air Arsenal (design only) who were unable to meet the demands of wartime expansion. Mitsubishi built some 2,400 'Bettys', Nakajima produced 1,200 'Kates', 1,268 'Jills', 906 'Frances' and 498 'Myrts', Kawanishi produced 382 flying boats, and Aichi turned out 1,294 'Vals' and 1,819 'Judys'. The Hiro Naval Air Arsenal also built 500 'Judys'.

Yamamoto therefore coaxed the Mitsui, Sumitomo and Hitachi conglomerates into aircraft manufacture. The main difficulty was the shortage of skilled workers, many of whom had been drafted into the Army or assigned to government work during the 'national emergency' in China. The Navy therefore had to get skilled workers reassigned to aircraft work. They had some success: for instance, Hitachi Aircraft produced many training aircraft, although not enough even to approach the huge US effort.

As well as lacking the basic resources (raw materials, skilled designers and technicians, factories and flight crews, etc.) for mass production, the Navy also experienced problems in the production of next generation aircraft for the same reasons. For instance the Yokosuka/Aichi D4Y Suisei 'Judy' dive-bomber (360mph, 750 miles range) was delayed (specification 1937, production 1941) by structural and undercarriage retraction weaknesses, and because engine production was lagging behind. Furthermore, having been designed for speed (to fly with the Zero), it carried a mere 682lb bombload. Despite a new engine (350mph, 944 miles endurance) it was far less successful than the older Dauntless and was relegated to high-speed reconnaissance.

Although excellent designs, such as the Nakajima B6N Tenzan ('Jill') torpedo-bomber and the Nakajima C6N Saiun ('Myrt') scout, continued to be produced, they often arrived too late, having been delayed by engine and production difficulties. Because of overheating and vibration in its first engine, the 'Jill' (prototype 1942) did not replace the 'Kate' in numbers until the Marianas, whereas the Avenger had been in service since 1942.

Similarly the replacement for the 'Zero', the 390mph Mitsubishi A7M Reppu, had problems and the prototype with an improved engine did not fly until October 1944. It never did go into mass production, the Navy adopting instead the 400mph Shiden which began to reach the carriers in the autumn.

As with carrier construction, Japan's aircraft production was only really geared to conduct a short war. Despite the raw material difficulties, production did steadily increase, though nothing like that of America, from 5,088 in 1941 to 28,100 in 1944. However, engine production failed to keep pace and became the bottleneck by the spring of 1944. The position rapidly deteriorated from June 1944 under the impact of raw material shortages and became disastrous from November because of the B-29 raids.

The carriers in the first half of the war had to rely mainly on existing aircraft types flown by crews who had been chosen very selectively, intensively trained and hardened in the war in China. During the second half, the main problems for the Navy werre not the lack of new aircraft types but a disastrous lack of aviation fuel and, above all, of experienced air crew from 1943. By 1944 new carriers and aircraft were available, but even if fuel had been available, trained crews were not.

Fleet Personnel and Training

As with aircraft production, Japan lagged behind America in the training of large numbers of pilots and aircrew. Her first naval pilots had been sent to schools in France or America or both. On their return they established the first Japanese naval air station at Oppama near the Yokosuka naval base, Tokyo Bay. From then on the Navy trained its own pilots. This was put on a systematic basis in 1921 when the Sempill Mission established basic air training at Kasumigaura along the lines of Cranwell. Specialised training was undertaken at the Oiita (fighter) and Yokosuka (bomber) Air Corps.

The majority of the pilots were enlisted men. Few officers and even fewer reserve (non Academy) officers were trained. For instance in December 1927 Sub-Lieutenant Fuchida (later leader of the Pearl Harbor raid) joined a class of officers at Kasumigaura that consisted of only ten pupils of whom two were soon killed in accidents and only three survived the war.

The enlisted pilots were given a 30-month educational course before undergoing eight months of flying training (divided between basic and operational) of more than 100 hours, plus ground school which gave them a wider knowledge of the theory of flight and engine design than their American counterparts. The officers were selected after at least two years at sea and therefore did not need any general education, but they did have a two-month ground course before a ten-month flying course (150–175 hours).

Qualified pilots then went to an Air Corps for additional training, before assignment to a front-line shore-based unit. Only after considerable experience and 'above average' ratings could a pilot be considered for carrier assignment. The Navy introduced a system of rotation to give its front-line, including carrier, pilots combat experience in China.

The Navy trained very few pilots in the 1920s and even in the 1930s as few as 100 a year. During the early 1920s naval aviation was given a relatively low priority and the battle fleet was still the favoured means of promotion. However, by the late 1920s aviation had become very popular with the younger officers and enlisted men and there was no shortage of applicants.

The Navy, however, continued its rigorous selection and training procedures (including physical fitness). In 1937 only 70 enlisted applicants (including Saburo Sakai, a leading ace) were selected from 1,500 for the ten-month course and only 25 completed it. This reflected the values of the Navy which expected to select only the cream of Japanese youth and stressed physical fitness. Entrance to the Naval Academy at Etajima was also very competitive and its training too stressed physical fitness. The Navy sought quality personnel to compensate for any lack in quantity.

Thus the naval pilots, and especially the carrier pilots, represented an élite corps with an average of 800 hours' flying, with a maximum of 1,500 and minimum of 200–300. By December 1941 there were about 3,500 naval pilots of whom about a third were carrier qualified. There were not enough pilots to man all aircraft and establish an adequate reserve.

The inability of Japanese naval aircraft to absorb punishment, not identified in China, led to heavy crew casualties which exacerbated the crew shortages. Thus for Pearl Harbor the lack of qualified fighter pilots led to their diversion from the Third and Fourth Carrier Squadrons, assigned to the Southern Area, and even of instructors from the Yokosuka Air Corps which provided specialised training and study. This therefore affected the pipeline of fighter pilots even though the fleet took over some of their training.

In August 1941 it was planned to train 15,000 pilots a year. However, this was far too late. During the first six months of the war, with the conquest of the Southern Area, carrier pilot losses were low and were made up from the land-based 11th Air Fleet. In March 1942 many of its pilots were sent back to Japan for carrier training.

In the second half of 1942 at the battles of the Coral Sea, Midway, Eastern Solomons and Santa Cruz, and throughout the New Guinea and Solomons campaign, the Navy suffered a disastrous attrition (more than 7,000 by the end of 1943) of its experienced land- and carrier-based air personnel. The carrier losses were made up by the training system and the existing and new carriers were brought up to strength.

However, in April 1943 the carrier air groups were transferred to Rabaul because the 11th Air Fleet had suffered heavy losses, and in turn lost more than 250 pilots for little return. They had to be withdrawn on 16 April. As a result the average Japanese pilot's flight hours declined from 700 to 500 hours whereas the US figures climbed from 305 to 500. The carrier pilots were again committed to Rabaul by the new CinC (Koga) with similar results. Thus by May 1944 on average the Japanese carrier pilot's flight training hours had fallen to 275, a near 50 per cent drop, compared to the US pilot's total which had again risen to 525 hours.

These losses could not be replaced by the training system. The Navy's main response to the war was to increase the enlisted intake and begin large-scale recruitment of reserve officers. However, neither the general education course for enlisted men nor the ground school course for officers were cut. Thus the production of large numbers of pilots was too slow. The small number of recruits with a technical and educated background was also a problem.

After the high losses of 1943, in the autumn the Navy cut the operational training of pilots and sent them straight to units after a reduced intermediate training. Pilots were given a brief conversion and tactical training with their unit before becoming operational with about 100 hours of flying. Although this meant a rapid increase of pilots with front-line units, combat (due to inexperience) and training losses (lack of qualified instructors) also rose steadily. In the spring of 1944 the Navy therefore returned to the old training syllabus. By late 1944 the oil situation was so bad that pilot training was affected and this worsened in 1945.

Thus when the expected American fleet drive across the Central Pacific began in late 1943, the planned Japanese defence was crippled. It lacked the requisite pilots for the land-based air groups, for attrition of the US fleet, and for the carriers without which the Navy could not expect to win any decisive battle, the keystone of its defensive plans.

Like the Royal Navy, the IJN lacked the resources to produce the carriers, aircraft and personnel to match the huge industrial strength of America. As against China and Russia, the Japanese planned for a short war and thus concentrated on providing an élite force. Once the élite carrier force had been destroyed, the rest of the Navy was at the mercy of the rapidly growing power and size of the US fast carrier force.

4. The Carrier War, 1939–1945

In the Second World War, American, British and Japanese carrier operations differed greatly from one another, and reflected their respective preparations during the previous thirty years. Of the three, the British experience was most varied, their carriers fighting in Home Waters, the Arctic, Atlantic, Mediterranean and Far East. The climax of the carrier war, however, came in the Pacific.

US Carrier Air Power in the Pacific

The Japanese 400 carrier aircraft strike on Pearl Harbor ended any pre-war notions of reliance on, and tying the carriers to, the battle line. Five US battleships were sunk (later three were re-floated) and the remaining old battleships retreated to California. This left two new fast battleships, five carriers (*Ranger* and *Wasp* were in the Atlantic) and their escorts plus the submarines to hold the line until reinforcements arrived. Everything now depended on carrier air power.

Unlike the Japanese, the Americans operated their carriers in separate task forces, each with her own screen of cruisers and destroyers, as did the hard-pressed Royal Navy. They had no alternative, given the emergency and the many operations needed to defend bases (such as Guam and Wake), protect convoys along the lines of communication – and to hit back.

There was also a fear that AA and fighters could not adequately defend a concentration of carriers and that dispersion was a better policy. This fear increased after early losses: *Saratoga* (damaged by a submarine, January 1942), *Lexington* (sunk, Coral Sea, May 1942) and *Yorktown* (sunk, Midway, June 1942). Even when carriers were operating in consort, each retained her own screen, and they separated before the attack, their aircraft meeting over the target, much like the Japanese *modus operandi*.

The only early exception was the raid on Lae and Salamaua, New Guinea, led by Rear Admiral W. Brown (Commander Scouting Force) with Captain F. C. Sherman (CO, *Lexington*) as his air adviser. Sherman deployed *Lexington* and *Yorktown* in one formation, but this was not tested by air attack. *Lexington* was lost at Coral Sea and Sherman's influence was temporarily lost. Moreover, Brown was not a carrier commander after April.

In December 1941, when Admiral King became Commander-in-Chief, he had three main tasks: implementing the 'Germany first' policy, defending the Atlantic supply lines upon which it depended, and prosecuting the long-planned Pacific offensive against Japan.

Anglo-American planning (December–March) for 'Germany first' called for Operation 'Gymnast' to occupy French North Africa; Operation 'Sledgehammer', September 1942, for a second front if the Soviets collapsed, and Operation 'Round Up', second front in France in the spring of 1943 (exploiting Sledgehammer's beachhead if implemented). These operations required seagoing landing-craft, of which 8,200 were ordered (later increased). These clashed with existing programmes including carriers, but Roosevelt refused to abandon this or other building.

Securing the Atlantic sea lanes, under heavy U-boat attack, depended on extending the convoy system from the transatlantic routes to coastal and Caribbean routes. The problem was the lack of escorts (and patrol aircraft). Existing building and the landing-craft programme pushed back construction into 1943. The first destroyer escorts and escort carriers arrived during the crisis of March 1943. More escorts, better intelligence and co-ordination by the newly created Tenth Fleet (May) opened the way for offensives in Europe.

With Europe and the Atlantic getting first priority, King's initial Pacific strategy was to hold the West Coast–Hawaii–Samoa–Australia line against an expected Japanese offensive at Samoa or the Ellice Islands to cut communications with Australia, so he garrisoned the South Pacific bases and harried the Japanese with carrier raids. Once the Japanese were halted he planned, since ships for the Central Pacific would not arrive until mid 1943, a South Pacific offensive using land-based air power to boost the carriers.

Thus *Yorktown* was diverted from the Atlantic to the Pacific and King used carrier raids (*Lexington* against Wake, *Enterprise* and *Yorktown* against the Gilberts and Marshalls, and *Hornet* and *Enterprise* on Tokyo, 18 April) to upset Japanese plans. *Yorktown* and *Lexington* also escorted troop convoys to the South Pacific.

King knew from intelligence that Nagumo's Indian Ocean offensive had left only two carriers in the Pacific. This prompted him and Admiral Nimitz (CinC Pacific) to commit Task Force 11 (Rear Admiral Fitch in *Lexington*) and Task Force 17 (Rear Admiral Fletcher in *Yorktown*) against the Japanese offensive at Port Moresby. The Battle of Coral Sea (7–8 May) resulted in *Lexington*'s loss, but turned back the Japanese invasion. Admiral Fletcher was not a carrier specialist and his handling of the carrier operation reflected his inexperience, but their aircraft sank the carrier *Shokaku* on the 7th. Like Sherman, Fitch kept the two carriers under one destroyer screen, but when attacked they manoeuvred independently which weakened the defence and both were hit, *Lexington* being abandoned.

After Vice Admiral Halsey had launched Army B-25s to bomb Tokyo (*Enterprise* and *Hornet*), the Japanese planned to attack Midway and destroy the US carriers. King expected another attack on Moresby and sent Halsey's carriers to the South Pacific.

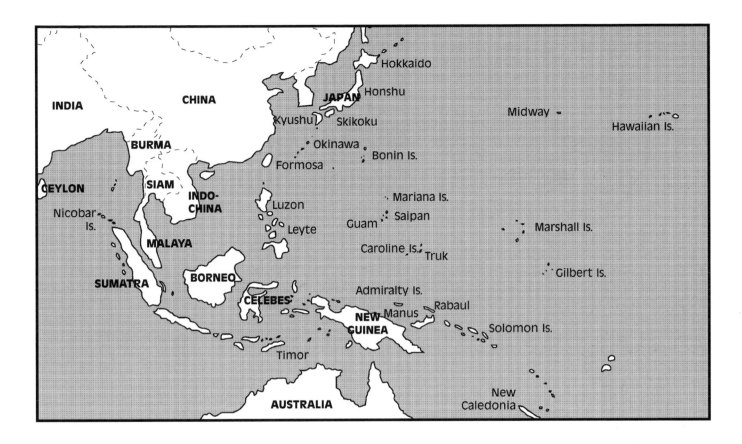

The Pacific Theatre, 1941–45.

Nimitz, convinced by his intelligence that Midway was the target, recalled Halsey himself. King agreed to his plan to ambush the Japanese carriers, so long as their own were not unduly risked.

With Halsey ill and Fitch at San Diego to fetch back the repaired *Saratoga*, Fletcher (TF16) was again senior carrier commander. This meant that everything rested on the inexperienced Rear Admiral Spruance (TF17), another cruiser commander, chosen by Halsey and guided by his chief of staff (Captain M. Browning), who acted independently of Fletcher and allowed Captain Mitscher, CO of *Hornet*, to do so too.

It was Browning who reckoned that an early strike would catch the Japanese carriers with their decks loaded with aircraft. Spruance took the risk, and although the Devastator torpedo-bombers suffered terrible losses, they enabled the Dauntless dive-bombers (undetected at high altitude) to sink all four Japanese carriers. Fletcher's strike was less effective and *Yorktown* was prematurely abandoned because of inefficient damage control procedures.

The Battle of Midway, 4–6 June, was the first US victory and the Japanese would never recover from their losses of four carriers and 253 aircraft. *Yorktown*, on the other hand, was to be replaced by the *Essex* and *Independence* classes. For a while there was a lull; the Japanese offensive had been blunted and the Americans had few resources. Neither side could afford more losses and needed to re-group. After the loss of *Lexington* in the Coral Sea and *Yorktown* and the Japanese carriers at Midway, King ruled that multi-carrier formations were unsafe and that each carrier must have her own commander and screen. By contrast, the Japanese decided on task forces of three carriers after June 1942.

In July 1942, King received permission for a limited offensive (replacing 'Sledgehammer', now abandoned) from the Joint Chiefs of Staff (JCS) to pre-empt the Japanese and clear the Solomons, New Guinea and Rabaul. General MacArthur wanted Navy carriers to support his New Guinea advance, but having lost two carriers to air attack (poor fighter and AA defence), King and Nimitz did not agree. As a compromise, the Navy, with fleet carriers under Nimitz, would clear the Solomons and Rabaul while MacArthur advanced along New Guinea.

The Marines landed unopposed at Guadalcanal and Tulagi on 7 August and began the famous naval and air battle of attrition that cost many men, aircraft and ships. Three US carriers were involved: *Saratoga* TF61 (Fletcher, Task Group 61.1), *Enterprise* TG61.2 (Rear Admiral Kincaid) and *Wasp* TG61.3 (Rear Admiral Noyes). But the battle-weary Fletcher's handling of the carriers lacked offensive spirit and mobility; he was tied down to the landings and faced the five Japanese carriers at Rabaul. King blamed Fletcher for the disastrous Battle of Savo Island on 8/9 August, because he withdrew the carriers a day early, which allowed Japanese surface ships to sink one Australian and three US cruisers.

Fletcher then allowed Nagumo to take the initiative in the Battle of the Eastern Solomons, 23-25 August. *Enterprise* was damaged for the loss of the light carrier *Ryujo*. After damage to *Saratoga* (31 August) and the loss of *Wasp* (15 September) both to submarines, Fletcher and aviator Noyes were relieved. With forces committed to the 'Torch' landings in North Africa and the first *Essex* carriers delayed by landing-craft programmes, King committed his last carriers, *Hornet* TF17 (Rear Admiral Murray) and *Enterprise* TF67 (Kincaid) plus two new battleships. He also replaced Vice Admiral Ghormley (CinC South Pacific) with the aggressive Halsey.

At the same time, Yamamoto committed Nagumo's four carriers to secure Guadalcanal. In the ensuing Battle of Santa Cruz which lasted two days, the US carriers repelled the Japanese fleet, *Hornet*'s air group damaging *Shokaku*, which withdrew to Truk. The cost was damage to *Enterprise* and the loss of *Hornet*. The new battleships were a great success, shooting down many aircraft. Sherman in the spring of 1943 concluded that air defence required multi-carrier task forces, but Ramsey (Captain of *Saratoga*) and Halsey disagreed, given King's ruling on carrier formations and flight efficiency problems.

Saratoga, now the only carrier in the South Pacific, was withdrawn by Halsey and surface and land-based air reinforcements decisively defeated the last attempts by the

USS *Wasp*: a detailed view of the island, with bridge, flag bridge, offices and galleries etc., as seen shortly after the ship had commissioned in May 1940. (US National Archives)

Japanese to reinforce the island in the Battle of Guadalcanal in December. This victory coincided with Stalingrad, El Alamein and the 'Torch' landings which turned the tide on all fronts.

The Guadalcanal campaign had tied the carriers to confined waters, denying them their mobility, and single carrier task forces had ensured inadequate air defensive measures. The handling of the carriers by Fletcher and Kincaid (not aviation specialists) had also been of mixed quality. In October Towers replaced Noyes in the new post of ComAirPac and thereafter ensured that all carrier commanders were aviators. Kincaid was despatched to recapture the Aleutians in early 1943. Meanwhile land-based aircraft engaged the Japanese carrier aircraft deployed ashore at Rabaul and by April forced Yamamoto to withdraw them.

King's patience was sorely tried by the slow progress and heavy losses in the South Pacific. He therefore switched to land-based air operations against Rabaul and committed the carriers to the open waters of the Central Pacific (the Gilberts and Marshalls). At Casablanca King failed to support General Marshall on Operation 'Round Up' (the invasion of France in 1943) since the British Mediterranean policy freed Allied shipping for the Central Pacific offensives.

King assured Nimitz, committed to a slow build-up in the Solomons, that the construction programme now allowed a drive through the Central Pacific in 1943. He and Marshall agreed meanwhile (March) that Halsey (Solomons) and MacArthur (New Guinea) would converge on Rabaul using Army troops and aircraft. King also assured Marshall that the carrier losses suffered in the Solomons would not be repeated in the Central Pacific, and that much depended on the first landings, in the Gilbert and Ellice Islands.

King developed a strategy to bomb, blockade and invade Japan. Operations in 1943 and 1944 would secure the Marshalls and force a decisive fleet action. The next phase (Luzon–China–Formosa) would sever Japan's supply lines to the East Indies and recapture the Philippines. The Trident Conference in May accepted this, and in June King ordered Nimitz to take the Marshalls and Truk (Carolines) by early 1944. Nimitz decided to take the Gilberts in November, and the Marshalls in February 1944.

After Guadalcanal the burden of operational planning was gradually shifted from Washington to Hawaii. In early 1943 King had felt that Nimitz was insufficiently aggressive, but eventually changed his mind. He assigned Nimitz a schedule of operations (agreed by the JCS), had meetings with him, usually at San Francisco but sometimes in Hawaii (as in September 1943), to issue fresh instructions and Nimitz would brief him on the latest operational plans.

By January 1944 King's confidence in Nimitz was at its height and he delegated operational planning to him, subject to approval, and even agreed that Towers, a rival

USS *Essex*: a close-up view of the island of the new class, December 1942. Note the 5-inch guns in twin turrets forward and aft of the island, offset to keep the deck clear. (US Navy)

from Moffett days, should become Nimitz's deputy. However, King kept a firm grip on naval air appointments and logistics.

The key to implementing the Central Pacific offensive was new technology which solved the problems of vulnerable carriers and the heavy losses of 1942. Technical advances in communications held the key to implementing multi-carrier formations. British experience in the Mediterranean against large shore-based air forces had much influence and their invention of radar (radio detection and ranging) was crucial.

Radar allowed superior general navigation and surface ship tracking, and enabled ships of a multi-carrier task force to maintain station at high speed even in poor weather and at night. Thus the task force could maintain an interlocking AA defence of the carriers. Each new carrier and ship of the screen was fitted with radar and older ones were steadily modernised. Information was collated by the Combat Information Center (CIC) which supplied it to the bridge and air plot, the centre for air operations.

Radar (by air plot) was essential to co-ordinated AA fire, although control was still by visual means. However, the 5-inch 38 calibre DP, Swedish 40mm Bofors and Swiss 20mm Oerlikon guns provided a devastating barrage which, with fighters, allowed the task forces to survive heavy air attacks. As a result of British experience, the Bofors and Oerlikons replaced the 0.5in machine-guns. The *Essex* class, as completed, were fitted with seventeen quadruple 40mm mountings and 65 or more single 20mm guns. The 20mm, however, proved to have insufficient stopping power against the Kamikaze.

The *Essex* class also had twelve 5in in twin turrets with a range of 10 miles and 12–15 rounds per minute. The effectiveness of this gun was increased fourfold by the VT (proximity) fuse at the end of 1942. Developed by the Americans after 2½ years, it meant that a near miss was usually sufficient to bring down an aircraft.

Radar was also essential to the direction of defensive fighters. Each *Essex* class carrier was fitted with Mk 4 air-search radar which revealed the position, composition and formation of an air unit. But it could not detect low-flying aircraft and was replaced in early 1944 by the new Mk 12. In the early summer of 1944 the Mk 22 radar began to be installed and improved fighter direction even more. The new radars arrived just in time for the Marianas where fighter direction destroyed Japanese attacks. Nevertheless there were still problems with low-level detection caused by hasty installation and Rear Admiral Clark (TG58.1) instituted visual fighter directors in his carriers to spot and intercept low-level attackers. Later, when faced by the Kamikaze, it was found that there was a deficiency in the detection of aircraft at extremely high altitudes and it became necessary to revert to the visual system.

In late 1943 the US Navy adopted the British IFF (Identification Friend or Foe), a device fitted in the aircraft that signalled its identity; henceforth any aircraft that did not respond was assumed to be hostile. Thus the Fighter Director could vector fighters to intercept enemy formations. Another important feature was the YE homing beacon installed in carriers which transmitted a Morse letter for each 15-degree segment of a given circle. On hearing this a pilot could find his carrier and the volume of the signal increased as he drew nearer.

Fighter direction was also transformed by radio improvements. Previously ships could talk to pilots by radio, but the enemy could listen-in and there was only one channel. Now they had a very high frequency (VHF) radio which could not be eavesdropped, with four channels for ship-to-ship, fighter direction, air group and training at sea. Effective assignment and use, to avoid overcrowding during combat, took time to develop.

During 1943 the roles of air group aircraft also changed. The scout/bombers lacked the range and size to carry radars and their scouting role was gradually taken over by the larger torpedo-aircraft. By early 1944 fighters could also be fitted with light radar but were seldom used for scouting, being deployed instead as fighter-bombers. Thus in US carriers reconnaissance was sacrificed for offensive missions.

The new *Essex* class carriers also had more fighters. The original pre-war air group consisted of eighteen fighters, 36 scout/dive-bombers and eighteen torpedo-aircraft (25:50:25). After Midway the number of fighters was increased. The *Essex* class then doubled the fighters (36) and carried the same bomber numbers (40:40:20). The *Independence* class carried 24 fighters and nine torpedo-bombers and the *Midway*s were to have 36 fighters, 48 dive-bombers and 36 torpedo-aircraft.

In mid 1944 the *Essex* air groups were changed again to carry even more fighters: 54 fighters, 24 dive- and 18 torpedo-bombers. By mid 1945 the *Essex* class had 32 fighters (four night), 24 fighter-bombers, 24 bombers and 20 torpedo-aircraft; the *Saipan*s 48 fighters; the *Independence*s 32 fighters; and the *Midway*s 73 fighters and 64 bombers. This greatly increased the fleet's fighter defences against the Kamikaze.

One weakness was in carrier night-fighters. At Guadalcanal the forces were harried by Japanese night-bombers and McCain, the land-based air commander, as Chief BuAer began development of a twin-engined night-fighter (Grumman Tigercat). Meanwhile radar-equipped Corsairs under Commander W. J. Widhelm were tested in the Solomons in late 1943. Although Nimitz suggested that each carrier have a night-fighter detachment (four Corsairs), Towers preferred to await the trial tests, and so carriers lacked night-fighters at the Gilberts.

The multi-carrier task forces not only provided maximum defence but also concentration of offensive power to neutralise or isolate enemy bases which could be bypassed or captured. This in turn relied on adequate and mobile logistics.

Carrier operations in the vast Pacific required a constant supply of oil, aviation fuel (avgas), replacement aircraft and aircrew, ammunition, ordnance and spares. During October 1943 Nimitz ordered Commander Service Force Pacific Fleet (Admiral W. L. Calhoun) to form two Service Squadrons (Servron) for the Central Pacific.

For the Gilberts and Marshalls most ships were staged from Pearl Harbor, with a few from Funafuti in the South Pacific, but the fleet tankers, of Servron 4 under Hoover, refuelled the carrier task groups on their way to and from air strikes. Even for the

Gilberts thirteen oil tankers (each carrying 80,000 barrels of oil, 18,000 avgas and 6,800 diesel) were needed, and as the distance of operations lengthened more and more were required.

For operations beyond the Marshalls it was clear that the fleet and its logistics would have to use an advance base in these islands (Majuro). A major unit (Servron 10) was formed at Pearl Harbor exclusively to supply the carriers and their escorts from Majuro when it was captured. In June 1944 TF58 moved its bases from Majuro and Kwajalein to Eniwetok, Manus and Saipan, and finally, Eniwetok only, in November. In October Servron 10 moved to Ulithi. Servron 10 embraced everything needed to supply carriers and their bases: store ships, tankers, tenders, hospital and barrack ships, harbour craft such as lighters, barges and tugs, drydocks and defensive warships (subchasers). Early in 1944 escort carriers were added for escort duties and to ferry replacement aircraft.

By late 1944 the fleet was served by Servron 2 (repair and salvage ships), Servron 8 (service vessels at Pearl Harbor), Servron 10 (oilers), and Servron 12 (harbour facilities). For increasingly long-range operations an At Sea Logistics Service Group (34 oilers, eleven CVEs and 45 escorts) was formed. Three groups of oilers constantly moved between Ulithi (refuelling) and the fleet (periodically oiled and supplied with replacement aircraft) which greatly extended its mobility.

With the fast carriers expected to be operating off the coasts of Japan and Iwo Jima by February 1945, Servron 6 was created in December 1944 to supply food, ammunition, general stores, personnel and salvage. Servron 10 continued to operate oilers and service ships from Ulithi. In February Guam and Saipan were abandoned for Ulithi and then Leyte (in April). The fleet used Eniwetok, Guam and Ulithi until moving to Leyte in June.

The provision of aircraft, their servicing, repair and spares in the combat zone were first provided by service squadrons, but Towers realised that the aviation logistics needed re-organisation to accelerate the huge numbers of aircraft arriving in the Pacific. He therefore asked on 26 August 1943 for control of aviation logistics and Nimitz placed all shore-based Carrier Aircraft Service Units (CASU) under ComAirPac on 17 September.

The carrier-based CASU remained the same and for flexibility were interchangeable with those that were shore-based. For the large *Essex* class ComAirPac enlarged each CASU to seventeen officers and 516 other ranks. The CASU was part of the ship's company not the air group and in 1943 centralised all maintenance ashore or on a carrier, squadrons thereafter having few maintenance personnel of their own. Great savings in supply, flexibility and standardisation were offset by a loss in the *esprit de corps* fostered in squadrons, and a decline in the daily availability of aircraft.

Logistics in the Pacific. The carrier fleet depended on supply and repair both at sea and in harbour. Advanced fleet bases had many types of vessel; some are seen here with *Enterprise* in 1945. (US Navy)

Despite these changes, aviation logistics suffered from sheer numbers, the lack of policy on when to repair or withdraw aircraft from combat and a lack of method in spares distribution. This problem was recognised after the Gilberts and the new DCNO (Air) (McCain) took action in February 1944 to formulate an aviation logistics policy.

In late 1943, with the Japanese fleet and its aircraft massed at Truk, Rabaul and other island bases, and unaware of its full air losses, the US fleet still expected a formidable adversary in the Central Pacific. Moreover, the amphibious and carrier doctrines of the Fleet Marine Force and US fleet were still largely untried. The build-up of forces, especially of carriers, took first priority.

The *Essex*, first of the class, set the path for each new carrier. After an initial trials cruise in the Caribbean, each carrier was inspected and passed by ComAir Atlantic Fleet (Admiral P. L. Bellinger), and passed through the Panama Canal to ComAirPac.

USS *Bataan* (CVL-29), March 1944: an air view showing her smaller island, armament, the deck park typical of US practice and the more cramped conditions of the light carriers. (US Navy)

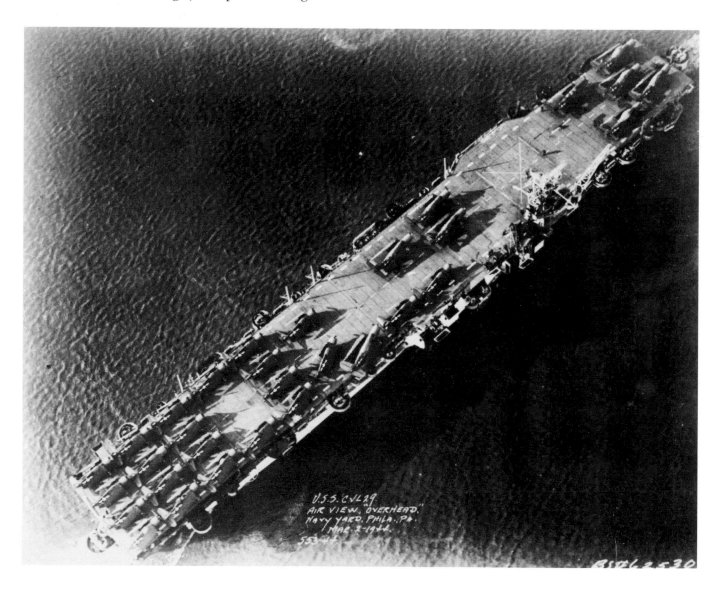

An air group was assigned either on the East Coast or by ComFleetAir West Coast. The carriers then began working-up while en route for Pearl Harbor (and later, Majuro or Leyte).

The first new carriers acquired combat experience on the early raids (for instance, Wake Island), but later new carriers were slotted into task groups where they learned from veteran air groups. Although Halsey (CinC South Pacific) requested carrier reinforcement, the new carriers (*Essex*, first in May, *Yorktown*, *Lexington*, *Independence*, *Princeton* and *Belleau Wood*) in mid 1943 all went to Pearl Harbor.

With the arrival of the new carriers Spruance, with Towers' help, issued in June 1943 a new fleet doctrine, PAC 10, which stressed flexibility in carrier operations and concentration for air defence, citing the success of British carriers in the Mediterranean and the losses of US single-carrier task forces. Thus multi-carrier task forces, favoured by Sherman, were accepted. However, formations for offensive operations were left to the air commanders. This doctrine was revised by USF 10A on 1 February 1944, but the essentials, tactical concentration of carriers in task groups and assigning tactical flexibility to the carrier commander, remained the same.

On 16 August Towers and the senior carrier aviators decided that the carrier groups of one *Essex* and one *Independence* class carrier should be increased to two or three *Essex* and one or two *Independence*s. Towers informed Nimitz on 21 August that the carriers had to be concentrated to gain command of the air, attack Japanese forces and bases and cover amphibious and fleet operations. He also argued that specialised air operations required commanders or their chiefs of staff to be aviators.

For the Gilberts invasion in November the Central Pacific Force (Spruance) had eleven carriers and Nimitz hoped for a decisive battle to destroy the enemy's six. Spruance planned to capture the Gilberts in a swift assault using the carriers to soften up the defences. Then he hoped to have a set-piece decisive battle.

To prepare the way for the Gilberts, to support Halsey's advance to Bougainville and to test the new carrier task force, Nimitz authorised some carrier raids. On 22 August Rear Admiral Pownall (Commander Fast Carriers, an aviator) left Pearl to neutralise the air bases of Marcus Island with Task Force 15 (two heavy and one light carrier, one fast battleship and screen). This force pioneered the circular formation with carriers in the centre, an inner circle of battleships and cruisers and an outer screen of destroyers for maximum AA protection. There was also a submarine lifeguard for ditched pilots.

The raid was launched at dawn on 31 August. The first sweep of fighters strafed enemy aircraft on the ground, while the Avengers (2,000lb bombs) and Dauntless (1,000lb fragmentation bombs) hit airfields and installations. *Essex* and *Yorktown* refuelled and re-armed their aircraft for second strikes. There was little opposition to test the defences of the new carrier formation. Pownall, fearful of risking his ships, refused to stay to rescue some airmen or bombard the island and rapidly left enemy waters.

At the same time Radford (CarDiv 11) led Task Force 11 (*Princeton* and *Belleau Wood*) to cover the occupation of Baker Island as a base for land aircraft against the Gilberts. Next Pownall took TF15 (*Lexington*, *Princeton* and *Belleau Wood*) on 18 September to soften up the Gilberts, take photographs for the assault and test a carrier force with mainly light carriers. Attacks by aircraft from Kwajalein air base in the Marshalls were expected, but in the event the raid provoked little reaction. Again Pownall withdrew quickly. Afterwards he called for a fleet fighter direction doctrine to standardise procedures and four night-fighters aboard each carrier. Again Towers refused because night-fighters were unavailable.

Another air raid on Wake under Rear Admiral A. E. Montgomery tested even larger carrier formations. Task Force 14 consisted of *Essex* and *Yorktown* (Montgomery), *Independence* and *Belleau Wood* (Rear Admiral Ragsdale) and *Lexington* and *Cowpens* (Rear Admiral Radford). Montgomery experimented with groups of six, three and two carriers. These were supported by seven cruisers, 24 destroyers, two oilers and a lifeguard submarine.

The Task Force had three times the bombers of previous assaults and stayed to launch attacks on 5 and 6 October. These were met by 30 Zeros and the Hellcat proved its superiority. Moreover, 24 aircraft were sent from the Marshalls to attack the carriers, but were driven off by Ragsdale's CAP. The cruising formations and defensive measures were successful and the three-carrier group was adopted for the Gilberts.

Towers and his chief of staff (F. P. Sherman) concluded that the carriers could withstand Japanese air defences if their mobility were fully utilised to destroy the aircraft at the Marshalls' air bases and then provide close support. However, Spruance and Rear Admiral R. K. Turner (Amphibious Commander) wanted the carriers to concentrate on supplying close air support to the troops.

For the Gilberts Spruance also had five new fast batttleships which were to add their heavy AA to the carrier task groups' defence because of a shortage of screen cruisers and destroyers. The carrier commander had tactical control of the battleships, but if the enemy fleet arrived they were to form line of battle under Spruance for the set-piece surface action against the Japanese battleships that he had planned.

However, Turner and Spruance assigned the fast carriers to help the escort carriers (Rear Admirals Ragsdale and Mullinix) support the troops on the ground under the direction of the Pacific Fleet Amphibious Aircraft Support Unit (Captain H. Sallada). Its doctrine, experience and communications were still weak, but Spruance wanted an intense, rather than lengthy, pre-landing bombardment so that the Japanese fleet would not be alerted and intervene before the landing could take place.

Spruance planned to remain off the Gilberts to provide air support and be ready to meet the Japanese fleet. The battleships would then detach for a surface battle while the carriers provided air cover and took out any enemy carriers. Spruance was confident that the battleships would defeat the Japanese surface fleet and later landings would then be unopposed. Thus Pownall (TG 50.1) was stationed to intercept Japa-

Flight-deck operations, *Enterprise*, February 1944. Hangar maintenance and flight-deck personnel were vital for the carrier's offence and defence. Note the use of a Jeep and the 'vulture's' row above. (US Navy)

nese aircraft and neutralise their southern Marshalls air bases; Radford (TG50.2) to cover the Makin landings; Montgomery (TG 50.3) those at Tarawa; and Rear Admiral Sherman (TG50.4 *Saratoga* and *Princeton*) to neutralise Nauru, escort the troop convoys and act as reserve.

Pownall, Radford and Montgomery protested to Spruance that to wait for the Japanese advance would place the carriers at risk from air and submarine attack. Anti-aircraft protection (five battleships and six cruisers) was strong, but there were only 21 destroyers for eleven carriers. Experience from the Solomons had shown that using mobility to attack the enemy at source alone provided safety from air and submarine attack. Spruance, a battleship specialist, was determined to arrange for a set-piece surface battle and refused to change his dispositions.

The lesson of mobility was clearly illustrated when Halsey sent Sherman (TF38 *Saratoga* and *Princeton*) to cover the Bougainville landings on 1 November. Operating from open waters, the carrier aircraft hit the Japanese airfields on the island and then withdrew to refuel. Halsey's force turned back four local cruisers, but then another eight cruisers reached Rabaul from Truk. To prevent these cruisers attacking the Bougainville landings, Halsey sent all his 97 carrier aircraft to attack Rabaul, expecting heavy air and AA opposition, while land-based fighters protected the vulnerable carriers.

On 5 November, with 52 Hellcats trained by Commander J. C. Clifton for close escort, 23 Avengers and 22 Dauntless attacked and damaged six cruisers. Despite the presence of nearly 400 Japanese aircraft at Rabaul, the escorting Hellcats held off the Zeros and only eight aircraft failed to return to the carriers. On the same day Nimitz sent Montgomery's TG50.3 (*Essex, Bunker Hill, Independence*) to reinforce Halsey and to hit Rabaul again. Sherman favoured one task force, but Halsey ordered him to attack from the north and Montgomery from the south. The latter sent a full strike while his carriers were covered by two land-based Corsair squadrons including VF17 (Commander J. T. Blackburn) which had trained on *Bunker Hill* and so landed on her with arrester hooks to refuel.

The second air strike on Rabaul on 11 November confirmed the striking power and defensive abilities of the new carrier groups. Sherman's group did little damage because of poor weather, but TG50.3, later in the day, damaged another cruiser and sank two destroyers. The 90 Hellcats were able to hold off 68 defending Zeros. The Japanese launched 120 aircraft at the carriers, which had only their own and destroyer AA because the cruisers were supporting the troops on Bougainville. However, five fighter squadrons intercepted the first wave and AA accounted for 24 attackers.

The two raids on Rabaul proved that troop landings should be protected by the carriers using their mobility to attack the Japanese fleet and air bases. Moreover, the multi-carrier groups survived heavy air attack even without battleships and cruisers, the US fighter pilots and aircraft (Hellcats and Corsairs) now being superior to the Japanese. The Helldiver also proved itself and the Avengers had torpedoed enemy heavy ships, though their torpedoes were still beset by malfunctions. These lessons, however, came too late for the Gilberts; the plans could not be changed because the other carrier groups had left Pearl Harbor the day before the second strike.

The Gilberts offensive proved a great trial for the carriers. On 18 November Montgomery's carriers worked over Tarawa and on the 19th Pownall's hit the airfields of Mili and Jaluit (south Marshalls), Radford's Makin and Sherman's Nauru. Three hours before the assault the surface ships and carrier aircraft began to bombard Tarawa. The results were poor because inadequate briefing (Montgomery's group were absent at Rabaul) and inexperience meant that aircraft did not concentrate on a target long enough to ensure its destruction.

As the carrier commanders expected, their defensive stations for ground support drew heavy Japanese attack and revealed serious weaknesses. The main Japanese tactic was to send torpedo-bombers to attack at night by the light of flares. To warn of Japanese air attacks each task group deployed a picket destroyer with radar to direct defensive fighters. Because of Towers' decisions only Radford had a night-fighter unit, three aircraft formed on his own initiative, part of *Enterprise*'s veteran Air Group 6 (Lieutenant Commander E. H. O'Hare).

On 20 November 'Betty' torpedo-bombers from the northern Marshalls attacked Montgomery's task group off Tarawa and torpedoed *Independence*, which required six months' repairs. Even worse, on the 24th the CVE *Liscombe Bay* was sunk by a submarine with the loss of Rear Admiral Mullinix and 643 crewmen. By contrast, when on 26 November 30 'Bettys' attacked Radford's group, O'Hare's two Hellcats and radar-equipped Avenger broke up the attack, though O'Hare was killed in the process. This meant that night-flying was abandoned until the arrival of special units.

The day after *Independence* was damaged, Towers requested Nimitz to rescind the restriction on carrier mobility and allow them to attack the Marshalls air bases which were sending off the Japanese torpedo-aircraft. Nimitz therefore ordered a strike on the Marshalls as soon as possible. The carriers were needed until the 23rd when the main atolls (Betio, Makin and Apemama) fell; organised resistance had come to an end by the 28th.

Spruance could now proceed against the north Marshalls to safeguard the Gilberts and its shipping against further air attacks. Sherman's TG was left north of the Gilberts while Pownall took his own (*Yorktown, Lexington, Cowpens*) and Montgomery's TG50.3 (now *Essex, Enterprise* and *Belleau Wood*) to neutralise and photograph Kwajalein, the major base of the north Marshalls. A strike from the north on 4 December surprised the Japanese who were expecting attacks from the south.

Because of faulty intelligence and a new target co-ordinator, the first sortie, although sinking four merchant ships and destroying 55 aircraft in the air and on the ground, left many long-range 'Bettys', capable of attacking the task force, unscathed. Pownall therefore declined a second strike and withdrew. As a result the carriers endured a night of torpedo attacks, without night-fighters, during which *Lexington* was hit by a torpedo. Worse was only averted by superb ship manoeuvring and AA fire.

In the meantime Sherman (TG50.4 *Bunker Hill, Monterey*) covered a battleship bombardment of Nauru's airfield where more Japanese aircraft were reported and then (as TG37.2) transferred back to Halsey's command to strike Kavieng, New Ireland, on 25 December, and 1 and 4 January as part of the plan to surround Rabaul. Targets, however, were sparse.

Refuelling at sea – here from the tanker *Sebec* (AO-87) – was the key to the power of the carriers and the ability of the US Navy to mount its Central Pacific offensive. (US Navy)

The carrier operations around Rabaul and the Gilberts proved that carriers, if not left vulnerable to land-based aircraft, had great offensive power and could successfully defend themselves. However, their correct use depended on mobility, and resolute and aggressive leadership which Pownall had not shown.

Just before the invasion of the Gilberts the Allies met again at Cairo and Tehran (November–December 1943). The Combined Chiefs agreed to King's Pacific plans for a sea (submarine and mining) and air blockade and bombardment of Japan from bases in the Formosa–Luzon–China area, followed by invasion in 1945. In the Central Pacific, Truk, the Carolines (mid July 1944) and the Marianas (October) were to be secured while MacArthur advanced along New Guinea to Vogelkop (August). Halsey would eliminate Rabaul.

This was a compromise between King's and MacArthur's plans and allowed a dual advance to the Philippines–Formosa–China axis to choke Japanese communications with the East Indies. Further operations could then be decided. Proven carrier mobility and offensive power also allowed the planners to consider bypassing major Japanese bases such as Rabaul (there had been minor leapfrogging in the Aleutians and Solomons). Thus the priority was now the Marshalls and Truk.

On 3 January King briefed Nimitz about his latest assignments: to cut Japanese supply lines to the oil and raw materials of South East Asia and the East Indies (Luzon or Formosa) and secure bases in China for bombing and invading Japan. The key was to advance along the line Marshalls–Carolines–Marianas to provide bases for the fleet to strike to Luzon–Formosa–China and the B-29s to bomb Japan.

Nimitz and his planners decided to bypass the south Marshalls (Mili and Jaluit) and capture Wotje, Maloelap and Kawajalein (north Marshalls). Towers and F. P. Sherman (Cincpac planning officer) suggested securing Kwajalein only and using air power to neutralise the rest of the Marshalls. Spruance and Turner, not forgetting the night air attacks of the Gilberts, wanted to secure the other bases.

However, Nimitz had sufficient confidence in land and carrier air power to bypass the other Marshalls bases and prevent interference from the Carolines or Marianas. Thus only Kwajalein and the fleet base at Majuro were taken. While Nimitz decided to bypass major air bases (Marshalls), Sherman (Truk) and Halsey (Rabaul) also recommended bypassing key fleet bases. In January 1944 Towers agreed with bypassing Truk and also missing out the Marianas to advance to the Bismarcks–Admiralties–Palaus (July)–Philippines (August). Nimitz therefore suggested to King an advance from New Guinea to Luzon and abandoning the Marianas offensive.

At this time MacArthur also argued that the Marianas would delay the advance on the Philippines. The Gilberts operations, although a carrier success, had been costly in troops and there was a question whether the Central Pacific offensive would be too bloody. Nimitz therefore suggested substituting Palau for Truk. At Pearl Harbor (27–28 January) representatives of Central, South West and South Pacific Commands agreed on a New Guinea–Bismarcks–Admiralties–Palaus–Philippines advance. King however would not place Halsey's carriers under MacArthur and the USAAF wanted bases in the Marianas for B-29s to bomb Japan. All depended on which of the routes, Central or South West Pacific, would prove the most costly.

In December the Marshalls planning began and the arguments over carrier deployment continued. Spruance again feared a Japanese reaction if he committed the carriers too early. He and Pownall planned a two-day shore bombardment before the landings on Tarawa, but the latter insisted that the new battleships defend the carriers until the day before the landings. Towers and the other carrier commanders all agreed that the battleships should provide the two-day bombardment and Pownall had to agree. However, Spruance, who feared the Japanese fleet at Truk, eventually omitted the battleships' first day of bombardment.

Nimitz replaced Pownall – owing to his lack of aggression – with Mitscher as senior carrier commander. The latter also objected to Spruance's tying the carriers to a two-day pre-assault bombardment and close support of the troops ashore. Again Spruance refused to change his plans because fire support for the assault forces at the Gilberts had been inadequate. Towers recommended preliminary land-based air attacks for weeks beforehand. J. H. Hoover's land-aircraft began attacks on the Marshalls in January, but failed to destroy the airfields or defences. As Spruance would not commit his battleships until two days before the assault, the main burden again fell to the carriers.

The Gilberts' close air support techniques were improved and the fleet and escort carrier aircraft constantly strafed the enemy from low level to within ten feet of the advancing Marines. The problems of communications for controlling close support at the Gilberts was overcome by new amphibious command ships (AGCs) pioneered in the Mediterranean. The Commander Support Aircraft now had his own centre with an enlarged staff and improved communications.

In the Marshalls there was an AGC for both landings, each with a Commander Aircraft Support who controlled Target CAP, air target selection, and strengthened Support Air Control Units ashore for liaison or if communications failed. Pilots were also given extensive pre-attack briefings when each was assigned specific targets.

Given the Japanese night attacks at the Gilberts, Radford, as Tower's chief of staff, formulated a night-fighter policy and on 16 December 1943 issued a training scheme for every carrier to provide at least two night-fighter teams (one or two Avengers and two Hellcats). Every air group was to experiment until a doctrine was evolved.

Night training was placed under Commanders J. L. Phillips, who had assisted O'Hare, and Widhelm from NF75 in the Solomons. The main idea was to use ship fighter directors and radars to avoid another O'Hare tragedy. *Enterprise* with her new radar and Avenger (one)/Hellcat (two) team began the process. By 8 January each carrier had a team. *Enterprise* and *Intrepid* were assigned the special Corsair teams (four aircraft each) which had now arrived and *Yorktown* and *Bunker Hill* four Hellcats each which had not been specially trained.

Spruance also suggested strengthening the daytime carrier defence by increasing the CAP fighters, but Towers refused since the advantage of multi-carrier TGs was the requirement for fewer defensive fighters and their assignment to strike groups for strafing and escort. Moreover, Japanese daytime air attacks were few until the Philippines.

In January 1944 TF58 sortied for the last time from Pearl Harbor (being based in the Central Pacific thereafter). It now included twelve carriers (with the arrival of light carriers *Langley* and *Cabot*), 650 aircraft and eight fast battleships. On 29 January the carriers attacked the Marshalls and the battleships left the screens to bombard the beaches on 30 and 31 January. They were relieved on the 31st by seven old battleships, their escorts and eight escort carriers (Rear Admirals Ragsdale and Davison).

Rear Admirals Reeves', Ginder's, Montgomery's and Sherman's TGs were assigned Maloelap, Wotje, Roi and Kwajalein respectively. The airfields were hit while most Japanese aircraft were still on the ground and the few that took-off were soon destroyed. Once the aircraft on the ground had been strafed, an unchallenged command of the air was achieved on the first morning. Pounding the defences was then the main priority while Sherman (Eniwetok) and Ginder (Maloelap and Eniwetok) prevented Japanese reinforcements flying in.

From the 31st the AGCs directed close support of the assaults. Majuro was secured on the 31st and Kwajalein on 4 February. On the 3rd, Mitscher's carriers had withdrawn except Ginder's TG which continued to suppress Japanese aircraft on Eniwetok. The Marshalls operations went like clockwork. The carriers flew more than 4,500 sorties, losing only 44 aircraft, ensurng much weaker resistance than in the Gilberts due to the direction of the AGCs to which their offensive power was fully harnessed.

Apart from the airfields, the main gain was the acquisition of the fleet base at Majuro, 2,000 miles closer to Japan than Pearl Harbor. Servron 4 was merged into Servron 10 which was then based at Majuro. The tankers now went straight there, bypassing Pearl Harbor. ComAirPac also established a replacement pool for carrier aircraft which were ferried to the carriers by the escort carriers now assigned to Servron 10.

The weakness of the Japanese defence, despite the close proximity of Truk, induced Spruance to land on Eniwetok (1 May) to gain its strategic air base. First the main Japanese base at Truk (scheduled for March) had to be neutralised. Spruance flew his flag in *New Jersey*, but Mitscher in *Yorktown* had control of air operations. If the Japanese fleet approached, Spruance would assume command of the six fast battleships which Vice Admiral Lee (ComBatPac) would form into a battle line. Mitscher led the largest (nine) carrier strike against a fleet base of the entire war. US naval intelligence knew little of Truk and everyone hoped to repay the Japanese fleet for the attack on Pearl Harbor.

TF58, comprising TF58.1 (Reeves, *Enterprise*, *Yorktown*, *Belleau Wood*), TF58.2 (Montgomery, *Essex*, *Intrepid*, *Cabot*), TF58.3 (Sherman, *Bunker Hill*, *Cowpens*, *Monterey*), left in mid February. TG58.4 (Ginder, *Saratoga*, *Princeton*, *Langley*) covered the Eniwetok landings. On the 14th the carriers refuelled and the oilers returned to Kwajalein to top-up from commercial tankers for the post-strike refuelling which became standard practice.

On the 17 February 72 fighters were launched before dawn from 90 miles out. Mitscher initiated an all-fighter sweep because they were needed to escort the bombers and eliminate any enemy fighters. In the event they encountered heavy AA opposition and about 80 Zeros of which about 50 were shot down for the loss of four Hellcats. A further 150 were strafed on the ground, but some 100 of these escaped damage. The US pilots, tactics and aircraft were now clearly superior. The Japanese ships (only two cruisers, two destroyers and fifty auxiliaries and transports) were caught in harbour. The bombers sank about 140,000 tons of shipping. In contrast Spruance's two battleships, which with two cruisers and escorts engaged the Japanese warships escaping harbour, sank one cruiser and one destroyer.

For the first time the US carriers launched a night attack when twelve Avengers of VT10 (*Enterprise*) used their radar to sink another 60,000 tons of shipping with 500lb bombs. This attack was led by Lieutenant Commander W. I. Martin who had pioneered night torpedo attacks. During the same night, however, one of six 'Kate' torpedo-bombers eluded the night-fighters and hit the carrier *Intrepid* which had to be escorted to Pearl Harbor for lengthy repairs to its steering gear. Night-fighter direction still lacked conviction.

On 18 February the carriers launched more sorties against shore installations, meeting only light AA, and retired having lost seventeen aircraft and 26 aircrew. The final score against the Japanese was about 300 aircraft, three light cruisers, four destroyers, two transports and thirty merchant or auxiliary ships. In the meantime Ginder, having attacked Eniwetok on the 11th and 13th, returned with the escort carriers (Ragsdale) on the 17th for the pre-assault bombardment and landing. Resistance ceased on the 22nd.

After refuelling on the 19th Mitscher detached *Enterprise* to strike Jaluit on the 21st and led his remaining two TGs to attack the Marianas. On the final run-in (21–22 February) the TF was spotted by a 'Betty' which escaped, but Mitscher now had the confidence to continue the attack despite repeated torpedo attacks. Moreover, although night-fighters were available, he did not launch them. This was because of their failure to protect *Intrepid*. He also objected to night operations because they kept his air department up at night and aircrews could not get their rest. Mitscher therefore restricted night training, which denied the night-fighter pilots their practice and led to deck crashes which further fed his reluctance. A proposal that night-fighter carriers be adopted had

Crash! A typical accident aboard USS *Essex* in 1944. Often, such accidents were caused by combat fatigue and the difficulties of landing faster, heavier modern aircraft. Note the large numbers of deck crewmen. (US Navy)

been made, but this had not yet been taken up by Towers or Mitscher. In the meantime the attacks were beaten off by AA and evasive ship manoeuvring.

As before, Mitscher launched pre-dawn fighter sweeps which shot down most of the 74 interceptors that came up and strafed aircraft on the Saipan, Tinian and Guam airfields. The bombers sank some enemy transports and drove the rest out to sea where more were sunk by waiting submarines (45,000 tons total). Photographs were also taken for future landings. The US pilots and aircraft were far superior, losing only six aircraft as against 168. By now the naval pilots were scoring an average of thirteen kills to one against the Japanese.

After the seizure of the Marshall Islands the US fleet was into the heart of the Japanese defences. Moreover, the islands had been taken for only a third of the losses incurred at the Gilberts, and the strike on Truk had neutralised its naval base and

USS *Saratoga*: a detailed view of her profile as altered by January 1944, with the increased anti-aircraft armament highlighted. These extra weapons were to be needed against the Kamikazes. (US National Archives)

shown that the Japanese fleet was not the force it had been. Allied strategists now realised that the Central Pacific offensive could be accelerated if Truk was bypassed for the Marianas. Towers also concluded that the carriers, rather than being tied to the landings, should use their mobility and power to destroy the enemy's air power and fleet before they could interfere with amphibious operations.

Meanwhile MacArthur had secured (February–March 1944) the Admiralty Islands with the fleet base of Seedler Harbour in Manus Island. This was wanted by MacArthur for Vice Admiral Kincaid's Seventh Fleet (Philippines) and by Nimitz for Halsey's Third Fleet (Formosa). In March the JCS decided to continue a two-pronged advance, the Japanese being weaker than had been anticipated. Bypassing Truk, Nimitz was to seize Saipan in June and Formosa in February 1945. MacArthur would advance New Guinea–Mindanao, bypassing Rabaul and Kavieng. Both would use Manus as a fleet base.

Nimitz therefore planned for the carriers to bypass Truk for the Marianas (June) and Palaus (September) and assist MacArthur's operations at Hollandia, New Guinea (June) and Mindanao. Whether Luzon or Formosa would be the next objective was left open. However, King had secured agreement that the main emphasis would be on the Central Pacific and an accelerated attack on the Japanese perimeter.

The carriers' support of MacArthur's Hollandia landing would be difficult because there were large air bases in the area and aircraft could also attack from the Palaus. General Kenney's land aircraft were given the job of neutralising enemy aircraft on New Guinea and Mitscher those from the Palaus. As usual Spruance (flag in the cruiser *Indianapolis*) was in overall command, with Lee to command the battleships in any fleet action. The power of the carrier task force was increased by the TGs being upgraded to four carriers each, starting with Montgomery's (*Hornet*) and Ginder's (*Langley*). TF58 left Espiritu Santo on 23 March for a southern approach designed to avoid Truk's reconnaissance aircraft, but these located the TF on the 25th. The fleet's AA guns again beat off Japanese night attacks.

The pre-dawn fighter sweep on the 30th achieved command of the air; 30 Zeros were destroyed in the air and more aircraft on the ground, and the US fighters joined the attack on merchant shipping in harbour with very effective strafing. The Helldivers (now two squadrons) carried more bombs and so had a greater percentage of hits in dive-bombing than the SBDs. The Avengers concentrated on low-level bomb and torpedo attacks, sinking one destroyer. Co-ordinated attacks from many directions gave surface ships, at anchor or manoeuvring in confined waters, little chance.

The Avengers also successfully pioneered the laying of air mines, including delay fuzed, which claimed some victims and trapped the remaining shipping at Palau for six weeks until they had been swept. During the mining the Avengers were slow and vulnerable and the experiment was not repeated by carrier aircraft, the job being undertaken with great success by land aircraft.

On the 31st Montgomery's and Ginder's TGs returned to Palau where they caught another 60 aircraft flown-in for reprisals, while Reeves' TG attacked Yap. On 1 April it was the turn of Woleai and Ulithi, but Palau proved to have the most targets. For the loss of eighteen aircrew and a few aircraft (26 more aircrew were rescued by life-guards) more than 30 aircraft, one destroyer and 28 other ships were destroyed. The Palaus were neutralised and Hollandia's northern flank had been secured.

As a consequence of the destruction of Japanese aircraft in New Guinea and the landings being supported by units under command of the Seventh Fleet, the carriers found few worthwhile targets. The TF left Majuro on 13 April with all three TGs now having four carriers. Mitscher used his night-fighters to intercept Japanese night attacks and to keep their troops awake. On the 24th the carriers withdrew to Manus. However, the land-based Liberators which had taken over the bombing of Truk from 29 March 1944 encountered heavy opposition.

Mitscher therefore launched another raid on Truk on 29 April. The pre-dawn fighter sweep provoked a major battle with 60 Zeros, intense AA and a torpedo attack on the carriers which was beaten off by the CAP and AA. The attackers returned on the 30th. Ninety enemy aircraft were destroyed in the air and on the ground for a loss of 26. Thus Truk was finally eliminated as a major air base though it still retained formidable AA defences. On their way home the surface ships were detached to bombard Sarawan and Ponape covered by Clark's TG.

For the next step of the Central Pacific campaign the US Fifth Fleet was the largest in history, the core being fifteen fast carriers and seven new battleships. Naval intelligence was aware that the Japanese fleet now had new carriers and air groups roughly equivalent to half the US strength. Nimitz believed that the Japanese, after refusing battle in the Gilberts and Marshalls, must use these to defend the Marianas. He was confident that the US fleet had the advantage in all classes of ship and aircraft plus veteran commanders, ships' companies and air groups. So the US fleet eagerly sought battle and hoped to destroy the Japanese fleet or maim it to the extent that it would no longer pose a threat to subsequent amphibious operations which would be further from US bases and closer to Japanese ones.

The question was how to achieve this victory. Spruance had spent three tours at the Naval War College in 1926–38 where, like the British and Japanese at their Staff Colleges, he had re-fought Jutland. He still wanted to form a line of battle of the new battleships (Lee) and fight a classic, traditional surface action. Spruance also had the new weapon – the fast carriers which before the war had been expected merely to take care of the enemy carriers and provide air cover and spotting for the battle line. Whether the carriers would be able to sink enemy battleships had been controversial.

By 1944 the aviators were sure that they could not only sink enemy carriers but also their battleships. The fast carriers had already sunk Japanese carriers, cruisers and destroyers, and battleships had been sunk by aircraft in harbour (Taranto and Pearl Harbor) and also at sea (*Prince of Wales* and *Repulse*). The carriers, however, were very vulnerable to surface ships, aircraft and submarines. They therefore had to keep their mobility and retain strong surface escorts.

An excellent view of *Saratoga*'s large funnel and island and of her heavy armament. (US Navy)

Spruance, however, had to protect the amphibious operations (more than 600 vessels) as well, and if the Japanese fleet attacked these it would threaten the troops ashore and set back the Central Pacific offensive. He was well aware of the problems caused by Japanese interventions during the Solomons and Gilberts campaigns. For this reason, as at the Gilberts and Marshalls, Spruance favoured the strategy of remaining close to the amphibious operations and allowing the Japanese fleet to come to him.

At Midway and Guadalcanal, in a calculated risk, King and Nimitz had taken the offensive against the Japanese fleet. They were continuing to take risks, but they supported Spruance's strategy because they believed that the Japanese fleet would have to intervene in an endeavour to put a stop to the Pacific offensive. This stance posed two problems: Spruance's inexperience of aviation matters and his lack of a senior air adviser on his staff to make up for it. King had appointed a surface specialist (A. A. Burke) as Mitscher's chief of staff, but still had not given Spruance an aviator as his.

Moreover, as Towers predicted on 13 June and Nimitz informed Spruance, the Japanese could use their longer-ranged aircraft and bases in the Marianas to keep their ships out of range of US aircraft, and the battleships would never get near the enemy. If Spruance wanted to destroy the enemy fleet he had to take a risk and allow the carriers to close the enemy, rather than wait for them to come to him. But this called for the adoption of a strategy based on initiative (of the carrier commander and air group leaders), mobility and long-range weapons, rather than the traditional line of battle, with the CinC in control, for which he had been trained.

Unlike the situation in the Gilberts and Marshalls, the amphibious command ships with fighter-direction teams, using a CAP from seven escort carriers (157 aircraft), although inexperienced, now covered the landings and freed the carriers. The CVEs could also provide – the destroyers now being armed with the latest sonar – anti-submarine patrols. Their air patrols and ships' radar could also locate any enemy surface ships.

However, the old battleships only had a radar coverage of 30 miles, little more than the Japanese big gun range. If the Japanese battleships evaded the air search, there would be little warning before they started shelling the landings and transports. Then, too, CVEs had short decks so their Avengers could not employ their torpedoes. The Japanese had sent their two *Yamato* class super-battleships to attack MacArthur's shipping at Biak. Thus Spruance could not allow its fleet to slip past his forces.

USS *Bunker Hill* (CV-17; 1943). Even fleet carriers on the way to Pearl Harbor to join the fleet were used to ferry aircraft, as here, September 1943. (US National Archives)

As a preliminary to the Marianas, Mitscher sent Montgomery's TG to attack Marcus and Wake (20–24 May) to prevent their support of the Marianas and to gain experience with assigning targets to pilots in pre-attack briefings so as to cut down bomb wastage. The operation was a success, but the pre-attack target selection was not because each target was unique and air group commanders had to assign primary targets.

On 15 June the Fifth Fleet landed troops on Saipan. TF58 had left Majuro on the 6th for pre-dawn sweeps and strikes (12th) on Saipan and Pagan (Rear Admirals Reeves and Harrill), Tinian (Montgomery), Guam and Rota (Clark). Mitscher had also implemented an afternoon strike on the 11th to pre-empt night attacks and keep the Japanese guessing. This swept the skies clear of Japanese aircraft of which about 150 were destroyed in the air or on the ground.

The carrier aircraft then attacked shore defences under heavy AA fire for the next three days before the landing. Mitscher wanted to conserve his bombs for the expected naval battle, so the Avengers used rockets, but they were very vulnerable to AA during their long approach so the faster Hellcats took over the rockets. The carrier aircraft also located two convoys and sank ten merchantmen and four escorts. Meanwhile the new battleships pounded Saipan on the 13th until relieved by the old battleships next day. Although the support of the old battleships and carrier aircraft was the best and heaviest yet, resistance was still tenacious and the division earmarked for the landing on Guam had to be committed.

The US fleet prevented the Japanese High Command sending in convoys of reinforcements and their first reaction was to send aircraft from the Bonins and Jimas to support a proposed fleet attack. Spruance had anticipated this and on the 14th ordered Mitscher to send two carrier TGs (Clark and Harrill) to hit the Volcano Islands for two days (16th–17th). In the event, the sortie of the Japanese fleet caused Clark to strike early (15th–16th) in order to return in time for the expected fleet action. This severely curtailed the Japanese effort to mass its land-based aircraft in Guam to attack the US fleet.

Spruance knew almost as soon as the Japanese fleet left harbour and he alerted Clark and Harrill to concentrate again with Mitscher. On the evening of the 15th two submarines reported that the main body was clearing the San Bernardino Strait and that the *Yamato*s were heading north-west. Spruance concluded that the Japanese were using their traditional tactics of dividing their fleet to lay a trap, but in fact they were concentrating.

Anticipating a battle, Spruance and his chief of staff (C. J. Moore) conferred with Turner (amphibious commander). All battleship specialists, they decided to reinforce the fast carriers with eight cruisers and 21 destroyers, to position the seven old battleships and three cruisers west of Saipan against a Japanese flanking move, and withdraw all amphibious forces except landing-craft unloading and CVEs and destroyers supporting the troops. Spruance gave Mitscher the task of destroying the enemy carriers. He also ordered Lee to form his line of battle fifteen miles ahead of the carriers to avoid confusion during the battle and to engage the enemy fleet or destroy its stragglers.

During their passage south on the 17th to join him, Mitscher ordered Clark and Harrill to search for the carriers 350 miles to the south-west. On the same day Montgomery and Reeves left the support of Saipan to the escort carriers. Having failed to find the enemy carriers, Clark wanted to continue south-west to come behind them and catch them in a trap with Mitscher in front. There was some risk because the US carriers would be split and the Japanese could concentrate on either Clark or Mitscher and crush each in turn. However, it was unlikely that they had the strength to do so and their escape route would be closed. Harrill, however, did not have the nerve for the scheme.

Meanwhile Mitscher expected the Japanese fleet to advance by the Davao–Palau–Yap route (south-west) or across the Philippine Sea (west). On the night of 17/18 June a submarine reported a large force to the west and Spruance, taking this to be the Japanese main line of advance, intended to advance westwards to destroy their fleet. Mitscher therefore advanced westwards with Lee in the van, Harrill covering him and, twelve miles astern, Clark, Reeves and Montgomery in a line abreast. His plan was for the TF to close the range on the Japanese (who had longer-range aircraft), allow the battleships to get in the first blow by night and then launch a dawn strike.

However, Lee, fearing Japanese night tactics and torpedo attacks, and conscious of the Americans' lack of night operational training, declined a night action, though this was his best chance of a surface action in the age of aircraft. So Mitscher retired eastwards during the night of 18/19 June, which curtailed his chance of closing the range. He would have to steam eastwards (into wind) away from the Japanese to launch and retrieve his aircraft, while they could continue to advance westwards while launching.

At 2200 hours on the 18th, Mitscher received an intelligence report of a radio interception 300 miles to the west. He therefore planned to return westwards at 0130 hours on the 19th so as to be within 200 miles of the Japanese fleet for an 0500 hours launch aimed at destroying the main body of the Japanese fleet.

If the Japanese sent a battleship force round his flank to attack the Saipan beachhead he expected Oldendorf's seven old battleships and three cruisers plus the seven CVEs (Rear Admirals Sallada, Bogan) to deal with it, with assistance from a fast carrier strike eastwards if necessary. Moreover, if the Japanese detached their battleships their six carriers would have a greatly weakened AA defence. Thus both forces were likely to be crushed.

Spruance, meanwhile, had decided to keep the carriers close to the Marianas, in case the Japanese force to the west was a decoy. Not being an aviator, he did not fully realise that the carriers, even though further west, could still strike the main Japanese body even if it turned out to be in the south-west (heading for Saipan) rather than to the west. Moreover, keeping the TF off the Marianas deprived the carriers of their mobility and prevented their striking the Japanese carriers while the enemy's longer-ranged aircraft (and land-based aircraft from Marianas) could strike.

Spruance lacked a senior aviator on his staff during the decision-making process. Even more unfortunate was the fact that he received so little intelligence on the 18th. For long-range reconnaissance he relied on 27 submarines patrolling Bonins–Marianas–Formosa–Philippines and off Tawi Tawi, long-range patrol aircraft (five Mariners from a tender at Saipan and twelve Liberators at Los Negros, Admiralty Islands) and Army bombers. He also had shore-based radio direction finding if the Japanese used their radio. For tactical reconnaissance he relied on carrier scouts. Nevertheless, a report from a Mariner flying boat which located the entire Japanese fleet on radar at 0100 hours on the 18th did not reach him until seven hours later.

Like Jellicoe's at Jutland, Spruance's plans were upset by the shortcomings of his battle intelligence. The submarines notified Spruance that the Japanese fleet was at sea, but, with periscopes, could not accurately report its composition, and their reports took time to reach him from Submarine Command. The Navy patrol aircraft had serious radio problems, and the Army bombers, through lack of training, had great difficulty in accurately reporting the location and composition of naval forces.

Over-emphasis on the strike function had led the reconnaissance squadrons, long-viewed as the eyes of the fleet, to neglect their primary function. The old Dauntless (59 aircraft) did not have radar and had not been used for reconnaissance since the Gilberts. The Helldivers (174 aircraft) were designed primarily for dive-bombing and the early versions did not carry radar either. The first carrier with radar Helldivers (*Hancock*) was shaking-down in the Caribbean, and not all Helldivers were fitted until the end of 1944. In the meantime 27 Avengers with radar (32-mile range) undertook scouting duties but were comparatively slow. In addition, 24 Hellcats and three Corsairs, fitted with radar for night-fighting, could have been used, but their radar was unreliable.

Therefore, although the carriers had great striking power in the Avengers (torpedo/bombs), Helldivers (bombs/cannon in later version) and Hellcats (light bombs), their scouting was poor. With inadequate intelligence Spruance would not take risks because he could not be certain as to the whereabouts of the Japanese fleet and was obsessed by the fear that they would get past him and play havoc with the landings.

On 19 June, having not yet received the reported position of the Japanese fleet, Spruance asked Mitscher to neutralise Japanese land-based air at the Guam and Rota airfields. Mitscher sent some fighters, reinforced when it was reported that enemy aircraft were taking-off (35 were shot down). At 0950 hours the first Japanese strike appeared on US radar. Interception by the CAP (Hellcats) was co-ordinated by the TF fighter direction officer (Lieutenant J. Eggert) and his four TG colleagues. Mitscher recalled his fighters from Guam and launched all his strike aircraft to orbit off Guam and damage its airfields so as to clear the flight-decks for fighter operations by his 450 Hellcats.

The combat with the inexperienced Japanese pilots, which lasted until 1500 hours, was so one-sided that it became known as the 'Marianas Turkey Shoot'. Lieutenant A. Vracia (VF16) became an ace with six victories and Air Group 15 (Commander D. McCampbell) scored an impressive total. The few Japanese aircraft that got through met intensive AA fire. The only result of four strikes was one hit on the fast battleship *South Dakota* and some near misses. The Japanese carriers lost 330 aircraft of 354 launched.

By contrast the US carriers lost only eighteen fighters and twelve strike aircraft, but Mitscher estimated that the Japanese could still have 200 aircraft and nine carriers which had not been located (apart from submarine reports). Although Spruance still felt some concern for Saipan, he recalled the amphibious ships and allowed Mitscher, who left the reluctant Harrill to cover Guam and Rota with night-fighters over their airfields, to take up the pursuit at 2000 hours.

During the night of the 19th Mitscher, while steaming north-west, did not launch any aircraft to search for the Japanese fleet because he wished to rest his air groups, but mainly because he had failed to develop any night search capability. At dawn on the 20th air searches to the north-west began. For long-range search he still relied on the Mariners operating from Saipan. The Japanese fleet was not found until 1540 hours (by an Avenger of VF10, *Enterprise*) and Mitscher was informed at 1605 hours that it was 275 miles WNW of TF58. By this time only 30 minutes of daylight remained for an attack, after which the pilots would be faced with the hazards of landing-on in darkness.

Mitscher at once ordered two full strikes and at 1621 the carriers turned into the wind. A strike of 215 aircraft (84 Hellcats, 54 Avengers, 51 Helldivers and 26 Dauntless) led by Lieutenant Commander B. M. Strean was launched from every carrier, except the CVL *Princeton*, in a record ten minutes. After it left, a corrected position (60 miles further north) for the Japanese fleet was received and Mitscher cancelled the second strike which now had no time to attack.

After two hours (300 miles) the enemy fleet was sighted at 1840 hours. With only 30 minutes of daylight remaining, attacks were made with little attempt at co-ordination or target selection. Even worse, few Avengers carried torpedoes because of the Devastators' fate at Midway, and torpedo practice had been neglected in favour of constant attacks on land targets. Their bombs tended to do little damage, as was the case when the carrier *Ryuho* was hit by VT10 (*Enterprise*). Bombers damaged *Junyo* and the CVL *Chitose*. The dive-bombers of VB1 (*Yorktown*) and bombers of VT2 (*Hornet*) set *Zuikaku* ablaze. The only squadron armed with torpedoes was VT24 (*Belleau Wood*) and one of its torpedoes sank *Hiyo* after two hours, showing what might have been.

The surviving 190-odd aircraft then had a two-hour, 250-mile flight home in the dark. Those who ran out of fuel before reaching the carriers or made an error of navigation in the moonless night had to ditch, the crew climbing into their rafts and hoping for rescue. Those who reached the carriers, found them lighted up according to standard night-landing procedure. Mitscher went further, ordering searchlights on and night-fighters up to guide them in. For two hours from 2000 hours aircraft landed-on or ditched beside the carriers, damaged aircraft being dumped to clear the flight-deck. During the 21st TF58 continued the pursuit, picking up ditched aircrew on the way, and Lee's force covered by two carriers was detached to clear up any enemy stragglers. However, no further contact was made and the pursuit was abandoned on the 23rd.

The result of the strike had been one carrier sunk, three badly damaged, one slightly damaged plus two oilers damaged and scuttled. The losses were twenty aircraft shot down and 60 ditched or discarded overboard. Of the aircrew, 101 were recovered near the carriers and 62 during the pursuit. Thus 49 aircrew and 100 aircraft were lost plus six ships' company in shipboard accidents. Although Mitscher had destroyed 475 air-craft for the loss of 100, which were quickly replaced, the Japanese carriers were still largely intact, only *Hiyo* being sunk. So the fleet's objective of destroying the Japanese fleet was not achieved, nor was it realised that Japanese carrier air power had been annihilated as a result of its aircraft and pilot losses.

Deck-edge lift, USS *Leyte* (CV-32; 1946): a close-up view of the feature pioneered by the *Essex* class and used extensively in modern designs. Note the hangar closed by blinds. (US National Archives)

Although Nimitz's main aim had been the destruction of the Japanese fleet, Spruance had made the Saipan beachhead's safety his priority. He had underestimated the ability of air power to strike in any direction. A more aggressive policy would have allowed TF58 to position itself 250 miles west of Saipan where it could still cover Saipan and strike the Japanese carriers. If they were sunk their aircraft could not attack Saipan. Spruance and his staff, too surface-oriented and lacking carrier expertise, did not fully appreciate carrier potential and their need for an aggressive strategy.

A dawn strike on the Japanese force, even if divided, as Spruance feared, would have annihilated the carriers, given the superiority of the US aircrew and aircraft and ample daylight for a co-ordinated attack. Lee's force could also have finished off any stragglers. Although there would have been more risk of losing carriers to Japanese strikes, the radar-directed Hellcats and AA guns were more than a match for the inexperienced Japanese pilots and their inferior aircraft. The point however was that the Japanese carriers would not have survived to fight another day. Hampered by lack of good intelligence, Spruance had played it safe but had allowed the Japanese carriers to escape. Thus they remained a factor in later US operational planning, including the assault on Leyte.

After the battle, which had revealed the lack of night search, night attack and night landing capability, all carrier pilots were required to qualify in night landing and a carrier night task group was formed in July 1944. In August the newly repaired *Independence* left Pearl Harbor with an extemporised night air group, to join the group which included *Enterprise* and *Bataan*, headed by newly promoted Rear Admiral M. Gardner. Meanwhile training was undertaken on *Saratoga* and *Ranger* by Hellcats (completely replacing Corsairs) and Avengers.

Carrier aviation was also strengthened by other decisions. King finally forced Spruance, Kinkaid (Seventh Fleet under MacArthur) and Lee to accept aviator chiefs of staff. In November 1944 ComBatPac was abolished in favour of two battleship squadrons: 1st (old battleships, Rear Admiral Oldendorf) and 2nd (fast battleships, Vice Admiral Lee). Finally in December ComAirPac (now G. A. Murray) was upgraded to Vice Admiral.

After Saipan the fast and escort carriers supported the seizure of Tinian and Guam (July–August) and the former also raided the Palaus in preparation for future operations and the Bonin and Volcanoes to keep down shore-based aircraft. Meanwhile in mid 1944 the next phase of the campaign was debated and it was decided that land-based support was needed.

MacArthur was to advance Morotai–Mindanao–Leyte–Luzon and Nimitz Palaus–Leyte–Formosa–China (Amoy). Nimitz, Spruance and Turner wanted to take Luzon in order to secure Manila Bay as a base for the Formosa operations, but King argued that Eniwetok would be a sufficiently advanced base for a direct move to Formosa or even Japan. However, with Operations 'Overlord' (Normandy) and 'Anvil' (South of France) in full swing, there would be insufficient shipping and landing-craft for Formosa until 1945; on 8 September 1944 King agreed to the Leyte landings, followed by Luzon or Formosa.

When the operations in New Guinea ended, Halsey was transferred to the Central Pacific. Admiral Spruance (Fifth Fleet) and Admiral Halsey (Third Fleet) now alternated operations and planning to ensure that the Japanese remained under continuous pressure. Mitscher would be Spruance's carrier commander, and J. S. McCain, King's DCNO (Air) in Washington, would be Halsey's over the heads of Towers (now deputy CinCPac) and F. C. Sherman. Mitscher remained in overall command until after Leyte while McCain learned the ropes as a TG commander. King and Marshall disagreed on a Supreme Commander in the Pacific and so Army operations (Philippines) came under MacArthur and naval operations (Central Pacific) under Nimitz.

In expectation that resistance and fleet operations would intensify as they drew ever nearer to the Japanese mainland, the US fleet was expanded and improved. During the summer and autumn seven more *Essex* class carriers arrived, with improved AA armament (40mm Bofors replacing 20mm Oerlikons) and the other carriers were also upgraded.

In August and September Halsey had to support the landings at Morotai (MacArthur) and Peleliu (Nimitz) and whittle down Japanese air power in the Philippines and other bases. He undertook carrier raids on Mindanao and Leyte and as a result of the light opposition Nimitz bypassed Mindanao for Leyte and Formosa for Luzon–Iwo Jima–Okinawa.

For the landings on Leyte on 20 October Nimitz ordered Halsey, with his sixteen carriers and more than 1,000 aircraft, to make the destruction of the Japanese fleet his first priority so as to prevent interference with the landings. Halsey's first move was to destroy Japanese aircraft on Okinawa, Formosa, the Philippines and Kyushu. He started with Okinawa on 10 October, moved on to Formosa on 12–15 October, and the Philippines on 12 and 15–19 October. These attacks in fact wiped out the Japanese land and carrier aircraft reserve (committed to Formosa), but Halsey, expecting more resistance, arranged for rest and replenishment in turn at Ulithi, starting with McCain's TG38.1 (five carriers).

Early on the 24th Halsey learned that two submarines had torpedoed three Japanese cruisers in the Palawan Passage. After carrier scouts had sighted two Japanese battleship groups, Halsey covered the three approaches to Leyte with his TGs – Luzon, Sherman's TG38.3; San Bernardino Strait, Bogan's TG38.2; Surigao Strait, Davison's TG38.4 – and recalled McCain's TG.

Carrier aircraft began to attack both Japanese groups. The South Force (Surigao Strait) was then left to Oldendorf's old battleships and the aircraft concentrated on the Centre Force (San Bernardino Strait). They sank the super-battleship *Musashi* and damaged others and the Force turned away at 1400 hours. Japanese aircraft, instead of covering their surface ships, attacked Sherman's TG and sank the light fleet carrier *Princeton*. Halsey, believing the Centre Force to be badly mauled and planning to detach

Funeral, light carrier USS *Cabot* (CVL-28), November 1944. The price paid for victory was heavy. Note the small island with typical decoration and log of claimed air victories. (US Navy)

Lee's battleships if it returned, concentrated his energies on finding the Japanese carriers.

At 1640 hours Helldivers from Sherman's carriers located the decoy Northern Force 190 miles away. Halsey decided to take his force, including Lee's battleships since he expected heavy air attacks, to destroy the Northern Force's carriers. He did not change his mind when a Hellcat night-fighter from *Independence* reported the Centre Force heading back for the San Bernardino Strait, because he assumed that Kincaid (Seventh Fleet) would cover it. Kinkaid, however, thought that Lee's battle line would do this. During his night advance Halsey, like Spruance, was chiefly concerned lest the Japanese carriers sneak past him.

Meanwhile Oldendorf and PT boats destroyed the Southern Force in the Surigao Strait, while the Centre Force, unopposed, passed through the San Bernardino Strait

and at 0645 hours was sighted visually by the CVEs off Samar which were soon being bombarded. The CVEs had few bombers in the air so Kinkaid and Rear Admiral C. A. F. Sprague (CVE CO) appealed to Halsey for help. At first Halsey ordered McCain to the rescue and then sent his battleships south, covered by Bogan.

At dawn Mitscher launched his strike against the ill-defended Japanese carriers and sank *Zuikaku*, *Zuiho* and *Chitose* in textbook co-ordinated attacks while *Chiyoda* was abandoned. Halsey ordered his surface units to finish off *Chiyoda* (sunk by cruisers) and the escorts. This delayed ordering the battleships south again and his reluctance to divide his force meant that the Japanese heavy escorts and the Centre Force's battleships escaped. Luckily for Halsey, Centre Force withdrew at 1300 hours, having sunk only one CVE (*Gambier Bay*) and three escorts for the loss of three cruisers, but believing that several fast carriers had been sunk and that any shipping had fled Leyte. Kamikaze were deployed for the first time and these sank another escort carrier (*St Lo*) and damaged others.

The Centre Force's retreat to Manila was not stopped despite heavy attacks by McCain's carriers during the afternoon, which inflicted little damage; a night strike launched from the night carrier *Independence* failed to find it, and a dawn strike by McCain and Bogan sank one cruiser sunk and damaged another.

As a result of the battle the US Navy had destroyed nearly 50 per cent of the Japanese forces committed: four carriers, three battleships, ten cruisers and nine destroyers. Moreover, the Japanese had also sacrificed their land-based and carrier aircraft to give Centre Force the chance to attack the Philippines bridgehead, which was not taken. However, even if they had gone into Leyte Bay they would have been confronted by Oldendorf's old battleships, supported by McCain, and then Lee's battleships coming south with Bogan.

King was furious that Halsey had been decoyed away by the Japanese carriers, leaving the transports open to the battleships, and blamed Kinkaid for not sending air searches to locate the Central Force. Only the escort carriers and Japanese hesitation had prevented achievement of their objective of attacking Leyte. Their plan had worked perfectly in luring Halsey away and his lack of communication with Kinkaid and refusal to divide his force had allowed them in.

Although Halsey had been a carrier commander from 1939 to 1942, had taken over tactical command and was prepared to take risks, he lacked Spruance's quality of meticulous planning, Mitscher's recent experience with the huge forces involved in 1944, and a specialised aviation staff. Thus he failed to co-ordinate with Kinkaid, divide his forces or dash north and then south again in time to destroy the Centre Force as well as the Northern Force. However, communications with Kinkaid were very slow and Halsey had not had carrier experience since 1942. Moreover, Kinkaid, also inexperienced in large-scale operations, left too much to Halsey and failed to locate the Centre Force.

After the battle the CVEs and some fast carriers had to remain off Leyte until 30 October to cover the troops ashore. Thus the fast carriers faced their first Kamikaze attacks, causing great damage and casualties to *Franklin* and *Belleau Wood* though rather less to *Intrepid.* To prevent further attacks on the beachhead, Halsey attacked airfields on Luzon and troop convoys to Leyte throughout November, during which *Lexington, Intrepid, Essex* and *Cabot* were hit by Kamikaze and *Hancock* was damaged by a near-miss. Halsey therefore insisted on no more operations until better counter-measures were devised.

This meant more fighters for CAP, in place of bombers, but the only sources were the new Bearcat, which would not reach squadron service until May 1945, or the USMC. The Marines, who earlier had rejected carrier service, had tired of keeping bypassed islands quiet and wanted to provide their own air support for their amphibious landings. So in August Towers agreed to the training of Marines for CVEs and a Marine Carrier Group Command was formed in October.

In November Mitscher suggested switching some of these Marine pilots to the fast carriers and on 2 December King ordered ten squadrons to qualify on *Saratoga* and *Ranger* immediately. As a result the carrier air group bombers (fifteen Helldiver, fifteen Avenger) were again cut to allow 73 fighters. The Marine Corsairs would fly CAP and the Hellcats serve as fighter-bombers. As a temporary expedient, for January 1945 only, *Essex* and *Wasp* were given 91 fighters each! As squadrons of 73 planes were unwieldy they were split into fighter and fighter-bomber (VBF) squadrons. The carrier conversion of Marine Corsairs resulted in heavy pilot and aircraft losses at first because of deck crashes.

Further measures introduced by McCain were radar picket destroyers (TOMCATs) sixty miles ahead of the carrier formation for early warning, with their own CAP and scouts; special low-altitude dawn and dusk CAPs; and constant fighter patrols over enemy airfields, day and night, to prevent Kamikaze taking-off. These new tactics were exercised at Ulithi from late November.

On 19 December, Night Carrier Division 7 (Gardner) was activated and soon afterwards *Enterprise* left Pearl Harbor with her new Night Air Group to join *Independence* in January. The latter proved too small for night operations, returned to Pearl Harbor for a day air group and was replaced by *Saratoga* which could also operate 24 day fighters. *Bataan* also went to Pearl to work up a night air group. When *Saratoga* was badly damaged off Iwo Jima on 21 February, the new *Bon Homme Richard*, still in US waters, was designated her replacement and arrived in June.

Meanwhile King continued to oppose the Luzon operation because he felt that the Philippines would fall anyway once Japan did and that taking them would delay the advance to China. He favoured taking Formosa, with its air bases, and then bases in China, but the requisite shipping and troops could not be found until the end of the war in Europe. Nimitz preferred neutralising Formosa with carrier air power and taking the Bonins and Okinawa to provide airfields for B-29 strikes on Japan. King therefore agreed to MacArthur taking Luzon, to keep up momentum, while Nimitz advanced to Okinawa.

Kamikaze damage limited Halsey to three TGs during the Luzon operation of 9 January, but support of the landings was now left to the large numbers of CVEs formed into the Escort Carrier Force, Pacific Fleet (Rear Admiral C. Durgin, from the Mediterranean in December). The fast carriers were to destroy enemy aircraft on Luzon and keep the Kamikaze from taking-off. On 18 December, while seeking to refuel, the carrier task force (TF) was hit by the first of 'Halsey's typhoons', losing three destroyers and many aircraft.

From 30 December to 9 January Halsey returned to stifling the Kamikaze by attacking the airfields on Luzon, Formosa, Pescadores, Ryukyus and Okinawa, but the Kamikaze still managed to sink a CVE (*Ommaney Bay*) and other ships at the Luzon landings. The TF also suffered heavy operational losses, mainly from inexperienced Marine landings. The senior TG commanders were critical of the inexperience, sloppy methods and vague instructions of Halsey and McCain (acting merely as his deputy).

In mid January Halsey took the TF into the South China Sea to search for remaining Japanese warships, especially battleships, which might threaten the Luzon landings. Ranging from Singapore via Camranh Bay to Hong Kong, the carriers found few targets and no warships. Returning to attacks on Formosa, the Pescadores and

Kamikaze! With the decimation of élite carrier air crews and the failure to produce replacements of quality and in numbers, suicide tactics were adopted. Here a 'Kate' is destroyed by US anti-aircraft fire. (IWM)

Sakishimas (21 January), the TF suffered heavy Kamikaze reprisals, *Ticonderoga*, a picket destroyer and *Langley* being hit. *Hancock* was also damaged by a landing accident.

By 30 January naval responsibilities for the Philippines had ended. These operations had cut the Japanese communications to the East Indies, given the fleet a base at Leyte and allowed a sustained blockade of Japan by air and sea. The carrier TF had remained at sea for record periods despite the Kamikaze. Attention now turned to the final encirclement of Japan under Spruance and Mitscher.

The debate as to exactly how the final defeat of Japan was to be accomplished was still in full cry during the winter of 1944/45. The B-29 bomber offensive from the Marianas had opened in November, and US submarines had cut the Japanese lines of communication to the East Indies and decimated their shipping by early 1945. However, the large Japanese armies in China and Japan remained intact and would fight on. King was still advocating landings in China (Chu Shan), but Marshall was in favour of hitting the Japanese mainland direct (Kyushu) using Iwo Jima (February) and Okinawa (April) as air bases. Russian intervention in China and lack of support forced King to agree to the latter in November 1944. Nimitz was to be the naval commander and MacArthur the Army commander.

Although Halsey, Nimitz and King were still anxious to finish off any Japanese warships and convoys they could find, the lack of such targets relegated the fast carriers' main mission to support of amphibious landings plus softening-up the mainland in preparation for the invasion. Instead of attacking isolated island objectives, the fast carriers were now required to take on and remain in range of continental air power, which meant more fighters, picket destroyers, night carriers and logistical support to meet the anticipated Kamikaze.

For the Iwo Jima landings, close air support was to be under the Marine aircrew on the CVEs and the fast carriers were to defend against the Kamikaze and strike airfields in Japan to prevent aircraft there from interfering. At dawn on 16 February 1945 Mitscher launched fighter sweeps over Tokyo and Honshu and, against heavy opposition, more than 300 Japanese aircraft were destroyed for the loss of 60 US aircraft. The bombers attacked many targets, but, in poor weather, were unable to find any shipping. Mitscher then moved to bombard Chichi and Iwo Jima prior to the landing on Iwo Jima on the 19th.

On the 21st Kamikaze attacks inflicted major damage to *Saratoga* and sank a CVE (*Bismarck Sea*), which meant that the only night cover now available would be provided by *Enterprise*. The fast carriers withdrew on the 22nd, followed by the CVEs on 11 March. Another strike on Japan was ruled out by the weather and so Okinawa was attacked and photographed for the coming landing.

To prepare for Okinawa Mitscher returned to Ulithi, where *Randolph* was damaged by a Kamikaze by night. Although the night carrier *Bataan* arrived, Mitscher would not operate a night carrier TG. On 18 March the TF began operations against Kyushu and the remnant of the Japanese fleet at Kure. Kamikaze damaged three carriers, but two Japanese carriers (*Amagi* and *Ryuho*) and the battleship *Yamato* were damaged. The

Hellcats also met a small number of the superior Kawanishi N1K1 Shiden fighter. Next day Kamikaze badly damaged *Franklin*, *Wasp* and *Enterprise*, all of which had to be sent back to Ulithi. The first two, like *Saratoga*, had to return to the USA. As a result Mitscher allowed Sherman the five-carrier TG for which Sherman had been pressing for some time.

Mitscher now began round the clock bombing of Okinawa until the landing on 1 April, which provoked nearly 400 Kamikaze to attack the carriers on 6 April. The Japanese also sent the battleship *Yamato* from Japan on a suicide mission (it did not have enough fuel to return). On the 7th Mitscher flew-off search-strikes of Hellcats (500lb bombs), Helldivers (1,000lb bombs) and Avengers with torpedoes. Ten torpedoes sank *Yamato* and five of her nine escorts in what had been the battleship's swan-song, and the death knell of the Japanese Navy.

The Kamikaze exacted some revenge by damaging *Hancock* (7 April), *Enterprise* (11th), *Intrepid* (16th) and many picket destroyers. *Hancock* and *Enterprise* had to return to Ulithi. Until the end of May Mitscher continued to fly missions in support of the troops in addition to attacking the Japanese mainland and Sakishima Gunto (assigned to the British TG). The TGs were rotated to Ulithi in turn for rest periods. While the British armoured flight-decks could absorb Kamikaze hits, the US carriers suffered heavy damage which put them out of the battle: *Bunker Hill* on 5 May and *Enterprise* on the 14th. The carriers remained in the same area, only 350 miles from Kyushu, for three months which took a heavy toll of the pilots and ships' companies which were not rotated like the air groups.

On 28 May Halsey and McCain again took over and headed for Japan, but yet another typhoon on 5 June damaged *Hornet* and *Bennington*, other surface warships and 76 aircraft. Operations continued until 10 June when the carriers returned to Leyte after a 92-day Okinawa campaign which brought land-based medium bombers and fighters within range of Kyushu. Work studies into anti-aircraft missiles began and a Special Defense Section (A. A. Burke) was established in Maine to come up with counter-measures against the Kamikaze.

Halsey's new job in Phase 1 of Operation 'Olympic' (the Kyushu landings) was to soften up Kyushu for the invasion scheduled for 1 November, which he, alone of the senior admirals, supported. King and Nimitz preferred a less costly air and sea blockade. However, more *Essex* class carriers were due with more 40mm AA guns, and the new, longer-range 5in/54cal (from April 1945) was being added to their armament. In strikes against Japan from 10 July, however, Halsey met very little air opposition because the Japanese were conserving their aircraft for the anticipated invasion.

On the 24th and 28th Halsey launched strikes on the Mobile Fleet laid up in harbours and destroyed the remainder of the Japanese fleet (three battleships, three carriers and three incomplete carriers). In early August the last raids of the war were undertaken on Honshu, to destroy suicide aircraft and to help the Russians, and against Tokyo on the 15th.

As well as the Japanese, the fast carriers under Halsey also had to face two typhoons, the second of which (5 June 1945) produced this severe damage to USS *Hornet* (CV-12). (US Navy)

In the meantime Spruance planned Operation 'Olympic' (Kyushu) to be implemented by Vice Admiral F. C. Sherman, his new carrier commander, who replaced Mitscher on 15 August, Towers having replaced the unsuccessful McCain as Halsey's carrier commander the day before. On 24 October two carrier TFs (38 and 58) would be formed under Towers and Sherman. The first, together with the British TF37, would conducted long-range operations throughout the Japan homeland while the latter, with Durgin's CVEs, supported the landings. The atom bombs brought everything to a halt.

The triumph of the fast carriers in the Pacific owed most to the pre-war development of carriers, aircraft and personnel, and to four senior naval officers. King, unlike his predecessor Stark, was not wedded to the 'Germany first' policy, but supported Marshall in calling for an offensive in France in 1942 or 1943 so that war in Europe could be terminated swiftly and attention switched to the Pacific. Moreover, he en-

259

sured that a limited offensive would be waged in the Pacific to wrest the initiative from the Japanese. When the British refused an early operation in France, King took the chance to divert more resources to the Pacific.

At first he adhered to a 'South Pacific' strategy, but after Guadalcanal reverted to the old Plan Orange (a Central Pacific offensive). The key to his strategic plans was taking risks to halt the Japanese offensive and then to penetrate their defensive perimeter. His confidence was based on his knowledge of carriers and acceptance of their increasing dominance in naval warfare due to his own specialisation in aviation, albeit as a 'latecomer'. By 1943 his faith in Nimitz, Halsey and the carrier commanders was such that he left operations to them.

Whereas Nimitz lacked an aviation background, he had studied the logistics of the Pacific at the Naval War College, had a steady character, picked able men, wielded them into a team by his tact and delegated to his commanders with whom he did not interfere. Nimitz was also aggressive and willing to take risks, and he acted as a buffer between the impatient King and the commanders.

He made decisive contributions to strategy as well. In 1942 he persuaded King to mass carriers in mid Pacific to ambush the Japanese at Midway. Later he was bold in bypassing Rabaul, Truk, the outer Marshalls, Formosa and China in favour of the Kwajalein, Iwo Jima and Okinawa route. However, Nimitz's role in the tactical handling of the fast carriers is more controversial and he had a difficult relationship with Towers, and the latter's chief of staff (Rear Admiral Forrest P. Sherman) acted as intermediary.

The key aviators were Towers and Mitscher. Towers fought Nimitz's and Spruance's conservative preference for outdated battle-line tactics. This enabled acceptance of the fast carriers' ability to spearhead the Central Pacific offensive and the leapfrogging of major fleet bases such as Rabaul and Truk. As Nimitz's deputy from February 1944, he ensured full acceptance of aviation in Pacific strategy and the advancement of qualified aviators. Mitscher was quite simply the greatest commander of fast carrier forces in history; neither Pownall, Halsey nor McCain could match him. As a result of their efforts and those of the men of the air groups and ships' companies of the fast carriers, naval warfare was changed for ever. The process had been given a jump-start on 7 December 1941.

The Japanese Offensive

In January 1941 Yamamoto considered attacking the US fleet at Pearl Harbor and ordered a preliminary report by Rear Admiral T. Onishi, Chief of Staff 11th Air Fleet, one of the Navy's few aviator admirals and a consistent advocate of carrier aviation. The fleet staff was divided into four study groups to work out detailed plans. Air operations were assigned to the Air Staff Officer (Commander A. Sasaki) and his assistant (Lieutenant-Commander K. Inoguchi).

Onishi talked to two air staff officers, Commander K. Maeda on his own staff at Kanoya, and Commander M. Genda of the 1st Carrier Division, in *Akagi*. Maeda, a torpedo specialist, was consulted about Pearl Harbor's shallow water and Genda for his original and daring thinking on aviation. To keep the carriers out of danger, Yamamoto envisaged a one-way torpedo strike, the pilots being recovered by submarines. Genda argued that this would be a waste of aircraft and pilots who would be needed for a possible US counter-attack; that relying on torpedoes alone was risky; and that the US carriers must be sunk as well as the battleships.

Genda advocated the concentration of six or more carriers, which he argued would replace battleships, to launch their bombers in two large waves escorted by long-range fighters to ensure command of the air over the target. This concentration would also allow enough fighters to defend the carriers from any counter-attack while the strike was under way.

In February Genda produced a plan for Onishi which stressed complete surprise (a Japanese tactic used at Port Arthur in 1906) to assure maximum damage and carrier safety. By concentrating on the US carriers and land-based aircraft, remaining battleships, lacking air cover, could be eliminated at will. All available carriers, bombers and fighters would be deployed at dawn to ensure success as night attacks had not been perfected and dive-bombing was more reliable than torpedo- or high-level bombing. He pointed out that refuelling at sea must be developed if Pearl Harbor was to be reached. He also advocated occupying Hawaii because he wanted the US fleet to be destroyed rather than merely damaged and contained, as was Yamamoto's original idea.

Genda's plan was adopted by Onishi, except for the seizure of Hawaii since all available forces were needed for the Southern Area. In his report to Yamamoto in March 1941 he also advocated high-level rather than dive-bombing to avoid heavy casualties and stressed a northern line of advance to escape detection. The plan aimed at destroying the US Fleet and its air power rather than taking out the installations, oil tanks, dry docks and bases which in the absence of a plan to seize Hawaii alone would have driven the Pacific Fleet back to the West Coast.

The Navy Ministry Aeronautics Department's air torpedo expert, Commander F. Aiko, was enlisted to solve the problem of using torpedoes in shallow waters. In the name of the Minister he ordered the Yokosuka Air Corps, in charge of specialist training, to improve the torpedo hit rate from 70 to 100 per cent.

In April Onishi's plan and all intelligence were given to the First Air Fleet which was formed on 10 April to concentrate the carriers. Neither the CinC First Air Fleet (Vice-Admiral C. Nagumo) nor his chief of staff (Rear-Admiral R. Kusaka), both non-aviators, had confidence in the logistics of Yamamoto's proposed operation, but realising their lack of air experience left matters to the Air Staff Officer, Genda.

Nagumo, however, did set targets for the First Air Fleet's basic training (1 July) and combat readiness (1 September) to enable it to operate as one unit. He also used fleet manoeuvres to test Genda's concept of concentrating the carriers. Until this time the two carrier divisions had operated separately. By 1936 the tactic of launching their

aircraft from different areas to converge over a target was accepted because it fitted in with the traditional fleet tactic of dispersing to encircle and ambush an enemy fleet.

Nagumo operated the two divisions in box formations next to each other to co-ordinate defence and the launching of strikes. The main weakness was the lack of battleships or cruisers in the escort which meant that the defence relied mainly on fighters for which the Japanese had not developed radar. Thus the box formation was designed for sustained attack ashore as at Pearl Harbor and Midway. If carrier opposition was expected the carriers were to be dispersed as before.

Intensive aircrew training ashore was undertaken to solve the problems of accurate high-level and shallow-depth torpedo bombing. For torpedoes low-level flying (40ft) was developed and for high-altitude bombing 16in shells were adapted. Since the IJN's bomb sight, based on a German design, relied on operator skill, emphasis was placed on tight formations and intensively trained crews. High-altitude bombing accuracy was raised from 10 to 33 per cent. During the first six months of 1941 the dive-bombers re-equipped with the 'Val' Type 99 and under training accuracy rose to 50–60 per cent. The fighter pilots were trained to extend their range from the carriers from 100 to 300 miles in order to escort the bombers.

To prepare for the annual manoeuvres, and the Pearl Harbor attack, Genda also recruited the Navy's top pilots: Lieutenant-Commander M. Fuchida to train and lead the combined First Air Fleet's air groups in battle, Lieutenant-Commander T. Egusa the dive-bombers and Lieutenant S. Murata the torpedo-aircraft. The fighter leader, Lieutenant-Commander S. Itayu, was already with the fleet. In September the new 5th Carrier Division (Rear-Admiral C. Hara), consisting of *Shokaku* and *Zuikaku,* also joined the First Air Fleet, their completion having been accelerated.

The 1941 manoeuvres and war games were moved from November/December to September to demonstrate the Pearl Harbor scheme to the Naval Staff and allow adjustments to plans and training according to the results. During the War Games (11–20 September) the Pearl Harbor plan was enacted twice. In the first surprise was not achieved and the carriers and aircraft suffered heavy casualties. In the second, by timing the advance to avoid US air scouts, surprise and air command were achieved and five battleships and three carriers sunk. However, one Japanese carrier was sunk and another damaged during the withdrawal.

Because of poor high-level bombing Genda decided to arm these bombers with torpedoes to attack the US battleships (hoping to sink eight) and to divide the dive-bombers between the carriers (three) and land-based aircraft. The problems now were to obtain good intelligence of the US fleet in harbour, to achieve surprise for the attack and to withdraw the carriers safely.

During 11–13 October Yamamoto conducted more exercises, aboard his flagship *Nagato,* to test further the Pearl Harbor plans. In these games the strike force consisted of only three carriers, since the Naval Staff continued to allocate the 2nd Carrier Division and possibly *Akagi* to the Southern Area. As a result only moderate damage was inflicted on the US fleet.

The war games focused the carrier air groups' training on greater weapon accuracy. By October the Yokosuka Air Corps finally achieved successful high-altitude bombing with 16in shells from 9,843 feet. This meant that the 90 'Kate' bombers available were divided between torpedo (40) and high-altitude (50). The ablest crews were assigned to the torpedoes. The high-altitude bombers were split into ten formations for close

A Japanese Zero attacks. The pilot tried to smash onto his target but crashed into the sea. American development of AA proximity fuzes and radar fighter direction was crucial for carrier defence. (IWM)

formation flying and to attack as many targets as possible. The dive-bombers used the old battleship *Settsu* as a target, modified the bomb releases to accommodate 500lb bombs and pioneered release at closer range to improve accuracy.

As the 5th Carrier Squadron had just been formed, its aircrew were assigned to high-altitude bombing and dive-bombing of airfields which needed less training than attacking ships. Night carrier launches, approaches in the dark and even night torpedo launches were also featured to allow a dawn attack. Each group practised twelve hours a day using terrain similar to Pearl Harbor.

As no Japanese carrier had ever refuelled from a tanker at sea (the Japanese fleet was designed for short-range operations in home waters), this was to be a major logistical concern for the Naval Staff. To prove its feasibility and procedures the fleet also began to train with oilers at sea and *Kaga* was refuelled at sea in September.

The other grave concern was the security needed for the task force to approach unseen and not suffer heavy losses before the launch. In the event the passage of the forces for the Southern Area operations deflected attention from the carriers.

The carrier air strike of early 7 December 1941 was very successful in the elimination of the US battleships (one beached, four sunk and three damaged) and land-based aircraft because there was little airborne opposition. Of more than 400 aircraft committed, only 30 were lost. But the Japanese did not locate the US carriers (*Enterprise* was supplying aircraft to Wake, and *Lexington* to Midway, while *Saratoga* was at San Diego), and all but two battleships were salvaged.

At the table war games the task force was adjudged to have suffered heavy losses during the withdrawal so Nagumo was not anxious to linger, especially as the whereabouts of the US carriers were unknown. He broke off the attack and headed for his refuelling rendezvous, before returning home, leaving the US fleet base largely intact.

Immediately after the attack the carriers were deployed as promised in support of the Army in the Southern Area, since land-based air did not have the range or strength. The fast carrier task force was broken up as carriers were assigned to cover landings at Wake, Rabaul, Kavieng, New Guinea and in the Dutch East Indies. The light carrier *Ryujo* also supported the Philippines operations.

Nagumo's carriers neutralised enemy naval bases, raiding Darwin on 19 February and Trincomalee on 5 April, and shipping was sunk in the Bay of Bengal. After the fall of Singapore, Trincomalee was the base of the British Eastern Fleet, much weakened in the interests of strengthening the Mediterranean Fleet. Nagumo's carriers sank the last British carrier in the East, *Hermes*, on 8 April.

From now until April 1942 the carriers mainly supported the Army ashore, in box formation for concentrated power. Apart from attempts to destroy the Allied fleets at Pearl Harbor, Darwin and Trincomalee, there was little opportunity to deploy in a fleet action, except against the British fleet. Even then an action was avoided. The carriers did not practise their own attacks on enemy naval forces or disperse to meet an enemy attack. They also lacked the AA protection afforded by a combined formation with the

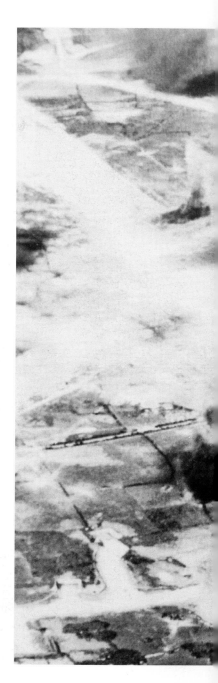

Hirara Airfield, Sakashima, 1945. The Japanese Navy always planned to supplement its carriers in the defence of its perimeter by using 'unsinkable' island airfields to shuttle land-based bombers. (FAAM)

battleships because the Naval Staff still planned for the battleships to win a decisive battle with the Americans in the Pacific.

The Japanese strategy after the conquest of the Southern Area was essentially to destroy the enemy fleet. Naval Staff plans called for a defensive perimeter: Wake–Marshalls–Gilberts–Solomons–New Guinea. The fleet could then operate from Singapore, Rabaul or Truk and land-based aircraft from the nearest islands would whittle down and destroy the US fleet.

To help the Army round out the perimeter, Hara's 5th Carrier Division (*Shokaku* and *Zuikaku*) were to cover the invasion of Port Moresby, New Guinea and the southern Solomons. A light carrier was to support the landings. However, due to their intelligence from decryption of Japanese codes, the Americans deployed their two carriers which resulted in the first carrier battle in history, the battle of the Coral Sea, on 7 May 1942. The Japanese sank one carrier (*Lexington*) and damaged another, but *Shoho* (covering the landings) was sunk, *Shokaku* was badly damaged, and 70 aircraft were lost. *Shoho*, in a prefigurement of events at Midway, was rapidly consumed by fire and sank within minutes.

There were important strategic results: although the Solomons had been secured, the invasion of Port Moresby was abandoned and the carrier division was no longer available for Midway (*Zuikaku*'s air group had to be reformed). The scene was also set for attritional warfare in the South West Pacific. Contrary to Japanese plans, it was their land-based and carrier air groups, and not those of the attackers, that were to be bled white.

Rather than wait for the US fleet to gather strength Yamamoto sought to finish the job started on 7 December and particularly to sink the last three US carriers and neutralise Pearl Harbor. The plan was for the Combined fleet to cover the capture of the Aleutians and Midway. If the US carriers rushed north to relieve the Aleutians they would meet either Nagumo's carriers or Yamamoto's battleships, operating separately, and be destroyed. Occupied Midway would then be used by the 11th Air Fleet to pound Pearl Harbor.

The plan was too complicated and dissipated Japanese forces. Above all it did not concentrate the carriers or defend them with the battleships, and tied them to defensive operations. The First Carrier Striking Force (Nagumo, four carriers of the 1st and 2nd Carrier Divisions) were to cover Midway, the Second (Kakuta, two carriers of the 4th Carrier Division) the Aleutians and *Zuiho* the Midway landings, and *Hosho* would remain with the battleships which were too far back.

Genda wanted the carriers concentrated, and Yamaguchi suggested three balanced task forces with three carriers, battleships, cruisers and destroyers. Yamamoto refused, nor would he wait until July when the 5th Carrier Division and possibly the new *Hiyo* would have been ready. Thus the carriers were tied to the military landings without tactical flexibility or battleship protection.

The US carriers did not rush into the lion's den as planned, and in the meantime Nagumo adopted the box formation so that his bombers could soften up Midway. When his scouts finally found a US carrier Nagumo refused to attack at once, despite Yamaguchi's urgings and US attacks, because he had too few fighters. He remained in formation (defended only by two battleships, three cruisers and eleven destroyers) and began to refuel and re-arm his bombers when they returned.

At this moment the US dive-bombers caught the Japanese fighters (at low level to decimate the US torpedo-bombers) by surprise. Direct hits on each carrier ignited aircraft, aviation fuel and ammunition. Uncontrollable flames then sank *Akagi*, *Kaga*, *Soryu* and *Hiryu*.

The carrier backbone of the Japanese naval air arm was destroyed because the planners tried to invade the Aleutians and Midway before securing command of the air and sea and because they failed to protect the carriers with all available AA platforms. As a consequence the carriers were at last concentrated and combined with the battleships and cruisers to provide AA protection. Using their multi-carrier experience, they were deployed in three carrier task forces throughout the Solomons campaign.

As a result of Midway the 11th Air Fleet was moved from the Marianas to Rabaul rather than Midway, and the Japanese were committed to a trial of attrition in the South Pacific. When the land-based aircraft failed to win command of the air from the US land-based aircraft, Yamamoto committed the carriers' air groups at Rabaul to operate against New Guinea. This too failed to stem the tide and on 16 April he had to recall the remnants. Two days later Yamamoto died when his aircraft was shot down.

Following the losses at Guadalcanal, New Guinea and the Solomons, the Japanese Navy had to abandon any hope of destroying the US fleet and go on the defensive. However, while the Americans were expecting large reinforcements, the Japanese fleet could only expect the two *Chiyoda* light carriers in late 1943 and no more carriers until 1944. Although they still had six carriers, only two were large (*Shokaku*s) and four light (*Zuiho*, *Hiyo*, *Junyo* and *Ryuho*) while their air groups had been robbed of many experienced pilots. Nor was a cadre system organised to replace them promptly.

The Japanese pilots lost the training edge they had had, and their average flight hours were now equalled by the US pilots. Moreover, the Japanese aircraft advantage vanished with the arrival of new US aircraft (Hellcats, Hellcats and Avengers). Japanese industry proved unable to produce new types as quickly or in equal numbers. Furthermore, because aviation fuel was in short supply as a consequence of tanker sinkings, the 2nd Carrier Division was withdrawn to Singapore to train its new pilots.

Thus in the autumn of 1943, although expecting a US offensive in the Central Pacific, the Japanese fleet at Truk had only the three carriers of the 1st Carrier Division available, and US forces were moving through the Solomons towards Bougainville which was within fighter range of Rabaul. The aggressive new CinC Combined Fleet, M. Koga, hoped to reinforce and hold Rabaul, suck in the new American forces and delay the Central Pacific offensive or a decisive battle until more carriers were ready. In contrast, the Americans hoped that he would commit the last of his carriers to defend the Gilberts and enable them to destroy the rest of his fleet in a decisive battle.

When the US carriers hit Wake in early October the Japanese fleet sortied from Truk (mid October) to the Marshalls to meet the expected Central Pacific offensive. Finding no enemy fleet, it was concluded that the Wake raid was a diversion to draw the Japanese fleet from the Solomons and all efforts were concentrated on Rabaul's defence. When Halsey landed troops at Bougainville on 1 November, Koga commit-

ted the 173 aircraft of the 1st Carrier Division at Truk plus eight cruisers and four destroyers to Rabaul to attack Halsey's force.

However, seven cruisers were damaged and two destroyers lost to the US carrier air raids on Rabaul on 5 and 11 November. This meant that the Japanese had not only failed to destroy the Bougainville landing, but also that their battleships were deprived of their screen. On 13 November Koga, as Yamamoto before him, had to withdraw his carrier aircraft from Rabaul. After two weeks the 1st Carrier Division had lost 50 per cent of its fighters and nearly all its bombers in the actions over Rabaul and Bougainville. Without its carrier aircraft and cruisers the fleet was unable to intervene in the Gilberts. Deprived of its main air defence, the outer perimeter was lost.

Koga's only resource was the land-based aircraft of the Marshalls and the last of the carrier fighters (32) which were also sent. Seventy-one of the Marshalls aircraft were lost attacking the US forces off the Gilberts and most of the carrier fighters were finished off. After the loss of the Gilberts the Japanese continued to defend Rabaul. In January 1944 the aircraft of Admiral Joshima's 2nd Carrier Division were sent there from their training at Singapore, although these were the last trained carrier pilots available. For the third time, Japanese carrier pilots took heavy casualties from the Solomons land-based aircraft. Thus before the invasion of the Marshalls the Japanese fleet was again without carrier pilots.

When he heard of the US fleet's arrival at the Marshalls, Koga ordered the major Japanese surface ships to retire from Truk to Palau. Only 150 land-based aircraft were left to defend the islands. These proved no match for the 650 US carrier aircraft. When the US carriers approached Palau the Japanese fleet, forewarned, retreated again to Singapore, Borneo and Japan. Admiral Koga himself was lost when his aircraft crashed in poor weather en route for Mindanao. With even fewer land-based aircraft in defence, the large numbers of merchant ships at Truk and Palau were left to the US fleet's mercy and more than 330,000 tons were sunk.

The basic flaw in the Japanese dependence on its chain of 'unsinkable' carriers was their lack of mobility and the difficulty in concentrating aircraft at the decisive point. The only way was to deploy very large numbers of aircraft, but this was not possible due to their inability to match US production and replace the heavy losses of the Solomons.

After the retreat of the fleet from Truk and the Palaus, the new CinC Combined Fleet, Admiral S. Toyoda, took command in May 1944 from a cruiser in Tokyo Bay. He and his staff sought to halt the next offensive (either in the South West or Centre) before the US fleet reached Japan's threshold. In February the Naval General Staff had formed a new inner line of defence which was to be held at all costs.

It was based on 1,600 aircraft at the seven air bases on Guam, Tinian, Saipan, Rota (Marianas), Babelthuap, Yap (Palaus) and Iwo Jima. These all came under Kakuta (First Air Fleet) at Tinian. The local surface commander was Nagumo. The problem was that most of the aircrew were inexperienced trainees, many of whom were lost in crashes while being switched from one crisis point to the next.

The Combined Fleet, in the year up to April 1944, had lost one battleship, five light cruisers and twenty-five destroyers, but had received only two light cruisers and nine destroyers as replacements. The main hope now rested in the carriers of the Mobile Fleet (J. Ozawa) at Tawi Tawi in the Celebes. On paper this was a fine force comprising nine carriers, five battleships, seven cruisers and twenty-eight destroyers, but it would be opposed by fifteen US carriers

The carriers were *Taiho* (new, armoured), the *Shokaku*s (1st Carrier Division), *Junyo*, *Hiyo* and the light carriers *Ryuho* (2nd Carrier Division) and *Zuiho*, *Chitose* and *Chiyoda* (3rd Carrier Division). The last six were all conversions from merchant ships or auxiliaries carrying relatively few aircraft. The 4th Carrier Division comprised the hybrid battleships *Hyuga* and *Ise*, which were not ready for battle.

Worse still, although 1st Carrier Division had 207 aircraft, the 2nd and 3rd had only 135 and 90 respectively. The last carried mainly fighters, their decks being too short for heavy bombers. Moreover, although there was a new version of the Zero, which was still inferior to the Hellcat, and some new torpedo-bombers ('Jill'), these air groups mainly deployed inferior aircraft: the 'Judy' (dive -bomber), 'Kate' (torpedo) and 'Val' (scout).

The situation concerning aircrew was grave. The 1st Carrier Division had lost most of its veterans at Rabaul and the Marshalls, and by May 1944 most pilots had had less than five months' training. The 2nd, trained at Singapore in the autumn of 1943, had more survivors of Rabaul, but the newest aircraft were assigned to the novice pilots of the 1st Carrier Division. The 3rd had only recently been formed and its pilots had less than three months' flight time.

Furthermore, the airfield at Tawi Tawi was incomplete and these pilots received little training in May, let alone any chance for the air groups to perfect tactics. Therefore the nine Japanese carriers with their 450 aircraft represented a force that was inadequately trained and inexperienced in combat. Ozawa did at last have radar in each carrier for air defence, but its operators were inexperienced.

Given the shortage of oil for the fleet and the need for large numbers of land-based aircraft to equalise the US advantage in fleet aircraft and experienced pilots, the Japanese High Command hoped that the main US offensive would come in the South West Pacific. It therefore devised Operation 'KON' in which it was planned to ferry troop reinforcements to the probable point of MacArthur's next attack and then concentrate the Mobile Fleet for a decisive naval battle to halt the US advance.

In the event the fleet failed to reinforce Biak with troops and Saipan was invaded on 15 June. Nor did the *Yamato* class battleships succeed in attacking MacArthur's transports. Operation 'KON' was cancelled in favour of Operation 'A-GO', designed to force a decisive battle off the Carolines or Palaus. In the event the Americans leap-frogged ahead to the Marianas, and on 11 June Toyoda ordered land-based aircraft to concentrate there.

Nobara Airfield, Miyako Shima, May 1945. The Japanese defence ultimately failed because Allied carrier aircraft sank their carriers, destroyed the aircraft being shuttled-in and made airfields unusable. (IWM)

Ozawa's plan was for Kakuta's land-based aircraft (when concentrated at the Marianas) to attack the US carriers so as to wear down their air groups and damage or sink some of them. Ozawa would then use the greater range (by 200 miles) of his air groups to attack the US carriers without endangering his own. His aircraft would land at Guam, refuel and strike the US carriers again on their return. Toyoda vetoed any idea of an attack on the Saipan beachhead which Spruance so feared. Ozawa also favoured concentration for a stronger defence as learned at Midway.

However, the plan failed in its execution. It was affected by losses at Biak and poor weather. Above all, as part of operations to isolate Saipan the US carriers had raided the Japanese aircraft staging-points at Iwo Jima, Chichi Jima, Guam and Rota on 15–19 June, and the Marianas themselves. Thus Kakuta could only amass about 50 aircraft at Guam (not the 500 planned) because he could not further weaken the defence of Truk, Yap and the Palaus. However, to save face, Kakuta still assured Ozawa, who proceeded according to plan, that his aircraft had inflicted heavy losses on the US carriers.

On 13 June Ozawa's force left Tawi Tawi and passed out of the San Bernardino Strait into the Philippine Sea where the *Yamato*s (Kurita) joined forces. During the night of 18/19 June Ozawa split his force into a van and main body. The van consisted of Obayashi's 3rd Carrier Division, three light carriers each with its own screen and a total of four battleships, nine cruisers and eight destroyers, 100 miles ahead of the main body which consisted of two groups: 1st Carrier Division screened by three cruisers and seven destroyers, and 2nd Carrier Division with one battleship, one cruiser and eight destroyers.

This disposition had two objects. It allowed the seaplanes of the heavy surface ships in the van to search for the enemy. Also the three light carriers, with few strike aircraft, mostly fighters and heavy AA gun protection, would take the brunt of any US carrier strikes while Ozawa's heavy carriers launched a counter-strike. However, the price was dispersion of his few destroyers and inadequate anti-submarine screens. As a result the flagship, the new armoured carrier *Taiho* was hit by a torpedo from USS *Albacore* and *Shokaku* by three torpedoes from USS *Cavalla*. Both carriers sank as a consequence of poor damage control and avgas fumes respectively.

At twilight, when the main body was 400 miles from TF58, Ozawa launched reconnaissance seaplanes from his heavy ships in the van to locate the US carriers. Starting at 0830 hours he then launched four strikes: 45 fighter-bombers, eight torpedo-aircraft and sixteen escorts (the van), the 1st's first strike (53 bombers, 27 torpedo and 46 escorts), the 2nd's strike (25, 7, 15) and the 1st's second strike (46, 6, 30).

The Japanese carriers lost 330 aircraft of the 354 launched: 233 in combat or wrecked on landing at Guam plus 22 lost with the two carriers sunk and another 75 which returned but were too badly damaged for further use. In addition sixteen surface-ship seaplanes were lost and another six rendered unfit for service. Ozawa intended to continue his strikes on the 20th, but because of his losses he abandoned the plan and withdrew at 2000 hours. During the US carrier strike of the 20th a further eighty aircraft were lost. Ozawa tendered his resignation but it was not accepted.

The fall of Saipan in early July led to the fall of Tojo's government and the naval leaders concluded that defeat was inevitable. The High Command expected the Americans to land in the Philippines next (about November 1944) which gave four months to train new air groups and replace *Shokaku*, *Taiho* and *Hiyo*. Thus the carriers were recalled to Japan while the surface ships (Second Fleet) remained at Singapore. In early August *Unryu* and *Amagi* (new *Unryu* class) joined *Zuikaku* in the 1st Carrier Division. In October they were joined by a third sister, *Katsuragi*. The 2nd Carrier Division was dissolved and *Junyo* and *Ryuho* transferred to the 4th with *Ise* and *Hyuga*. The 3rd Carrier Division still comprised *Zuiho*, *Chitose* and *Chiyoda*.

By November Toyoda and Ozawa again had five heavy and four light carriers plus the *Ise* class. Moreover, the fleet was due to receive the first 400 of the new 400mph Shiden ('George') fighter. Again the main problem was the lack of pilots, but land- and carrier-based training was sharply curtailed by the lack of aircraft and ship fuel, due to the heavy submarine sinkings of tankers. The scanty training managed in the Inland Sea resulted in many crashes and deaths among the under-trained pilots.

It was fairly clear that the carriers stood little chance against the US fleet. Captain E. Jyo (*Chiyoda*), with the approval of Admiral Obayashi, suggested suicide tactics. Ozawa did not take up the idea, but Onishi, commander of land-based aircraft in the Philippines, did.

In July 1944 the Navy and Army agreed to commit all their combined resources to defend the Philippines and keep open the supply line of oil from the East Indies. This meant committing all land-based aircraft and the Mobile Fleet which would join the Second Fleet (battleships, T. Kurita) at Singapore once the carriers had worked up. Toyoda and Ozawa hoped for some respite until November by which time their aircrew would have had that much more training.

When Halsey's carriers began their attacks on Formosa on 12 October, however, Toyoda committed the land-based aircraft of the Second Air Fleet (Admiral S. Fukudome) and flew to Formosa to direct the defence. Despite heavy losses, over-optimistic claims of US losses led him to commit the aircraft of 3rd and 4th Carrier Divisions (Obayashi and Matsuda). The Hellcat pilots made short work of these under-trained pilots and more than 500 Japanese aircraft were lost in four days.

These losses meant that Ozawa had no carrier aircraft to attack the landing at Leyte on the 20th, and he recommended using the carriers as bait to allow Kurita's battleships to slip in and attack the landing forces. Toyoda therefore ordered a Central Force (four battleships, seven cruisers under Kurita), via the San Bernardino Strait, and a Southern Force (two battleships, four cruisers under S. Nishimura), via Surigao Strait, to converge on Leyte on the 25th while Ozawa drew Halsey off. Few of these ships were expected to survive the US carriers and battleships, but were sacrificed to keep the supply of East Indies oil open.

Ozawa took only the 3rd Carrier Division (*Zuikaku*, *Zuiho*, *Chitose* and *Chiyoda*) with enough aircraft (116) for one strike (landing in Luzon) plus two battleships and three cruisers as escort. He left the Inland Sea on the 20th. At the same time every available aircraft was flown to the Philippines, and Onishi (First Air Fleet, Philippines) mobilised his Kamikaze.

The plan worked perfectly, for the loss of all four carriers and Nishimura's Southern Force, but Kurita lost his nerve and failed to press his suicide attack after sinking a CVE and some escorts. Moreover, Toyoda's premature committal of his air forces to Formosa meant that little damage was inflicted on Halsey. Onishi's Kamikaze had some success against the US CVEs and these were now to be the last-ditch weapon. As a result of the battle Kurita was dismissed from his appointment as President of the Naval Academy in December, and Ozawa replaced Toyoda as CinC Combined Fleet in March 1945.

In theory Ozawa still had five carriers (1st Carrier Division, Rear-Admiral K. Komura: *Unryu*, *Amagi*, *Katsuragi*, *Junyo* and *Ryuho*) with the new *Shinano* (commissioned mid November) to join them. These were to act as a fleet in being to threaten US operations. However, after Formosa and Leyte, the carriers were again without pilots (now fewer than 150 hours each) and the losses of tankers to submarines meant that there was very little fuel for operations. Lack of fuel and B-29 raids also slowed down aircraft production and the development of new aircraft types.

Finally, in the absence of escorts, the US submarines were able to pen the remaining Japanese warships in harbour, having sunk *Shinano* (29 November) and *Unryu* (19 December) and badly damaging *Junyo* (9 December). Although carrier building continued, on 1 March 1945 the last carrier divisions (1st and 4th) were disbanded and construction of new ships was abandoned. The remaining carriers were abandoned in Japanese harbours where most were badly damaged by Halsey's air attacks. Thus the vaunted Japanese carriers ended with a whimper.

Japan's last throw rested in the Kamikaze, flying converted bombers or the specially built Ohka (piloted bombs with 2,400lb of explosive). Fukodome, impressed by Onishi's unit during the Leyte battle, made him his chief of staff and began raising suicide units on a large scale. The unskilled carrier and land-based pilots now needed just enough training to guide their aircraft one way to hit either carriers or their destroyer pickets. Ferocious attacks on the US carriers were made in late October, and three were damaged. During the landings at Luzon, Iwo Jima and Okinawa US carrier and destroyer losses steadily mounted, but this made little impression on their vast resources.

During the Pacific war the Japanese carrier forces went from almost continuous victories to almost complete annihilation by December 1944. The victories were based on the formation of an élite force which had been highly trained in war conditions in China. However, this force had serious flaws: a lack of experienced senior carrier officers, poor damage control and inadequate protection against avgas fumes.

Thus the inexperienced Nagumo made serious mistakes at Pearl Harbor and Midway and many carriers were lost when Japan could ill afford to lose any. On top of this, successive CinCs Combined Fleet squandered their élite pilots and later replacements by committing them to land bases where they were rapidly lost. Above all, as Yamamoto had known, Japan could not compete with the industrial might of the USA and lacked their war production experience of 1914–18. After mid 1942 it was always a case of too little, too late.

British Carriers, 1939–1945

The British carrier experience was similar in some respects to that of the Americans and the Japanese. As with the Americans, re-armament came late, the few carriers had to be committed to the Atlantic and Pacific and faced huge odds in the early years. Like the Japanese, reliance was placed on a small, élite force, there being insufficient industrial power to implement the huge expansion needed to keep up with the US Fleet. However, the Fleet Air Arm also had major commitments in the Mediterranean and could rely on massive help from US Lend-Lease.

The Early War Years

In September 1939 the FAA had seven carriers: *Ark Royal* and *Furious* with the Home Fleet; *Glorious* in the Mediterranean; *Eagle* in the Far East; *Argus* for training; and *Hermes* and *Courageous* in reserve. However, these carriers provided merely 177 obsolete aircraft, including only 30 fighters (Skuas and Sea Gladiators). *Ark Royal* alone was modern, though six more were building. The Admiralty made the situation worse by using *Ark Royal*, *Hermes* and *Courageous* to hunt U-boats, resulting in the loss of the last on 17 September.

Although carriers played a part in the hunt for the 'pocket-battleships' *Admiral Graf Spee* and *Deutschland*, the FAA's first real test came when the Germans invaded Norway. Their missions were to protect units of the Home Fleet from the land-based Fliegerkorps X because the area was out of range of RAF fighters. However, on 9 April 1940 *Furious* could not attack the damaged cruiser *Königsberg* because she lacked fighter defence against the Luftwaffe although on the 12th she did launch the first air-torpedo strike of the war (eighteen Swordfish) against German destroyers in Trondheim (no hits due to shallow water). That afternoon she also sent her Swordfish to bomb ships in Narvik. Six aircraft were lost for no results. The first large warship to be lost to dive-bombers, *Königsberg*, was sunk on 10 April by shore-based Skuas at Bergen.

Although damaged by bombs *Furious* continued to operate until late April when *Ark Royal* and *Glorious* arrived from the Mediterranean. By this time the Home Fleet had failed to stop the German invasion. On 24 April *Ark Royal* launched 29 Swordfish and ten Skuas against shipping in Trondheim and damaged some ships and aircraft, but she soon had to retire to Scapa to embark more aircraft, particularly Skua fighters because of heavy losses.

On the 24th *Glorious* delivered RAF Gladiators to northern Norway to support the troops, but these were soon destroyed. In May *Furious* and *Glorious* delivered more RAF fighters, but the fall of France on 28 May led to the evacuation of Norway, including the RAF Hurricanes, covered by *Glorious* and *Ark Royal* (none of the RAF pilots had ever landed on a carrier before). On 8 June while heading south, *Glorious* and her escort ran into the battlecruisers *Gneisenau* and *Scharnhorst* and, being unable to launch due to the RAF aircraft, were sunk.

With the fall of France and Italy's entry into the war on 10 June, Force H (Admiral Sir James Somerville), including *Ark Royal*, was based at Gibraltar to secure the Western Mediterranean and prevent the French fleet at Mers-el-Kébir falling into German hands. On 3 July *Ark Royal*'s Swordfish were used to mine the entrance and spot for the guns which sank or damaged three capital ships, but an attack by six aircraft with torpedoes failed to prevent *Strasbourg*'s escape. On the 6th the Swordfish, escorted by Skuas, returned to finish off *Dunkerque* but she was eventually patched up and reached Toulon. Meanwhile *Hermes* on the 8th launched six Swordfish against the battleship *Richelieu* in Dakar, gaining one torpedo hit which was sufficient to keep her in port.

In August Force H departed for Dakar with Free French troops under General de Gaulle to take over a possible U-boat base and the *Richelieu* from the Vichy French. After negotiations failed, *Ark Royal*'s Swordfish and Skuas attacked the battleship but failed to damage her because of heavy AA fire and fighter opposition. It was left to a battleship to hit her. The force withdrew and *Ark Royal* returned to England for repairs in October.

When Italy joined the war, Hitler left the Mediterranean to the modern Italian fleet (lacking only a carrier) and the Regia Aeronautica. The key to the Mediterranean was Malta, which commanded both British and Italian communications to Egypt and Libya, and so her supply was a priority. In the absence of promised RAF Hurricanes, her air defence against the Regia Aeronautica, which began bombing in June, consisted of three Sea Gladiators and twelve Swordfish from the training carrier *Argus*, withdrawn from France.

The Regia Aeronautica detailed most of its aircraft to attack Malta, and on 2 August *Argus* made the first of many carrier runs to Malta to deliver fighters (Hurricanes) while *Ark Royal* made a diversionary attack (eleven Swordfish) on Sardinia. During the operation the British fleet was shadowed and again bombed by Italian aircraft. *Ark Royal*'s Skuas shot down two of the attackers. In September a merchant convoy from Egypt was escorted by the Mediterranean Fleet to Malta while *Ark Royal* of Force H and the new *Illustrious* again attacked Sardinia. *Illustrious*, with a battleship and two AA cruisers to provide heavy AA fire, then joined CinC Mediterranean (Sir Andrew Cunningham) off Malta. These aircraft and merchant convoys to Malta continued throughout 1940 and 1941.

Despite his few resources Cunningham was determined to eliminate the threat of the Italian fleet. To face them he had *Eagle* and four old battleships plus Force H.

However, *Eagle* only carried seventeen Swordfish and no fighters. To protect the fleet her Commander (Flying), C. Keighley-Patch, obtained three old Gladiator biplanes and trained some of his bomber pilots.

On 9 July 1940 while escorting two convoys from Malta to Egypt, he got his first chance off Calabria where the Italians had deployed two battleships and fourteen cruisers against three battleships, five cruisers and *Eagle*. After suffering damage to a battleship and a cruiser in a surface action, the Italians withdrew with the British in pursuit. As envisaged pre-war, *Eagle* launched a Swordfish torpedo strike to slow down a fleeing enemy fleet but it failed in its task. Afterwards the British fleet was subjected to high-altitude formation bombing by the Regia Aeronautica which lacked torpedo- or dive-bombers and made exaggerated claims but did little damage. This encouraged Cunningham to think the fleet could operate despite the lack of fighters.

Illustrious (Rear-Admiral Lyster (RAA) had commissioned in April and worked-up off Bermuda. Her arrival added a new dimension to the fleet; in addition to her eighteen Swordfish, she carried fifteen new Fulmar fleet fighters and the first carrier radar for fighter interception. The Fulmar, although well armed, proved a disappointment since it was slow, had a poor rate of climb and had a limited ceiling.

On his arrival Lyster proposed to Cunningham a carrier strike on the Italian fleet in Taranto harbour. In 1937–39 Lyster had been captain of *Glorious* in the Mediterranean when Ramsay (RAA) during the Abyssinian Crisis of 1935 proposed to the CinC (Admiral Fisher) an attack on the Italian Fleet in Taranto with Fairey III bombers and Blackburn Ripons (torpedoes). To keep the carrier(s) out of range of Italian aircraft, the aircraft were to use Janina airfield in Greece for a night strike and then return to the carrier(s).

The plan was not fully developed, but in 1938 the new CinC (Admiral Pound) asked Lyster to prepare a Taranto plan for *Glorious*'s squadrons which were highly trained in night flying. Lyster thought *Glorious* could carry out a refined plan and training was begun in the utmost secrecy. When he became First Sea Lord Pound recommended the plan to Cunningham (his successor) in August 1939.

By then *Glorious* had been sunk, but *Illustrious* had brought auxiliary fuel tanks to extend the Swordfish's range and the RAF had three US-built ex-French Martin Maryland long-range reconnaissance aircraft at Malta which could reconnoitre the Italian harbours. At the same time two new and two modernised battleships joined the Italian fleet outnumbering Cunningham six to four. The attack was scheduled for Trafalgar Day (21 October), but was delayed by a hangar fire in *Illustrious* and the Italian invasion of Greece on the 28th.

In the end *Eagle* was inoperable and *Illustrious* was the only carrier that sailed on 6 November. On the 11th she and her screen left the main force for the launch-point (170 miles out) and that night launched two waves of twelve and nine Swordfish (eleven with torpedoes) led by Lieutenant-Commanders K. Williamson and J. W. Hale. The Italian fleet was taken by surprise and neither the torpedo nets nor a balloon barrage prevented a successful attack.

Despite a heavy AA barrage, the Swordfish, aided by flares, sank the new *Littorio*, *Conte de Cavour* and *Caio Duilio*, though the first two were repaired in four and six months respectively. Only two aircraft were lost and *Illustrious* escaped unscathed, and in the meantime a convoy got through to Malta, Another result was the Italian fleet's withdrawal to Naples where it had less influence on events. Apart from the British attacks on the French fleet, this was the first operational attack on battleships.

In December 1940 General Geisler's anti-shipping Fliegerkorps X arrived in Sicily from Norway to harry the fleet and shipping at Malta. Its Stukas badly damaged *Illustrious* while covering Operation 'Excess' and again at Malta. Saved by her armour deck, she was sent to the USA for a ten-month refit. With *Eagle* in the South Atlantic, *Ark Royal* was now the only carrier in the Mediterranean.

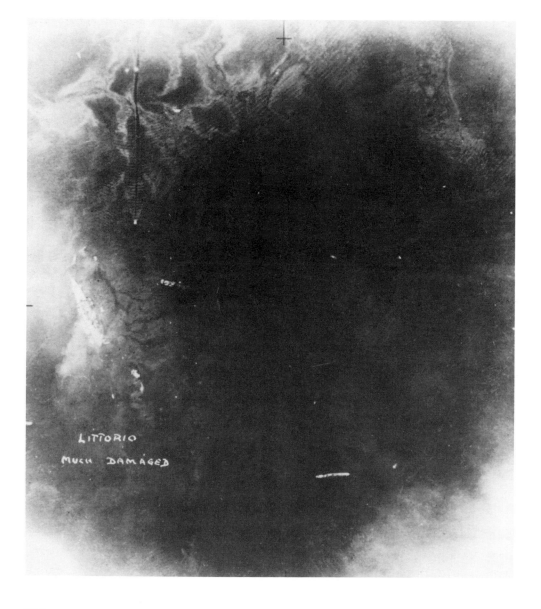

Taranto: a reconnaissance photograph showing the Italian fleet crippled by the few Swordfish of *Illustrious* on 11 November 1940. Ironically, this example encouraged the Japanese to attack Pearl Harbor. (FAAM)

In March 1941 *Formidable*, with Rear-Admiral D. Boyd as RAA, arrived to replace *Illustrious*. The fleet was now also covering convoys to Greece and on the 27th she left to intercept the Italian fleet, which was attempting to interfere, off Cape Matapan. *Formidable* launched two strikes (six Albacores and two Fulmars, then three Albacores, two Swordfish and two Fulmars), and one torpedo damaged *Vittorio Veneto*. Despite another strike, the battleship escaped, but the fleet sank three cruisers and two destroyers, the FAA having damaged one of the cruisers.

In February, March and April 1941 *Ark Royal* was deployed to search for the German battlecruisers *Gneisenau* and *Scharnhorst* without success, but later this proved to have been ideal practice during the search for *Bismarck*, which, together with a cruiser, entered the Atlantic in late May and sank the battlecruiser *Hood*. The hunt was joined by *Ark Royal* and the new *Victorious* which launched nine Swordfish on the 24th but the only hit inflicted slight damage. It was fifteen Swordfish from the veteran *Ark Royal* on the 26th that gained two hits, one of which jammed *Bismarck*'s rudders, allowing her to be sunk by the warships.

After this success disaster quickly overtook the Mediterranean carriers. *Formidable* was committed to the battle of Crete on 25 May with twelve Fulmars and next day was attacked by Stukas and badly damaged by two bombs. From June the British used *Victorious*, *Ark Royal* and *Furious* to supply massive aircraft reinforcements to Malta. However, *Ark Royal* was sunk by a single U-boat torpedo on 13 November 1941. With *Furious*, *Illustrious* and *Formidable* damaged, *Victorious* with the Home Fleet, *Eagle* in the South Atlantic, *Argus* training and *Hermes* and *Indomitable* (working-up) in the East, no carrier was left in the Mediterranean. Moreover, the Germans switched another Fliegerkorps to Sicily.

To continue covering convoys to Malta, during the height of Rommel's victories, and to deliver Spitfires, *Argus* and *Eagle* were pressed into service from February 1942. As a large carrier was needed to deliver large numbers of Spitfires, the USS *Wasp* was borrowed from the Home Fleet for two successful trips in April.

After failure to get convoys through to Malta in June, four carriers (*Furious*, *Eagle*, *Victorious* and *Indomitable*) were assembled in August for Operation 'Pedestal', to provide a 72-fighter cover for *Furious* carrying 38 Spitfires. The Spitfires and five (of fourteen) merchantmen were delivered, but *Eagle* was lost to *U 73* and *Victorious* and *Indomitable* were damaged (the latter badly) by aircraft. However, sufficient aircraft had been delivered to enable the forces at Malta to continue interdicting Rommel's supplies for the time being.

Operation 'Torch' (the Allied landings in Morocco and Algeria) sprang the trap on Rommel. The Western Force (Atlantic) was covered by the USS *Ranger* and four CVEs. In the Mediterranean the British mustered *Formidable*, *Victorious*, *Furious*, *Argus* and three CVEs. The emphasis was on fighters to cover the landings (out of range of land bases): 35 Martlets (Wildcats), seven Fulmars, 42 Sea Hurricanes and 45 Seafires which were being deployed for the first time. In the event opposition was light, but operational losses were heavy, especially with the Seafire (because of its landing characteristics and undercarriage design), and the escort carrier *Avenger* was sunk by *U 155*.

'Torch' was the first of the major landings in Europe. Sicily (July 1943) was covered by *Formidable* and *Indomitable* in case the Italian fleet sought to interfere, and the latter was damaged by an Italian torpedo-aircraft, the only success achieved by the Regia Aeronautica against British carriers. At Salerno *Formidable* and *Illustrious* covered the Support Carrier Force (the repair carrier *Unicorn* used as a light carrier and four escort carriers) supporting the landing. The main problem was posed by German radio-controlled bombs. Operation 'Anvil' (South of France) was covered by TF88 (Rear-Admiral T. H. Troubridge) which consisted of nine CVEs (two American). This ended major carrier operations in the Mediterranean.

From 1942 the Home Fleet's main task was to cover the Arctic convoys to Russia. Most of the air cover and ASW work for these was provided by escort carriers such as

Fleet Air Arm offensive on German shipping at Kilboth, Norway, 5 May 1944. This was part of a series of carrier raids on the Norwegian coast and the battleship *Tirpitz* by the Home Fleet in 1944–45. (FAAM)

Fleet Air Arm deck crews bombing-up Barracudas and Corsairs for operations against *Tirpitz,* off Norway, 1944. Note the ever-present escort for AS, AA and rescue duties. (FAA)

Avenger, Vindex and *Nairana.* The fleet was needed to counter the heavy German surface ships, especially *Tirpitz,* in Norway, which at any time could sortie to maul a convoy or try to break out into the Atlantic. In March 1942 *Tirpitz* attempted to attack convoys and *Victorious* launched twelve Albacores but poor weather and heavy AA prevented any hits. Lack of carriers prevented further attempts.

From early 1944 the Admiralty planned to sink *Tirpitz* using *Victorious, Furious* and four CVEs, (*Emperor, Pursuer, Searcher* and *Fencer*). The fleet carriers had 42 Barracudas escorted by 40 Hellcats, Wildcats and Corsairs, and first attacked on 3 April inflicting fourteen direct hits that required three months' repairs. The raid was followed up on 24 April and 14 May.

When *Victorious* was sent to the East, she was replaced by the new *Indefatigable* and *Implacable* which carried twice the number of aircraft. With *Furious* they continued the attacks against *Tirpitz.* On 17 July they launched 44 Barracudas escorted by 48 Cor-

sairs, Hellcats and Fireflies, but the former were too slow to surprise the defences. In three more raids on 22, 24 and 29 August, 242 aircraft attacked her but without a single hit. This was a direct result of the Barracuda's lack of speed and inadequate bomb-load. The RAF had to finish the job.

The British Pacific Fleet

At the Cairo Conference of December 1943, the British pressed for a squadron in the Pacific by June 1944 and a fleet in 1945. King (US CNO), dubious about their logistic capability, resisted a British say in Pacific strategy and a share in the final victory. The only British participation had been the Eastern Fleet's (Admiral Somerville, *Formidable* and *Indomitable*) sparring with Nagumo in April 1942 and *Victorious*' loan (May–July 1943) to operate with *Saratoga* while *Enterprise* was refitted.

King's distrust of British strategy and motives meant that he strove to limit them to the South West Pacific backwater. However, by the Quebec Conference (September

HMS *Implacable* (1944), one of the improved *Illustrious* class, with greater power, four shafts, more AA guns and a larger air group, used against *Tirpitz* and in the Pacific. (IWM)

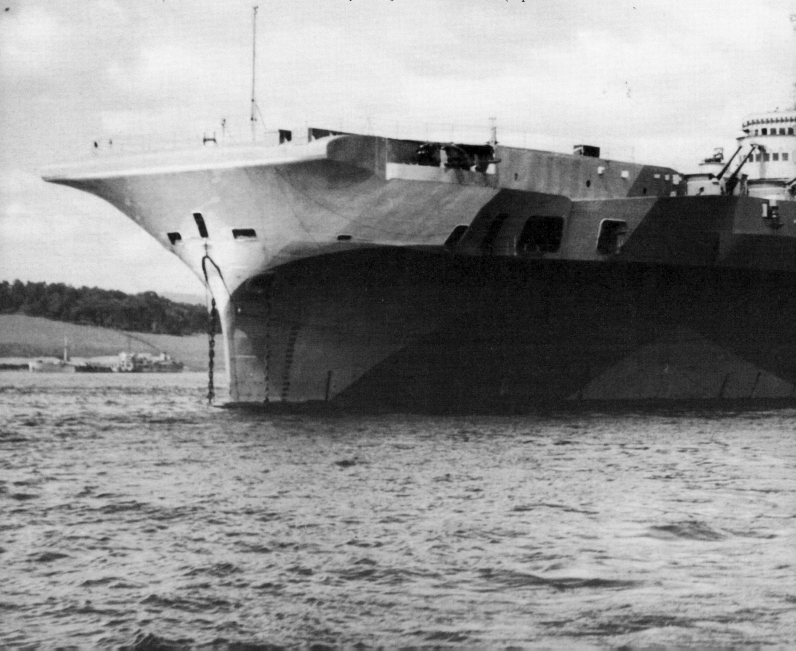

1944) the British had large naval forces available and Roosevelt accepted Churchill's offer of a British Pacific Fleet for the Central Pacific. It began operations in February 1945 and indeed experienced great logistical problems.

In April 1944 *Saratoga* was lent to the British to indoctrinate them in Pacific techniques, and with *Illustrious* attacked Sumatra. This was followed by British carrier raids on the Andamans (June), Sumatra (July, August, September) and Nicobars (October). On 22 November the Eastern Fleet was split into the East Indies Fleet (four CVEs) and the Pacific Fleet (Admiral Sir Bruce Fraser) with *Illustrious* (replaced by *Formidable* in April 1945), *Victorious*, *Indomitable* and *Indefatigable*. These raided the Sumatran oil refineries in December and January to gain large-scale carrier and operational experience.

After this the fleet moved to Manus where Vice-Admiral Sir Bernard Rawlings (second in command) commanded at sea (since Fraser was senior to Nimitz and Halsey) and Sir Philip Vian was the carrier commander, Both were veterans of the Mediterranean, but not aviation. The fleet was supported by TG112 or the fleet train, a motley group of oilers, repair and maintenance ships plus six CVEs.

Vought Corsair fighter. After the US Navy rejected the aircraft for use on its carriers the FAA, desperate for high-performance fighters, pioneered its use against *Tirpitz* and in the Pacific. (IWM)

For the Okinawa operations as TF57 in late March, the fleet's job was to keep the Ryukus (Sakishima Gunto) and Formosan airfields quiet, alternated with some raids on Japan. During refuelling their place was taken by US CVEs. Although the Kamikaze occasionally hit the carriers their armoured flight-decks saved them from serious damage, again proving its worth. On 25 May TF57 withdrew to Sydney to replenish and prepare for the Japanese campaign.

The main weaknesses of the British Pacific Fleet were insufficient 40mm Bofors, capable of stopping Kamikaze, lack of radars equal to the US model (only *Indomitable* had one) and night-fighters to prevent the Japanese filling in bomb craters by night. The arrival of *Implacable* with Avengers and Hellcats in June gave the fleet a night capability. The light fleet carrier *Ocean* was also designated a night carrier. *Implacable* (75 aircraft) worked-up by raiding Truk in mid June.

Spruance and Nimitz agreed to the TF's incorporation into the US fast carrier Task Force since they had shown themselves capable of undertaking operations in the Pacific. As TF37, the fleet joined the US carriers on 16 July for attacks on Tokyo which continued until Japan surrendered. While Halsey concentrated on destroying the heavy unit remnants of the Japanese fleet, the British were used on other targets. For an attack on a destroyer the Canadian Corsair pilot, R. H. Gray, was awarded a posthumous VC.

During the first three years of war the Royal Navy was so short of carriers that it had to rely on the old *Argus*, *Furious* and *Eagle* as late as Operations 'Pedestal' and 'Torch' and the *Tirpitz* raids of 1944. The four armoured carriers laid down just before the war had to be spread too thinly and take much damage. In Home and Mediterranean waters the Royal Navy eventually triumphed over the German and Italian fleets and air forces but at great cost. In the Pacific the British carriers were just one task group of many. The failure to equip the FAA adequately between the wars was to cost Great Britain and the Allies dearly during the Second World War. In the end the personnel triumphed over the failings of the carriers and their aircraft.

Index of Ships

Page references in **bold type** indicate illustrations